SING OUT!

GAYS AND LESBIANS IN THE MUSIC WORLD

By the same author:

HOLLYWOOD GAYS (Barricade Books)

BETTE DAVIS SPEAKS (Barricade Books)

HOLLYWOOD LESBIANS (Barricade Books)

HOLLYWOOD BABBLE ON

THE LAVENDER SCREEN

LEADING LADIES (UK)

HISPANIC HOLLYWOOD

CONVERSATIONS WITH MY ELDERS

THE FILMS OF JANE FONDA

SING OUT!

GAYS AND LESBIANS IN THE MUSIC WORLD

Boze Hadleigh

Barricade Books Inc.
New York

Published by Barricade Books Inc.
150 Fifth Avenue
Suite 700
New York, NY 10011

Library of Congress Cataloging-in-Publication Data

Hadleigh, Boze.
   [Vinyl closet]
   Sing out! : gays and lesbians in the music world / by Boze Hadleigh
      p.   cm.
   Originally published: The vinyl closet. San Diego, CA : Los Hombres Press, c1991.
   ISBN 1-56980-116-9
   1. Gay musicians. 2. Homosexuality and music. 3. Closeted gays. I. Title.
ML385.H14   1997
780'.86'64—DC21   97-33026
                                             CIP

Printed in the United States of America.

10 9 8 7 6 5 4 3 2 1

For Ronnie—whose name produces musical vibrations

Contents

Foreword/Leonard Bernstein   1

Preface/Vito Russo   3

Introduction to the Second Edition   5

Introduction   11

The Music Lovers   27

Crooners   61

Songbirds   109

The British Are Coming!   165

Bring On The Dancing Boys   211

...Sing Out!   245

Epilogue   319

Index   323

"Being in the closet takes a terrible toll on your spirit. Every time you change pronouns or stifle a comment about your home life, you cause another microinjury to your soul. When you add up all those bad feelings and all those lies, you damage your self-esteem, your sense of yourself as a valuable human being, and your ability to contribute to the world. Stress is not healthy. Denying reality is not healthy. The damage we fear will come to our career, our lives, and our families from coming out doesn't hold a candle to the damage we do to ourselves every time we hide in the closet."

—k.d. lang on March 1, 1997, upon receiving the Creative Integrity Award from the Los Angeles Gay and Lesbian Community Services Center, presented by Ellen DeGeneres, who soon after came out on TV and in real life.

Foreword
by Leonard Bernstein

When I was 13, my father obtained tickets to a benefit at the Temple. Rachmaninoff! I was in heaven. For me, great music has always been a blessing, and I was privileged to have as mentors Aaron Copland, Dmitri Mitropoulos, Serge Koussevitsky and other sound immortals.

My own first symphony was *Jeremiah* (1942), the formal beginning of a lifelong affair with creating music. From an early age, I was aware that much of the most sublime music ever created derived from the efforts and souls of homosexuals. Our world feels free to enjoy this ageless music time and again, but not to acknowledge even the simple, mutual humanity of composers, conductors, singers and other gay artists.

Of course, the world is not to blame for what it doesn't know, and the affectional inheritance of gay artists is never made known to the vast majority of the public. This is where Boze Hadleigh's true contribution rests—in educating our minds and hearts. He did this in the film-themed *Conversations With My Elders,* and now in the music-themed *The Vinyl Closet.*

If there are any benefits to semi-retirement, one of the most positive and enjoyable will be the reading of books and manuscripts which my work has too often precluded. Boze, I look forward with barely suppressed pleasure and with high hopes to reading your entertaining and revealing material!

October 5, 1990
New York City

Author's note:

Leonard Bernstein's kindness was legendary, and his support of the gay community was long-standing. In 1982, when the New York *Native* was foundering, Manhattan's only gay paper turned to Lenny for help. Tom Steele later declared, "We were trying to tell the truth about a burgeoning epidemic—and the truth is seldom lucrative or popular."

Bernstein replied, "Keep the candy store going. Take care of this house." Steele recalls, "Lenny was, in certain ways, everyone's father, husband, brother, lover, friend, but for the *Native,* he was a savior."

In 1989, the conductor-composer-activist declined a presidential medal of honor, in protest against the National Endowment for the Arts' decision to withdraw a grant from a gay-oriented AIDS art exhibit in New York. The funds were restored due to his and others' protests, but Lenny wasn't reinvited to the White House, where he was to receive his medal. . . .

P.S. He passed away five days after announcing his retirement from conducting and performing (he still planned to compose and teach), upon his doctors' orders. Lenny died October 14, from a sudden cardiac arrest.

October 31, 1990
Beverly Hills

Preface
by Vito Russo

There are three kinds of pianists: Jewish pianists, homosexual pianists, and bad pianists. ——Vladimir Horowitz

The Vinyl Closet takes up where both my book *The Celluloid Closet* and Boze's *Conversations With My Elders* leave off. Both books were movie-themed and dealt with the gay content of and contributions to motion pictures over the years. Mine was about the films, Boze's about the filmmakers.

The Vinyl Closet is about both the music and the music-makers. It has enough inside "dirt" to break a vacuum-cleaner, and yet enough historical and social context to render this a significant work about popular music and to a lesser degree classical music and the dance.

As the author explains, the essential difference between actors and singers is that actors do act. They play other than themselves, while singers' public images are much closer to their private realities. Music isn't so heavily laden with romantic symbolism as are film and TV, and so its creators and interpreters are freer to deviate openly from the sexual and affectional

3

norms and pretenses of Hollywood.

Music is not as consciously influential an art form as is film, for film teaches us how to react and behave, and is thus powerful propaganda. Seldom do songs take on a message, although it can be argued that singers participate in heterosexual propaganda every time they sing a "silly love song."

Rock and pop stars, however, are international icons and role models, and to the degree that they reject traditional sex roles and gender imagery—for instance, iconoclastic k. d. lang and androgynous Boy George—they are social revolutionaries. Starting immediately after Stonewall, pop/rock has gone androgynous, even if in the 1980s it retrenched a bit. The late '80s saw the start of an alarming rise in pop/rock bigotry in lyrics and outspoken homophobia on the part of certain music stars.

This anti-gay backlash via misguided singers, composers and closeted gay record executives must be countered by gay boycotts and campaigns to curb homophobia. Racism, misogyny and anti-Semitism have been largely erased from popular music—though of course rock is inherently anti-feminist. But we must not allow music to become the new and worldwide forum for anti-gay hatred. Fortunately, music is far more easily influenced by protests and boycotts than film.

If Hollywood seems no closer than in the past to easing up on its homophobia, and if Hollywood stars are as firmly closeted as ever, then we must now turn to music to help spread the message—via its openly gay artists and all-embracing lyrics— that *Gay Is Okay*. Rock began in the counterculture, and so-called lavender rock has proven—in England, America and elsewhere—that alternative music can be very profitable. Both commercially and, more importantly, socially.

If today's movies are made for heterosexual male teens, then music should still be, and can be, for Everybody!

Introduction to
the Second Edition

"...and I wrote only half of what I saw."—Marco Polo

In the almost seven years since the first edition of this book was completed, much has happened in the volatile music world. The key word in this Ellen/Elton era being: *out*.

Among those who have since come out as gay or bi: Elton John, k.d. lang, Melissa Etheridge, the more prominent of the two Pet Shop Boys, the Indigo Girls, Janis Ian, Pete Townshend, Courtney Love, Chastity Bono, Marianne Faithfull, Jill Sobule, Fred Schneider, RuPaul, Neneh Cherry, Michael Feinstein, Barbra Streisand's son, Jerry Herman, Bob Mould, and Michael Stipe, sort of.

Among those outed: George Michael (partly by himself), Mick Jagger, Tracy Chapman, Nathan Lane, Dusty Springfield, Luther Vandross, Madonna's brother (by Madonna), Ty Herndon, Van Cliburn, Judy Garland, and *Rolling Stone* founder/publisher Jann Wenner, who left his wife and kids for a younger man—no wonder this first book about gays, lesbians, and bi's in the music world couldn't get reviewed in *Rolling Stone* back in 1991!

Some have gone the opposite route of outing: Whitney Houston married a guy and had kids, the artist formerly known as Prince had a kid and got married to its mother, and Michael Jackson married two females and got a kid.

And of course the deaths, too many of them premature and AIDS-related: Freddie Mercury, Rudolf Nureyev, Kurt Cobain,

Gene Kelly, Peter Allen, Village People founder Jacques Morali, Truman Capote's partner Jack Dunphy, Michael Callen, Larry Kert, Carmen McRae, Howard Ashman, Laura Nyro, Maxene Andrews (of the Andrews Sisters), John Curry, Joe Layton, Lincoln Kirstein, John Cage, Emile Ardolino, Gerry Mulligan (Johnny Mathis's likely lover), Tiny Tim, Paul Jabara, Miles Davis, and Leonard Bernstein.

Transitions: then, *Kiss Of The Spider Woman* was a flop; now, a Tony-winning hit. Then, Chastity Bono was the closeted daughter (and would-be singer) of an Oscar-winning actress and a washed-up singer-restaurateur, attending the Grammys as Michael Jackson's "date;" now, she's a media liaison for GLAAD (Gay and Lesbian Alliance Against Defamation), while her father is a congressman opposed to gay rights. Virulent homophobe Axl Rose of the anti-gay Guns 'N Roses in 1992 participated in an AIDS fundraiser honoring the late Freddie Mercury and in '93 was chosen to give the Rock 'N Roll Hall of Fame induction speech to his longtime hero, openly gay (no longer "bi," no longer contractually married) Elton John.

More transitions: Tipper Gore went from being best known as a lyrically censorious Washington Wife to the Vice President's Wife, now openly supportive—like her husband Al—of gay rights. The 1996 movie *Beavis and Butt-head Do America*'s soundtrack featured Engelbert Humperdinck crooning "Fly High, Lesbian Seagull" (gay sex has been observed in more than sixty species of mammals, apart from birds; of all people, Cole Porter wrote, "Birds do it . . ."). The song was written in 1978 by Tom Wilson Weinberg as a response to Anita Bryant's homophobic campaign against gay teachers and gay citizens, period. Ironic that the song wound up in a film criticized as sexist and antigay.

It's worth remembering that Ellen (DeGeneres and her TV alter ego) first came out *singing*. Months before she officially came out, after she heard ABC planned to put her show on hiatus or cancel it before she got a chance to come out, she ad-libbed at the end of a music-themed episode, "So here's what I have to say: 'And by the way, I'm *gay*! It's okay! I'm gay! I'm gay! I'm gay!'" The audience at the taping erupted in cheers and applause, but the network and its owner, Disney, were reportedly furious. Ellen's song adlib never aired. The point being that

Ellen didn't get to come out till she got permission. The mass media still invisibilizes gay people and characters. A few examples:

Disney heterized *Hercules*. The Greek demigod was bisexual. One doesn't expect an animated musical to deal in truth, but fictional and historical figures are still routinely resexualized in nonjuvenile films. A&E's *Biography* series often leaves out subjects' nonheterosexuality. A recent A&E bio of Judy Garland also left out Ann Miller's factual in-passing comment that Judy's second husband Vincente Minnelli was "AC/DC."

Jim Nash, president and cofounder of Wax Trax! Records—with his business and life partner Dannie Flesher—told OUT magazine, "The music industry's weird. It's the most homophobic industry, yet so many gay people are involved in it, not only as artists but also as presidents of record companies." And it's still a fact that *male* gay-themed songs—unlike, say, Jill Sobule's "I Kissed a Girl"—are officially and unofficially banned from most radio stations' airplay. As are many of the more open and/or flamboyant gay singers, Boy George among them.

And the religious self-righteous still destroy not only gay music and openly gay singers' CDs—not always the same thing—but albums by Barry Manilow, the Bee Gees, the Beatles, Alanis Morrissette, Billy Joel, and Don McLean . . . as happened in early 1997 at Minneapolis's Central Christian School, with a local evangelist helping students to sledgehammer and burn the albums and CDs of the above-mentioned artists.

The music world moves quicker than the movie world, no question, but much remains to be done . . . in a word, *equality*, for those who make the music and those who listen to it. Music is said to intoxicate the ear and the soul. It should also satisfy the conscience.

June 5, 1997
Beverly Hills

9

Introduction

"Music hath charms to soothe the savage breast." — Traditional

Homosexuality. It exists. In the music industry. So does heterosexuality, a less well-kept secret.

Or is it still a secret? Compared to the Hollywood closet, that is. Consider:

Throughout 1987 rumors swirled like recalcitrant crows over a scarecrow about the nature of Whitney Houston's sexuality.

The same year, a biography of the late Jacqueline Susann revealed for the first time in print the novelist's bisexuality, and her affair with actress Carole Landis and her possible affair with the great and very deceased Ethel Merman. Ethel, AC/DC?! Sing it ain't so! Everyone knew Merman was mannish, perhaps a tenth as feminine as, say, Mary Martin. But could she truly have been anything but a self-professed heterosexual?

So are they all, with few glittering exceptions, self-described and reiterated heterosexuals. Who but the perverse Mick Jagger would wish to be thought non-straight? In my gay Hollywood book *Conversations With My Elders,* Cecil Beaton noted his belief that Jagger—with whom he once dropped acid in the 1960s—preferred to be thought bi, yet was essentially heterosexual. When *High Society* magazine queried whether Jagger was or wasn't, the pouty rocker countered with a humorous and explicit defense of bisexuals, "the fastest-growing population in the world."

In 1989, rumors still proliferated about the sexuality of pop icon George Michael, whom the free-wheeling British press had frequently dunked in lavender ink. On American television, Michael was confronted with The Big Question. Like Olympic-gold diver Greg Louganis at about the same time, he neither confirmed nor denied, but said it was nobody's goddamned business.

And, ideally, one's sexual orientation (or lack of it, or excess of it) shouldn't be anyone's business.

But it is, it is! To managers, promoters, record producers, et al.; it's literally their business, or so they believe. If a singer, so the prevailing wisdom goes, is thought or even suspected of being gay, sales will plummet and careers will go belly up. In the 1950s it was whispered that Arthur Godfrey fired a male singer live on his TV show as much for intimations of the singer's alleged homosexuality as for Godfrey's abiding jealousy.

In today's mellow-macho rock world, purple mascara is okay, but purple prose and whiffs of lilac aren't. At the most, a singer may admit to being "bi," a breed which Rock Hudson felt is as ephemeral as leprechauns. Therefore when David Bowie and Elton John and Joan Baez came out, they were officially *bi*-sexual—fans might presumably have misgivings, but would still *buy* their albums. So, when a George Michael retains his integrity, he does it by not saying No. . . .

Yet, to Middle America, bisexual is nearly equivalent to gay. For the average record-buyer or *Entertainment Tonight* watcher, the thrill or taboo of alternative sexuality is so strong, so indelible, that one gay affair during a lifetime of skirt-chasing may get a lothario labeled "bi" and thought of as "queer" (as was said of Bowie in *Saturday Night Fever*).

But music performers have always been considered non-mainstream, even extreme, and despite their sexual pronouncements, Bowie and John remain at the top of their fields. Elton's music videos continue typically androgynous and peopled by Calvin Klein clones. The speculations have hardly hurt Whitney's white-hot career, nor will George Michael's likely suffer, even with notoriously fickle teenyboppers.

And the latest John Lennon bio, with its revelation of Lennon as more or less bisexual, will affect his sales and legend not a whit(man). Though, of course, self-righteous critics will keep "defending" Lennon's memory against author Albert Goldman, and allege that the book's non-heterosexual passages are libelous or, worse, propaganda—which is simply whatever the majority disagrees with.

Fact: in the flickering firmament of top music stars, only Johnny Mathis has come out—in 1982, already—as unself-consciously and honestly gay.

That the average American has yet to hear this headline-grabbing fact is due to the nature of the media, which up- holds and mirrors solely heterosexual images, unless stereotypical and offputting gay ones. Rock Hudson told me, "Trust me, Boze, America does not want to know." However, he later said that America must know, "whether they want to or not—to accept people for what they are."

Does America Want to Know?

I believe so, otherwise the rumors would remain whispered, as in the '50s and '60s, where today they're printed more boldly and often than ever, and with less result. The gossip business has never thrived as now, and though still unofficially homophobic, it's no longer so true of the media that—as Will Rogers once said in a different context— "Powerful interests are at work, keeping the truth from the public."

Nonetheless, it's one thing for a Liberace or Boy George to be teased or baited in print. Men who wear rhinestones must expect to get scrutinized, or worse. Males are also the butt of sexual wonderings-aloud more often than women, and not just because there are fewer female singers. The phrase "family man" has various implications, though few if any guarantees. Conversely, the phrase "family woman" seems redundant. It takes more for a female to be suspected of, or asked about, sexual non-orthodoxy.

Or, as the Chinese saying goes, The first time you hear a rumor, you don't believe it. The second time you hear a rumor, you don't believe it. The third time, you believe it.

Yet some stereotypes have fallen by the wayside. Earrings, once the province of pirates and precious males, are now commonplace, almost unremarkable. And no one jokes about Spring-steen's first name, though once upon a not so long ago time, whole comedic routines were built around anyone who hap-pened to be named Bruce.

Consider: The Boss—note that his first name is, though, rarely invoked; it's either The Boss or Springsteen—was cap-tured in a widely reproduced Janet Gough photo, in the parking lot of Tower Records on Sunset Boulevard in West Hollywood, emerging with a rental video of *Kiss of the Spider Woman,* of all movies. But, not so big a deal (even the stodgy Academy awarded William Hurt for playing a gay stereotype).

It *would* have been a big deal, had the general media picked up the following tidbit from a 1986 issue of the *Advocate:* "Springsteen . . . shocked crowds to their feet midway through his four-hour shows. As he finished 'Thunder Road,' he would dive to his knees—sliding the length of the stage to the side of his massive black bass player, Clarence Clemmons.

"Springsteen would look up pleadingly, and Clemmons would bend down—the two men locking lips for 15 seconds.

"Rock 'n roll always sounded like it burst out of a soul-shattering midnight rendezvous between a black field hand and a white juvenile delinquent. In one spectacular, liberating ges-ture, Springsteen enacted those implications."

This is not to say that Bruce or Clarence is gay. Or that they're 100 percent heterosexual (is anyone?). The point is, this is the world of music, which is wider, freer and more real than the Hollywood scene. Men ostensibly heterosexual, or possibly bisexual, can indulge in all manner of gestures, get-ups, accesso-ries, poses and public announcements. Sex and reputations are a lot more fluid on the musical scale than on thin, potentially jagged celluloid.

No movie star has ever come out of the closet voluntarily. Several famous singers have, at least half-way. Of course, most comings-out occurred at the height of the Sexual Revolution, pre-Reagan and pre-AIDS. And more importantly, pre-video. Music then was a basically aural pleasure, where only movies and TV were visual—thus, *their* romantic leads didn't dare come out and shatter the fantasies of some house-wife in Poughkeepsie.

Today, music videos have made music, at least on television, almost as visual as acting. Especially for rockers of MTV calibre. By contrast, a Johnny Mathis, rarely if ever seen in a music video, and devoted to what Margo Channing called "unyielding good taste," is far less affected. . . .

Still, one factor in the comparative honesty of music versus dramatic performance is that an actor is doing just that—acting. He isn't playing himself, but a character, an image. A singer isn't playing anyone but a possibly gaudier, louder version of himself. A singer emotes in a more sincere way than an actor reading lines and posing behind conventional mannerisms.

Also, a music career can soar virtually overnight. Most star actors are the products of years of struggle, and every feature film or TV series is a time-consuming committee endeavor costing roughly a few dozen millions. Albums are far cheaper to create and market, and require fewer buyers to make a profit.

An album may star practically anyone, any type, romantic or otherwise. A singer can turn out a few dozen albums in one decade, if the desire and the demand are there. Even a movie superstar isn't likely to make more than one film a year, if that. Albums can afford to specialize; movies must appeal to the broadest possible audience. As the very specialized *and* very successful Boy George put it, "People who get into singing want to express themselves. People who go to Hollywood want to make a pile of money or go on an ego trip."

The blending of music and motion pictures is of course more conservative, more sexually disingenuous, than music alone. Hollywood be thy name.

Consider: the top two movie musicals featured gay or bisexual leading men *and* women. Yet none of these performers has a remotely gay image, although one remains contractually single.

Hollywood figures that if you can star in a musical, you can profitably go on—like Streisand or Sinatra—to star in nonmusicals, which invariably demands a heterosexual image. Ergo, stars with dubious images must be refashioned for the screen, i.e., Prince, whose song lyrics sometimes crooned bisexuality, but whose *Purple Rain* film debut depicted him as a non-stop straight stud and featured *de rigeur* anti-gay slurs and demeaning though fleeting pansy portrayals.

In the music industry, sexual speculation is a long-time staple. Just as rock 'n roll has black roots but usually wears a

19

white face, so disco and other aspects of contemporary music harbor gay psyches within straight drag——not unlike the Village People. Perceptions and tolerance levels vary, but innuendo has always greeted tuneful trailblazers.

Elvis, in the old days, was considered by moralists as both dangerous and effete. The Beatles were similarly labeled when they burst upon the American scene; not a few disc jockeys rejected the Fab Four as akin to a musical tortilla——cold, flat and foreign. The Beatles initially attracted as much attention for their then-girlish hairdos as for their new-fangled music.

But in music, more than movies, talent will out, and eventually the music is heard and appreciated, while the gyrating hips, the mod hairdos or the kabuki makeup of a Boy George are taken almost for granted, as the singer's outer persona is relegated to the sidelines of his career's ascendancy (particularly on radio). Even in a Boy George, the desire to startle may be forgiven because it is so guileless and eager, and is practically a commercial requirement these days.

Of course, *too* sensationalistic a private life, or drug addiction, or consistently declining sales——once a performer strikes out in new musical directions——can again push the product into the background and bring the personality back into the critical foreground, as happened with Elvis and Boy.

Controversy and sexual exploitation are part and parcel of music journalism. But they are selective and cling more tenaciously to the unwed or the iconoclastic. In 1987, while the Whitney rumors were sprouting like French truffles, the *Sun* bannered "Gay Loves of Tina Turner!" The front-page piece in Europe's top-circulation paper declared that "Rock Queen Tina Turner is a bisexual who has had a string of lesbian love affairs."

In 1988, at the height of gossip about George Michael, a court case concerning Engelbert Humperdinck was ignored by most newspapers but suggested that the least complicated thing about the singer was his name. The *Hollywood Kids,* aka "the divas of dirt," reported that the big E "fired a sexy dancer in his show because she was too tall. 'No way,' claims the dancer. She's suing the Hump, claiming sexual harassment.

"In fact, making a lurid story even more so, when the dancer took the witness stand she told the court that Engelbert was AC/DC and was having a torrid affair with the man who has been blow-drying his hair for the past seven years!"

Amazing as they seemed, the stories about Tina and Engelbert were buried in an avalanche of print about the younger, unmatrimonied stars. One record executive puts it this way: "If you're a gender-bender, like the guy in Duran Duran who wore all that makeup, or like k. d. lang the country singer, the press tries to excuse you, whether you're gay or not. For, the press dearly wants you to be heterosexual.

"But if you 'persist' in not marrying or at least going 'round and 'round with one member of the opposite sex, they 'punish' a performer by printing some of the rumors. And sometimes even gender-bending heterosexuals run scared. . . ."

In Nick Rhodes' case, he finally took a wife. In Ms. lang's case, she explains that dressing and looking like a comely youth is "just the natural way I present myself." But as Dolly Parton exclaimed in *TV Guide,* "It sure is a far cry from Kitty Wells to k. d. lang!"

Ready acceptance of social, let alone sexual, innovation in the entertainment industry is as hard to find as sugar in a sand dune. However, it does occur, and lasts just as long as the money keeps rolling in. The changes are reflected in the following music stars' comments, which comprised a 1986 round-up by the author in *First Hand* magazine, titled "Gay Melody."

> *Annie Lennox* of the Eurythmics. "Music has become more visual; added to the political climate in Britain and the States, this is an inhibiting factor. However, much of the current musical rebellion is a direct reaction to the Thatcher government. . . . I think more singers will come out, mostly in groups or bands. But not individual singing stars—not if they have acting ambitions."

> *Elton John* surprised—and disappointed— many fans by marrying in 1984. Soon after, he appeared publicly in Tina Turner drag. Those close to the chart-topper say he is pro-gay and still considers himself bisexual. "I may have suffered a bit, career-wise, in the short run (after coming out in *Rolling Stone*). But not in the long run. . . . Most singers lead rather insular

lives anyway, and I figured that the few name-callers were betraying their own unhappiness by being forced to put someone else down to keep themselves up."

Tina Turner. "It's funny, because the sensitive souls who you'd think might be gay, from the way we've been taught to guess, keep denying it. Then you have these butch, incredible men, and some of them are gay, and if there's gossip about them, they don't give a damn. . . . I think being secure as a person has a lot to do with your public image and what you say about it."

Larry Steinbachek was part of the original three-gay-man Bronski Beat (singer Jimmy Somerville left to form his own duo, then went solo). "I think sales finally caught up with David Bowie. Once he got big sales and made the cover of *Time,* it was a radicalizing process. But in the wrong direction. . . . I mean, it's daft to call yourself a liar, isn't it?"

Grace Jones, now a some-time film actor, was earlier an androgynous disco diva. She also raised eyebrows, among other things, by posing semi-nude in a sapphicly suggestive black-and-white layout in *Hustler* magazine. "The time just came when you couldn't keep a lid on people's sex personalities anymore. It's an explosion! Most of the record-buying public are mature enough to accept it, and now most of the top male singers are ambiguous. Why not keep people guessing? . . . Straight men love female androgyny, although they won't say it. It is easier to be female and into androgyny; it causes less of a stir."

Paul Rutherford was one of Frankie Goes To Hollywood's openly gay lead singers (two singers, three music-men). Frankie's most infamous song, the explicit "Relax," was banned by the BBC before becoming an international hit. "We're into success. It's what every honest musician wants. We don't want to lose the gay crowd or the straight crowd. We made our statement, but we can't go on telling about our private lives forever."

Jon Moss, Culture Club's drummer, was even better known as Boy George's alleged lover. "I had to laugh when a girl (a top singer) whom we all know is gay, got married, and married a boy (younger) who's even prettier than she is. . . . And while Springsteen's probably hetero, he does kiss a black man in his concerts, so I think people had better start reevaluating their stereotypes, and not divide everyone into neat little categories. This is part of what Culture Club and today's music are trying to undo. . . ."

Much can change in the world of popular music in two or three years, and the purpose of this book isn't to keep up with trends or highlight the latest lavender acts. Nor is the intention to reveal anybody's sexual orientation or generalize about homosexuality in music or necessarily examine the private lives of those who have passed on. Nor to weigh the contributions of gay people in pop music; it's tough enough to gauge a living individual's waxing and waning influence, let alone the generations of an entire population.

But the truth is that contemporary music would be vastly different without the input and style of gay men and lesbians, also bisexual men and women. Yet lately, despite the increasing impact of sexually and socially committed performers, many audience members seem to be stuck in the past. A 1988 *Rolling Stone* survey found that 75 percent of its readers don't consider homosexuality, in their friends or co-workers, "acceptable." This may reflect the fact that, more than any-thing else, AIDS has infected people's minds.

British hetero socialist Billy Bragg, sometimes described as the UK's electric answer to Woody Guthrie, has championed gay rights on his recent *Save the Youth of America* tour:

"I was so outraged when I read *Rolling Stone's* [poll] that

I've brought it up every night in concerts," he told a reporter. "These aren't just gay rights, they're human rights."

Boy George, who used to verbally fence with the press over his confessed "bisexuality," has hardly used the word since his over-publicized drug bust, and is now a singing activist. His boldest single was "Stop Clause 28," a protest against the most sweeping piece of homophobic legislation by the Thatcher regime—the song was banned on UK radio.

Rock 'n roll's image is sex and drugs, but as Boy George has pointed out, "There's also this myth that straight people make love, while gay people—or 'homosexuals'—only have sex." This might explain why there's not been a book or study about gay singers, composers, etc. From Stephen Foster, Larry Hart and Cole Porter to choreographers Jack Cole and Michael Bennett, from Maurice Chevalier to Nelson Eddy and Ricky Nelson, the story of non-heterosexual musicians is about far more than sex.

The open secret of gays in music hasn't allowed the closet door to disclose more than a glimpse of the varied musical chairs within. In an industry that cherishes and even flaunts its extremes, sexual variation still bears a stigma. The rock world has yet to fundraise or raise consciousnesses against AIDS on a level remotely approaching the *We Are The Word* effort. Even though, ironically, far more African heterosexuals will die of AIDS than starvation. . . .

Liberace was the first music star to die of AIDS. The following year, TV aired two factually limp Liberace telebios. The producer of one informed *People* magazine with a straight face that his production wouldn't admit that Liberace "was patently homosexual—that would be gross." Even in death, a showman could show only so much.

The two TV films communicated more about Hollywood's Rambo rhumba mentality than Liberace or the industry in which he was considered an eccentric but savvy and legitimate performer about as "controversial" as the blue rinses sported by most of his adoring and apparently indulgent fans.

But if Bowie has recanted and Elton has stood behind his very public marriage, Johnny Mathis is still going strong, Boy George has thrown caution to the winds, George Michael isn't saying for certain, Joan Baez has written explicitly about her same-sex affair, and k. d. lang is not in the market for a beau or a husband—not even in *People*.

Why *The Vinyl Closet?*

Because unlike Everest, it wasn't there. The individuals were and are there, but the Presence has gone unacknowledged. The personalities and lifestyles have been camouflaged by fearful press agents, zealous editors, greedy record executives, intimidated performers, and innocuous little words— the opposite-sex pronouns in all those "silly love songs." In the swinging '60s and the acerbic '70s, progress was being made. Then came the aching '80s and AIDS.

"Today's music world is a frightened and confused place," feels the openly celibate Morrissey, formerly of Britain's The Smiths.

This book isn't a last word on gay people in non-classical music, and doesn't even include everyone in music who was or is gay. Nor is everybody in this book gay or bi. It's not a Who's Who or a Who Had Who, and isn't meant as a collection of biographies, though it does include missing, sometimes crucial pieces of earlier, more judgmental biographies.

I flatter myself by thinking of *The Vinyl Closet* as a beginning. Only a beginning. But hopefully also an end—to the social and moral equivalent of Johnny One-Note.

October 5, 1990
Beverly Hills

25

The Music Lovers

"Music is the brandy of the damned."—Bernard Shaw

"I Am What I Am"

It may have started with the mythological Orpheus, Greece's greatest musician, who sang his musical creations to winsome young men. Like the average Greek, Orpheus was contractually wedded, but the gods smiled down on bisexuality and indeed themselves quite often partook. Zeus, king of the gods, abducted the irresistible cupbearer Ganymede while incarnated as an eagle, and melodic paeans to their love were sung throughout Greece and Italy until the Christian era, when same-sexuality was punishable by death. As remained the case in most Western countries until the 19th or 20th centuries.

With the 1920s, things began to hum a bit. Partly thanks to two brilliant gay lyricists, Lorenz Hart and Cole Porter. In 1921 a big scandal about gay sex in the U.S. Navy actually hit the headlines—at a time when "sex," let alone gay sex, wasn't mentioned in mixed company or the media. Coincidentally or not, 1922 yielded the hit song "My Buddy," a sensual celebration of, supposedly, military buddies.

Probably the first song to use "gay" to mean *gay* was "Don't Ask" in 1926 by George and Ira Gershwin. Ira was the lyricist, George the composer, and George—the genius of the two—was almost certainly gay or bi. "Masculine Women! Feminine

29

Men!" was also heard in 1926, via singer Frank Harris. In 1930 Larry Hart's "Ten Cents A Dance" included "pansies" in a purportedly heterosexual dance hall. Ruth Etting performed it as a disillusioned taxi dancer. The '55 version by Doris Day in an Etting film bio substituted "dandies" for "pansies" but still mentioned her "queer romance" with one. Also in the pansy mode, Hermione Gingold's Broadway revue *Sweet and Low* featured "When a Pansy Was A Flower," and Bea Lillie warbled "I Always Say Hello (To A Flower)," which catalogued the qualities of particular flowers——"Hiya, 'cinths!"——for instance, "pansies never fight."

Just as Oscar Wilde's green carnation was a dandy symbol and a covert badge of gayness in the 1890s, so in the '20s the red necktie became a sexual color code. Music historian Rudy Grillo noted that the red tie's meaning was commonly known by the time it was deployed in "What! No Women?" (1926) and "Gotta Go To Town" (1931). Gay men therefore stopped wearing them——score another one for the closet.

The most lasting color to take over affectional symbolism was lavender (and sometimes purple). Cole Porter used "a dash of lavender" as a sexual code in "I'm A Gigolo." So did the unknown writer of "Lavender Cowboy," about a "tenderfoot" losing his life while trying to prove his manhood. Porter's "You're The Top" was one of his catalogue songs about "top" people, places and items. Among them, "the purple light" seen at night in Spain, that is, the purple lights outside gay bars, then as now in many cities around the world.

Gender-neutral songs which could be sung to either sex were, as today, rare exceptions, i.e., "Gay Love" in 1929, sung by the original Crooner, Bing Crosby, whose then-daringly lilting voice thrilled millions of romance-bound listeners of both genders. More common were songs in which the female singer discovers her romantic object is "queer," a "pansy" and so on, much to her dismay and vindictiveness. A gay composer-lyricist like Porter omitted such homophobia, as in his "I'm Unlucky At Gambling," in which the sophisticated lady finds out her favorite croupier is gay and shrugs it off to happenstance.

Porter went further with lavender lyrics than anyone in America (unlike Hart, he accepted and was happy with his gayness). In "I'd Rather Be Spanish (Than Mannish)" he wrote of

30

gay bullfighters—and bulls! In "Farming" the cow isn't calfing because the bull is "beautiful" but gay. And of course "My Heart Belongs To Daddy," which made a Broadway star of Mary Martin, was written from the perspective of a gigolo whose sugar daddy "treats it so well." (*It*, notice.)

Larry Hart worked with and was much influenced by Richard "Stodgy" Rodgers (who later loathed talented Stephen Sondheim). In 1940 Rodgers & Hart's "Zip" had its singer sniping disdain for deep contraltos or men with alto voices because "Zip—I'm a heterosexual!" (Well, isn't that *special*.)

By the '50s, things were real touchy again. One illustration was the title change of "Lavender Cowboy" to "Delicate Cowboy." Even the lyrics were updated, to reflect a troubled and sometimes paranoid society's fascination with psychoanalysis. The now "inwardly troubled" cowboy tries to "conquer his complex" by buying two six-shooters, then rides out "sidesaddle" singing a tune "light and gay," but still ends up a "delicate" (not "lavender") dead cowboy.

With the '60s, things were looking forward, not backward, and Leonard Bernstein and Stephen Sondheim created "Somewhere" (for *West Side Story*), a universal expression of lovers' yearning for a better, more tolerant time—in this case, a hetero but half-Hispanic pair. When Barbra Streisand put out "Somewhere" as a single and video in the late '80s (from her *Broadway* album), it was still a song inspiring to gay couples but visually inclusive of everyone but gays.

Of course some songs which may have been composed without any gay intent were "appropriated" by gay music lovers, like "Secret Love"—"At last my heart's an open door. . . ." Gay audiences took meaning where they found it. After the war, words said more. The *On The Town* team of Bernstein, Comden & Green described "Christopher Street" —"Life is gay, life is sweet/Interesting people on Christopher Street." Songs either "innocent" or implicit were joined, especially post-'60s, by overt songs. Some were insightful, like Dory Previn's "Michael, Michael" about an overcompensating gay male. Others were inciteful, like Frank Zappa's stereotypically satiric "Bobby Brown."

(However, Zappa is heartening proof that the uninformed and temporarily bigoted can be enlightened into tolerance and a pro-gay stance. He later led the anti-crusade vs. the Washington Wives who wanted to censor rock lyrics, particularly gay ones, and asserted, "My attitude towards anybody's sexual persuasion is: without deviation from the norm, progress is not possible.")

And in the '70s the Village People sang the rousing pre-hit "I Am What I Am," while in the '80s *La Cage Aux Folles* the Broadway musical featured "I Am What I Am" —this one by Jerry Herman—a drag queen's gutsy self-affirmation, urging everyone that it was high time to "open up your closet. . . ."

"The Nutcracker"

Gay composers? A partial list would have to include:
Peter Tchaikovsky and his brother Modeste, Ludwig Van Beethoven, Sir Arthur Sullivan, Cole Porter, Claude Debussy, Maurice Ravel, Lili Boulanger, Nicola Porpora, Charles Tomlinson Griffes, Gerald Tyrwhitt-Wilson (Lord Berners), William Flanagan, Hans Werner Henze, Percy Grainger, Porter Grainger, David Diamond, Samuel Barber, Leonard Bernstein, Stephen Sondheim, Edvard Grieg, Thomas Augustine Arne, Modeste Mussorgsky, Jan Ladislav Dussek, Carl Czerny, Arcangelo Corelli, Jean-Baptise Lully, . . .

Also, Frederic Chopin, Frederick Delius, Benjamin Britten, Noel Coward, Stephen Foster, Aaron Copland, George Fredrick Handel, Manuel De Falla, Francis Poulenc, Gustav Mahler, Franz Schubert, Ivor Novello, Virgil Thomson, Ned Rorem, Reynaldo Hahn and Camille Saint-Saens—who when asked if he were homosexual responded, "Oh, no, no, no, no, no! I am a pederast!" And dozens more, especially among modern composers for Broadway and film.

Modeste Tchaikovsky was a fine composer, but his ten-years-older brother Peter Ilyich (1840-93) was a genius. So much for Modeste. Cholera dramatically and prematurely ended a life made all the more tortuous by Peter's Russian Orthodoxy, which convinced him that his homosexuality was sinful. He was also unsure of the worth of his output, which included the ballets *Swan Lake, The Nutcracker* and *Sleeping Beauty* and *The 1812 Overture.* Perhaps *he* should have been named Modeste.

Yet his first name wasn't totally *inapropos.*

Vassily Sapelnikov (born 1868) became a leading pianist of his day after studying with Tchaikovsky and climbing into bed with him. Gay historian Martin Greif (*The Gay Book of Days*) has cited the composer-pianist's fondness for "duets with his students." The great Peter became the blond Vassily's patron as well as his instructor, and wrote about their intimate relationship. He also *knew* the poet Apukhtin and had a lengthy affair with Vladimir Shilovsky while a professor at the Moscow Conservatory.

As for sanctioned relationships, Tchaikovsky did marry— a "nymphomaniac." Ken Russell's 1970 film bio *The Music Lovers* cast Richard Chamberlain(!) as Peter and Glenda Jackson as his wife. Out of habit, it focused on their meaningless marriage and dwelt on the composer's self-tortures while practically ignoring (or trivializing or stereotyping) the gay liaisons which no doubt soothed his dolorous way.

Tchaikovsky's romantic relationship with his blond-maned nephew Vladimir Davidov, to whom he dedicated his *Symphony No. 6 in B-Flat Minor,* was unrequited. But it was Beethoven (1770-1827) whose ardor for an unresponsive nephew bordered on lunacy. Much of the last thirteen years of Ludwig's life centered on his ward Karl; he'd ousted his widowed sister-in-law, Karl's mother, from joint custody after numerous court battles, and even forbade Karl to see her, which may have led to the youth's unsuccessful suicide attempt in 1826.

Karl got his own back and probably hastened the deaf composer's death the following year. To escape the avuncular dictator, Karl joined the army. Ludwig insisted on accompanying him on the 100-mile journey to Vienna for enlistment. Karl took the ailing genius on a twelve-hour carriage ride, then abandoned him in a cold, dank inn for three days. There, Beethoven contracted the pneumonia from which he died. (The relationship was the subject of Paul Morrissey's 1987 film *Beethoven's Nephew.*)

Beethoven was one of the few great gays who could be called a woman-hater. He regarded all women as "diseased whores" and even his friendships were all with men. For a time, he'd lived with Stephen Von Breuning. . . . When he dedicated the *A-Major Violin Sonata, Opus 47* to George Bridgetower there was such a public row about it that he re-dedicated it to Rudolf Kreutzer. . . . Beethoven dedicated the *C-Minor Piano Concerto* to his good friend Prince Louis Ferdinand of Prussia, who was in love with Jan Ladislav Dussek. . . . Carl Czerny was a pupil of Beethoven, whose *Opus 111 Sonata* was nicknamed *The Uranian Sonata* by 19th century German and Austrian gays (*Uranian* meant "homosexual" before that word gained currency in the late 19th century).

Like Oscar Wilde, Arthur Sullivan (1842-1900) was Irish. Unlike Wilde, he understood the hypocritical English nature which tolerated homosexuality in high places so long as it was free of visibility or comment. Sullivan, unlike his heterosexual English partner William Gilbert, was knighted by the eponymous Victorian. Gay dancer-choreographer John Cranko, who created *Pineapple Poll* in 1951 to music by Sullivan, asserted, "It should have been Sullivan & Gilbert. . . . The composer is far more crucial than the lyricist; his work can stand alone.

"But both men, though temperamental opposites, were good for each other. They complemented each other, and yoked together toward a common musical goal they produced timeless treasures." Much like Rodgers & Hart.

Edvard Grieg (1843-1907) was heterosexualized for the limpid bio-film *Song of Norway*. Ex-elementary schoolers may recall his name from "Anitra's Dance," played in music appreciation classes which often also featured Percy Grainger's "Country Gardens." Grieg enjoyed a passion for the blond Aussie and confessed, "I love him like I love a young woman." The same bisexual refrain was uttered about Percy by American poet Vachel Lindsay.

Jean-Baptiste Lully (1632-87) was an Italian composer-violinist in Paris, eventually appointed Director of Official Music for Louis XIV, the Sun King. Even then, the casting couch was a tradition, and it was known throughout European art circles that playing musical chairs—or beds—with Lully was quite salubrious to one's career. The very active Lully has been commemorated on a French postage stamp for "having helped to sow the seeds of classical music in France."

"The Trout"

Handel (1685-1759), who anglicized his name from Georg to George after settling in England, is best known for the *Messiah,* though he also wrote on Jewish themes and composed the exquisite *Water Music.* Geographically and emotionally, he got around. His famed affair with Johann Mattheson was brief, ended by the tenor's greed and temperament—he challenged Handel to a duel, but neither was hurt. On the gay Gian Gastone's advice, Handel tried the Italian scene, where he struck romantic gold via composer Alessandro Scarlatti and his composer son Domenico; both were lustily bisexual family men. They introduced Handel to the Arcadians, an elite group with mostly gay members.

In Italy, the German composer resided with among others a prince and a cardinal. In Naples, the gay composer-diplomat Agustino Steffani urged him to go to Hanover, where he became Kapellmeister of the Court until moving to England, where he dwelled with a Mr. Andrews before managing to co-habit with an earl. In time, Handel gained his own munificent household, where all the servants except the chambermaids were male, essentially good-looking or good-cooking, for Handel grew with his output.

Rumor has it that somewhere in a private collection in Britain there exist several love letters written by Handel to a prominent royal of the time. Rumor also contends that the current royal family pays the letters' owner to keep them exclusively Private in his collection!

"Take people as they are, not as they should be," wrote handsome 19-year-old Franz Schubert in his diary in 1816. The happily—for us—prolific composer (1797-1828) of *The Trout, Die Winterreise, the Impromptus (Opus 90 and 142), The Unfinished Symphony (No. 8 in B-Minor),* etc., died unhappily at 31 from the syphilis which had plagued him for years. At 26 he'd been hospitalized for the venereal disease which in those days was a virtual death sentence, then experienced a painful two- to three-year convalescence. In 1982 Martin Greif wrote, "Far more is known about this great composer's music than his life. . . . But there is no knowing the real Schubert without knowing the friends with whom he lived from his early teens.

"Almost all never married, with the exception of one who married at 60. The others were suicides. That Schubert traveled in a circle that was predominantly gay seems fairly certain. . . . That he himself was gay is more than likely. There is no evidence to prove otherwise."

More information has since come to light, and even establishment scholars are beginning to admit the man's bi or, more likely, homosexuality. At 18 he lived with a poet-lawyer. At 19 with an actor aristocrat who'd performed in drag under a pseudonym. Other intimates included a tenor, a playwright, a painter, and Anselm Huttenbrenner, in whose arms Schubert died. Franz had had "a dominating (sexual) aversion to," as Huttenbrenner put it, "the daughters of Eve."

That it took so long for Schubert's non-heterosexuality to be acknowledged was due to two factors. First and less importantly, his music only became widely known long after his death, at which time acquaintances and biographers chose to bathe the past that was Schubert's young life in a golden, often sterile, glow. Second, historians and textbook pushers fixed upon those biographies whose versions came closest, via omissions or outright lies, to the officially desired "truth."

The truth, as Oscar Wilde noted, is rarely pure and never simple. "The truth about Hollywood's biographies of gay and bisexual composers," said actor Jerry Dodge, "is that their so-called art mirrors not nature but the average audience." And so with history. Dodge, who appeared in stage musicals like *Hello, Dolly* and *George M!,* used to "carry about my person" a piece of folded paper on which was typed the great 16th century Florentine artisan Benvenuto Cellini's retort to a contemporary who called him "you dirty sodomite:"

"Would to God I did know how to practise so noble an art, for one reads that Jove practised it with Ganymede in paradise, and here on earth there use it the greatest emperors and the grandest kings in the world. . . ."

"I can't remember who sent me that quote from Cellini's memoirs. . . . It might have been (English musical comedy songwriter) Lionel Bart (who wrote *Oliver!*) . . . But the main point is, a man stands up to his detractors, and tries to let the truth shine out, whenever courage allows."

Paris in the 1920s was where truth was most freely allowed

to shine out, and American composers and other artists flocked to the City of Light to escape U.S. puritanism and Prohibition, and enjoy the then-favorable exchange rate and France's lack of anti-homosexual laws. The homophobic but possibly gay Ernest Hemingway called Paris "a movable feast," Thomas Wolfe "an enormous treasure-hoard of unceasing pleasure and delight," Jules Romains "a place and time without equal in the history of the world." Gay artists from Cole Porter and Noel Coward—who dubbed the influential crowd "Nescafe society"—to Reynaldo Hahn found that sexual and artistic freedom went hand in hand there.

Hahn, a Jewish Venezuelan, was Marcel Proust's first known lover. The handsome composer-singer (1875-1947) declared, "If anything, Napoleon was boldly pro-homosexual, and the Napoleonic Code is a boon to half of this city's creative inhabitants. . . . Plato held that the young man who is beautiful doesn't really appreciate his beauty until it is perceived by the older man and then reflected back to the youth.

"It is the same with self-worth and creativity—in a civilization which perceives our humanity, we can see reflected our own potential, and more vividly and confidently create beauty and lasting art for all the world."

"Oh! Susanna!"

Stephen Foster was the first gay American composer to a-chieve fame. In his short life (1826-64) he composed multigenerational down-home classics like "Oh! Susanna!," "Camptown Races," "Old Folks At Home," "Old Black Joe," "My Old Kentucky Home," "Beautiful Dreamer" and—ironically, for it's often held up as "proof" that he couldn't have been gay—"Jeannie With the Light Brown Hair." To quote Ned Rorem, Foster, born on the Fourth of July, was the "hit-maker of his time." Alas, in that pre-ASCAP era the bucks went to the singers of his songs, and the composer was left without a performing rights fee or legal recourse.

Foster outraged Victorian morality by leaving his wife and offspring to go live with a handsome composer named George

Cooper, again ironically best remembered for the barbershop quartet standard "Sweet Genevieve." The 1939 Foster biofilm *Swanee River* upheld the Victorian tradition by erasing Foster's homosexuality and the love of his life from the story. Rather, the Pittsburgher is feebly impersonated by Don Ameche, who lives a routine life and writes his Southern songs—in between spooning with Andrea Leeds —so that minstrel man E.P. Christy (Al Jolson) can bring them to life.

A lesser known American composer was Daniel Gregory Mason (1873-1953)—"Quartet On Negro Themes"—whose lifemate was Virginian composer-pianist John Powell (1882-1962). The short-lived Charles Tomlinson Griffes (1884-1920) is all but forgotten, save for his occasionally revived "The White Peacock" and "The Pleasure Dome of Kubla-Khan." Henry Cowell (1897-1965) was renowned as "the master of the tone cluster" and according to historian Paul Moor was "this country's first internationally celebrated composer." In the 1930s Cowell's fame turned to domestic notoriety when he served a sentence at San Quentin State Penitentiary because of a "sodomy" conviction resulting from a "morals" charge. "America treats most of its artists like shit," said Samuel Barber, "and its bigots like royalty." Or presidents. . . .

(In *Christopher Street* magazine Moor wrote, "Of this century's leading American composers, about half have been gay—an astonishing, possibly unique statistic in music history.")

Virgil Thomson (1896-1989) moved to France in 1920 and for two decades there composed songs, sonatas, quartets, symphonies, the ballet *Filling Station,* film scores, and the opera *Four Saints In Three Acts*—the latter in collaboration with Gertrude Stein. With World War II he returned to the States, where for fourteen years he served as critic for the *New York Herald Tribune* (Ned Rorem was his in-house copyist, earning $20 and two orchestration lessons a week). Thomson was also a well known author of books about music; Rorem called him "this century's most articulate musicologist."

Marc Blitzstein (1905-1964) was a liberal activist during a period when "it was more dangerous than genteel." Along with Thomson and Aaron Copland *(Appalachian Spring),* Blitzstein forged an American classical music independent of European traditions. He also created popular Broadway successes, and performers like Bea Arthur, Eve Arden, Carol Channing and Evelyn Lear got their big breaks in Blitzstein shows. Today he's principally remembered for three things —his 1936 opera *The Cradle Will Rock,* assessed by more than one critic as "America's second-greatest opera;" his translation of Brecht's *The Three-penny Opera,* and his headlined murder.

Blitzstein was always drawn to rough trade. A devotee of bars, baths and quickie relationships, in 1964 he was on the Caribbean island of Martinique working on an opera about the murderers Sacco and Vanzetti. One night in a bar, he picked up two Portuguese sailors who, after sex, robbed and beat him to death, at 59. His work is seldom revived today, and it's been suggested that this is due to his manner of death (which however hasn't hurt Joe Orton's plays any). Blitzstein's legacy includes the *Airborne Symphony,* composed during WWII, and his 1949 opera *Regina,* based on Lillian Hellman's *The Little Foxes.* The work of the handsome composer, born in the City of Brotherly Love, is marked by a transcendent social conscious-ness which eschewed poverty, exploitation and injustice. In 1937 the government padlocked a NYC theatre to prevent performance of his Depression era labor opera *The Cradle Will Rock,* which raised uncomfortable questions about the sacrifice of jobs, futures and "the little people" to big business. John Houseman recalled, "Marc, Orson Welles and I were passionate about putting it on, so that night we marched the cast up Broadway to the Venice Theatre near the park. We were deter-mined to rock the cradle, as it were, and present the work to the public . . . and we did!"

The actor-producer agreed that since his death Blitzstein "has become a neglected figure, unjustly so, because of the cultural higher-ups' incomprehension or hypocrisy."

Samuel Barber (1910-81) had a career span of over fifty years. He began composing at 7, essayed his first opera at 10, and at 13 was admitted to the Curtis Institute of Music. His output embraced the Pulitzer Prize-winning opera *Vanessa* and the popular *Adagio For Strings,* written at 26. Barber became one of the most often performed American composers in the interna-tional symphonic repertoire, and his specially commissioned opera *Antony and Cleopatra* opened the brand new Metropoli-tan Opera House in 1966. In contrast to Blitzstein, whose closest emotional tie was to his sister, Barber, whose gayness was an open secret, lived for many years with operatic composer Gian-Carlo Menotti *(The Medium, Tamu-Tamu)*, who wrote *Vanessa's* libretto and worked with Samuel on other works.

Ned Rorem (born 1923) came out in the mid-'60s in his *Paris Diary*, a kiss-and-tell memoir of a handsome gay man navigating French cultural circles in the '40s and '50s. It was a long way from Indiana, where he'd been born to a Quaker family. A composer, critic and diarist—as Mae West said, "Keep a diary, and someday it'll keep you"—he's written numerous books on music, such as *Settling The Score,* and though a writer of church music, states, "I do not believe in God, but I do believe in poetry." A gay celeb and role model, Ned shares his life with choirmaster James Holmes, whom he met on a blind date in 1967.

"I can't imagine life without Jim. He is my dearest friend, the only person I consult about anything. He is smarter than me, and I rely utterly on him."

Was George Gershwin gay? "Is the Rhapsody blue?" ask some. "No proof," say others. (On the other hand, where's the proof that somebody is "straight?" Saying it doesn't mean it's necessarily so, and having offspring isn't conclusive evidence, as gay 37-year-old composer David Edgar Walter found out; his father Dr. Sam Walter, an organist and composer, was also gay. David's works include *Crazy Dinosaurs, Lavender Requiem* commemorating gay victims of the Nazi holocaust, *Calamus,* a song cycle of gay poems by Walt Whitman; and *Edward II,* from the play about the gay king by gay Elizabethan Christopher Marlowe.)

Gershwin is considered by many to be America's greatest composer, but his sexuality is an unofficially taboo subject. Biographies excuse his not having wed by claiming he was too busy or didn't live long enough (1898-1937), and trot out photos of his female friends ("girlfriends") while enthusing over his "dates" or alleged "affairs" with actresses like bisexual Paulette Goddard—but after all, that's what gay men do in Hollywood: get seen with famous beauties (sometimes themselves bi or lesbian).

George Gershwin idolized Ravel, and was prepared to go to Paris to study with him. Maurice wisely—or shyly—wrote back that he shouldn't, else "you would stop writing good Gershwin and start writing bad Ravel."

Ned Rorem mused, "It's fun to ponder the implications of lines like 'I want to bite my initials on a sailor's neck' or 'all the sexes from Maine to Texas,'" by Ira, and to what extent if any George influenced his brother's lyrics. Nor did George, like a typical hetero male, have a "steady" girlfriend, though he was close to his Hollywood masseur and before he actually needed one, had a handsome male nurse living with him. Like the Gershwin song title says, "It's Hard To Tell."

"Candide"

Orchestra conductor Dmitri Mitropoulos (born 1896) once told gay composer Porter Grainger, "I was born in the 'Gay '90s.' Make of that what you will!" His profession he summed up as "Utopia! You stand proud, looking at well-dressed gentlemen making beautiful music, and telling them what to do."

Lehman Engel (born 1910) was the most popular conductor in American musical theatre and author of the autobiography *This Bright Day.* His praise for his post was more qualified than the Greek's was. "There is ego gratification and deflation, owing to the volatile personalities drawn to music. . . . Some come to make music, others to make merry or even each other, still others to make life hell for everyone else!" For instance:

"Listen, Tommy, I'll take care of the music. You just stick to sucking cock!" So screamed soprano Eileen Farrell at conductor Thomas Schippers (1930-77) after he reprimanded her during a rehearsal at the Metropolitan Opera. Proving that correcting a soprano is harder than Jesse Helms' heart.

Another conductor, Leopold Stokowski (1882-1977), would probably have strangled the bitch-diva. By all accounts he was a man of dark moods and blinding ambition. Thus he latched onto Greta Garbo and as usual the press couldn't see the double-lavender for the stars and romantically dubbed them pink-and-blue. When aristocratic Leo took a wife, it was Gloria Vanderbilt, no less (she later wed *Talk* magazine critic Wyatt Cooper).

One of his platonic girlfriends was writer Anita "Gentlemen

41

Prefer Blondes" Loos, who snapped, "Nowadays gentlemen prefer gentlemen!" in the '70s. "In 1936 Stokie came to Hollywood to appear in *100 Men and A Girl.* I befriended him. . . . He asked me to take Garbo to Bullock's Wilshire to buy her some decent clothes. Said she dressed like a stevedore. . . . He also told Gloria what to wear," long before Murjani put her into jeans.

Stokowski's enemy was competitor Artur [*sic*] Rubinstein, who provided a *feud* details in his memoirs *My Many Years.* Their enmity's germ was "a comment casting aspersions on Stokie's manhood," said Loos' lips. "I don't know when it began, but at a party after Stokie won an Oscar, Rubinstein called him Leona. The word spoke volumes, all of them libelous. And it got back to Stokie what Rubinstein had said." Today Stokowski is remembered in conjunction with *Fantasia* (remember him and Micky Mouse on the podium?), for which he won his 1941 Oscar.

Conductor Vs. Diva, Part II: Peter Feibleman's Lillian Hellman bio *Lilly* recounted the time she attended a party celebrating the unveiling of a painting of Leonard Bernstein. The portrait was ooh-ed and aah-ed over by other guests, but Hellman, who spoke nothing but her mind, growled, "What in hell is everybody talking about, it's an awful painting—it makes Lennie look like a middle-aged fag—I think it's the worst mess I've ever seen in my life." Bernstein's wife eased the other guests away as the playwright muttered, "Now look what I've done." *(Lilly* also revealed her lesbian affairs.)

But Bernstein got in the last word, in 1988. "Most people do think of me as just another pinko faggot, a bleeding heart, a do-gooder." Pause. "But that's what I am."

Anglo-Irish actor Max Adrian appeared in Bernstein's *Candide* and films like the musical *The Boyfriend* (with Tommy Tune) and *The Music Lovers.* "Lennie is highly gifted and highly sexed. He's sincere about wanting to be himself, but also very attracted to the fame and stardom that can come to somebody as gifted as he is." This may have been Adrian's explanation of the gay Bernstein's marrying and having children.

Like Vladimir Horowitz, Bernstein (born 1918) was uncloseted during his lifetime in an '80s bio, Joan Peyser's *Bernstein.* The book was an eye-opener not only about the composer-conductor's life but gay contributions to music via Aaron Copland, Gian-Carlo Menotti, Samuel Barber, Marc Blitzstein, Virgil Thomson, Dmitri Mitropoulos, David Diamond, etc. Many of the subjects were still alive, but despite Peyser's befuddled approach to gayness—and superficial treatment of Bernstein's affairs with, for instance, actor Farley Granger—it brought home to diverse readers the fact that modern music wouldn't be remotely the same minus its gay creators and interpreters.

An anonymous friend of Bernstein opines, "The book was ass-backwards. She made out like Lennie was tortured about his sexuality. Hooey. That he was more creative when he was married or at home with the kids. Double-hooey. If Lennie has suffered at all, it's been because of society's and the music establishment's commandments that he fill the heterosexual mold. He tried to, because he was *that* ambitious."

Lennie the virtuoso lived the life of Riley-plus from the word "go." His first deluxe apartment was immortalized by director friend Irving Rapper in his music-themed 1946 film *Deception*. Bette Davis' apartment in it was modeled on Bernstein's: "We had a trash-can outside the elevator on the way up to the apartment, and Bette said, 'Why the trash-can?' and I said, 'Well, Lennie Bernstein's first penthouse was like this.' The apartment was exactly like Bernstein's, the big studio windows and so on—everyone remembers that set."

For years, Bernstein served as conductor of the New York Philharmonic. He also composed operas and symphonic works. His and Jerome Robbins' ballet *Fancy Free* became Broadway's *On The Town*, with a sailor motif of sorts. In 1949 it was transferred to the screen with Gene Kelly. When in Hollywood, Bernstein often spent Sunday afternoons and evenings at Kelly's home, where the clique included Judy Garland, Jule Styne, Betty Comden and Adolph Green, and gay actor Keenan Wynn. The gang would play volleyball, charades and enjoy casual supper together.

Bernstein was Oscar-nominated for the score of *On The Waterfront*, 1954, but became most famous for *West Side Story*, which culminated in a 1961 Oscar-sweep for the movie version. Leonard had co-written the Broadway musical's lyrics with young Stephen Sondheim, in addition to composing the music, but realized that the youth's lyrical contribution was significantly greater. So he contacted his agent and music publisher and insisted that the score be reprinted and his name removed as co-lyricist——with Bernstein as composer and Sondheim receiving sole credit as lyricist. WSS made Sondheim a star in his own right, and Bernstein's agent Flora Roberts marvelled, "What Lenny did is unheard of in the theatre. Too many people get credit for things they don't do, much less remove their names."

Max Adrian felt, "It is very rare indeed what Lennie did for Stephen. And I know that a great deal of that generous act's motivation was the feeling and camaraderie that one gay man can feel for another."

A——Single Man

A is half of a successful music-making team which has had regular triumphs on Broadway, in Hollywood and overseas. He cheerfully announces in his suite at the Beverly Hills Four Seasons, "All of Musicland, if they know me, know I'm gay!" But he's not officially out, and doesn't plan to make it a matter of record "because Broadway is more morally conservative than it's been in some time, especially now that the musical of *Kiss of the Spider Woman* flopped so heavily. And Hollywood's always been anti-gay. Even its gays are anti-gay, like that (a movie mogul) who recently tied the knot."

H: you're a single man or . . . ?

A: Well, I'm *a* man. But not exactly an "eligible bachelor," because I'm not eligible——to women——and not a bachelor. I've got someone, more or less, though exceptions have been known to be made. . . .

H: Um, how if at all does being gay affect your musical output?

A: I think it's an intrinsic part of who I am and what I feel. I think it's a big part of why I am so creative.

H: Yet your finished product doesn't have a noticeably gay perspective. . . .

A: That's because I have to sell it on the marketplace. I'm——we're——hired to sell to the public.

The Music Lovers

H: The predominantly heterosexual public.

A: When I say "public," it's like saying "straight."

H: Interesting, that public means hetero, and so gay must mean private. . . .

A: At least until AIDS is over with.

H: You say most musical people know you're gay. Has AIDS meant a little less openness on your part?

A: No, I wouldn't do that. When you're known, well, you're known—you can't go back on it. It's not really like changing your hair color!

H: Besides which, times of adversity seem to bring more openly gay artists to the fore.

A: That's absolutely the case. Look at England ever since Thatcher got in.

H: Do you have any favorite young singers these days?

A: (shakes his head smilingly) *If* you can call that singing. . . . I think some of them are handsome. Or clever. Or have a good gimmick—like that Steven Morrissey, who's working the celibacy angle and also the anti-royal bit.

H: Who among singers do you physically fancy?

A: That's just it—today's singers are no loverboys. If they have looks, they don't become singers, they go into acting. And if not acting, television.

H: What can you tell me about your own fascinating life, since we can't talk about your career?

A: Well, mostly I like to talk about other people, not me. I find me dull! Our music, I love, but that's for listening to. But you'll find that the music bunch is a *very* sexy bunch, and unlike actors they spend more time doing it than talking about it or pretending to do it.

H: For instance?

A: You may have heard of a gay composer called David Diamond? He had love affairs with Carson McCullers—she was bi, a great writer—and her husband.

H: Threeways?

A: (nods, then claps)

H: Trios turn up a lot in music, don't they?

A: *L'amour*, the merrier!

H: I read in one of Ned Rorem's books that the composer Francis Poulenc used to chase local youths in Morocco, in the same time-worn tradition as Saint-Saens and Delacroix. . . .

A: The painter Delacroix?

H: I assume he's the one famous Delacroix.

A: Ah, but that leaves out something quite positive, because Poulenc was consumed with love for Pierre Bernac, who was a baritone.

H: Not a tenor?

A: Fortunately for him. (laughs) But he and Bernac were together some 25 years, working, doing the art-song bit touring Europe. Gossip tends to leave out important relationships like that.

H: So do biographies.

A: *Touché*.

H: You and your partner, are you . . . ?

A: I'd love to tell you some great stories about him, but you're a writer, so . . . can't.

H: I'm sort of used to that.

A: (suddenly, vehemently) What I can't abide are the hypocrites!

H: Like who?

A: I'm thinking of a particular man, Mr. Broadway. That's how he wants to be known. A director. Gayer than springtime, but he'd hate to have *you* think so, and he hides behind his wife and family. I can assure you, *he* would not have met to talk with you, even off the record.

H: And Musicland all knows he's gay?

A: (nods)

H: So who does he fool that matters? The "angels" (money-men)?

A: Not even them, I hope. (laughs) But screw him— he's Mr. Pretentious. I *don't* want to talk about him.

H: You brought him up.

A: . . . I think it's important for you to know his type exists. Oh, the stories I could tell!

H: What do you think of Stephen Sondheim?

A: Very nice man. Crushingly talented. For the purposes of your book, not 100 percent on integrity—he wrote a movie called *The Last of Shiela* (1973) with Tony Perkins. Even though *they* wrote it, it was *not* pro-gay by any means!

H: That was long ago, though.

A: Stephen still isn't writing any shows on gay themes, if I'm not mistaken . . . .

H: Was Fritz Loewe of Lerner & Loewe gay?

A: Aye.

H: I always thought Lerner & Loewe were at least on a par with Rodgers & Hammerstein.

A: Wonderful teams.

H: Loewe did all that glorious music (*My Fair Lady, Camelot, Gigi*), yet he got far less press than [Alan Jay] Lerner. How come?

A: First, Fritz was his nickname—he was really Frederick. And he was the far less colorful one, although Alan was the one who got married eight times and thought women had a definite place. He used to say that the only way to get over one woman was to get atop another one!

H: A tasteful man.

A: *I* didn't like him, but he was a nifty writer—of lyrics and scripts. (claps hands to signal end of subject, then sings, "Forget your genders, come on, get happy. . . ." to the tune of Judy Garland's "Forget your troubles, come on, get happy . . .")

H: Your own lyrics?

A: (laughs) My very own.

H: How do you rate Jerry Herman?

A: How do I . . . ? Charming man. Loves money and *earns* it. Do you know his work?

H: Who doesn't? I think it's incredible how many beautiful tunes he's done—words and music (for *Hello, Dolly; Mame* and several others). I went to a benefit that honored him in January of 1989. It was for AIDS Project Los Angeles. Lucille Ball was there, watching her daughter perform.

A: I'm surprised Jerry would even speak to her, after what she did to his songs in that movie *(Mame)!* But that's Jerry for you—no hard feelings, ever.

H: You live longer that way. Sometimes.

A: *I* think so. Ingrid Bergman said the key to a felicitous life is good health and bad memory. Then she died of cancer. (sighs loudly, then laughs) Let's banish the gloom. . . . Say, do you know *Babar the Elephant?*

H: Not personally.

A: Silly! Francis Poulenc did the music to that.

H: No kidding.

A: Now, do you know about P? (a record mogul whom the media romantically linked with one of his female singers) Right now, he's in the middle of all this fuss about those homophobic acts on his label, denying like crazy, but if people only *knew*. . . . Back in the early days of AIDS— possibly *before*— he used to drive his black Porsche into the back alley of a porno bookstore in North Hollywood and pick up young boys there every day. . . .

H: Of course you mean young men, right? Why do people say "boys?"

A: That's not the point. I'm not saying P's a pederast. I just think it's so funny he's so aloof from the homophobic lyrics in his own business, yet there he was, such a whore-monger, and *still* functioning!

H: But presumably not still whoring.

A: No, we're *all* careful now.

H: Tell me, was Vincent Youmans gay?

A: Young man, when you're in love, the whole world's gay! (gets up, moves toward bar) Now, I'd like to propose a toast. . . .

H: Oh, God. Not to the ladies who lunch.

A: You have to speak up, I can't hear you. (uncorks champagne) But so long as you can hear *me* . . .

"Grease"

Pianist Paul Jacobs was the first prominent musician to die of AIDS, at 53 in 1983—almost the age of Debussy, the composer for whom he felt the greatest affinity.

The most notable AIDS death in music was Liberace, 67 in 1987. What made it even more of a headline-grabber was the corpse's unwillingness to come out of the closet. On his deathbed, he'd threatened to sue anyone who said he had AIDS or was gay. After his death, there was a tug of war between his last requests and the local coroner; Liberace lost.

When the Wizard of Ooze released his '80s autobiography, *The Wonderful World of Liberace,* he claimed his virginity had been taken by an older woman called Miss Bea Haven —droll, huh? The non-public version was offered in the posthumous bio *Behind the Candelabra: My Life With Liberace* by Scott Thorson with Alex Thorleifson. "Lee" had told Scott about a football player with the Green Bay Packers.

"He was the size of a door, the most intimidating man I'd ever seen. Every time I looked out in the audience, there he was, smiling at me. . . . One night he asked to drive me home. That's the night I lost my virginity." Thorson was the ex-lover who broke the *National Enquirer* story about being kicked out by the pianist whom he then sued for palimony.

One of Liberace's few flings with a fellow celebrity was with Rock Hudson in the early '50s, when Lee's TV show was seen in more homes than *I Love Lucy* and Hudson was a struggling contract player at Universal, where he was labeled the Baron of Beefcake because of his willingness to do bare-chested publicity photos. Hudson apprised this author that Lee was a so-so lover, generous and attentive, but "too patronizing" and inclined to be "dictatorial and jealous."

By the '60s, according to talk show host Carl David, Liberace was "cruising the Akron store on Sunset Boulevard with his little doggie in hand, dressed all in white—Lee, I mean—and trying hard to pick up Mexicans on the store's parking lot. He was quite flamboyant and daring." Flamboyant but not daring in his public life. He habitually dressed and acted the nance, while negating his gayness.

"I tried to get him on my show," said David. "He was definitely intrigued and rather flattered. But terrified. *(Lifestyle Update)* is a gay cable show. Obviously he didn't know the media, because he was afraid that some prime-time show might run an excerpt of my show, with him on it! I told him, 'Lee, I should only live so long.'

"He'd done a few B-movies but thought of himself as a multi-media darling. He wasn't—he was a musical showman. A pianist. A two-dimensional Personality, as opposed to a one-dimensional type like Rock Hudson." In the same vein, Warren Casey stated, "Acting brings greater fame but exacts a steeper price. Acting is pretense, on and off the screen. But music is performed on a stage or a record, and that's it." True enough, music stars like Ned Rorem, Leonard Bernstein and Vladimir Horowitz—to name a few—have been printed up in their lifetimes as gay and didn't suffer for it professionally; in Rorem's case, his light-purple prose memoirs made him more celebrated than before.

One typically finds that when a music personality enters film, he or she suddenly becomes more worried about the Image and conforms more desperately to the double movie-star-sexual-standard. Casey, an author-lyricist who collaborated on the musical *Grease*, explained, "Sergei Diaghilev the ballet impresario lived his life as high and mighty and flighty as he pleased. His head was literally so big he had to have hats made to order! But he's the one who said, 'The public sees singers and musicians as entertainers. No more, no less. But the public takes picture stars as their role models!'" Apparently the public values what it sees more highly than what it hears.

In 1988 Warren Casey planned to attend the Rock and Roll Hall of Fame induction ceremonies (where Little Richard cooed, "I just love the Supremes. They remind me of me."). He died of AIDS that year, having told friend Carl David, "I always saw Liberace as an embarrassment to gays. That was an opinion. What I can't forgive is how he treated his private life as so shameful that even in death he wanted it secret. He could have done so much good, telling the world with dignity that yes, he had AIDS, and so do thousands of good, creative, successful people.

"Instead, he carried on like a cowardly fruit, right into the grave."

The incredible lightness of being Liberace. . . . But enough about a mega-millionaire who died of AIDS yet willed not one cent to combat it or to help fellow PWAs.

The year after his death, nephew Lester Lee Liberace, 33, was ordered into a state mental hospital for seven years after stabbing his sister Ina Liberace, 28, in the stomach with an eight-inch kitchen knife. *The Hollywood Star* and other sources had cited Ina as actress Kristy McNichol's girlfriend. Not long after the death, his relatives were planning a shopping mall in Las Vegas, to be named after their benefactor. But before the mall could be commenced, a gay bar had to be kicked off the site. Liberace's family told the press that they'd had no choice in the eviction, since they didn't want persons "of that kind around. . . ."

"Bolero"

Those crooning pianists called cafe singers run the quality gamut from Vegas-y self-parodies to class acts like Bobby Short and Michael Feinstein. Short, a musical prodigy born in 1924, worked as a sophisticated youth at Harlem's famed Apollo. In the book *American Singers* he reflected, "Apollo audiences were used to Pigmeat Markham, Butter Beans and Susie, and Moms Mabley. . . . They didn't care about my white tie and tails."

Later, when his generation was into boogie-woogie, he "thought it was cheap" and instead drew inspiration from Hildegarde, billed as "the incomparable Hildegarde." "She was the queen. . . . She had the slickest nightclub act. It was produced down to the last sigh. Even down to a blue spotlight that brought out the color in the red roses that invariably stood by her piano." Like Short, she favored Broadway scores, Cole Porter, the Gershwins and Noel Coward.

Mabel Mercer was another influence, as Short "absorbed" the style of great singers while fine-meshing his own. He found a professional niche at the fabled Cafe Gala, the soigné nightclub on Sunset Boulevard where gay movie colonists hung out with East Coast couples like Cole Porter and Monty Woolley and Lena Horne and Lennie Hayton. Short worked there during the late '40s and early '50s. "I fell into a velvet-lined rut." He became the Gala's star attraction, the stars' entertainer of choice.

But he didn't attract Hollywood stardom. One night, singer-actress Olga San Juan turned to Leonard Spigelgass and inquired, "Who is this Bobby Short? Why isn't he in films?" Spigelgass replied, "He's too chic."

A letter in the November, 1988, *Hollywood Kids' Newsletter* recalled Halloween night: "As I was walking near San Vicente Boulevard I spotted three men in outrageous drag. Looking closer, I realized that the three in question were none other than Jm J. Bullock [*sic*] of *Hollywood Squares,* Michael Feinstein the popular pianist, and Richard Simmons the fitness freak! I followed them for quite a while and am *sure* it was them. . . ." The letter was signed Kind of a Drag, West Hollywood.

In the gay community, Feinstein is known for his frequent support at AIDS fundraisers, e.g., a 1988 benefit for HERO (Health Education Resource Organization) at which he and comedian Paula Poundstone performed (she was denied booking on the Johnny Carson show because she was "too androgynous"!). The gala raised over $170,000, including a $7,000 personal contribution from Michael Feinstein.

In the entertainment world, Feinstein is known as the top cafe singer since Bobby Short. "Please don't bend my ear with punk or funk," he croons, "it's junk." Back when his peers were worshipping the Beatles and Stones, Feinstein idolized the Gershwins. He worked his way up the hard way— and the Steinway. The young Ohioan was employed by the reclusive Ira Gershwin, who was annotating Gershwin material for deposit in the Gershwin Archive at the Library of Congress. After that scholarly job, Feinstein fused his pleasing baritone, sparkling blue eyes and love for Gershwin tunes into a multi-media career that includes TV, recordings and live performances on Broadway and elsewhere.

Harold Bauer was a renowned pianist who'd befriended Claude Debussy and Maurice Ravel and interpreted their music. One of his concert offerings which sent a *frisson* of forbidden pleasure through many audiences—it was once banned in Boston!—was Debussy's *Chansons de Bilitis* (it was composed in 1897, with text by gay French poet Pierre Louys). Was Bauer romantically involved with Claude or Maurice? Bauer told a friend who told a biographer, "When I think of Ravel, I think of his *Bolero*. To some, it's invigorating, to me, draining."

Thanks to the movie *10*—which featured Robert Webber as a gay composer—'80s audiences rediscovered *Bolero* as music to make love by. It was first given as a ballet in 1928 at the Paris Opera by Ida Rubinstein. Bisexual author Colette described Ravel's "delicate, rodent's hands . . . and his gaze would flit over the surface of things like a squirrel's. . . . He liked loud ties and frilly shirts."

In 1975 it was noted at Ravel's centenary (1875-1937) that he was "the most played modern composer." Most of his substantial royalties go to the widow of his brother's widow's second husband—another gay will for straight relatives and acquaintances. . . . Roger Nichols wrote in "Ravel Remembered" that "He loved the Paris night life, was often in his corner at *Le Boeuf sur le Toit* or *Le Grand Ecart*, reveling in the decorations, the lights shaded with multi-colored cellophane, the Negroes, the saxophone and Clement Doucet at the piano."

Alma Mahler, Gustav's over-protective wife, felt, "He was a narcissist. He came to breakfast rouged and perfumed, and he loved the bright satin robes that he wore in the morning." Ned Rorem said of Ravel, "The two most frequent questions: Was he Jewish? Was he homosexual? (One assumes he couldn't be both!)" Ravel himself divulged, "Basically the only love affair I ever had was with my music."

A *ménage-à-trois* may or may not be considered a love affair, but Ravel was said to be part of one with Catalonian pianist Ricardo Viñes (1876-1943) and Manuel De Falla (1876-1946), Spain's greatest composer since the Renaissance. Picasso thought Viñes *(Nights in the Gardens of Spain)* the shyest man he'd ever met, "even smaller than myself, and as modest and withdrawn as an oyster shell." De Falla was a friend of Diaghilev and his then-lover Leonide Massine. The three collaborated on the ballet *The Three-Cornered Hat,* and De Falla was observed to stare frequently at the dancing Massine in unrequited, very quiet passion.

Viñes and Ravel entered the Paris Conservatoire in 1889 and were close friends for years. Studies may not have been all they shared; Viñes' diary entry for Thursday, 23 November, 1888, read, "I played a scale in thirds and octaves. In the evening we went for the first time to the home of the boy with long hair called Mauricio, 73 rue Pigalle on the 5th floor." Thirds and threesomes figured prominently in the shy Spaniard's life!

Vladimir Horowitz (1904-89) was yanked out of the closet in 1983 by biographer Glenn Plaskin. The husband of Toscanini's daughter informed this would-be interviewer, "The music press, I talk to. The book-sellers, no!" Ironically, the pre-eminent pianist had once chided gay composer Vincenzo Bellini for having chosen as heterosexual a subject as Romeo and Juliet for his opera *I Capuleti e i Montecchi* (which debuted at Venice's La Fenice in 1930) and then having over-romanticized it!

"I Wanna Hold Your Hand"

Brian Epstein was a gay record store owner in Liverpool who prided himself on being able to fill any customer request.

One day some three decades ago, a fan came in and asked for a record called "My Bonnie" by the Beatles. (Actually, the group was only a backup band on that song.) Epstein searched for the obscure record, didn't have it, and went to see the group at the Cavern Club, some 250 steps from his front door. The rest, as they say, is history.

Bob Wooler, disc jockey at the CC, contended, "If Epstein was not homosexual, the Beatles wouldn't have happened." The shy youth had a crush on the Beatles and doggedly pursued a recording contract for them, then became their manager and created their Look by getting them out of leather and into suits—an unusual look for rock 'n roll, but one which helped them cross over and become an intergenerational, international phenomenon.

Epstein knew that the conservative suits were needed to offset the "girlish" hair which alarmed parents and moralists of the time. (Only Moe Howard of the Three Stooges had gotten away with such a 'do, since he was sexless and not meant to be taken seriously, except by Larry and Curly.)

Epstein had a particular crush on John Lennon, and in 1963 they went to Spain together and apparently had a brief affair there, as Peter Brown suggested in *The Love You Make*. In *The Man Who Made the Beatles: An Intimate Biography of Brian Epstein,* Ray Coleman negated the affair, because Lennon was heterosexual-—the author was unaware that one experience doesn't make one homosexual, or even a practicing, let alone perfected, bisexual. (Epstein had a sad propensity to fall for straight men, and once he could afford them turned increasingly to drugs for solace and to counter his business responsibilities.)

At any rate, when Epstein and Lennon returned to Liverpool, Bob Wooler insinuated to John that something sexual had happened between the pair, and Lennon beat Wooler so badly that he had to be hospitalized. Had nothing happened, the insecure bully probably wouldn't have punished Wooler so severely for guessing correctly (see the *Brits* chapter).

Brian Epstein died at 32 from "an accidental drug overdose." Called "the fifth Beatle," his fantasies and tastes revolutionized the look and sound of modern music from the '60s on. But don't expect an Epstein biofilm during the ex-Beatles' lifetimes. One Hollywood producer who optioned the Epstein story finally gave it up after repeatedly failing to obtain the necessary waivers from the three once-fab survivors.

Music producers like Epstein and creators like *W* often impress their sexuality into their musical product. *W* is a formerly very successful rock lyricist. "Do you ever wonder why so many fictional heroines in movies and novels have masculine or genderless names? I used to wonder. It's because a lot of the writers are gay men who must follow the formula of using a heroine, so they turn their male fantasy into a woman for the public, but make her very spunky and brave. . . .

"I've written some songs with female titles to them, but in music the names tend not to be butch, 'cause we can't fool them with a picture of a girl on the book cover or an actress playing the part. . . . I'd wanted to do a song about an ultimate gender-bender, like Billy Tipton, who turned out to be a woman. But I was told by the record execs that it's *too* radical—that it *might* work as a TV movie instead."

When Billy Tipton died in 1989 at the age of 74, "his" secret gender was finally out. The baby-faced, barely eyebrowed jazz entertainer died of an internal hemorrhage, for years having refused to see a doctor in spite of a serious ulcer condition. In 1962 Tipton had married a stripper and later adopted three sons—the ex-wife after his death informed the tabloids that she'd never known that her husband of eighteen years had been a woman!

The elaborate ruse may have been born of Billy's desire for a career as a musician in an era when women only sang songs, or, uh, inspired them. Ex-wife Kitty explained, "There were certain rules and regulations in those days if you were going to be a musician." Tipton, a saxophone and piano player, worked with the Jack Teagarden, Russ Carlyle and Scott Cameron bands, then formed the Billy Tipton Trio in the '50s and performed in nightclubs all over the western U.S.

Drummer Dick O'Neil, who worked with Billy in the '50s, allowed that there were "cracks about his face and high singing voice. But I would almost fight anybody who said that. I never suspected a thing." As time went on, the musician felt she needed more of a "cover," and acquired a wife, then a family. Prior to Kitty, Billy had introduced some girlfriends to the boys in the band. After her death, one associate wondered if Tipton "may have been a little 'lez.' Who knows?"

One adopted son posthumously realized, "He had so much to protect, and I think he was just tired . . . of keeping the secret." Billy, who didn't confide her secret to the boys or leave any written explanations, died broke and virtually forgotten by an industry in which she'd never been a star. Another son said, "You can imagine the pressure he lived with. Maybe that's what gave him the ulcer that ended up killing him/her." Tipton's story was optioned by a major film production company for television—from the Unobservant ex-wife's point of view. . . .

A gay screenwriter who used to free-lance for music publications reveals, "Music personalities are the worst-served of any personalities by writers, publishers and producers. Unlike lots of movies, almost no songs get based on true stories, which carries over into singers' real lives. Publishers and Hollywood don't care about the truth, and the public doesn't demand it." Tipton's story will thus most likely omit any whiff of lavender and dwell upon Billy's heartening but fatal balancing act of careerism and nuclear family unit. It will titillate middle-American viewers while pleasing cautious advertisers by pulling good ratings (but no Controversy) via its bowdlerized novelty.

Frank Zappa once described rock journalists as "people who can't write, doing interviews with people who can't think, in order to prepare articles for people who can't read." In that world, which includes the big and little screen, singers and musicians are never gay, only eccentric.

"Something For The Boys"

Lorenz Hart (1895-1943) was "Bewitched, Bothered and Bewildered." For years Broadway's leading lyricist, he was the first partner of Richard Rodgers, and despite the equal commercial success which Rodgers found with Oscar Hammerstein, many found the latter's lyrics sappy. The gay Hart wrote lyrics that were "tough and muscular," said one critic, compared with Hammerstein's "verses that a marcelled dowager could have submitted to *The Ladies' Home Companion*." Hammerstein was hetero and a six-footer, while Hart was barely over five feet tall, or four-foot-nine, depending on your source.

It was a toss-up which Hart regretted more, his shortness or gayness. He cloaked both with wit and a brittle butchness which led him to become "grotesque and alcoholic," according to columnist Lee Graham. The bittersweet is evident in many of Hart's songs, like "My Funny Valentine," "Where Or When?" and "The Lady Is A Tramp." Hart's rages over his lack of height (not stature) signalled an increasing melancholia. He "was given to disappearing for days at a time," said an early biography, which elsewhere admitted that "he had no success at all with the female sex."

Not that he ever gave up wanting to change. Vivienne Segal, 90 in 1988, had been a star on Broadway and was Hart's favorite performer. He wrote "Bewitched . . ." for her to introduce in *Pal Joey* in 1940. Shortly before his death, he proposed to her. In 1988 she recalled, "I loved him, but not that way." Lee Graham believed, "As much as he could love any woman, Hart loved Vivienne, but the emotion stopped short of sexual desire." It was Hart who wrote "Falling In Love With Love". . . .

Through his lifetime and beyond, Hart's inherent "secret love" was a carefully guarded secret. Maurice Chevalier, who starred in Hart's film musical *Love Me Tonight,* opined, "He was a tiny man with a great big fury. . . . If he had not written hundreds of beautiful songs, no one would have liked him." Musical actor Dan Dailey got his first big break via a quick affair with Hart, and told this writer, "He disliked himself before and after sex, and his partners during."

That emotionally tempestuous double-life didn't prevent him from averaging two Broadway musicals a year during the last twenty years of his life—in 1926 he wrote six! In the early '30s, Hart went to Hollywood, as any successful lyricist or composer eventually did, but considered his two years there an unpleasant waste. By 1943 his moods, alcoholism and health had lost him Richard Rodgers, who found a new partner and a new lease on success via *Oklahoma!* It was a new era for more naturalistic American musicals, but Hart declined to continue creating, and though he wished Richard well, took to his bed.

Months later, he was dead. It took 35 more years before the homosexuality he'd been made to feel so inferior about was mentioned in print, in a biography.

Those good old, bad old days were described by Broadway playwright and screenwriter *(Gypsy, A Majority of One)* Leonard Spigelgass in the book *Rodgers & Hart—Bewitched, Bothered and Bedeviled.* "Homosexuality in that period had two levels: one, it was held in major contempt, and the other was that among Larry Hart's kind it was the most exclusive club in New York. That's terribly important to realize—that it was a club into which you couldn't get. . . . I mean, no ordinary certified public accountant could get in the Larry Hart, Cole Porter, George Cukor world. That was *the* world. That was W. Somerset Maugham. That was Cole Porter. That was Noel Coward.

"That was *it* if you were into that, and I remember those houses on 55th Street, with the butlers and carryings-on. . . . You were king of the golden river! That was it! In spite of the attitude towards homosexuality in those days. On the one hand you said, 'They were homosexual—oh, my, isn't that terrible!' On the other hand you said, 'My God, the other night I was at dinner with Cole Porter!' Immediate reaction: 'Jesus Christ, what did he have on? What was he wearing? What did he say? *Were* you at that party?'

"So you had this ambivalence . . . ."

An ambivalence which the media still perpetrates. A 1990 PBS-TV special, *You're The Top: The Cole Porter Story,* was singled out by *TV Guide* for its "sheer frankness." In other words, the word "homosexuality" was actually used, once— in one of two references to Porter's gayness; the other was the "goldenboys" lying around his Hollywood pool (which Lorenz should have visited). Narrated by Bobby Short and featuring Michael Feinstein, Saint Subber, etc., the program was steeped in references to The Marriage and The Wife. "The Cole Porter we never knew!" gushed one reviewer. And still don't.

Porter (1893-1964) was to the manor born. A contentedly spoiled only-child, he left Peru, Indiana, for Yale, where he briefly studied law to please his maternal grandfather, a milliner. He then switched to more liberal Harvard to study music. Gay pal Monty Woolley *(The Man Who Came to Dinner)* introduced him to New York's theatre scene before Porter moved to Paris after the disappointing flop of his first Broadway show, the 1916 *See America First* (which was Clifton Webb's debut). Until the last years of his life, Cole spent part of each year living in palatial splendor in Paris and Venice.

In Europe he met Linda Lee Thomas, an elegant Kentucky divorcee whose first husband had repeatedly beaten her, then settled a fortune on her. The 1919 marriage made headlines, specifically, "Boy With $1 Million Weds Girl With $2 Million!!" Eight years Cole's senior, Linda made no sexual demands whatever, and put his career first.

Back in America, the frog-eyed genius' successes began to pour forth: *Anything Goes, You Never Know, Something For The Boys, Kiss Me, Kate; Can-Can,* film scores like *The Gay Divorcee, The Pirate, High Society, Les Girls,* and hundreds of songs from the provocatively titled and therefore temporarily banned "Love For Sale" to "Night and Day," "Begin The Beguine," "Blow, Gabriel, Blow," "Let's Do It," "I Love Paris," "Miss Otis Regrets," "True Love," "I Get a Kick Out of You," "Just One of Those Things," "I've Got You Under My Skin," "It's De-lovely" and "In the Still of the Night."

Cole's lovers included blacks and whites, gays and bi's, rich and poor, famous and infamous, gondoliers, California beach bums, and at least one greedy wine steward, as Truman Capote famously related:

"He was Italian . . . a nut-brown man . . . with oiled hair and the sexiest jawline. . . . He was Southern, so they called him Dixie. . . . Cole's approach was creative: he invited Dixie to his apartment under the pretext of getting advice on the laying in of a new wine cellar—Cole! who knew more about wine than that dago ever dreamed. So they were sitting on the couch—the lovely suede one Billy Baldwin made for Cole—all very informal, and Cole kisses this fellow on the cheek, and Dixie grins and says, 'That will cost you $500, Mr. Porter.'

"Cole just laughs and squeezes Dixie's leg. 'Now that will cost you $1,000, Mr. Porter.' Then Cole realizes this piece of pizza was serious; and so he unzippered him, hauled him out, shook it and said, 'What will be the full price on the use of that?' Dixie told him $2,000. Cole went straight to his desk, wrote a check and handed it to him. And he said, 'Miss Otis regrets she's unable to lunch today. Now get out.'"

Another—consummated—lover of Porter's, according to *The Gay Book of Days,* was Jackie Kennedy Onassis' womanizing father John Bouvier! Also Cary Grant, whom Cole chose to portray him in the propagandistic biofilm *Night and Day* (in which even Monty Woolley, who also introduced Cole to male bordellos, played a heterosexual Monty Woolley).

In 1937 tragedy struck. During a riding accident, Cole's horse fell and broke both his legs. The pain lasted the rest of his life—also psychically, for the vain, pleasure-loving aesthete was forced to rely on canes, braces, wheelchairs and in 1958 to undergo an amputation which put a voluntary end to his creativity and after which he became a recluse at his sumptuous apartment up in the Waldorf. (Linda and Cole had separated, but changed their minds in 1937. In the '50s, both were invalids, though Cole got around more. Linda died at 70 in 1954.)

As with Coward and other institutions of their day, Cole Porter after the war was considered old-hat. He was said to be out of touch with public taste (particularly with his 1950 musical *Out Of This World,* which boasted "vast expanses of scantily clad males" that spelled trouble in Boston), and critics greeted his every new effort with the refrain, "not up to his old standards," alluding to his glittering '30s heyday.

But then came a new run of hits on Broadway and in film, and television variety shows—with Hollywood royalty performing Cole's songs—reminded the nation that Porter had never really gone out of style (and never would) and that his sole rival for the title of Greatest American Songwriter was Irving Berlin, who like Cole was the only Tin Pan Alley giant who did both the words and the music. But where Berlin's art was simplicity, Cole Porter's was sophistication. He forced the American musical to grow up, and made our lyrics sexier and more fun:

"He was sly," said Dan Dailey. "He wrote 'Let's Do It' ("Birds do it, bees do it . . . "), and it was naughty but clean. Everyone knew what Cole meant—sex!—but he wrote 'Let's do it, let's fall in love.' Cole loved sex, but he enveloped it, like his life, in glamour and romance and optimism."

Crooners

"I have had sex with men; does that make me gay?" ——Rod McKuen

"I'm A Man"

The Circle Star Theatre in San Carlos, California, late 1987. Fabian's "Good Time Rock 'N Roll, Volume IV" concert.

My memory floats forward over the waves of shaboom to a mid-'80s TV talk show where Frankie Avalon good-naturedly admitted that there'd been Rumors because he and Fabian lived together in the early '60s. At last count, the former Teen Angel had eight offspring, and as for "the Fabulous Fabe," he was one of *Playgirl's* first celebrity centerfolds—way back when they didn't display their centerpieces.

Also in the Circle Star audience is Steve Warren, an entertainment journalist. He recalls "painful high school memories of the days when I was seemingly the only gay person in the city of Philadelphia." Despite several teen singing stars who emerged from Philly, "We didn't have role models then. I was attracted to other boys and fooled around a little, but I would see Liberace on television and think I couldn't be one of *those* because I didn't act like *him*."

After Fabian sings a few bars of "old time rock 'n roll" and unsuccessfully attempts to get the middle-aged audience to croon along, he gives up and introduces Frankie Ford. Later, Warren writes, "In the army a man told me he knew someone who had tricked with Ford in Korea. I was impressed. I didn't

63

know then that there's no one you can name who some gay person won't claim tricked with someone he knows.

"It could be true about Ford. . . . He wears a magenta lamé jacket and a keyboard scarf and says things like, 'If I'm reincarnated, I wanna come back as a crawfish. It's the only creature in the world where they suck your head and eat your tail!'" Ford sings a Little Richard medley before performing his own hit, "Sea Cruise."

During intermission someone volunteers that Chubby Checker once worked in a record shop in drag. Soon after, he sang both parts on *Samson and Delilah,* impersonating the latter in a garish red wig. "You won't find the song on his greatest hits package," noted Warren. "Chubby was a funny guy until 'The Twist' got him taken seriously."

Back on stage, Fabian reprises some of his hits—"Tiger," "Turn Me Loose," "I'm A Man"—then reminisces about when "I wore white buck shoes and real tight mohair pants. I still have brain damage from those pants." Discovered on a South Philly doorstep, Fabian Forte was signed to a contract largely because of his looks and promotability. In 1959 he made his screen debut in *Hound-Dog Man.* Said one male co-star, "The boy's beautiful. He sings too. If he cooks, I might marry him."

The final act in the concert is Little Anthony, who jokes, "You can call me Anthony. I'm 45 years old, I've got eight kids, four grandkids, and you're still calling me 'Little.'" Warren: "It's lucky he gave us his heterosexual credentials. He sounds gayer than Frankie Ford, with his falsetto singing and a comic delivery somewhat like Flip Wilson's as Geraldine.

"Last year at Fabian's 'Good Time Rock 'N Roll, Volume II,' the Platters' lead singer Paul Robinson ad-libbed to a man in the audience, 'I saw you in a queer bar. Of course I was just looking in. I wasn't inside like you were.'"

On either side of the sexual fence, "queer" was a '50s obsession. It was the first decade in which the closet door opened a crack to shed some light on the worlds of song and film. But only a crack—i.e., the first American film with a gay character was *Suddenly, Last Summer* in 1959 from Tennessee Williams' play. However the villainous Sebastian never appeared *in toto;* one glimpsed an arm here, a leg there, his back, . . .

In the mid-'80s the '50s-style "Johnny, Are You Queer?"

became a radio hit in Southern California. Until TV reported the phenomenon and irate parents saw to it that the song, aimed at teens, died of Controversy. From Northern California, Sylvester told me over the phone, "I hear Josie Cotton sang 'Johnny, Are You Queer?' to a gay audience, then made a real lame apology. Honey, I'd hate to have her nerve in my tooth!"

Sylvester grew up in the '50s and unfondly remembered, "I deeply, truly regretted that I could never have a pompadour. In those days a boy singer could become a star just on the strength of his pompadour! My mother says it was the most flamboyant time. In some ways it was more flamboyant than today. . . . And a hell of a lot of the pretty-boy singers that came up then were AC/DC or gay. But always closeted.

"My favorite singer among whites was Frankie Avalon. I nearly died in 1965 or thereabouts when I saw him in a cheap musical called *Ski Party* where he actually wore drag!" Of course, Hollywood drag was always a comical means to a hetero end, and Avalon and Dwayne "Dobie Gillis" Hickman only wore dresses to convince nymphets Deborah Walley and Yvonne "Batgirl" Craig that they, too, were just plain sorority girls (very plain). Who later woo and win the real girls.

"When Frankie sang a song in that movie, I nearly creamed in my pants—because it was titled 'Lots, Lots More.' Ooh, hon-ey-chile!

"Pants on boy singers in the '50s got tighter than ever. And there was nothing more flamboyant or sexy than a white boy with slicked down hair and tight pants and white shoes!" To think, Pee-Wee Herman would have been a sex god in the '50s. . . .

"Menergy"

There were two reigning disco divas created by gays in the '70s. One was Donna Summer, who disowned her original audience en route to the religious and commercial masses. The other was Sylvester, who never had a prayer of finding a place in the mainstream sun (Gustav Mahler believed, "Mediocrity lies on the mainstream."). Nor did Sylvester eschew his biggest fans, or cloak his sexuality in anything but drag and exuberance. When he died of AIDS in 1988 he was 42 but looked and acted 22.

His first hit record was "You Make Me Feel . . . Mighty Real" in 1969, the year of Stonewall. He followed it with fourteen more records and five gold songs and one platinum. Born Sylvester James, he performed with San Francisco's drag act the Cockettes in the early '70s, and dwelled in the city's gay-dominated Castro district. "I love living here, doing what I always wanted—earning my living as a male soprano.

"Honey, I'd never want to be a eunuch, but people forget the *castrati* of Italy. Hundreds of years ago they lived like royalty and were idolized as singers of perfection."

Like his idols, Sylvester sometimes performed in venues such as the San Francisco Opera House and "those great classy joints in Europe—beautiful places that made me feel beautiful." His meaty, beat-y, bouncy songs included "Menergy," "Do You Wanna Funk," "Rock the Box" and more laid-back tunes like "I Need You" and "I'm Not Ready to Fall in Love Again."

"He soars beyond gender," said one critic. But not far enough for Warner Brothers Records, which at one point asked him "to butch it up a little" for his new record cover. The result? "Immortal" boasts the singer in flame-colored wig, rhinestone jacket and . . . heels, lying on his back, literally having the last laugh.

"I may look like a darker, shorter Liberace," he explained in '88, "but honey, we are *not* soul sisters." Unlike the Sultan of Kitsch, Sylvester bravely announced to the press that he had AIDS and marched in the 1988 San Francisco Gay Pride Parade—in a wheelchair.

"Back in 1977 I was feeling low, and then one day I heard a song, out of nowhere, sung by an honestly gay black man named Carl Bean. It was titled 'I Was Born That Way.' It just made me feel like I had to go on no matter what, and try and inspire or at least comfort others. . . . I decided I could either get bitter or I could get myself a better life."

After his death, Sylvester was honored at two Bay Area benefits. Patti LaBelle dedicated the last night of her Circle Star Theatre engagement to him. She sang her song "You Are My Friend," which he had covered, and introduced Gladys Knight in the audience (Knight had sung with Dionne Warwick &

Friends on the AIDS fundraiser "That's What Friends Are For"). At San Francisco's Galleria, several singers teamed to sing Sylvester's "Dance——Disco Heat" and "Mighty Real" while a slide show illustrated his career highlights and his old costumes hung about the hall, glittering reminders of a life that was more than flash.

Little Richard (Richard Wayne Penniman) did surface for a time in the mainstream. That was in the 1950s, when rock was new, people were sexually naive, and America didn't know what to make of or quite how to label frightening newcomers like Elvis Presley——with his banned-in-Boston hips——and Little Richard——with his eyeliner, wild-man antics and womanish demeanor. In 1956 Richard had his first big hit, "Tutti Frutti." He energetically shored up his rock rep with "Lucille," "Jenny, Jenny," "Long Tall Sally" and "Good Golly, Miss Molly" (the feminine names fooled a lot of people in those days).

LR made Jerry Lee Lewis seem timid by comparison, but his fans——never minding their parents——loved it. Until he was gone, after just a year and a half of fame. Asked why he had quit so abruptly, he offered, "That was my Living Flame period. But when the Russians put Sputnik up in the air, I felt that God was speaking to me."

In the interview book *Off The Record* he explained how he got past plain clothes. "I took my mother's brooches and pinned them on. . . . I would go on stage with a ring on, and whenever I was singing I would stick my finger up in the air so you could see the ring. I kept it on until my finger turned green.

"I met a singer in Atlanta called Billy Wright at a club called the Royal Peacock. It was Billy who made me realize that I wasn't dressing. . . . Billy had on green and gold shoes and green suits, and I thought this guy was fabulous. . . . He knew how to make up and I didn't. So I started to copy him. He became my idol, and finally I got some flash shoes and Billy gave me my first suit, my pretty suit."

As to his material, LR admitted, "People wanted to add a writer to clean up my lyrics, but my lyrics weren't dirty. They were sort of how Prince's lyrics are today."

Though he was a big draw live, Richard was little-heard on radio and records. "Pat Boone started covering my tunes while they were still hot, and the pop stations would play his version and kill mine from ever having the chance of crossing over. You'd go into the record shops and there would be his version but not mine . . . and Pat was covering them so fast. Pat was also covering Fats Domino and many others."

The racism in early rock was brought up at the New Music Seminar in 1988. Someone stood up and angrily stated, "We must remember that the father of rock 'n roll, Little Richard, was black." Then a brave soul got up to add, "The father of rock was black *and* gay. Everyone is trying to bury that."

In his autobiography *The Quasar of Rock*, LR confessed his well-known gayness and revealed that whenever he'd had sex with a woman he'd "always fantasized it was a man." During a 1989 talk show appearance he was asked about this quote and replied, "That was because my girlfriends were all so ugly!" When an audience member suggested LR ought to pay a visit to imprisoned James Brown—"the sweetheart of cell block 5"— Richard stomped to the edge of the stage and shouted at the heckler, "*You're* uglier than James Brown. So shut up!"

The some-time singer had renounced his sexuality in favor of his interpretation of his religion, and became a celibate and a minister. But he couldn't be other than his exuberant self, and in the 1980 documentary *The Little Richard Story* he proclaimed, "Elvis may have been the king, but I am the queen!"

In 1986 he made a comeback as more or less himself in the hit comedy *Down and Out in Beverly Hills*. Director Paul Mazursky reassured potential viewers, "The funniest rumor about LR these days is that he's considering converting to Judaism." On the *Tonight Show* the singer voiced his hopes that his life story would be brought to the silver screen. Who did he want to play him? He had only one choice. "Michael Jackson."

As a presenter at the 1988 Grammys he berated academy members for never having honored him with an award, and at the Rock and Roll Hall of Fame's fourth annual induction ceremonies he showed up to praise inductee Otis Redding but instead wound up eulogizing his own career more than the late Redding's! During the ceremonies' finale, a jam session featuring "30 hams," Richard got up on stage and "cowed even Mick Jagger, continually screaming 'Lucille' like such a maniac that the assembled finally kicked into the song just to shut him up." Critic Adam Block called him a "screaming, unhinged queen."

68

Crooners

During a 1989 Seattle engagement, Richard hit the stage garbed in a silver cape, black crepe and enough makeup to fill even Zsa Zsa Gabor's crevices. He mounted the shiny piano and ejaculated, "I'm gonna scream like a white woman!" And did. After that, he cocked an eyebrow, limped his wrist and snapped, "Shut up!" before laughing like a hyena in heat. His closing medley included Elvis' "Hound Dog," Fats Domino's "Blueberry Hill," Jerry Lee Lewis' "Whole Lotta Shakin' Goin' On" and even Aretha Franklin's "Chain of Fools" in which the singer croons the belief that for five passionate years "You were my man!"

He did this while pacing the piano for a quarter-hour and dangling his rhinestone bracelets before the ecstatic crowds, then tossing them into the throng like cracker crumbs to goldfish. "Even Liberace pales beside the Queen of Rock 'N Roll!" *The Advocate* limned two significant facts about LR. "No matter how often he has rejected his sexuality . . . he remains an irreducible queen, and that queeniness is essential to everything astonishing and liberating that he has brought to our music and culture." And "His entire career at Specialty Records lasted less than a year. He cut most of his hits in one burning session, but the shock waves are still going out, over thirty years later."

Webster's definition of a quasar is "a starlight object that emits powerful radio waves."

"Bad"

Michael Bennett, the gay creator of the Broadway musical *Dreamgirls,* was often asked whom he envisioned in the anticipated screen version of the thinly disguised story of the Supremes. More than once he half-joked, "Michael Jackson or Prince, for the Diana Ross part."

In the December, 1989, issue of *Movieline,* Stephen Rebello wrote, "Two supernovas born to play the Ross role are Prince or Michael Jackson. Lord knows, Prince could vamp, coo, primp and do that reach-out-and-touch-someone stuff to filth.

"When Ross made her big screen splash in *Lady Sings the Blues,* marketing experts spent a fortune deciding whether to whet audience interest with: 'Diana Ross *Is* Billie Holiday' or

'Diana Ross *As* Billie Holiday.' No such question arises around *Dreamgirls,* for Michael Jackson *is* Diana Ross. . . . With the savings in mascara, why not pay Jackson to write a decent song or two for the score? And no, neither Janet nor LaToya will suffice."

In the early '80s, before Prince's stellar breakthrough as a singer and some-time actor, I was shopping at Sears in San Mateo, California. In the TV/stereo department, with two teenaged girls ahead of me at the cashier's. One girl was purchasing among other things a Prince record, when her friend suddenly looked at the LP and squealed, "Ugh! I heard he's a faaag!" Her friend snapped her gum and shrugged, "I like his music." The other girl shuddered elaborately.

Who and what is Prince Rogers Nelson? Early interviews included fabrications about his age, racial background, parents and real name. Some of his early lyrics were boldly bisexual. Others, like "Sister" on the 1980 album *Dirty Mind,* were incestuous, prompting media speculation about how autobiographical his work really was. Sometimes Prince went spiritual, as when he wrote about how it feels to fall in love, "not with a girl or boy," but with heaven.

He combined pouty tomboyishness with stylistic effeminacy—the highest men's heels, the laciest collars, the most mascara this side of Piccadilly, . . . Androgyny earned him attention as a singer, but when he made his film bow in *Purple Rain,* his vehicle proved misogynistic and homophobic. As a film star, he was increasingly linked with beautiful women, such as Vanity (née Denise Matthews). "One thing I cannot handle is the macho man. I look for a man to have some feminine qualities. When they can't cry or feel sorry, it's like, Gimme a break, boy. *Pow!"* she exclaimed, punching her fist into her palm.

The five-foot-three boy-man shocked general audiences with his girlish attire, some of which was however merely neo-Versailles drag, for Mozart is said to be his idol. His penchant for purple—or loud lavender?—alarmed many who believe rust and mildew are the only "masculine" colors. Others applauded Prince's audacity. During a 1988 London concert that was part of his *Lovesexy* tour he was urged on by Boy George, who was in the audience shouting, "Come on, girl! Good on you, girl!"

The *Lovesexy* album featured Prince in the luxuriant buff.

Critics railed against him for even wishing to be depicted as a sex object. Said *RPM* magazine, "His narcissism nauseates and needles less flirtatious men."

Prince had already alienated several peers by declining to participate in the *We Are the World* fundraising song/video whose central characters were Diana Ross and Michael Jackson. *Night & Day* commented, "Just as well. . . . There wouldn't have been room in the studio for his security harem. And what with Michael, Diana and Prince all in a row, it might have looked more like a Supremes reunion." However, Prince's biggest gaffe-of-the-rich-and-famous was when Elizabeth Taylor invited him to her Bel-Air home. According to *Vanity Fair,* he infuriated his hostess by having his security people case her house before visiting her and then, having arrived, refusing to talk to her.

Michael Jackson by contrast seems well-mannered (though Kate Hepburn told him it was rude to wear sunglasses indoors), asexual and less the arrogant recluse, more the sad eccentric whom nobody can figure out. Both performers are soft-spoken to the point of inaudibility, both are girlish and love to dress up, and both are control freaks. When Jackson received a star on the Hollywood Walk of Fame, he reportedly agreed to show only on condition that it be placed directly in front of Mann's Chinese Theatre—the Boardwalk area of the Walk of Fame. (Only Streisand ever got away with not showing up for her new star!)

When he agreed to do *We Are the World,* he asked for and got "input." Re *Night & Day,* "He added the line 'As God has shown us by turning stone to bread,' very nearly turning a universal anthem into a Christian hymn, despite the presence of various Jewish and Buddhist artists." He was also granted unique permission to reshoot his portion of the video, the better to appear "more glamorous," said *Entertainment Tonight.* This, despite the sign posted outside the recording studio to "Leave your egos outside." And when the all-night session ended at 8 the next morning, the only people still in the studio weren't co-writers Lionel Ritchie and Jackson, but Ritchie and producer Quincy Jones.

Jackson's wacky escapades have filled hundreds of pages in the tabloids which often call him "wacky Jacko." For instance, following his 1988 Euro-tour he went to Disneyland disguised as a nurse in a white dress, white shoes and a wig. According to the

Star, he was with a 16-year-old friend and told attendants, "I'm here with my charge who tends to faint. We need a wheelchair." Thus, "They got the chair and got to go to the front of the line at every ride."

That same year, he displayed fundamental(ist) ignorance about how AIDS is transmitted and drew the ire of local tourist authorities when he declared in Ireland, "No way am I going to kiss (the Blarney Stone)——I might get AIDS, or something worse." Something "worse?"

In a 1984 *Time* cover story he went out of his way to deny rumors about his homosexuality or that he "condoned" it, then became the first person in history to call a press conference to announce that he *wasn't* gay! But six years later the rumors still proliferated, as for instance on a *Star* cover: "Dad Accuses Michael Jackson of Being Gay——Eyewitness Report." (In tacky tab-land, bi- and homosexuality, unlike heterosexuality, are something one is "accused" of, not something one is.)

The piece quoted paterfamilias Joseph Jackson, "You spend a lot of time with your friend over there," at a family picnic, "and a lot of time with other young men." Then Joe turned to the "good-looking blond man in his early 20s . . . and boomed, 'I think it's time for you to leave.'"

The *Star* noted, "He has a juvenile passion for toys [and] had cosmetic surgery that gives his almost hairless face a delicate, effeminate appearance; he maintains safe relationships with older, unavailable women including Diana Ross, Elizabeth Taylor, Sophia Loren, Liza Minnelli, . . . speaks in an almost feminine voice, sings nearly falsetto, and has never had a lasting relationship with a woman his age.

"Michael's 'dates' with Tatum O'Neal and Brooke Shields were suspiciously well-orchestrated, as was a dubious 'fling' with back-up singer Sheryl Crow."

'Nuff said?

Not quite. J. Randy Taraborrelli's Diana bio *Call Her Miss Ross* chronicled the two pals' not-so-close-as-everyone-thinks friendship. The author quoted a limo chauffeur, "I said, 'Mr. Jackson, would you like——' and he cut me off. He said, 'Please, call me Miss Ross.' So I did!"

Another time, Diana found Michael backstage at one of her shows, applying her makeup. She turned to an associate and exclaimed, "My God, that boy has got to stop fooling with his face! What is he doing?" Trying to look like you, she was told. "I look like that?"

In 1982 Jackson wrote the sexylove song "Muscles" for Diana's latest LP, about "the joys of a man's muscles 'all over your body.'" In the studio, Ross stated, "It's shocking to me that this guy can be so shy. Why does he have to whisper like that?" She teased one of her Los Angeles concert audiences, "'Muscles' was written for me by Michael Jackson. But I don't know whether it's supposed to be *his* fantasy or mine. . . . "

She told associate John Whyman, "I just wish he would be himself. I wish he would stop worrying about what people will think of him if he just got real."

Another report had it that Jackson wasn't trying to look like diva Diana so much as he was trying not to look like somebody he used to resemble:

"He has said privately that he has plastic surgery so he won't look like his father Joseph Jackson." The two have allegedly been estranged since 1981, after the last of their management contracts expired. Michael supposedly also resented how his father treated his wife Katherine, Michael's mother. And Joe was said to blame Michael for breaking up the family act, also for the way he looks and acts and speaks, and for not marrying.

Re Taraborrelli, Michael has confessed, "I'd do anything so as not to end up looking like him. I couldn't bear to look at myself in the mirror if I had to have my father staring back at me."

What does Jacko's superstardom say about our times? "The weirdos have taken over the business," declared Barbara Stanwyck. "Appearances have always been everything," rued Halston, "but now they're *too* everything." And on the dust jacket of Whitney Stine's 1990 book about her, Bette Davis mourned the lack of contemporary heroes. "Name *one* today! Michael Jackson?!"

"Tiptoe Through the Tulips"

British critic James Agate once mused, "Society *wonders* about male dancers, because they look superb. Very seldom do they wonder about male opera singers, for they don't." Fat or not, there has always been a disproportionate number of gay opera singers. One of the most famous was Danish Heldentenor Lauritz Melchior, who in the 1930s and '40s was almost a household name. He memorably played Tristan to Kirsten Flagstad's Isolde at the Met but gained wider exposure in some of MGM's worst musicals. One critic felt he was to cinematic opera what Jose Iturbi was to cinematic piano-playing!

Born Lebrecht Hommel in 1890, Melchior was one of the two great loves of British writer Hugh Walpole, who became his patron in return for services rendered. After he began living off the fat of the Hollywood land, Melchior was described as "Sophie Tucker in a suit." As his girth and reputation grew, he dropped his male lovers and eventually acquired three wives and two kids. Even so, Peter Lawford, who co-starred in *Two Sisters From Boston,* 1946, later revealed that the great Dane had more than once pinched his bottom!

Melchior also spent time with poet Hart Crane, Tennessee Williams' idol. Gay historian Martin Greif disclosed that the singer and the poet formed a *ménage-à-trois* during the shore leaves of an American sailor they'd befriended. (Speaking of men out of uniform, Melchior's New York residence, the Ansonia, in the '70s became home to the gay Continental Baths, where Bette Midler and Barry Manilow launched their musical careers.)

Though he strained endlessly to present a heterosexual image, Lauritz did make two laudable public statements. Another of his renowned roles was Siegfried: "The operas of Wagner might never have come into existence but for the patronage and encouragement of a young man who loved him, Ludwig II of Bavaria. They called him 'mad,' but he wasn't. Rather, he was mad for splendid music and madly extravagant in its pursuit."

Melchior eschewed the fictitious 1952 Hollywood bio of the gay Danish writer Hans Christian Andersen. "They have made of his sensitive and moving story a big lie which it does not really benefit anyone to believe."

Danny Kaye (né Kaminsky), who played Andersen, achieved Broadway stardom as a gay caricature in the 1940 Gertrude Lawrence musical *Lady in the Dark.* He didn't reprise the nellie photographer in the lavish Ginger Rogers screen version because Sam Goldwyn was grooming him for G-rated stardom (anyhow the role was so toned down that folks in Des Moines didn't "get" that he was gay, 'cause he really no longer was).

Kaye's gayness—or bisexuality—was an even better kept secret than his Jewishness. Goldwyn (born Goldfish) had ordered a nose-job after the name-change, but they compromised with a blond dye-job. The heterosexually unconvincing Kaye sang comic tongue-twisting specialty songs in several musicals. But before he became a screen star he recorded in 1942 a song, "Anatole of Paris," notable for its homophobia. *Christopher Street* explained, "With vicious humor, the lyric depicts a gay milliner as a frivolous misogynist and all-around nitwit. The lyrics were by Sylvia Fine, later Mrs. Kay. . . ."

When it came to specialty singing, no one was more rarified than Tiny Tim, aka Herbert Khaury, a personality peculiar to the late '60s and *Rowan & Martin's Laugh-In*. Co-host Dick Martin had a running gag that something must be "funny" about TT, but a bio of the period divulged the "sensational news" that the Lebanese falsetto singer had had same-sex. TT, who preferred to spell out words having to do with "s-e-x," owned up to a h-o-m-o-s-e-x-u-a-l fling in which he spilled his "s-e-e-d faster than anyone—in two seconds."

With his long stringy hair, rolling eyes, ukelele and quivery, piercing renditions of camp oldies like "Tiptoe Through the Tulips" (Tiptoe Through Your Two Lips?), Tiny held the American public's horrified attention for a few months before reaching his biggest audience not by singing but by wedding one Miss Vicki on the *Tonight Show* (they were married by a gay priest). Comfortably "solved," he was quickly forgotten. Gay trivia experts continue to keep his name alive, for instance Michael Willhoite in the *Gay Desk Calendar:* "Tiny Tim admitted to a homosexual experience once. Yeah, once. . . ."

The *1990 Gay Calendar* also included opera singer John Reardon, who made his Broadway debut at 30 in the 1960 musical *Do Re Mi. Dance Magazine* editor William Como confessed, "I always had the hots for Reardon, though I could scarcely believe he wasn't straight. When I was a kid I heard all the rumors about Valentino and Rudy Vallee, together. I didn't think such big stars could be gay! Then I met Jack Cassidy and when he made a pass at me I thought it *had* to be a joke."

But it wasn't, and the two had a "scorching" affair. "The only thing that surprises me anymore is that I still get surprised when I find out a particular star is gay or bi!"

Cassidy, who died at 49 in a fire, made his Broadway bow in *Small Wonder* in 1948. When he met future wife Shirley Jones he'd already fathered future pop star David Cassidy. The pair met in Europe while Cassidy was play-singing Curly in *Oklahoma* after release of the film version starring Jones. They had three handsome sons, among them pop star and Hardy Boy Shaun Cassidy and actor Patrick, who appeared in the outstanding 1990 AIDS-themed film *Longtime Companion*.

"I'm sorry, but Jack was a shit," Como told me. "One of the vainest prima donnas. . . . His biggest defeat in life was not being a huge star, and being married to a woman who for a while was sort of a star." Reportedly, when Jones chose to quit working to become a full-time mother, Cassidy wouldn't let her. "He loved the show biz whirl, and loved seducing VIPs of both sexes even if he had no intention of bedding them."

One of Jack's longer, more unusual affairs was with Cole Porter, described in Gerald Clarke's Truman *Capote* bio. Cassidy would offer his endowment to Porter and urge, "Come and get it." "Then he would stand away so that Cole, whose legs had been paralyzed in that awful riding accident, would have to crawl toward him. Every time Cole got near, Cassidy would move farther away. This went on for half an hour or 45 minutes before Cassidy would finally stop and let Cole have it."

Rudy Vallee (né Hubert Pryor) became a star via Valentino's death, which made possible his cheesy hit song "There's a New Star in Heaven." Rumors about their affair hurt Vallee's career, and his vogue passed quickly, until he and his megaphone were widely and derisively imitated as passé. The singer became a supporting actor in thirty-four films and opened a Hollywood nightery called the Pirates' Den. "It was a straight place, but Mr. Vallee often had a trail of fey young things following him about," said a former employee of the "very, very closeted" ex-star.

Once, Vallee stayed at the same Cleveland hotel as Beatrice Lillie. They walked his dogs together, and she subsequently informed a biographer, "That man had more good-looking 'nephews' than he could probably shake his stick at!" Even while married, Vallee would invite comely young chaps to visit his palatial Los Angeles home. One future restaurateur reminisced, "He'd sit me on his lap in his bedroom, after the others had left, and ask about my girlfriends. When I said I had none he tsk-tsk-ed and pretended not to believe me.

"He told me that he'd had this enormous success on Broadway in *How to Succeed in Business* and that he worked with Bobby Morse, who had several kids but was also fond of men. Rudy was big on gossip." (Robert Morse came out in *The Advocate* as bisexual, and won a 1990 Tony as Truman Capote in *Tru.)*

KLM

KLM are not his initials. But let's call him K for short. K is generally a doll of a guy. Especially if one leaves politics and religion out of it. His views on the subjects seem to have jelled during the Eisenhower era.

Physically, K has never been handsome. But he was a TV star, with more than one series of his own. The last one was canceled—despite an official story about low ratings—because nationally circulated rumors were linking him with a handsome gay movie star. K remains primarily a working singer who doesn't discuss his private life in his few media interviews.

He lives far from the outing crowd, in the most beautiful of states, with an apparently invisible lover. Before granting this brief and anonymous interview K had me sign an affidavit to never publish, under my own or any other byline, an interview—"in any media" (*sic*)—with (real name). Thus, if I used his real name, he'd have grounds for legal action and recovery.

After the paper is signed and witnessed, the third party (who he?) departs, and K and I sit in a room with a spectacular view. He smiles generously, almost handsomely, and asks me to commence, eager to "let some of the truth spill out" so long as it can't ever hurt him again.

H: Do you have a lover?
K: I do have a lover (grins). But I don't talk about him.

H: How long were you and the movie star lovers?

K: Quite a while. But off and on.

H: Publicly, you deny that you were more than acquaintances.

K: Publicly has nothing to do with the truth . . . .

H: I've found that out!

K: That's why I liked your book (*Conversations With My Elders*). It tells about the gayness in show business, but all the subjects are dead, so nobody gets hurt.

H: Thank you. But can I ask if you're completely over the shock of being canceled due to rumors?

K: You know they were more than rumors. . . .

H: Yes, but who could prove it?

K: Somebody had pictures.

H: Blackmail?

K: No, a white male (laughs).

H: Do you think most audiences today know about the rumors?

K: Older ones do, and that's most of my audience——the older crowd. Luckily for me, they don't want to believe it.

H: You haven't contractually wed. Do you get interviewers asking about that?

K: I make it a policy up-front to say I'm not going to talk about what I do away from the stage or soundstages.

H: Do you prefer singing to acting?

K: Much more. When I sing, I'm interpreting it solo. In acting, it's always a teamwork thing. Teamwork's nice if you're building the pyramids or something, but for me a little of it goes a long way.

H: Do colleagues treat a gay performer poorly?

K: . . . I already put in my team—I mean *time*——being part of a team. Socially, I don't mind being part of a team, one of the guys. There's no such thing in this business. No equals——it's anti-democracy, this business. You're either the star, who's the king, or supporting, which is the serfs. At best, you're a courtier.

H: You often play comedic roles——

K: (interrupts quickly) No descriptions. I'm a singer and an actor. That's as specific as I want to get.

H: Sorry. Do you think if you came out, it would hurt your career?

K: . . . Not too much.

H: It hasn't hurt Johnny Mathis' career, has it? So why not come out?

K: What for? Some bad publicity?

H: Do you think your audiences would desert you?

K: Not for the most part. But what for to come out?

H: When you were growing up, you had no living, open role models, I'll bet . . . .

K: Oh, that! (snickers) We all come up the hard way. Life is hard.

H: It can be made a little easier, with gay role models for young gay men and lesbians. That can make a big difference.

K: But if it ruins my career?

H: You said you thought it wouldn't.

K: (no reply)

H: It didn't Mathis' career, and frankly he's a bigger celebrity, though not an actor.

K: He's black.

H: What would that have to do with it?

K: I'm sure no one was very surprised that Johnny's gay.

H: Do you think they would be if *you* came out?

K: You can answer that for me . . . .

H: . . . I think many wouldn't be surprised. Many others wouldn't care, and many more would never hear about it because the papers don't like to spread it around that someone famous is gay unless they're dying of AIDS or get caught in a sex scandal.

K: Being of the media, you would know.

H: Alas, I do. And you, you're not really a big recording star, and frankly you aren't selling sex appeal.

K: You don't think I'm sexy?

H: What I mean is it's not your image.

K: Same with Mathis.

H: That's right, and it didn't hurt him. Or his record sales.

K: Well, I'm very comfortable, and I do not live in a closet, nor do I intend to alter my life for a silly announcement. I don't want to hand out sexual details to strangers.

H: One's sexual and affectional orientation isn't a detail. Like, if a man admits he's heterosexual, you still know very little about his sexual tastes or habits—just that the object is a female.

K: But Boze, I've found that once somebody finds out I'm gay—if they're straight—they suddenly feel they can take liberties. They become patronizing and start asking stupid questions. Like "Who's the 'wife' in the relationship?"

H: Stupid questions are caused by ignorance. You could tell them, It's not like that—we're equals.

K: I could. . . . But I'm not going to.

H: You sound a little bitter.

K: I'm surprised. Because I'm a lot bitter. This so-called gay community—what has it ever given me?

H: What does the straight community give straights?

K: Gays don't buy my records. They don't see me perform. They're just plain not interested. Not in me. Maybe in me and . . . *him. That,* for sure!

H: That part's curiosity. Everyone's interested in gay celebrity couples.

K: Well, my whole background is just . . . The gay lib thing, as I see it, it's for young people. I'm not young.

H: Is your life partner younger than you?

K: That's not saying much! (laughs) But let's close off this subject. I'm *not* coming out, because I never went *in* to any closet. I'm very happy, I live freely, . . .

H: When one can't be open with associates or the world about the gender of one's mate, one isn't living freely.

K: I can tell ya this, Boze, I am glad I am not living with you! (laughs) You're almost convincing me. But anyway, I'm living very nicely, and a few sacrifices don't inconvenience me much. Besides, as an actor, it's *all* about pretense.

H: There's less pretense in singing, isn't there?

K: Thank God for that! In acting you have to kiss the girl. In singing all you have to do is change the word from "he" to "she." (laughs) A small sacrifice.

H: Well, a short one.

"Stout-Hearted Men"

In 1929 while filming Paramount's first big musical *Innocents of Paris,* Maurice Chevalier (1888-1972) sang "Every Little

80

Breeze." The moviemakers criticized his performance and instructed him that in America when a man sings, he *looks* at the "girl." Maurice had ignored her and instead made fluttering breeze-gestures. He retorted that he'd become a huge star in Paris, the center of world culture, and didn't need the advice of unknown smalltowners. The row resulted in a stalemate.

Until Chevalier viewed the rushes in which he was cardboard-stiff with and quite aloof to "Louise." He gave in and became a sex symbol to early talkies audiences. But henceforth, every little breeze seemed to whisper about his private life. He was known as a mama's boy who prayed daily at her commemorative bust in his garden near Paris. He'd supposedly learned English from a "handsome and unattached" British POW while both were in a WWI German camp. And he was said to be more than an employer to his faithful valet Felix Paquet, who outlasted Maurice's brief childless marriage to an actress associate.

Chevalier's first crush on a star had been directed at singer Felix Mayol, a favorite of Marcel Proust. But Mayol's gayness hampered his post-war career, and Chevalier learned from the older man's "mistake." His manager concocted a romance with music hall queen Mistinguett, a publicity ploy which flattered the older woman while boosting the young man. Noel Coward, Chevalier's friend and frequent host, told the author, "Mistinguett kept her famous legs into old age.

"What she didn't keep were her heterosexual admirers. Most of the romantic young and not-so-young men surrounding her were lavender dandies who loved publicity. . . . Some were veddy close friends of dear Maurice."

In the summer of '39 the bisexual Duke of Windsor (England's former king) bet his wife Wallis that Chevalier was gay. We shall never know if he found out, or what means he intended to use, for Something happened. Chevalier recounted in his memoirs *The Man in the Straw Hat,* "During lunch at the Duke's, we heard over the radio that the Germans had invaded Poland. We were all stunned. Of course that meant that England and France were in the war. Now golf was out of the question."

After the war Chevalier was accused of collaborating with the Nazis (he was later more or less cleared). Of course his leading man days were by then over, but in the late '50s he made a big comeback as a cabaret performer and supporting film actor.

81

His *Gigi* co-star Hermione Gingold (they dueted "I Remember It Well") explained, "Monsieur Chevalier was a remarkable man. As an actor, he positively exuded charm. As a man, he was about as appealing as a pickled jellyfish."

Queried by a reporter about his one short marriage, Chevalier asserted, "I have preferred a successful career to success with women." As an elder, he was less vulnerable to public opinion's romantic requirements.

In old age he became a symbol of French culture and an asexual sex symbol for the blue-rinse set. When he turned 80 he was asked what it felt like? "Considering the alternative, it feels pretty good." The star's jollity, elegant accent, curled lower lip and straw boater were in constant demand, and he worked till he dropped. "I adore money!" he conceded, simultaneously denying stories that he was tighter than the bark on a tree.

Interestingly, Chevalier was a pessimistic nation's official optimist, perhaps its most popular export. However, within France, pessimistic entertainers like Edith Piaf were far more popular, for *le gai* Maurice represented a "typical Frenchman" who never existed!

Like Chevalier, Nelson Eddy (1901-67) played the game—marriage: 1, kids: 0. But he became friends with his older wife, and the marriage lasted a lot longer. Nonetheless, Eddy half-joked with Noel Coward (in whose *Bittersweet* he starred) that "Marriage is the tax on stardom." Coincidentally, Eddy made his 1922 stage debut in *The Marriage Tax* (and Coward loathed the film of *Bittersweet* more than any of his adapted works).

Also like Chevalier, Eddy was musically and romantically teamed with Jeannette MacDonald, who had little use for either man. She preferred hetero co-stars who genuinely swooned at her feet. But the duo toiled together in eight vehicles. They were known unofficially as the Iron Butterfly and the Singing Capon (JM was a rock-ribbed Republican, three of whose 1965 pallbearers were Nixon, Reagan and Goldwater). Like Astaire and Rogers, Eddy and MacDonald resented their fans' and studio's demands of constant twosomeness. Both professional pairs complained bitterly to friends but publicly insisted they were pals.

As with Astaire, the seemingly sexless Eddy's film career

declined after he broke with his opposite-sexed partner. In 1942 he left Jeannette-a Operetta and in 1943—released from MGM—made *The Phantom of the Opera*. Its ending finds Eddy walking off to a dinner date with Claude Rains, arm in arm. His final picture, in 1947, was a western at Republic, on Poverty Row.

Nelson had resisted Louis B. Mayer's entreaties to wed until finally giving in in 1939—to the divorcee of a leading film director. Like Astaire, Eddy just wasn't sex symbol material, and a wife couldn't change that; Mayer acceded in 1940, "Nelson has no 'It.'" Bea Lillie saw him perform at Philadelphia's Latin Casino and muttered, "There's less here than meets the eye," a line also attributed to Tallulah Bankhead.

Unlike audiences, critics had never warmed to Nelson, and he'd been labeled "personality minus" and chided for his "embarrassing lack of ease." There may have been cause—imagine having to start a love scene with the disdainful Iron Butterfly by chirping, "Your dream prince, reporting for duty!" Much more than MacDonald, Eddy was soon considered passé, and in the '50s and '60s made a career performing live. Hours after a show in Miami Beach, he died of a stroke.

Within years he was something of a camp joke, e.g., in Woody Allen's 1971 *Bananas* a Latin American prisoner is tortured into a confession by being subjected to repeated doses of Nelson Eddy singing "Naughty Marietta." For quite some time, the rumors had affected his reputation. The man who'd begun as a telephone operator was deemed "the ham of hams" by director Allan Dwan, who never specified why he "couldn't stand" the singer. Today, Eddie's most famous song outside of the duet "Indian Love Call" is the Canadian Mountie tune which starts, "Give me some men," and depicts stout-hearted males boldly fighting for "the right they adore," shoulder by shoulder. . . .

Well, he could dream, couldn't he?

"Whoopee!"

Eddie Cantor starred in some of the most child-like and delightfully unusual musicals Hollywood ever invented. Most are now forgotten, but only now can their campiness be assessed and marveled at for its then-daring. In his book *Can't Help Singin'* Gerald Mast pointed out how often Cantor kisses other men in his movies. In *Whoopee!* (1930) the pop-eyed Cantor observes about a topless Indian brave, "He's cute, isn't he?" In *The Kid From Spain* (1932), when caught in a women's college dorm, Eddie confesses, "I'm a naughty girl."

In *Kid Millions* (1934) Cantor is the effete runt in a family of macho brutes——Eddie as Cinder(f)ella with a wicked stepfather and three stepbrothers. A lawyer cum fairy godmother frees him from bondage. Said Mast, "The Cantor films save their ultimate weapons for attacks on Eddie's butt——not Chaplin's kicks or Keaton's pratfalls, but phallic thrusts by Roman swords, the horns of bulls, even the biting beak of a goose."

The creators and actors of those films may have been aware of their sexual implications, but not most of yesteryear's audiences. Besides, how could anything be amiss when Eddie always wound up——deliberately or not——with the girl? Yet in the '50s, during the "political" witchhunts, most of whose targets were Jewish and/or gay, Cantor was an intended victim. Happily, he escaped, for he'd been enormously popular in several media. But not before being grilled about his private life and his original name, Edward Israel Iskowitz.

Paul Robeson was an estimable but underrated singer-actor. His apotheosis was the song "Old Man River" in the 1936 *Showboat,* helmed by eccentric gay Brit James Whale ("Frankenstein"). Said Whale, "Mr. Robeson is an enormous talent. He is enormous. . . . " Robeson's other picture was *The Emperor Jones.* On stage he was best known as Othello, and acted more often in England, which was then less racist.

(When gay spy Guy Burgess was posted to Washington, D.C., he was advised about America's three taboos: the color bar, communism and homosexuality. "What you're trying to tell me, in a nut shell, is I mustn't flirt with Paul Robeson.")

Before he was punished via the witchhunts for being a politically active black, Robeson became the first major black star. His friend and host Ivor Novello told producer David Lewis (Whale's lifemate), "Paul is terrified of going too far, he's been so intimidated. . . . But with politics, he gets too angry to curb his caution." For decades there were rumors of Robeson's bisexuality, but it's possible he never had an affair with a white man. If caught, he would have been destroyed.

Gay Archives curator Jim Kepner recalls, "I met Robeson when I had to deliver something to him. He was in sort of a dressing-gown, and a sexual electricity passed between us. Nothing happened, but I sensed there was *something* there." Robeson wasn't about to give the FBI non-political material to use against him. Even so, he was hounded by the State Department through much of the '40s and '50s. In 1950 it revoked his passport so he couldn't leave the country to perform. He got it back in 1958, and promptly left for Europe and the USSR.

In the early '60s he moved to Harlem, where he became a recluse until ill health forced him to live with a sister in Philadelphia, where he died, nearly forgotten, in 1976.

Robert Preston, *The Music Man,* was a beloved entertainer for decades, though never a box office star. In latter years he speculated to the press that, "They said all manner of things about me in Hollywood, and your image and those stories have an impact on the size of roles you're given." At 15 he'd joined Mrs. Tyrone Power's stock company. Later he was part of Paramount's stock company, where he became very close to Alan Ladd, whose life he saved, and met the actress to whom he became affianced. It was his sole marriage and produced no offspring.

In 1982 he achieved his biggest comeback as the gay Toddy in the pro-gay musical *Victor/Victoria.* He sang a homophile number titled "Gay Paree" and earned an Oscar nomination as the pal who convinces Julie Andrews to become a female impersonator. In *People* magazine he declared that he didn't care if people thought him gay, and granted that such rumors had been rife "for years and years."

The year before, in another Blake Edwards film, Preston had also played gay, as a doctor in *S.O.B.* In 1982 he explained to *Paris Match,* "One of the few advantages of age is that one becomes less answerable to the moral standards of others. . . . Now, if someone asks if I am like the characters I portray, I can laugh and ask, 'Why shouldn't I be?'"

Unless a duo is as droll as Laurel & Hardy or as square as Barney Rubble and Fred Flintstone, male couples typically generate rumors. Just partners, or lovers? In the May, '90, issue of

First Hand, a review of a Robert Patrick play stated, "The 'beauty' in a pair of estranged lovers returns to his natural mate and their 'legendary' collaboration. Is this a bit of 'real history?' Were Simon & Garfunkel lovers who separated and then reunited?"

(The big question is, which of that duo could possibly be the "beauty"?)

In Hall & Oates' case, both were attractive, so the rumors were strong. In 1980 *Rolling Stone* at last inquired. Daryl Hall answered, "The idea of sex with a man doesn't turn me off, but I don't express it. I satisfied my curiosity about that years ago. I had lots of sex between the ages of 3 and 4 and when I was 14 or 15. . . . Experiences with older boys. But men don't particularly turn me on.

"And no, John and I have never been lovers. He's not my type. Too short and dark."

There were rumors about half of a sister-brother duo, the Carpenters. In 1989 *Film Threat* magazine profiled Todd Haynes' Carpenters documentary *Superstar,* which used Barbie and Ken dolls as actors(!). Interviewer Sheryl Farber asked about the film's vague reference to Richard Carpenter's private life. Haynes said it "could be interpreted as referring to his drug habit."

Farber: "Or his homosexuality."

Haynes: "Yes. But I don't have any solid evidence to what his private life entails, so I guess I could leave it open."

Rumors also crop up around high-pitched male singers. In an old monologue, Johnny Carson tittered, "I saw Wayne Newton and Liberace together in a pink bathtub. What do you think that meant?" The outraged Newton complained to Carson, who ended the "fag jokes." Then Newton turned around and made "fairy jokes" a staple of his long-running Vegas act.

Similar rumors have more or less plagued Neil Sedaka, Rockwell (whose 1984 *Somebody's Watching Me* featured pal Michael Jackson) and Andy Gibb, who before his premature death—obviously—declared, "The gays wonder why my brothers' voices are so high and my crotch so tight."

Rumors also accrue to the relationships between handsome young protegés of gay would-be impresarios like Sal Mineo, who "discovered" Bobby Sherman and promoted the sometime teen idol. Mineo also gave Don Johnson—who was a singer before he could act—his first big break, in the L.A. production which he directed and co-starred in of the gay prison drama *Fortune and Men's Eyes.*

Although Johnson would later deny he and Sal had sex, he and his sister allegedly lived with Sal for a time, and he told the press, "I don't differentiate between any of it—it's all love to me. I feel that you can get just as real a love from a guy as you can from a chick.

"I mean, if there were nothing but old whores and nasty old hard women around, I'd be out looking for some young, sweet little 15-year-old boy. But instead, I've got a young, sweet little girl, and that's enough for me right now."

A provocative gimmick like a guy named Alice gets rumors going and hate-mail churning, as Alice Cooper found out. Alice, né Vincent Damon Furnier, was the first to import glitter rock from Britain. Domestic tabloids reacted with loud indignation. "The weirdest thing about our band was that it was made up of athletes. Alice Cooper, 'the sickest band in America'—we were all four-year lettermen." Yet his female first name—which he legally adopted when he went solo—made him a joke and hate object. The lavender innuendos faded after the band got into shock-rock, performing with chickens and snakes and paving the ghoulish way for hetero-camp groups like Kiss.

Finally, rumors are impossible to scotch when a macho icon like Bruce Springsteen shocks crowds "to their feet midway through his four-hour shows." *The Advocate* reported, "As he finished 'Thunder Road' he would dive to his knees, sliding the length of the stage to the side of his massive black bass player Clarence Clemmons. Springsteen would look up pleadingly, and Clemmons would bend down—the two men locking lips for fifteen seconds.

"Rock 'n roll always sounded like it burst out of a soul-shattering midnight rendezvous between a black field hand and a white juvenile delinquent. In one spectacular, liberating gesture, Springsteen enacted those implications. Give the man the 'Come On Back to De Raft, Huck Honey' award."

In 1987 a photo by Janet Gough, reproduced in much of the national press, captured Springsteen in the parking lot of Tower Records in L.A., departing with a rental video of *Kiss of the Spider Woman.*

People never said a thing about "Kiss" or The Kiss. But perhaps Bruce is as open-minded as he is *broad*-minded?

"Cry"

Johnnie Ray (1927-1990) was the Prince of Wails, an androgynous blond who became a musical sensation in 1951. According to the *L.A. Weekly,* "He managed to arouse 12-year-old bobbysoxers and their fathers." But he almost didn't get the chance. After listening to Ray's "Whiskey and Gin," one Columbia Records exec announced, "I don't think she's gonna make it." Another couldn't visualize the concert potential of "a white boy who sings like a Negro."

Ray won fame at 23 with maudlin hits like "Cry," "Little White Cloud," "Please, Mr. Sun" and "Broken Hearted." He didn't merely sing about crying, he wept. Buckets. On stage he worked himself into "a quivering, emotional mess," and his fans were twice as devoted as Sinatra's wartime fans. Frank reportedly hated Johnnie's uninhibited guts.

One critic believed, "Ray is the missing link in American pop music between Sinatra and Presley—based in Frankie's tradition of bandstand entertainment, Ray devastated fans with the same controversial eroticism that Elvis later employed." Yet Ray was no sex symbol. Jonny Whiteside called him "a wraithlike towhead, stone-deaf without his ever present hearing aid, a soft-spoken and—by 1950s standards—effeminate lad."

Powerful '50s columnists put down Ray as a freak, including Dorothy Kilgallen until he made a friend of her; then her column and others chronicled the fake "romance" which boosted both parties. Less publicized was his brief early-'50s marriage, of which he said, "You call that a marriage?"

The general media loved to analyze Johnnie's emotional dynamism but almost never brought up his gayness, which was no big secret on his part. He was a regular at several gay restaurants in West Hollywood, including the French Quarter, where I first interviewed him in 1986 for an Australian magazine—he was more popular there and in England than at home in the '70s and '80s. The media was quicker to mention his problems with producers, pills and alcoholism. At 63 he died of cirrhosis of the liver.

J: I saw you at another restaurant, before this . . . .

H: . . . Also on Santa Monica Boulevard. I saw you too, and—separately—George Maharis. That was for dinner.

J: With a friend? (leers)

H: A good friend. But enough about me, as journalists say.

J: You know who I saw here the other day? We won't print his name, but . . . (Johnnie went on to describe a legally single ex-actor who did a famous, cute movie duet with Debbie Reynolds.) . . . He recognized me before I recognized him, and he came right up and kissed me on the cheek—this being a gay place—and said he'd been a fan of mine for so long!

H: That was nice of him.

J: It really was, because I still know the words to that duet he did. But he hasn't sung a note in years, outside the shower. He still looks good, considering his age. And he has several cats where he lives, back east.

H: Do I detect a trace of envy?

J: Does it show?

H: Is it true you came out to Hollywood to be an actor?

J: That was my goal. It's not what happened.

H: Some types of gay men have more success singing than acting . . . .

J: Oh, I know. I was pretty far-out. I scared the movie guys. Even Brando and Dean scared them at first. There was a space for far-out guys, but it was in music. . . . Much more exciting *then*.

H: What's dull about it now?

J: Everything's been tried. Everything's been exploited ten times over. When I was new, no one else would dare do what I did. Now people are ready to do any crazy or gross thing on stage, if it'll draw a crowd.

H: Long ago I heard that you were hoping to sell your life story to Hollywood?

J: I had that as a hope. But now I see it couldn't be. Not with any core of truth. Not just because the gay aspects, but the booze, the breakdowns, the carrying-on, the way I got figuratively screwed—a movie of all that would have made audiences turn against Hollywood forever.

H: In your heyday, according to the articles, you got standing ovations from people like Noel Coward and the Duchess of Windsor, among others.

J: (nods) At the Copa in New York. I've also done about 20 trips down to Oz (Australia) and I hold the record for headline engagements at the Palladium in London.

H: So you've been anything but washed up, these past many years.

J: Ehm, it's a matter of degree. I still get a good income from singing, but I'd have to die to get in the papers, *here.* They still interview me overseas.

H: Is it true you were friends with Marilyn, Noel and Sophie Tucker?

J: (smiles sardonically) "Friends" is a real big word. You'd have to define it. . . . I hardly knew Sophie Tucker, but I knew the others—and lots more big names in addition. *Friends*—I don't know if I'd call them that. They weren't there when I was in the depths, but why should they be? They had their own careers and their own problems. What's new? But most of the time I went it alone from choice.

H: What about lovers or companions?

J: I've screwed my way around the world eight times over, minimum. That's sex. "Love" is another giant word. I've scared off more than my share of nice guys. Anyway nice guys don't gravitate to guys like me, guys who're famous. We get the seekers—people who *seek* things. No one ever sought me out just for me, and I say that without any self-pity.

H: Who were your musical influences, growing up?

J: Kate Smith was a *big* influence! (laughs) She was, though—anyway I listened to her a lot. We listened to Billie Holiday, Rose Maddox, lots of them. My sister got into the big bands, so music came right into the house. I played the piano. I dreamed a lot. It wasn't so much my having some great love for music—I just wanted to be famous and live it up. Acting didn't bring it to me, so I sang my way into it.

You know what they called me then? I was the Nabob of Sob. Some disc jockey also said I was a "freaky kid." He said it on the air, and in those days it was a far-out thing to say about someone. I almost sued.

90

H: Were rumors about your private life widespread in the 1950s?

J: It was really such a perverted, paranoid time. They attacked me for everything, but almost always without saying why. Anyone who wasn't square was a menace to society. . . . But once I looked around from my own personal hell—all on my own—I saw a lot of other singers, actors, entertainers, were getting it in the chops too. So I felt better.

H: Misery loves company.

J: Well, you don't want to be the only one who's picked on.

H: Did you know Elvis well?

J: One of my biggest fans, that guy. I'm not bragging—look it up in the literature. He'd never admit it, but he was a big fan of mine. I was even too freaky for *him!* He'd come visit me at the Desert Inn, we'd talk. But what he didn't have was a knowledge of how to be friends. He observed, he borrowed, he asked—a sponge. But he wasn't a friend. Which was okay, 'cause he provided me with nightly fantasies. Just shaking his hand was a pretty hot stimulus!

H: You never tried to get him to—

J: Huh-*unh!* Suicide, that's what it would've been. It's not like now, where you can smile at a guy or lay the old hand on the thigh and he'll say he's not into that. If you'd done that then, you'd have to have a duel or something!

H: You were arrested twice. Can you tell me—

J: —about the arrest in the men's room? (shakes head) Right. "Morals charge." Trumped up. The other time, same thing, but in a bar, and I can never prove it, but they were both frames, and the guy that did it was a singer. A slob who thought I stole his audience, 'cause he bombed out when I became the biggest thing on wheels. He arranged both those times—and I survived them. That's what matters now.

H: Is it true that in 1964 you had only $40 to your name?

J: It's not only true, they misspelled that name. They still do. But I'm still here. *That* I can be proud of. And I'm never sorry for myself.

When Johnnie's L.A. home burned down in the early 1970s, Columbia replaced his gold records. But all of them were misspelled *J-o-h-n-n-y R-a-y*.

91

"Born In Africa"

In April, 1989, Philly Bongoley Lutaaya became the first prominent African to publicly declare he had AIDS. He was a singer who in 1988 became "the Bruce Springsteen of Africa" after recording "Born In Africa" and following it up with a sold-out concert tour. Lutaaya explained, "I decided to come out . . . to launch a campaign, a crusade against AIDS—a crucial act in Uganda, a poverty-crippled nation of 16 million where almost one million are HIV-infected (and where AIDS is primarily heterosexually transmitted).

"America does Africa a great disservice. . . . AIDS began in Africa, and America wants only to publicize it as something from gay men. But when the body count is made for AIDS around the world, and this terrible disease is conquered someday, everyone will see that most of the victims are not gay, and most of the victims are of the Third World."

Philly spoke and sang not only about the causes of and precautions against AIDS, but about the importance of tolerance and compassion, as in his song "Alone and Frightened." Over 70,000 fans attended his final concert in the capital city of Kampala. He died that year, aged 38.

"Sammy Davis, Jr. was 'unisex' before the word was even used on clothes," said Bob Fosse, who directed him in *Sweet Charity*. For decades, rumors abounded about Davis' unbridled sexuality and taste for all manner of sex acts. It didn't hurt that he was living proof that big things come in small packages. Hollywood columnist Jim Bacon wrote about the time he was at a urinal next to Sammy and Milton Berle (along with Forrest Tucker, Berle had the largest celebrity organ in Hollywood). Sammy nudged Milton and quipped, "If Truman Capote were here, he'd be singing 'Stranger in Paradise.'"

In a late-'70s issue of *Genesis,* a girlie magazine, it was Davis who admitted his passion for "long, smooth, beautiful cocks," which he supposedly viewed only in porno movies. About a decade earlier, "The Candy Man" used to haunt the gay-cruisy locker room at San Francisco's Aquatic Park, below the Maritime Museum. He hung around and literally got one eyeful. A fellow observer recalls, "I never saw him make a move on anyone, but he was all smiles with the handsome young whites."

One of Davis' biggest publicity stunts—though it may have been spontaneous—was when he kissed President Richard Nixon (although black, bisexual and Jewish, he'd converted to the Republican party). It was said that the singer-actor gravitated toward famous whites, and indeed he was the token black of the otherwise pale Rat Pack, among them fellow bi Peter Lawford (who had an acrimonious affair with Sal Mineo). And he nearly gave Columbia's Harry Cohn a heart attack by having a serious affair with Columbia's biggest star, Kim Novak, in the 1950s.

Cohn arranged a quickie marriage to a black dancer. It ended in less than six months, but Sammy had had no choice—Cohn had reportedly threatened Davis with extinction via the Mob if he continued with the valuable blonde. A subsequent marriage to Swedish actress Mai Britt gave him a chance to adopt two sons after their child Tracey was born, but according to London's *Daily Mail,* when he wed black dancer Altovise Gore in 1970 "he made only one stipulation—no children."

Sammy's penchant for flashy clothes and gaudy jewelry was well known. In 1981 he apprised Hong Kong's *Entertainment Times,* "I suppose I overdo the rings and necklaces. They're starting to call me the African Queen." It wasn't the sort of quote he'd have uttered in the U.S.

Davis also had a fondness for good lyrics, and avoided fads. "You won't find me imitating today's juvenile stars." Re Michael Jackson he noted, "I'd feel like a damned fool singing words like 'I'm bad, I'm bad, I'm bad, I'm bad.'" Sammy's was a class act, ended by throat cancer at 64. He'd joked, "My doctor told me smoking would take ten years of my life. I said, 'Yeah, baby, but only the last ten!'

"I smoke, and I can't help it, because I'm very oral. And I love it, man!"

Rick Nelson's bisexuality was better known—in the Industry—than Davis', but that wasn't saying much. "An army of publicity experts built me up in the '50s as a super-clean but highly erogenous teen idol," said Eric Hilliard Nelson (Hilliard was his mother's birth name) in *Talk* magazine. Ricky, who gained fame via his parents' eponymous sitcom, was the rock star next door, dull and inanimate until he opened his mouth to sing. That he played guitar and piano well was overshadowed by his singing, just as he always was by the inane TV series.

Nelson's last hit song was in 1972. But he was able to coast through the '80s on his '50s fame, for he was the first rock star created by television, and "My longevity is due to reruns." He added, "I was in my parents' shadow, then Elvis', and then the Beatles came along and wiped me and Elvis out completely. . . . But I stayed in music because it was all I knew how to do. Let's face it, I never really acted."

The affable and ageless hunk started his music career at Hollywood High, where he played drum and clarinet serviceably well. The book *Hollywood High* described him as friendly but formal with girls. In the mid-'50s, he preferred them to pay their own way on dates! A female student offered, "Ricky hated being called that, so it was always *Rick* to his face. Girls went for him on account of his being on TV; they weren't impressed by a pretty face. Not till he sang. Somehow the combination of a pretty face and a sexy voice set everyone on fire."

A male colleague, not quoted in the book, disclosed, "He was big about sexual experimenting. I *know*——because we did. He hated the mushy stuff but loved mutual climax and all that. I know he was drawn to at least one bisexual girl, and he dug party scenes." Doesn't quite square with the TV image, does it? Rick eventually bought Errol Flynn's Mulholland Drive home, aka the House of Pleasure because of its peepholes and countless orgies. Rumor had it that the singing Nelson brother took up where Flynn left off——just as intensely, but far more discreetly.

Flynn died at 50 a burnt-out shell, whereas Nelson was the model of healthy good looks despite a moderate drug habit. But at 45 he died in an airplane crash.

"I Am What I Am"

Esquire called Lou Reed's "Walk On the Wild Side" the theme song of androgyny. Reed's major benefactors were the patron saints of androgyny, Andy Warhol and David Bowie. Warhol's two greatest contributions to rock were the infamous Stones record cover *Sticky Fingers* (see the *Brits* chapter) and the quartet Velvet Underground which he recruited to provide music for his Exploding Plastic Inevitable shows in 1966.

VU member John Cale received a Tanglewood scholarship after a recommendation from Aaron Copland. In 1963 the Welsh-born Cale was part of a relay team of pianists who played Erik Satie's "Vexations" 840 times without interruption for 18 ½ hours. VU's drummer was a woman, Maureen Tucker, which caused the band to be taken less seriously by critics at that time, and Sterling Morrison was the fourth member.

Warhol and his aide-de-high-camp Paul Morrissey were the band's first managers, focusing as much on their Look and packaging as their sound. VU's first album cover was a peelable banana, an instant classic almost as notorious as the workable *Sticky Fingers* crotch-zipper. The quartet's nickname for Andy, which he didn't appreciate, was Drella, a combination of Dracula and Cinderella. In his own words, "I've created a monster." He and VU seldom saw eye to eye; the friction was exacerbated by lack of commercial success, due to radio stations' refusal to play their songs about gay and other "lunatic fringe" topics.

In 1970 the Velvet Underground broke up and singer-songwriter Reed (né Firbank) went his own way. East Coast critics crowned him the King Freak of New York, but it was his second solo album, *Transformer,* produced by Bowie, that yielded his only hit single, "Walk On the Wild Side." A self-proclaimed bisexual, Reed wrote about same-sex but was already distancing himself from the VU and Bowie. Asked about the band's "Sister Ray," concerning transvestites and their sailor boyfriends mainlining heroin at an orgy, he reportedly ignored the question.

He informed *Disc* magazine, "I'm *not* going in the same direction as David. He's into the mime thing and that's not me at all. . . . I wanted to try heavy eye makeup and dance about a bit. I've done it and stopped. I don't wear makeup."

Although Reed—who married and became what rock critic Adam Block called "a former homo"—didn't achieve mainstream success, Paul Nelson wrote, "Had Reed accomplished nothing else, his work with the VU would still have assured him a place in anyone's rock and roll pantheon."

Lou's 1989 comeback was the LP *New York,* in which he returned to familiar turf and earned his biggest sales in years. The song "Halloween Parade" is nominally about the annual Greenwich Village dragfest but really about the sad absence of former participants lost to AIDS. Also in '89, Reed and Cale collaborated on "Songs For Drella," a live presentation which many reviewers deemed a Warhol rip-off—"Reed is always either ahead of his time or joins the fray . . . too late."

Rock chronicler Judah Zachary asserted, "The Velvet Underground didn't sell many records, but everyone who bought one formed their own band." One such band was the then-shocking New York Dolls, a quintet of men now described (by Francis Davis in American Airlines' inflight magazine) as "five heterosexuals." Few if any thought so at the time! The stylistic successors to VU, the Dolls gloried in their drag and makeup and "looked like they had just stepped out of a Lou Reed song." Their few albums resulted in reams of publicity, far less sales, and member David Johansen evolved—or devolved?—into Buster Poindexter. Pre-Dolls, David had been part of gay theatre legend Charles Ludlam's Ridiculous Theatrical Company. Poindexter, says husband-father Johansen, is a character he's "more relaxed with."

Another early-'70s Amer-Glitter act was Jobriath, billed as "the first gay rock star." A "combination of Marlene Dietrich and Gary Glitter," Jobriath was big on publicity stunts that took Manhattan by storm-of-controversy but did little for his music. Openly gay Warners Records exec Ray Caviano explained, "I rose to the top within a fairly liberal business. But I'm not before the public, and Jobriath—who worked for and in front of the public—simply could not be openly gay.

"Then as now it's commercially smarter to keep 'em guessing. I'm proud of who I am, but performers have to represent so many things to so many people." (Caviano's twin brother manages Grace Jones and others.) Ray is contradicted by the anonymous head of his own record label: "Gay or bi, it's really the same thing to the great unwashed average public. And the media also doesn't become your cheerleader until you marry and have kids.

"That 'mystery' thing is crap. You can't hope to please even half of Everyone, so you just have to be yourself and let the limited publicity come after the fact of your music. Work on your music, then your image."

As gay drag stereotypes gradually withered, groups like VU and the NY Dolls were supplanted by the manly Village People, who were more in tune with modern gay men and less bizarre and threatening to general audiences. The VP achieved success with such solidly danceable and memorably hummable disco ditties as the Gay Pride anthem "Macho Man," "YMCA," "In the Navy," "Fire Island" and "I Am What I Am:" " . . . I did not choose the way I am. . . . People have the right to be just what they are. . . . I am what I am!"

Gay activists criticized the VP for being evasive and politically uncommitted. Since some or most of the members were gay, they were automatically ridiculed by the media, e.g., an "SCTV" parody in which each Village Person had a limp wrist. An inside source revealed, "VP were fairly open about being gay until (creator) Jacques Morali saw we were taking off and said we should clam up on the subject or it'd kill our record sales."

Assembled in 1977, the sextet represented Christopher Street's coolest fantasy figures—a leather man, a construction worker, a cowboy, a cop, a GI and a Native American. In their first year they struck gold with an album of songs whose titles were favorite gay hangouts. Then came their Liberace phase, flaunting their flamboyance on stage, disc and TV without labeling it. In 1979 they made a movie, *Can't Stop The Music*. It was released in 1980 and virtually killed all interest in the VP.

Fans rejected the movie because it was awful and/or featured too little of the VP. Flamboyant producer Allan Carr inserted a standard boy-meets-girl plot that overshadowed the group in their own screen debut, even though each member got to bare his chest at least once. The closest CSTM came to gay was the "YMCA" production number—re Ethan Mordden, its "stars and a horde of teenage brutes (purportedly) caused two fatal seizures, three heart attacks and 19 cases of aggravated drooling among Hollywood notables at an industry preview."

Just to make sure that audiences didn't get the Wrong (Is Right) Idea, each Village Person was assigned a girlfriend for their big musical number. Despite the revisions for straights, CSTM flopped big—of course: most of their real fans were gay! Critics were merciless, critiquing not so much the picture as the group's predominant sexuality. A less vituperative reviewer predicted, "By the year 2100, it's probably going to be hailed as the 'Gang's All Here' of the '80s."

Leather Man Glenn Hughes admitted that the only time restrictions were placed on the VP's private lives was "when the movie was in negotiation. Movie money is very conservative. . . . We had to keep a low profile . . . stay home and watch the late show."

Had the group rejected Hollywood and therefore survived, it's likely that more members would have come out, as Felipe "Indian" Rose technically did in 1983 in the gay *Bay Area Reporter* (the first VP album had already stated that Rose was discovered by Morali at the Anvil gay bar). Said Rose, "I'll tell the gay press I'm gay. If the straight press asks, we tell them it's none of their business. Or none of their fucking business, depending on how they ask."

In 1983 the reconstituted VP tried a comeback. But the timing—indeed the times—was all wrong: because of its gay associations, disco music had died a fiercely unlamented death in straight music/media circles. And AIDS had come out of Africa and settled in American minds as the allegedly Gay Disease.

"All The Time"

"I have had sex with men. Does that make me gay?" So asked poet-composer-singer Rod McKuen, a self-described "stringer of words." Martin Greif noted, "When he took a public stand against Anita Bryant's homophobia, he risked alienating millions of readers." (People like that read?) Friend Lou Thomas asserted, "'The Beautiful Strangers' in 1967 was his message about sexual fluidity. Rod agrees with ancient Greek philosophy that people are sexual, period. They're attracted to the individuals to whom they're attracted—and no labels, please."

McKuen's most famous song was "Jean" from the film *The Prime of Miss Jean Brodie.* He also collaborated with close friend Rock Hudson on the star's sole LP, *Rock, Gently.* Hudson pointed out, "I hate rock music! I love classical, also love songs, ballads, romantic music . . . When I decided to do an album, I knew it would require the assistance of a pro. Not just anyone——someone with a special, you know, sensibility." But the LP wasn't pushed, and few fans heard it.

A gay comedian commenting on the TV movie *Copacabana* told his audience, "Barry Manilow plays a heterosexual—it's science-fiction!" In the Whoopi Goldberg film *Burglar* her

Manilow tapes are stolen and used by the gay villain for "pillow talk"——the Rock Hudson kind. *All The Time,* included in Manilow's greatest hits collection, begins, "All the time I thought, There's only me," then describes a man reminiscing that he would have given everything he had if someone else had said, "You're not alone." It continues, "All the time I thought that I was wrong," contrasting the desire to be one's true self with the desire to "belong," yet wishing one had believed in oneself and "all I had. . . ." Including it was a brave decision, since "All The Time" was co-written with another man and the double-LP wasn't aimed at Barry's Continental Baths audiences . . . .

Jim Morrison of the Doors was the special guest at a 1970 New Year's Eve party hosted by Judy "Laugh-In" Carne. Another guest remembered, "In any room, he was the center of attention . . . Beautiful. Those eyes! That element of danger——like he'd strip naked in a trice. Yet he had this little-boy-lost quality. I'm sure he was confused, but he was like Mick Jagger——even straight guys found themselves receiving his sexy vibes."

Since his death at 27 in 1971 Morrison has become a cult figure, more so among straight rock fans whose historians hide the icon's bisexuality. Johnnie Ray felt, "Jim said 'Light My Fire' to a lot of people, so long as they were as handsome as he was. He told me so! His singing was like mine——sensual, outgoing. He was a screamer . . . They say he named the Doors after (Aldous Huxley's) book about mescaline. Not true." The name came from a line by gay English poet and artist William Blake: "There are things that are known and things that are unknown, in between the doors."

In 1969 Morrison's bad-boy rep caught up with him. Like Jagger, he was an occasional exhibitionist, plus his polysexuality put him on the FBI's and other lists. After a concert in Miami he was arrested for "committing an immoral act" during the show. Columnist Alexandra Tacht wrote, "Morrison finally did it. He culminated his career as a sex symbol of the decade by dropping his pants in front of umpteen screaming teenies in Miami. Exit Morrison, who hopped the country and left in his wake 35,000 teens turning on a Decency Rally behind Jackie Gleason and Anita Bryant to show that Miami is really a straight town."

Morrison and the Doors maintained that the incident never happened, that he was being persecuted for his lifestyle. His manager claimed, "The police had 150 photographs of the concert. None show any exposure."

The depressed Morrison wrote poetry and made some forays into film, for he'd been told he had celluloid potential. But during an extended stay in Paris he was discovered dead in his bathtub. Another mystery—or, for some fans, a "conspiracy"—for the exact cause of death was never found. Respiratory illness and heart attack were officially blamed. Jim's manager told *Sound* magazine in 1973, "I don't know to this day how the man died, and in fact I don't know if he's dead. I never saw the body and nobody ever saw Jim Morrison's body.

"It was a sealed coffin, so who knows. . . ?"

Through the '70s and '80s Morrison's murky saga was frequently optioned for the movies, and handsome stars like John Travolta and Tom Cruise pursued the role. In 1990 Val Kilmer got the plum part via writer-director Oliver Stone—in no doubt a heter-only version. Thus, information about the Lizard King diminishes over the decades. . . .

Some insiders believe Morrison would eventually have made a public declaration of bisexuality à la Bowie, Reed and Elton John. But "in *Europe*," insisted Johnnie Ray—as Brando, Richard Chamberlain, David Cassidy and others have done.

In 1970 Cassidy, Jack's eldest son, won pop star fame with the tamely bubble-gum-rock *Partridge Family* TV series. During the height of his success, he took his alleged boyfriend to Hawaii on a vacation. Also to Europe. One teenzine editor stated, "There were photos. . . . It was quite evident this was a couple, not just two guys."

In Germany, Cassidy confessed his bisexuality, but the news wasn't disseminated in the USA, back in those days before outing, AIDS and the-late-Rock-Hudson's-Secret. The singing actor caused domestic shock waves by posing semi-nude in *Rolling Stone,* and there were—again, very low-profile—rumors about Cassidy's friendship with then-unknown Sal Mineo protege Don Johnson. In 1989 David declared, "We go back a looong time."

Post-Partridge, Cassidy contractually wed (no kids). In 1990 *Movieline* asked if he'd ever dated anyone famous. "Never! I always stayed away from starlets, actresses and bimbos. I did marry and divorce actress Kay Lenz, although I realized never to do that again." Also in '90, gay novelist Dennis Cooper disclosed his long-ago Cassidy crush to the *New York Native*. "It had partially to do with his looks, and his bisexuality, which was pretty well known in the circles I traveled in. He as much as came out in the infamous *Rolling Stone* interview."

In the '90s, when the Hollywood Kids breathlessly inquired about the rumor "that you're one of the most well-endowed actors in tinseltown," David replied with tongue in cheek, "All I can say is, Big deal!"

Peter Allen was fond of telling talk show hosts that, like his latest LP, he was "Bicoastal." With a charming Aussie wink. Various of his songs told even more, and the 1983 book *Judy & Liza* by James Spada made known that Liza's first husband was gay. Spada later told *The Advocate,* "The manuscript was first screened by an attorney. I (only) had to cut a reference to Liza's drug use. A year or two later Liza checked into the Betty Ford Clinic for drug rehabilitation."

In a 1989 *Golden Girls* episode one of the foursome says about a corpse, "They found a tan, bamboo purse by his body." Another one completes the insinuation: "You mean he was on his way to a Peter Allen concert?"

When Allen starred in and wrote the words and music for the Broadway musical *Legs* (Diamond), half the town was waiting for him to fall on his face. Critics aimed their vitriol pens at the project—book by Harvey Fierstein—and the man. Even *Los Angeles* magazine chimed in, wondering, "Satire, camp or what! Torture." Reviewers devised witty headlines like "No Legs" and "Broken Legs," and the NY *Native* correctly guessed that *Legs* would be "practically dished to death."

Certain straight and gay critics trounced Allen for playing such a hetero stud. His countless gangster molls did seem more interesting when mouthing Fierstein's words. Even the *Native* was guarded—"You must really have to be a fan of Peter Allen's to put up with his voice, mannerisms and nervous habits for the two hours-plus of this show. But exactly *who* will admit to being a Peter Allen fan?" Not the *Golden Girls* writers. . . .

"Love Don't Need a Reason"

"Half the people who see my photo still don't get that I'm a man," said Divine (Harris Glenn Milstead). "I'm not kidding you, but countless housewives think that 'drag' means wearing extremely colorful clothes, like Cher."

Divine was on the verge of mainstream success in John Waters' 1988 film *Hairspray* when he died at 42 of weight-related problems. The counterculture's Lady Di was also a best-selling disco artist in Europe, with several albums to his credit. "I love doing cabaret and being on stage. People stare, but once they get used to 300 pounds of gorgeous, they listen."

Why didn't his music go over at home? "Marketing. Marketing is very important. Damn it!"

A combination of Joan Crawford and Sydney Greenstreet (which meant he could have co-starred with himself in *Flamingo Road*), Divine was best known for his films with gay directors John Waters and Paul Bartel. Especially the truly tasteless movie *Pink Flamingos*. He longed "to do musicals, because I have a fabulous sense of rhythm." In Bartel's 1984 *Lust in the Dust* with Tab Hunter, Divine played a way-out western chanteuse who crooned, "These lips were made for kissin,' these hips were made for blissin,'" with Mae Westian aplomb.

"All my life I wanted to look like Elizabeth Taylor," he said in 1981. "Now I find that Liz Taylor is beginning to look like me." In '87 he noted, "Liz is gorgeous again. But so am I—*and* I can sing!"

At the opposite end of the flamboyance scale was singer-songwriter and PWA Michael Callen. His *Purple Heart* LP contained a masculine cover of the Connie Francis gay cult favorite "Where the Boys Are," and the touching "Love Don't Need a Reason" (i.e., reproduction), written with Peter Allen and Marsha Malamet. Callen sang the latter at the ceremonies launching the 1987 AIDS Walkathon in Los Angeles.

Asked his reason for coming out, Michael related, "It never occurred to me not to be openly gay—using the right pronouns in a song and all that. . . . Several people along the way tried to convince me that I could be Barry Manilow. They said I had the Wonder Bread voice and could have a jingle career if only I wouldn't be so outfront gay. I would think about it for two seconds and would just laugh."

Callen had a firsthand perspective on AIDS, and firm opinions. "They want us dead. I call it passive genocide. . . . Clearly our lives are not valuable to them. . . . As long as we have a Republican administration, we're never going to get anywhere on this issue. A gay Republican in this day and age is a contradiction in terms. If they vote Republican, they don't care if their friends die. That's all there is to it."

Somewhere in between the apolitical Divine and Michael Callen are ex-lovers Romanovsky & Phillips. In 1981 they began singing and touring the country with their own songs —for their own label, Fresh Fruit Records—such as "I Thought You'd Be Taller," "Emotional Rollercoaster," "Waltz For the New Age" and more relevant material like "Living With AIDS" and "Be On the Safe Side." Likewise, Callen's *Purple Heart,* distributed by Fresh Fruit, includes the AIDS songs "Living in War Time" and "How To Have (Safe) Sex." (Fresh Fruit also distributes albums by Lynn Lavner, "the world's only left-handed Jewish lesbian leather act," creator of songs like "You Are What You Wear" and the moving homage to "Anne Frank.")

Ron Romanovsky and Paul Phillips' act blends multi-hued outfits just this side of drag with humorous, sometimes bitchy stage banter à la Sonny and Cher and their catchy tunes—three albums to date. After seven years they decided to call it quits as mates, and were amazed to find "a lot of criticism that we were not a couple anymore, just a duo. . . . Some fans suggested we should retain our romantic image on the stage, but that's counter to what we stand for: honesty."

The two have become role models for gay couples who have separated but remain good friends. Ron explains, "Seven years is a long time for any marriage, gay or straight. Besides which, we were at it twenty-four hours a day, living and working together." They now live apart but tour the world, performing at international Gay Pride festivals. The *Sydney Morning Herald* recently enthused, "The Mardi Gras committee could not have chosen two more delightful, entertaining yet politically committed ambassadors for their cause."

Sydney's *Daily Mirror* opined, "If Simon & Garfunkel were younger, very funny and very gay, you might have an act resembling Romanovsky & Phillips." Above all, the irrepressible blond and brunet team virtually created the genre of American gay men's music double-handedly.

In 1982 in *Us* magazine, Johnny Mathis casually came out. "No big deal," he affirmed, and it hasn't been a big deal to a career less dependent on visual, including video, images then on sheer vocal witchery and non-faddish ballads with heterosexual pronouns. Though a successful mainstream artist since the mid-1950s, Mathis never opted for the desperate Big Publicity Route of marriage, dating or being-seen-with—and therefore using—living heterosexual pronouns.

Rona Barrett called him "the greatest romantic singer of our time." Born in 1935, Johnny began lessons in voice and opera at 13 but planned to become a phys ed instructor. At San Francisco State he set records in track and field, and could have been the Carl Lewis (! . . .) of the '50s. He was headed for the Olympics while singing in local clubs. After much soul-searching, he chose music and signed with Columbia Records.

His first studio session was the same week as the Olympic tryouts in Berkeley. Johnny had left home for New York City and Columbia, telling his parents he'd be back in three days. He returned three years later, after indelible hits like "Wonderful, Wonderful," "It's Not For Me To Say" and "Chances Are." In 1958 Columbia released *Johnny's Greatest Hits,* which spent an unprecedented 9 ½ years on *Billboard* magazine's Top 100 list. Over 70 gold and platinum albums ensued.

Post-'50s, most of Mathis' songs weren't original hits, but covers of others' hits, e.g., Andy Williams' "Moon River," the Bee Gees' "How Deep Is Your Love." His first No. 1 single was the male-female duet "Too Much, Too Little, Too Late" in 1978 with Deniece Williams. Johnny also did subliminally gay songs like "All the Sad Young Men" and "A Time For Us," released in June, 1969, immediately before the Stonewall riots.

With the years, his fans became older—the same ones who'd bought his '50s hits or made out to his music in the early '60s before younger, hipper sounds took over. Today Johnny's sales strength is in his albums, not singles, and a majority of his fans are heterosexual.

Bill Como theorized, "To straight record-buyers, Johnny is a Voice. Period. To most older gays who know of him he's a sex symbol, a legend, a brother." Another reason his coming out

didn't affect him——apart from its not being widely reported——
was that, "Like McKuen, he came out once his time in the
limelight had already passed," re the *San Francisco Examiner's*
Barry Walters. Plus, since the '60s the mass media is much more
interested in the sexuality of under-40 hot-right-now stars.

Barbara Howar stated in 1988 that due to the rise of celebrity journalism periodicals are less loathe to reveal "the sexual
predilections of a Michael Jackson or a Whitney Houston." What
was once taboo is now merely iffy, thanks to inquiring minds and
Bigger Sales Dollars——although this doesn't mean the coverage
is other than drearily anti-gay.

Us' Alan Petrucelli probed Johnny about his loves. One was
"the best baritone sax player in the world. We had everything in
common." The sax player was 20, Johnny 16, but "in San
Francisco at 16 I was equivalent to 40 anywhere else." Of course
Mathis declared that he seldom had sex and only with "a very,
very close person. I go weeks, sometimes months, without
having sex, because I'm on the road. I wouldn't know how to
even find a sex partner!" Oh, Johnny, oh!

He added, "I've had little infatuations. But I finally met two
people, one in L.A. and the other in Louisiana. I love them both
very much but don't see them often——maybe twice a year. But
it's enough for me." At any rate, Mathis is the opposite of most
stars in that his public persona is quite shy, while in person he's
anything but.

He claims work is his All, and "I'm a hermit, with a lower
case *h*. Crowds make me very uncomfortable." Personally, he
prefers quality over quantity. "What is life for? To have *good*
friends."

However in his career he's managed to have both——steady
quality and stellar quantity. By coming out, and in a general
publication, he showed that he didn't value the opinions of
bigots above those of the gay community and his hetero well-
wishers. Like the song says, "I never bother with people I
hate . . . " That's (one reason) why the gentleman's a champ!

"Living in War Time"

In the beginning, many thought Elvis the Pelvis was a pansy. For a man to be so openly sexual, so sexy, so sexily free in his movements and stage presence was deemed radical. And weird. Then too, he didn't marry for the longest time, and had all those handsome if uncouth bodyguards separating him from the real world. That he was a mama's boy was a fact he was proud of—Gladys' devoted son never had another relationship as intense or faithful as the one with Big Mama.

Yet Elvis was a paranoid, right-wing homophobe. A natural blond, he dyed his hair black—more of a "man's" color. He detested liberals and feminists like Jane Fonda, also long-haired (therefore potentially queer) foreigners like the Beatles—who not incidentally toppled him from his sales throne and who unlike him created their own music and lyrics and didn't need a "Colonel" to stage-direct their careers. Ironically, Elvis sucked up to secretly gay J. Edgar Hoover by volunteering to spy on Fonda, the Fab Four and others for the FBI.

In 1987 Larry Duplechan observed that "though it's usually not remembered for this reason, Elvis Presley's 1957 classic 'Jailhouse Rock' contains rock 'n roll's very first lyrical allusion to homosexuality—and the only one for nearly fifteen years thereafter." After all, "No. 47 said to No. 3, 'You're the cutest jailbird I ever did see,'" etc. "Rock 'n roll" was a euphemism for sexual intercourse, and as hipsters knew, jailhouse "rock" meant jailhouse sex. But since society only hears what it wants to hear, it didn't notice. Then or now.

Marvin Gay didn't want anyone to think he might be. So he added a final "e." No mama's boy he, today his name is irrevocably linked with his father, who killed him.

Early in his career, country singer Merle Haggard walked off an *Ed Sullivan Show.* A bad move, but in his mind necessary, as he told the *New Yorker* in 1990: "I have never wanted to act like a pansy—you know, a tiptoe through the tulips sort of guy—and that was what was happenin'. (Backstage) there was all these fruiters runnin' around, and they had us doin' figure eights and all sorts of stuff."

Merle the pearl did apologize. Ignorantly. Said he didn't mean to "demean the gay movement or female impersonators or transvestites or guys with sex changes."

Journalist and radio interviewer Brandon Judell asked heavy metal group Mötley Crue whether they had any gay fans. "No, no," they protested. "Well, Tommy Lee had *one* . . . " Judell also pointed out that *Rolling Stone* and other music magazines "take for granted that there is no gay readership out there." *RS* and others also fail to put homophobic interviewees on the spot, as they do racists and anti-Semites. Thus, the hate-inciting lyrics of a Mark Knopfler or Axl Rose go unremarked and become unremarkable—acceptable. And the widely-covered controversy over the alleged obscenity of 2 Live Crew's sexist lyrics never even mentions the group's extreme homophobia and anti-gay lyrics.

Homophobia is becoming more vocal and visible in the music world. The sick minds range from small-timers like Audio Two to "the world's best-selling hard-rock group," Guns 'N Roses. If such a group is white, it's typically racist, anti-Semitic and homophobic. If black, it's anti-Semitic and homophobic. So the two groups which have possibly contributed the most (to culture, certainly to music) and definitely been persecuted the most remain the targets of immoral, unthinking majority-ites.

In "One In a Million" and other songs, Guns 'N Roses depicts gay people as aliens who come to America to spread AIDS. Public Enemy, a viciously anti-Semitic black group, pictures "First World whites spreading AIDS and syphilis" to the Third World—where AIDS began. A fascist-minded trio which would prefer all blacks to think alike, Public Enemy was challenged on radio about the diversity of the black community, which includes—as does every population—gay men and lesbians. Unfactually, they retorted that no word exists in any African language for "homosexual," "lesbian" or "prostitute" (as if the last had anything to do with the first two; guilt by false association).

Like the Nazis and other dictators (of countries and/or public opinion), such groups deal in Big Lies.

Meanwhile, Skid Road's Sebastian Bach shows up at a photo session wearing a t-shirt stating "AIDS: Kills Faggots Dead," and MTV makes video stars of some-time singers Sam Kinison and Eddie Murphy, two of today's bum crop of hate-comics—like Andrew Dice Clay—who verbally bash "fags and comics—like Andrew Dice Clay—who verbally bash "fags and bitches" all the way to the bank and inspire others to do the real dirty work.

The Audio Two song "Whatcha Lookin' At?" also incites anti-gay violence with its amateurish lyrics: "What's the matter witcha boy, are ya gay?" then warns that if he is, he can expect a punch in the face, for "Word to Giz, I hate faggots," who are compared to—easy rhyme—maggots. Nineteen-year-old lyricist Milk Dee informed the New York Post that he "wrote the lyrics after a gay man made a pass at him." Do we expect female songwriters cruised by straight men to then advocate universal castration?

Dee assured the *Post* that his group wants to be good role models for young kids. Asked how a lyric like "Gay mothers get punched in the face" sets a good example, Milk's brother/partner Gizmo declared, "We don't want the kids to follow the negative things that we're saying. It's not like our whole album is dedicated to beating homosexuals."

Again, the ten percent or so of kids who are gay—regardless at what age they realize or accept their inherent gayness—are, like gay adults, overlooked. And branded and targeted, in a decade in which gay-bashing and -murdering are more common—and, in the media, literally unremarkable (i.e., newscasts)—than ever before, aided and abetted by music and other media which painfully prove that as far as government and the system are concerned, "Our lives are not valuable to them. . . ."

Songbirds

"Girls got balls. They're just a little higher up, that's all."
——Joan Jett

"Society's Child"

In the early '70s, when I entered college and Joan Baez, the 1960s' preeminent female folk singer, *came out,* it caused a hell of a stir. Even in hypothetically hip circles. Perhaps some had thought of the woman who was called the voice and conscience of her generation as a sexless earth madonna. Or maybe the announcement of bisexuality was startling because Baez had been a star for so long and had so much to lose.

At the 1958 Newport Folk Festival, the 18-year-old nova already flamed passionately, singing as though silence were a wall and her lyrics the colors with which to cover it. Four years later, Baez made the cover of *Time,* an overrated but culturally significant honor.

At Woodstock, she sang, six months pregnant. Perhaps popular imagination only viewed bisexual women as glamorous and flighty, or as females who didn't have children.

Joan's courage shouldn't have come as a surprise. In the '60s she marched with Martin Luther King, Jr., and she sang in the bomb shelters of Hanoi during the 1972 Christmas bombings. Her song "Altar Boy and the Thief" took a sympathetic look at gay bar patrons, though it of course received scant critical attention (what the media always failed to note about artists like Baez, Janis Ian, Lou Reed, Rod McKuen, Elton John and David

111

Bowie was that not only did they each come out as gay or bi, they also wrote and sang songs about the gay or lesbian experience).

Most likely, the shock waves Joan caused were due to her folksy, pacifist image. Had she been a rock 'n roller, the impact of her coming out would have been minimized. As gay historian Martin Greif said, "Even schoolkids used to know that Janis [Joplin] did it with men and women both." With Baez, whose passionate ardor seemed reserved for singing and protests, even college kids were surprised.

But Joan, never a MOR megastar, never a sex symbol or feminine icon, went unscathed by her announcement, and lived to tell the tale in her 1987 autobiography, *And A Voice to Sing With*. She described only one woman-to-woman affair, but her attitude, à la Piaf, was I Regret Nothing.

"After an overdose of unhappiness at the end of an affair with a man," she wrote, "when I had a need for softness and understanding," she turned to another woman. However, during 1985's Live Aid concert, her heterosexual credentials were in good enough shape for her to "recklessly" flirt with Don Johnson, who soon after hooked up with Barbra Streisand.

Baez has remained single since her 1974 divorce, married to a career that has yielded over 50 albums and the one book. Not a few fans felt that in her book she tried to disassociate herself from lesbians, bisexuals and feminists—not to mention Jane Fonda, against whom she often was pitted by the press.

A letter to the *Gay Community News* opined, "*Voice* deifies Bob Dylan (an ex-lover) while trivializing Joan's year-long affair with 'surfer girl' Kimmie. . . . Since the affair occurred in 1962, why would Baez, if that was indeed her sole lesbian affair, call herself bisexual in the 1970s, but in the 1980s state that was her sole such affair?

"Or am I being commercially naive?"

There was recrimination from both sides of the reading audience, as certain readers discovered for the first time that Baez was, as the old saying went, multi-talented. "When Kimmie and I did finally make love," she recalled, "it was superb and utterly natural. It made me wonder what all the fuss was about, both society's and my own."

In the '80s, Joan remained pro-gay, and shared the stage with lesbian singer-activist Holly Near (a former anti-war colleague of Fonda's) to fight an anti-gay rights amendment in Los Angeles. In the late '80s Joan worked against the LaRouche-backed AIDS quarantine initiative while many other celebrities, including Fonda, literally hopped aboard the squeaky-clean, non-controversial Clean Water Initiative bus.

Baez came out during her marriage but made it easier for women like Janis Ian to come out, single. At her commercial height in the '70s, the short, wiry-haired Ian was a pop-folk singer in the brooding, pseudo-ethnic Baez mold. At 15 she became a pop star with "Society's Child." After some years away from the limelight, she returned with "At Seventeen," a catchy if downbeat evocation of the trials of teenhood for the unlovely. In time, Ian wed and became a mother and a very private person, again edging away from the limelight.

According to O (interviewed later in this chapter), "The two most disillusioning things for me in music—disappointments not related to my own career—were when Janis Ian married and the angst went out of her songs, and when Joan Baez went up to Don Johnson, in front of the whole world, and said, 'Hello, gorgeous. Could we discuss the possibility of rape?' When I heard that, my mouth dropped almost to the floor! *Rape*, mind you."

"I'm Still Here"

Back when I started this book, a friend in New York asked, "Whatever happened to Janis Ian, and what more can you tell me about her?" Well, after her brief eminence among the small corps of female singers-composers, then her new lifestyle—has she since changed it?—she's made comeback attempts. As for the *real* Janis, she was interviewed in *Star Treatment*, a quirky book about stars' psychoanalysis. She spoke about the trauma of coming out.

Her therapy she described as "coming to grips with what I was. Like, it wasn't hip to be bisexual. . . . No one around me could deal with it. I decided to be myself, whatever the cost. This was in 1967." In an interview, she inadvertently mentioned her dual sexuality, because she hated to lie. She compared herself with the David Bowie of that time. "Someone like David Bowie is committed to living his life as it is, whatever the changes he's going through. And that includes just being straightforward when somebody asks you about sex." That is, until one has to be straight to go professionally forward?

Sometimes one happens upon news of yesterday's stars of one-hit-spinners accidentally. In a June, 1988, issue of the *Hollywood Kids' Newsletter* I read, in the "It's True! Section," that "Alicia ('I Love the Night Life') Bridges is now a DJ in a lesbian bar in Atlanta called the Sportspage."

The fate of most women singers parallels that ascribed to actresses by Stephen Sondheim in *Follies:* They start out "sloe-eyed" vamps, then become mothers, and then "you're camp." Their career longevity is akin to that of the froufrou feathers on the front of a diva's slippers. From Kate Smith to Streisand, and whatever their differences, singers not male have typically been labeled and dismissed as "girl singers."

When successful, they were considered oddities by dint of their success, which many—like Connie Francis, controlled by a powerful male parent in the near background—couldn't handle. Marriage and/or motherhood often intervened, confirming the thesis that women only sang as a hobby, not a career. If bland or blandly pretty, like Patti Page or Olivia Newton-John, they risked being forgotten as they aged or faded into a wheat-haired haze.

If unusual, like a Streisand or Cyndi Lauper, only consistent sales and/or movie stardom could save them from becoming freakish fads. Whatever her style or substance, until recently a female singer was perceived or marketed as something which ignored her individualism and rich accumulation of detail.

Look at Ethel Merman, even. Her fame, demands and dominance made her feared and set upon by most non-gay critics. Early on, the "Merm" was institutionalized, and conclusions were drawn. For instance, via a pervasive stereotype, it was commonly assumed she was Jewish. "I am not of the Jewish persuasion," Merman often explained. Some fans suspected that behind the manly brashness lay an otherness, sexually speaking. Her very nickname rhymed with "sperm," and conjured visions of, say, a sperm whale, or at least something aggressively sturdy.

However, most fans were relievedly convinced of Ethel's

*like*ness by the marriages and offspring. After all, anyone willing to marry Ernest Borgnine *had* to be straight, right?

Merman's attitude toward gay men was emblematic of most show biz divas. She knew she needed them, and found their company useful—as "escorts"—and amusing, but she didn't approve of 'em, at least certainly not publicly (which is also true of a number of secretly lesbian singers and actresses).

On the other hand, lesbians did intrigue her. In the Jacqueline Susann bio *Lovely Me,* Jacqueline Seaman described Susann describing to a rapt Merman how in Paris Coco Chanel had made passes at her. The Merm was also eager to learn about Jackie's intimate relationship with blonde sex symbol Carole Landis.

What Ms. Seaman didn't include was Merman's decades-long fascination with and distaste for Mary Martin, a professional rival and feminine woman who despite more than one marriage (the second to a gay man) and more than one child, was a lifelong lesbian with once-famous girlfriends—among them Janet Gaynor, Oscar's first Best Actress—and a platonic friendship with Nancy Reagan, whose godmother was lesbian legend Alla Nazimova, once MGM's top-paid star.

In most everything written about her, Merman comes across as loud, coarse and cheap, even to the extent of insisting upon house seats at her musicals so she could resell them to scalpers. She was bigoted not only toward gay men, but also "niggers" and "Commie Jews." "Dykes," too. . . .

In her book, Seaman recounted the trouble a 50ish Ethel was having with the bumps and grinds in *Gypsy.* A sympathetic and experienced Susann visited the Merm's apartment wearing a bikini under her dress, and proceeded to shed the dress while rendering a heartfelt private performance for the woman on whom she had a "star crush." It may have been a one-sided crush, but according to Seaman at least one of Jackie's friends believed it was mutual. The friend remembered a Central Park West party:

"Everybody was very drunk. Jackie and Ethel were very drunk, and they lay down on a couch and they just made out in front of everyone." Jackie thereafter pursued Ethel with such fervor that her husband Irving angrily informed the 40-plus writer that she was too old for "schoolgirl crushes."

"You're The Top"

A different kind of harridan was Janis Joplin, whose stereotype of anything goes—chemically or sexually—was closer to the mark. Thanks to her wild woman image and her intense affiliation with rock 'n roll, Joplin's biographers haven't differed on her sexuality, only on its balance. In *Buried Alive* Myra Friedman declared there were "more men than women," while Peggy Casertas in *Going Down With Janis* wrote that there were "more women than men" (the title notwithstanding!).

Despite her rep, Janis was sensitive. Especially about her lack of looks and her androgynous allure. Enrolling at the University of Texas at Austin, she'd originally intended to become a teacher. She quit after her first year, when she was voted Most Ugly Man on Campus. Ever needful of attention, she fabricated boyfriends when they didn't exist, at other times faked celibacy to gain sympathy.

When a friend in Beaumont, Texas, asked how she'd been, she replied, "I haven't even been laid in six months, that's how good I've been."

Would she have 'fessed up to her lesbian affairs on paper, had she lived to tell? Sammy Davis, Jr., who admired her guts if not her music, once told the *Star*, "Janis wanted everyone to like her, man, not just the hippies and kids. She craved respectability." More than likely, her autobio would have reflected Swedish cartoonist Thorvald Gahlin's comment, "Whoever says you cannot change history never tried to write his/her memoirs."

Though AC/DC, Janis was by no means pro-gay. She railed against men whom she could only seduce with her voice, not her body. Photographer Francesco Scavullo revealed that after he worked with Joplin she happily blurted, "I'd expected you to be a fag!"—having formed a different opinion of the professional who did his best to make her look good.

The closest Hollywood has come to shooting Joplin's story was Bette Midler's debut film, *The Rose*. Lesbian kissing scenes were filmed, but against Midler's protestations were scrapped. A production associate noted, "The script was closer to Janis before it became Bette's movie.

"The producer had been romantically involved with Bette

and wanted the Janis allusions toned down, particularly the sexual ones, so it would be clearly Bette" and no doubt an unsullied, commercial blossom. *The Rose* fared well financially, but the re-tailoring to Midler's persona may have cost her an Oscar. Like Barbra Streisand (as Fanny Brice in *Funny Girl*), Bette was nominated her first time out. But Midler as Midler didn't cop the statuette.

The Rose spotlighted drug abuse, and it was said by some that Janis Joplin's steadiest lover was narcotics. And that sex was just another narcotic for her, something to kill the time and enhance the jaded senses.

Shortly before her death, she announced her engagement to a 21-year-old Berkeley student. Insiders said the impending marriage was publicity-engineered, or wishful thinking. Those closest to her felt that Janis' heart had long since been broken, for she'd used it too often.

The last night of her life was spent at Barney's Beanery on Santa Monica Boulevard in Los Angeles, a roadhouse since 1920 and a favorite hangout of Jean Harlow, John Barrymore, Clara Bow and James Dean. Not coincidentally, Janis had crushes on both Harlow and Dean.

On October 4, 1970, at the end of the bar, Janis had her last drink in public, after a late recording session with her Full Tilt Boogie Band. She departed about 12:30 a.m., and was dropped off at the Landmark Hotel in Hollywood. Seven months earlier she'd kicked a heroin habit. In the early morning hours of October 5th, she shot up some heroin and walked to the lobby to buy cigarettes. Back in her room, she overdosed and died, falling so hard to the floor that she broke her nose.

In O's opinion, part of Joplins' magic as a performer was "watching somebody who you knew had been through the wringer. Like Edith Piaf, she dragged herself up and out of the gutter. Watching Janis, you could see and hear that it was only her love of singing, and her desperate need to sing, that kept her barely hanging on."

Singing may have equalled survival for Joplin, but her troublesome celebrity was like an inextinguishable lantern whose light projected disturbing flames on the puddles of her life.

Ethel Merman was once asked to comment on the young divas of rock. She dismissed Grace Slick as "gimmicky but good," then spoke at length about how she didn't "get" Janis Joplin, concluding, "That girl has problems. . . . Bein' heard ain't one of 'em; like me, she gives an audience their money's worth.

"But when I sing, everything's comin' up roses. When she sings, it's a primal scream, for heaven's sake!"

Cole Porter once said, "I'd rather write for Ethel Merman than anyone else in the world." And so he did. Songs like "Blow, Gabriel, Blow," "It's De-Lovely," "I Get a Kick Out of You" and "You're The Top." Porter's quote about Merman was reproduced in her autobiography and on the back cover of her last major album. But the Merm didn't return the compliment:

"I don't have either a favorite song or songwriter. When George and Ira Gershwin, Cole Porter, Irving Berlin, Jule Styne, Steve Sondheim and Jerry Herman have written especially for you, how are you going to pick a favorite?" Possibly the choice is all the harder when most of the composers named are gay.

"Shadowland"

In 1987 I was interviewed for a gay cable-TV show, *Lifestyle Update*. The openly lesbian host, Melinda Tremoglio, told me about the recent taping at Universal City of a lesbian women's music festival, and how frustrated she'd been that lesbian cult singers like Holly Near and Cris Williamson had declined to appear on camera for the show. Why? Because they perceived *Lifestyle Update*, which had a male producer-director, as a male-dominated show. Said Melinda, "Normally, if people are wary about being on our show it's because of the rumor potential, although not everyone on our show is gay.

"But I can't imagine what sort of rumor Holly or Cris could be worried about!"

At times it seems that the uniting factor behind the women (or, to use their preferred spelling, womyn) of womyn's music isn't so much lesbianism as putting down penis-owners. Even after the fact: in 1977 several feminist musicians and technicians complained to Olivia Records about the presence of formerly male Sandy Stone, a record engineer who worked at Olivia. The group objected to Stone's employment at the female-owned and

-run company, at women-only events, and to the fact that she hadn't disclosed her former gender and had allegedly deprived a born-female engineer of potential employ at Olivia.

The company defended Stone, but the lesbian feminists' objections didn't die down over the next several years, and there were threats of boycott even though Olivia is the major purveyor of lesbian records.

Despite their strong sense of self, some of Olivia's singers, to quote the male-dominated *Advocate,* "dance around questions about their sexuality." One celebrated case was Cris Williamson, a pioneering lesbian singer-songwriter whose debut LP, *The Changer and the Changed,* is Olivia's best-ever-seller.

In September, 1989, she was interviewed for *Hot Wire* magazine. Asked if she'd been "forced out as a lesbian," she responded, "No one knows if I am or not. . . . I think some women are definitely lesbian, and that's their religion—that's what changed them. . . . It is not what has moved me most in my life."

In the January, 1990, issue she wrote, "I never meant to deny being a lesbian. . . . Truthfully, I was surprised at my own response. . . . It was a puzzle to me, after fifteen years of singing to lesbians, defending lesbians, and being a lesbian, that I found myself answering so defensively. I can only say that I have learned a great deal from the experience." She concluded, "I am a lesbian, and I remain proud."

So why the previous evasiveness? Rock critic Adam Block called it "That Stepford-zombie pop panic toward queers [which] is insidious and far-reaching." Perhaps too, singers like Williamson and Near are understandably cautious about overt statements in a medium which places lesbians at the very bottom of the totem pole and denies them the mainstream success that their talent merits.

Of course in show biz the Big Rumor is homosexuality, but it stalks, so to speak, fewer women singers than male ones. One reason is that there have been, till lately, fewer androgynous songstresses. Also, fewer female singers ever don drag. The latest big exception is country star k. d. lang [*sic*]. In the past, most country women have nestled in one of two basic grooves: the Partonesque floozy with a heart of grits or the plainer, Loretta Lynn-like brunette who suffers often and heartily.

Lang is neither of the above, and apprised *TV Guide,* "It's a good thing that I'm bringing a new style to country music, because it opens people's perspectives and breaks the barriers that women had to work within." Dolly Parton first broke through with a song titled "Dumb Blonde." It still took dozens more songs and several years to make her a star, moving from one medium to the next but always working within the parameters of her heavy wigs and thick makeup.

If lang stands out like a sore thumb in the femmy-frilly arena of country gals, her pure voice and unvarnished talent will obviate her becoming a fad or novelty act. She will likely cross over to other media, excepting motion pictures, more quickly than did Ms. Parton. But so far, as with Boy George, the media still snickers, taking a long, wondering look. The tabloid *Globe* decided, "Princely Queen of Country Is Out to Shock," then teasingly divulged that the singer's real name is Kathy Dawn "but don't ever call her that to her face!

"K. d. has brought genderbending to the world of country music. . . . Sometimes she looks like a cute teenaged boy in a tailored suit. She shuns makeup, has accented masculine features and maintains a closely cropped, mannish hair-style. . . .She shocks her audience by changing from a man to a woman on stage."

In 1983 lang won an award as "most promising newcomer" on the Canadian music scene. (Another Canadian singer under question at one time was Anne Murray, who said of herself on her own TV special, "I walk like a football player." The rumors were scotched by marriage and motherhood.)

Lang seems beyond rumors, and defines herself in unmincing terms. Regarding her *look,* "I like to pretend I'm a farmer, and sort of dress for chores—always ready to feed the cows, drive the tractor and fix the truck." No country stereotype, she informed *Us,* "I don't eat meat and I'm not a Christian and I don't have big, fluffy hair." A letter to the editor of San Francisco's gay *B.A.R.* newspaper stated at the time of the hit movie *Rain Man,* "If Dustin Hoffman and Tom Cruise had a son together, he'd look exactly like k. d. lang."

In 1990 k. d. was up for three Grammy awards, and was enthusiastically endorsed by Loretta Lynn, who'd sung on her '88 hit album *Shadowland.* When lang won big, she accepted her victory in a silver-embroidered dress coat and her trademarked boy-cut, labeling her Grammy "a piece of land where I intend to plant my seeds of hybrid country—and *this* land is fertile!" *The Advocate* approved. "Very Barbara Stanwyck. It was the queerest moment all night," especially since such "former fabulous troublemakers as Bette Midler and Lou Reed were there, looking as dapper and dull as account executives."

"Paint A Rumor"

From across the sea, the stunningly beautiful Annie Lennox of the Eurythmics has created an androgynous, pan-sexual mystique with her male impersonations and a butch stance that she perfected at the beginning of her stardom. Annie and Boy George made the cover of *Newsweek* together, in an article ostensibly about *The British Invasion, Part II,* but keyed to genderbending Brits.

Back when the Boy still dressed like a samurai rabbi and Lennox was less Marilyn Monroe-ish/girlish than today, Culture Club had bigger sales than the Eurythmics. The quartet also received immeasurably more publicity—its eye-catching and - opening lead singer was constantly doused in a shower of publicity. But Lennox's duo has lasted longer, building on each musical and video success while both musicians (Lennox and Dave Stewart) have done outside projects, including movie acting—in *Revolution* with Al Pacino—for Annie, who has what is definitely considered a movie face.

Sweet Dreams, the duo's breakthrough album, established Lennox's unconventional, chameleon-like quality. Sporting a black, shapeless man's suit and short-short David Bowie-orange hair, she crooned the title track. The video of the album's second hit, "Who's That Girl?" had her convincingly portraying both genders and at one point kissing herself on the lips. In songs like "Love Is a Stranger In an Open Car," "Paint A Rumor" and "The Walk," the love object's sex is never identified by a pronoun. Lennox and Stewart wrote their own songs, including the eerie love song sung to the late "Jennifer."

Interviewed in 1986, Lennox seemed defiant about the inevitable rumors. "I don't really care what they say." She did add that she was happily married (at that time) to a West German Hare Krishna.

Lennox and Stewart may have regarded her male drag as a fast-wearing gimmick or decided to broaden their appeal by eschewing it. At any rate, Lennox retained her close-cropped 'do, but her look has evolved into high-gloss—survival of the sleekest. After her sassy duet with Aretha Franklin, "Sisters Are Doing It for Themselves," she insisted that the strong-woman anthem wasn't feminist-themed, let alone a Movement classic like Helen Reddy's "I Am Woman."

Sleekly coltish and firmly mainstream from the start was Whitney Houston. Mom and apple pie were frequently invoked, the crucifix was usually displayed, and on a 1987 cover of *Us* magazine mama Cissy Houston was pictured "Worrying About Whitney." How come? The article gingerly touched on her daughter's attachment to an allegedly inseparable female secretary-companion. Houston senior denied the persistent rumors which even found their way into the typically reticent *Time*. "She's a loving, feeling girl," said the gospel singer, "and I know she wants a normal life. A mother just knows these things. . . ."

After Whitney ended her relationship with what *Us* called "her best girlfriend," there were further rumors when she befriended movie co-stars Jodie Foster and Kelly McGillis of *The Accused*. The gossip columns and British tabloids had a field day, as stories about the alleged triangle competed with stories about Brigitte Nielsen Stallone and *her* private female secretary. Through it all, Houston shattered records with consecutive hit singles, and kept her pristine public persona intact. She continues to wear the snug and flattering armor of her principles.

A senior publicist for Sony-owned Columbia Records (*not* Whitney's label) asserts, "In the music business, new stars are thought to be extremely vulnerable to public curiosity. Guided marriages still do take place. . . . Possibly the least vulnerable performer is an older, successful woman. Particularly a black woman, for black women's sexuality has always been taken for granted, even in the days when ladies were believed to lie on our backs and think of England or Uncle Sam."

As for male performers, "Oh, they're always vulnerable, at 18 or 80. In that regard, men are far more vulnerable than women."

Rumors have long swirled like vampire fog around ultra-androgyne-mon-amour Grace Jones, who sported a dangerously butch haircut long before Kathy Dawn twanged her first hybrid note. On stage, screen and record covers, Jones' unfeigned masculinity has made Eddie Murphy look like a simp in tight leather clothing. Unlike various disco and pop divas, Jones never denied her large—and mostly—gay following, nor did she do a Donna Summer-like spiritual turnabout against her biggest fans.

But the real Grace remains a dark enigma, though she's done physically revealing photo layouts in *People* and elsewhere paired with unrobed blond hunks and in *Hustler* paired with a blonde babe similarly clad in boxing gloves and little besides. Amazing Grace has held off the inquisitive by clarifying that she was one of twins, and that in childhood her twin brother had been the one to play with dolls, while she was a resolute tomboy. Jones' sexual orientation? She confessed that her brother is gay.

The front page of the March 31, 1987 *Sun* comprised two "exclusive" stories. One was "I Don't Trust Reds, Blasts Maggie" (Thatcher). Much more prominent was "Gay Loves of Tina Turner." A mini-skirted photo of Tina was captioned, "Sexy star. . . but Tina's really turned on by girls." A gruesome headshot of Ike was captioned, "I caught her in bed with a girl, says ex-hubby."

The *Sun* quoted various female friends of the singer and a former Ikette who declared, "Tina had two long-time relationships with women—one black and one white." Whether anyone believed the story is almost a moot point. True or false, it's not probable such a story, had it been printed in the U.S., could hurt Tina. Somebody younger, somebody mild as milk, or someone who hadn't paid their dues or had never wed, maybe—at least.

Among the people who never buy Tina Turner's albums, a more damaging story would have been her heartfelt odyssey from Baptist to Buddhist.

Yet, according to the record publicist quoted earlier, "The entertainment industry's fears aren't the average person's fears. I'm only half-joking, but in L.A., you live in fear that the IRS might find out you've been cheating them like you do your spouse. You live in fear that you won't be able to cover your Mercedes payments, and that you might be murdered—without all the attendant publicity.

"Probably the biggest fears in town are that your neighbors will find out you're a switch-hitter, and that your Nicaraguan cleaning lady will buy the house next door to you."

A secretly gay executive at MCA Records explains, "Even in our quote-unquote progressive business, people look at anything gay-related through a distorting magnifying glass. . . . There's more fear and apprehension than is warranted by the results. Over the long run, I don't think strong careers can be hurt by rumors or even by coming out. It's the homophobes who want you to think so, and too often we play into their hands."

The Rupert Murdoch-owned *Sun* is notorious for its homophobia, yet the most appalling thing about the Tina Turner story was its use of alleged bisexuality to somehow justify Ike Turner's wife-beating during the marriage. Turner seemed to defend his actions by reportedly saying, "I don't think she ever liked making love—except with women." Typically, the story used bi- or homosexuality as a means of besmirching an individual and casting doubt upon her prior statements.

The MCA executive points out, "There's always been prejudice of every kind. And will be. The only way to neutralize it, apart from legislating against it, is to stop giving it importance; if you're concerned with what a bigot thinks, you're helping validate his viewpoint."

The Story of O

O is a top singer, or was. She has been in a considerable commercial decline which, oddly enough, coincided with her contractual marriage to a gay male.

In the glory days, and despite her long-term girlfriends, O's image was almost as heterosexual as it is now. Like many female singers, she was romantically linked—by herself and the press—with her male manager, one of the several people in her life about whom she refused to talk.

H: Why did you agree to this interview?

O: It's a first of its kind book, so I don't mind being in on it, without my name or identity being used or exploited. . . . I think it's good for those interested in music to know something about the realities behind the facade.

H: Some of your fans, or former fans, say you're now keeping up a facade, with your chosen lifestyle. . . .

O: My friends know the reason for that.

H: Motherhood?

O: Yes.

H: Also a desire to be liked by a majority of the people?

O: That too.

H: You were very well-liked before.

O: Yes, but in some ways I'm old-fashioned.

H: No child out of wedlock?

O: Not for me anyway.

H: You wanted a father figure for your child?

O: I think it's important.

H: Your child is a girl, so is the father figure less important than for a boy?

O: I'm not sure. How can anyone know that?

H: And if your child is, or turns out to be, gay?

O: That would make no difference to me. Love is love.

H: But the conditions for tomorrow's gay generation aren't improved by parents—gay parents—who hide their identities behind a contractual union.

O: You're putting me on the spot.

H: Your fans put you on the spot, you put them on the spot, . . . It's all mutual. But what about it?

O: You mean the future?

H: Say your daughter eventually discovers she's lesbian. Wouldn't you want her to live in a world that's better and fairer than the one that led you to undertake what is sometimes called a lavender marriage?

O: Well, I doubt I'd have undertaken, as you say, this kind of marriage, or any marriage, if I wasn't who I am.

H: A star?

O: Someone with a big career. And responsibilities.

H: Responsibilities to yourself, as well.

O: The pressures are quite different, in this situation.

H: But to put it bluntly, your career is in the doldrums, has been for some time. Some say it's because you're focusing on your private life.

O: Others say some of my fans have deserted me. . . .

H: Do you think they have?

O: Some have, without question. Not just because I got married.

H: No. Some have gone over to relative newcomers like Madonna or Whitney Houston or Cyndi Lauper.

O: So what's the question?

H: Most entertainers who are gay but get married do so to boost their careers, although whether that's the result, after the publicity fades, is debatable. Do *you* think marriage has aided your career?

O: I'm not sure. . . . But I don't want to talk about my husband's career.

H: On the subject of wedlock—how locked in are the two of you?

O: Sexually?

H: And socially.

O: Socially, we have friends separately and together. But we *are* a couple. Sexually? Sometimes we go our own ways. I still have some friends from the old days. . . .

H: What about AIDS?

O: He gets tested regularly. Obviously, he practices safe sex. When and if he does it.

H: What if someday he happens to test positive?

O: I'll deal with him when it happens.

H: Deal with him, or it?

O: (laughs) I meant, I'll deal with that; we'll deal with it.

H: I see. You agreed to be interviewed, so what would you like to say?

O: . . . That the pressures on a singer who's a woman haven't changed very much over the years. I was always having to prove myself, and I always had to spend as much time on how I looked as I did on my singing.

H: Was it any tougher, being a lesbian singer?

O: Not as far as the public was concerned.

H: Do you think many of them wondered, what with you remaining single so long?

O: Maybe. But the media's very obliging. They always

paired me off with somebody, even people I'd never met! (laughs)

H: Is that being obliging, or dictating?

O: I suppose it's both.

H: How did male peers in the industry treat you?

O: Not everyone *knew*. . . . But most didn't react one way or the other, not once I was successful. Once I was successful, they stopped trying to hit on me. But that also happens with a star if she's hetero. Most men do become intimidated by female stars.

H: How do gay men in the business treat a diva?

O: About the same. They're always in awe. Not quite as contemptuous. I think on the whole, gay men can appreciate a woman's success more than straight men can.

H: What about the musical casting couch?

O: I didn't experience it. I was asked to, but I didn't. I never thought I was untalented enough to need it.

H: You've always shied away from controversy. Is the need to be liked a strong factor in your personal makeup?

O: Not more than most people, I don't think.

H: Switching subjects somewhat, there are numerous gay singers and groups these days, mostly in Britain. Why, though, so few lesbian singers?

O: Openly lesbian, or closeted?

H: You've got me; if they're not open, it's difficult to know—especially if the camouflage begins early.

O: Well, I think, again, it's sexism.

H: A word you rarely if ever use in public. . . .

O: I'm using it *now*.

H: Carry on. Please.

O: Men in music, or any aspect of entertainment, get a much bigger crack at success. And now, with AIDS, gay men are in a position that's forcing some of them to take action. So you have a few guys who are out and open about it. And a few always seems like a lot. . . . As for lesbians, we don't have that problem (AIDS).

H: Bisexual ones do. . . .

O: If their husbands or men are active. Or careless.

H: What about today's music industry do you deplore?

O: Right now, I don't have any big complaints. But a few years ago, when those conservative Washington Wives were trying to censor lyrics in albums . . . I was 100 percent against that, even though most of my material wouldn't have offended them. But I thought it obscene that a bunch of middle-aged, politically ambitious women would try and subvert what young people are listening to. There are few enough freedoms for kids and teens, as it is.

H: Do you think the heavy-metal rock groups were mostly to blame, as it were?

O: Yes, somewhat. But when somebody as MOR as Sheena Easton began singing about her "Sugar Walls". . . ! (laughs) I loved that song. It's so sexy. But those women were threatened by singers of our type becoming more sexually aggressive.

H You're very sexy. Are you aggressive?

O: Oh . . . not with men. . . .

H: Getting back to the would-be Capitol Censors, their leader, Tipper Gore, categorized homosexuality with drugs, bestiality and rape, even though the latter is by definition an act forced upon a female by a straight male.

O: That's their strategy, of any group like that. Anything they disagree with goes into the most odious category. I'm just hopeful we've heard the last of the Washington Witches. I mean, *wives*. (giggles)

H: I'm hopeful that you find happiness and continue to make your true feelings felt. Thanks for agreeing to talk.

O: Thank you.

"Let's Straighten This Big Thing Out"

In a 1987 article titled "The Gay Decades," Frank Rich listed ten pivotal phenomena in the homosexualization of American culture. The second, ahead of David Bowie's Ziggy Stardust alter ego, was Bette Midler. She, said Rich, was the person "that finally made camp kosher." It took a farcical straight woman training in a gay baths to bring gay humor to the masses.

Midler's alter ego was dubbed The Divine Miss M. She reveled in "trash with flash," in jokes that would have made Sophie Tucker blush (Midler rejected her stage persona after the birth of her own Sophie) and in "everything you were afraid your little girl would grow up to be—and your little boy."

Songbirds

After years of struggle on Broadway, and before that as a movie extra—she threw up on Julie Andrews in *Hawaii*—Midler at last found her niche, and her power base. As the celebrity impersonator in the film *Outrageous!* sang while doing Bette Midler, "Gay liberation was my salvation—steambaths are a girl's best friend" (sung to the tune of "Diamonds Are a Girl's Best Friend").

From the Continental Baths, Midler landed on *The Tonight Show*, then launched into albums, SRO one-woman shows, TV, films and producing, with marriage and motherhood as the surprising capper—and somewhat of a damper on her outrageousness, if not her escalating fortune; Bette is Disney's biggest box office star since Mickey Mouse, though as she's cheerfully admitted, even her toned-down over-40 incarnation wouldn't have been allowed past the studio gates by Uncle Walt.

Midler was the '70s' prima diva-icon for gay men, a Good Bitch Glinda gone delightfully wrong. A cartoonish woman imitating a gay man imitating a woman, she found her act was acceptable to heterosexuals because she served as a buffer between them and the sometimes alien humor she employed. With time, and the lack of any visible gay competition, Midler appropriated the humor as her own, using it to considerable effect in one Disney comedy hit after another.

That Ms. Midler and even Miss M. were never really suspected of being other than straight may have had to do with their motheringness and with Midler's casually pro-gay stance. From time to time, she poked gentle fun at gay men, while fellow diva Streisand made unkind and unthinking fun of gays in film after film and—according to Shaun Considine's *Barbra* bio—in one real life comment after another.

When Streisand eventually joined the fight against AIDS, she donated the proceeds of her non-hit single "Somewhere" to AIDS research. However, the video version of the Bernstein-Sondheim number about a better tomorrow contained not one same-gender couple among the numerous audience duos of all races, nationalities and ages.

In 1986 Barbra bought an option on the AIDS-themed play *The Normal Heart,* and the media feverishly speculated that she would produce it or co-star as the doctor in what would be the first major AIDS-themed film. Nothing happened. In 1988 playwright Larry Kramer revealed, "She gave up the rights in spring. She sat on it for two years, and finally we had to shame her to get the rights back. My lawyer said, 'Shit or get off the pot. We'll tell the world you are impeding it.' So finally we got a quitclaim." (The option went next to *Lenny* producer David Picker.)

Most gay-supported divas make at least a show of solidarity with their chiefest fans, fans who become crucial once— in the words of Lorelei Lee—"girls grow old," and heterosexual "men grow cold." Judy Garland's post-film comeback in live performances was largely due to her fanatical gay fans. Among the myriad gay men in attendance at her Carnegie Hall appearance on April 23, 1961, was Rock Hudson. Said the normally grudgeful Hedda Hopper, "Judy took a jam-packed crowd in Carnegie Hall in her arms and they hugged her right back—never saw the like in my life."

Merv Griffin later enthused, "Nothing in show business will ever touch it. No Broadway opening, no film premiere, nothing—Garland the performer and legend were one that night, and magic. . . . Judy left us standing on our chairs, weeping and cheering and totally, gladly drained."

Judy was familiar with gay and bisexual men well before 1961 and before gay directors like George Cukor, who oversaw her best screen performance in the 1954 *A Star Is Born*. Her father Frank was bisexual, a fact actually included in a telefilm about young Judy which starred Andrea "Annie" McArdle. Judy's husband Vincente Minnelli may have been bisexual, and as noted in *Conversations With My Elders,* Garland reportedly suspected, while making *The Pirate*, that her hubby was having an affair with her co-star, Gene Kelly!

Judy, whose only son is Joey Luft, and whose first son-in-law, in 1967, was Peter Allen, may have wed more than one gay man. . . . She died in 1969, the year of the birth of the gay rights movement at Manhattan's Stonewall Inn. Her funeral elicited the greatest outpouring of fan sympathy since that of Rudolph Valentino. . . .

By contrast, Mae West cold-heartedly played both sides of the fence. Her 1920s plays *The Drag* and *Pleasure Man* had gay themes or subplots, but in the most stereotypical way. Her notions remained rooted in the jazz age when she informed *Playboy* that gay men were "women, trapped in men's bodies."

In the '70s, in conjunction with publicizing her movie *Myra Breckinridge,* based on Gore Vidal's sex-change novel, West made a great verbal show of having been a forerunner of gay rights, a claim demolished by one-time Hollywood publicist Kaier Curtin in his book *We Can Always Call Them Bulgarians,* about lesbians and gay men as depicted in the American theatre.

"Non, Je Ne Regrette Rien"

Strangely enough, most gay icons, at least the singing female ones, aren't homosexual. Most make that very clear, from the outset. Unlike Edith Piaf, who until late in her life was content to let her more sophisticated aficionados wonder. Finally, she confessed that though she was "almost nymphomaniacally heterosexual," there had been a few *femmes* along the way. None of them fatal to her image; *au contraire.* But then she didn't have to work in Hollywood, or around it (i.e., the USA), *mais,* rather in France, where she grew up among prostitutes in a brothel.

Piaf was very close to a few women and may have had affairs with her female roommates. According to one biographer, "the little sparrow" used her vulnerability to get close to people, and sometimes went to bed with them to keep them in her orbit. Margaret Crosland wrote that "the sex act meant little or nothing to her." Piaf's most discussed woman-to-woman friendship began in 1947 when she made her New York City debut and met Marlene Dietrich, who later moved to Paris and attended her funeral in 1963; the two formed a mutual admiration society, at minimum.

Of course it was Piaf's heterosexual relationships, including the marriages, that drew the press' dizzy attention—particularly her *amour fou* boxer Marcel Cerdan (Maurice Chevalier always shed extravagant public praise on Piaf though she didn't much care for him; she'd once caught him trying to make a pass at Cerdan). In any event, insiders declared that Piaf sang more words of love than she ever spoke, and as for her magnificent, moving voice, she once complained to a fellow entertainer, "You can make people laugh, I can only make them cry."

Just as gay men could better appreciate Mae Western songs like "Let's Straighten This Big Thing Out" and "Easy Rider" than could the average woman, so gays responded the most enthusiastically to Carmen Miranda. "The Lady in the Tutti Frutti Hat" was a camp goddess from the word go. Just as Franklin Pangborn or Edward Everett Horton did vis-à-vis their leading men, so Carmen played a dumb-bunny wise-cracking pal and relieved her beauteous leading lady (invariably Betty Grable or Alice Faye) of the chore of comic relief.

The Portuguese-born Miranda was already a singing star in Brazil when Hollywood discovered her on Broadway, in *The Streets of Paris*. World War II closed off European markets to Hollywood pictures, and so Miranda was marketed by Fox to Latin American audiences. The film *Down Argentine Way* made a star of Carmen, who proceeded to do more for fruits than anyone since Waldorf and his nutty salad.

Too busy for love, Carmen had a screen image that was gaudy but asexual, as she spent most of her time prancing and mispronouncing. Off the screen, the bizarre foreigner wasn't expected by press agents and columnists to be as romantically active as homegrown stars. As for all her excess energy, wasn't that just typical of Latins? Little did moviegoers know, but Carmen was a big fan of coke—or, as Tallulah Bankhead once said, "Daddy always warned me about men and alcohol—but he never said a *thing* about women and cocaine."

In *Hollywood Babylon II*, Kenneth Anger divulged where Carmen stashed her coke supply: in a secret compartment in the platform heels of her ego-boosting shoes.

The uninhibited Carmen also had a penchant for natural air-conditioning. Like Marilyn a decade later, she favored the no-panties look, which was captured on film at least once. Hollywood's most famous suppressed still was of Carmen doing a dance turn with confirmed bachelor Cesar Romero, her co-star in *Springtime in the Rockies*.

Photographer Frank Powolny recalled, "It was a hot July day, and Miss Miranda knew the photographs would call for her to be quite active. . . . At one point in the action, Cesar swooped her up and twirled her about. . . . The entire session was very gay, with two such animated performers from south of the border. But nothing, or so I thought, out of the ordinary."

Powolny returned from his summer vacation after the roll of film had been developed. He found Fox in an uproar, for one of his shots revealed all—in one carefree moment of *cuanto le gusta*, Carmen, suspended in mid-air, was on total display through the slit of her full-length skirt! The 1941 still was clandestinely circulated around Hollywood for decades.

Was Carmen, or wasn't she? Which film title rang more true:*Something For the Boys*, 1944, or *A Date With Judy*, 1948?

Little has been written about Carmen's private life, far more about her queer couture. Until the late-'80s, there was no full-length biography in the English language. And most of the people who knew her socially or professionally are dead. But it was well known that she didn't mix with the movie crowd and was seldom seem with an eligible male, tinseled or otherwise.

One of Carmen's surviving co-stars, a fellow Latin, offers under cover of anonymity, "I believe Carmen was lesbian or a latent lesbian. . . . We had a lot in common, and got along famously. We even went out together a few times, while we were working. . . . I do know that she was very close to her lady friends, who weren't actresses and weren't necessarily all Latinas.

"The talk around town was that her marriage to producer David Sebastian was a business thing, for mutual benefit. I doubt he was anything but straight, and I don't believe Carmen did it to create that sort of image for herself. This marriage came quite late, and didn't last very long. Carmen already had an indestructible image of herself as Carmen Miranda. . . . I think she married at that point, after the war, because her career was in a serious downturn.

"We'll never know the exact truth about Carmen. But I know she could take or leave men, and was much more passionate about her lady friends, one of whom was a socialite known to be lesbian, even though long since married. . . . But above all, Carmen's career came first."

"Fairy Blues"

Singer Sippie Wallace once explained, "Blues and gospel, they're all the same. Where you say 'Jesus' in a gospel song, you just say 'baby' in a blues tune."

Likewise, there was plenty of easy substitution in the romantic lives of the great black female singers born in the late 19th and early 20th centuries. In *Tain't Nobody's Business—Homosexuality in Harlem in the 1920s*, Eric Garber wrote, "Ma Rainey, Bessie Smith, Ethel Waters and Alberta Hunter all maintained sexual and emotional involvements with women." As did Josephine Baker and Jackie "Moms" Mabley. "There's two things got me puzzled," sang Bessie Smith. "There's two things I don't understand; that's a mannish-actin' woman and a skippin', twistin' woman-actin' man." Or so she *sang*.

A literally bosom buddy of male-impersonator Gladys Fergusson, Smith had been initiated into lesbianism by blues singer Ma Rainey, née Gertrude Malissa [sic] Nix Pridgett in 1886, eight years before Bessie. On the road, Bessie often slept with gay women, including members of her performing troupe. According to Martin Greif, when she sang, "I know women that don't like men; it's dirty but good, oh, yes," "She was singing about the woman-lovin' woman she knew best—herself." Among Bessie's far-flung roster of gay male friends was composer Percy Grainger, who once averred, "The higher a singer's range, the better the lover."

Grainger reportedly introduced Bessie to "The Boy in the Boat," in which she warbled, "When you see two women walking hand in hand,/just look them over and try to understand:/they'll go to those parties—have the lights down low—/only those parties where women can go."

Ma Rainey wrote and performed her own "Sissy Blues" and the proud, defiant lesbian "Prove It On Me Blues." Prior to WWII, so-called race records were the main source of lesbian lyrics and such risqué song words as "pansy," "sissy," and "fairy" were semi-common in black lyrics before they were taken up by certain white lyricists. Race recordings were aimed at the Negro consumer and included titles like "Fairy Blues" and "Sissy Man Blues," in which gay men took the place of and were sometimes scorned by women afraid of losing their man to a "sissy."

Other alternative songs were "B.D (Bull Dykers) Woman Blues" by Bessie Jackson and "Freakish Man Blues" by George Hannah. One of Ma Rainey's most telling lyrics was "Went out last night/with a crowd of my friends,/they must be women/

'cause I don't like mens." Ethel Waters, who later got religion and became devout or fanatic—depending on your point of view—denied she had ever sung "songs like *that*," and in latter years refused to be directed by her Hollywood directors—she claimed God was her sole director.

In a 1988 *Christopher Street* article, Rudy Grillo noted that "Nowhere in the large number of volumes on the history of popular song in America can any mention of gays and lesbians be found: censorship by omission. Even those books written during the first (1922-34) peaking wave of gay-related song (for example, *The Facts of Life in Popular Song* by historian Sigmund Spaeth in 1934) discreetly ignore their existence lest the reader be offended and the subject legitimized."

Conveniently for Broadway moneymen and producers — sometimes themselves gay—such bisexual women as Ma Rainey, even if primarily lesbian, can be mounted on stage as hetero-sexual, without the need of inventing a male sex partner: again, censorship by omission.

The subject of the show *Ma Rainey's Black Bottom's* other lover-protegees included comic Moms Mabley and Josephine Baker, the "cinnamon sensensation" who was Paris' most exuberant and highly paid flapper of the 1920s. After fleeing the poverty and discrimination of St. Louis, "la Baker" found almost instant adulation in gay Paree, where she made her mark in a banana skirt, only. Her semi-nudity didn't overwhelm worldly Parisians. For one thing, as she herself exclaimed, "My breasts are like those of a 17-year-old boy!"

Baker's impact via her color and undress has often been analyzed. But she also took Paris by storm via her androgyny. Reviews of the 1925 *Révue Négre* asked, "Was it a man or woman? Black or white? Awful or marvelous?" Like Bea Lillie across the English Channel, Baker often worked in male drag in her early days, before gravity and respectability took their toll. Even now, in recent biographies like the other-wise excellent *Jazz Cleopatra,* Baker's private life is presented for the squares, as it were, rather than in its rounded fullness.

Baker was in great demand on stage, at parties and backstage. She modeled for Picasso and then some, and platonically befriended Ernest Hemingway—as did Dietrich; the self-advertised he-man appears never to have laid a famous beauty in his life! Eventually bilingual and ever-effervescent, Josephine partied all across Europe, most notably in Paris and pre-war Berlin. Later she was active in the French Resistance and sold all her jewels to fight the Germans.

Again, it was her affairs with *male* socialites, millionaires and sometimes royalty—among them a Scandinavian prince—that were chronicled in the press. In person, Josephine regaled her transplanted American friends Gertrude and Alice with details of her amitiés with Bessie and Ma. Stein confidant Samuel Steward has said that "Both black women had served as mother figures to Josephine, as well as lovers."

In France, la Baker was a screen as well as stage star, but her Gallic celebrity failed to cross back over the ocean till the sunset of her life. In 1935 Baker returned to America in a Ziegfeld revue starring Fanny Brice. Being billed behind newcomer Bob Hope was the first of several disappointments which made it clear that stardom was beyond her grasp within her own country. American critics were almost uniformly unkind, and because of her color, Baker was relegated to supporting bits within the show, despite all the advance publicity.

For decades, there were rumors that Baker was more than friendly with Piaf. Who knows? But in a posthumously published *Paris Match* article, a female servant of Baker's disclosed that "Mademoiselle Josephine preferred not to sexually mix with other singers. . . . She was more competitive than her beguiling smile admitted. When she did have a familiar lady friend, Mademoiselle liked to be the one pursued; she was innately feminine, always, and her . . . taste in women was customarily for somebody strong, tall, white and very capable."

Baker's signature tune was "*J'ai Deux Amours*" ("My Two Loves"). Officially, it referred to France and the United States, in that order. Unofficially, fans understood it to denote her matter of fact bisexuality—which, however, was cut from English-language editions of her autobiography.

Right-wing columnist Walter Winchell had it in for Baker partly because of her sexual neutrality. Also because of her "rainbow" collection of twelve adopted children of all races. But anti-miscegenationist Winchell would cite only political differences as the cause of his ongoing vendetta against the "Creole diva" who was more than once decorated for her valor and services to the nation by the French government. Columnist Dorothy Kilgallen once wrote, "Miss Baker never became as famous in these United States because we are admittedly sexual puritans, and a good thing, too! After all, it's the French who coined the phrase '*ménage à trois*' and who condone all manner of perverted couplings in and out of the gay show biz world of Paris' ooh-la-la performers."

"My Two Loves"

Josephine Baker, who gradually became as recognized a singer as she had been a dancer, often said that the one singer of her generation whom she really envied was Billie Holiday (née Eleanora McKay). Less well known in her time and setting as bisexual, Holiday was nevertheless widely known to have been raped as a girl and grown up in a brothel. Gay columnist Lucius Beebe felt that "Billie could have avoided most of her narcotics-related problems had she found a steady private partner, whoever that might be. . . . All her life, her basic problem was a piteous lack of self-esteem." This even extended to her inimitable singing style. She once explained:

"I don't think I'm singing. I feel like I'm playing a horn. I try to improvise like Lester Young, Louis Armstrong or someone else I admire." Yet despite the lack of Mermanesque confidence in her artistry, Billie had her pride; she earned her nickname of Lady Day when she declined to accept tips without using her hands in a very adult Harlem nightclub.

Baker's and Holiday's scarred childhoods had much in common, but Baker escaped, and found a new outlook elsewhere. Lady Day, even with her sublime vocal talent, was unable to surmount the negativity heaped upon her outside the nightclubs. The posthumous Diana Ross vehicle *Lady Sings the Blues* vastly oversimplified her personal life and merged several men into the fictional character played by Billy Dee Williams. Said *Blueboy* magazine, "If this movie is typical Hollywood hogwash, reshuffling facts the way a crooked player deals cards, it's also an anti-lavender wash."

(In the early '90s, Diana Ross undertook in her mid-40s to

portray Baker for cable-TV, even though Josephine had conquered Paris at 19 and been supposedly twice-wed by age 15. But then, in 1979 a 35-year-old Ross essayed little Dorothy on the big screen in the megaflop *The Wiz*. Call her Miss Ross, but not Little Miss Muffet.)

Billie Holiday has been misrepresented frequently, but Gladys Bentley has been all but forgotten due to so few of her songs having been put on record. Through the '20s and '30s, Bentley was a sought-after chanteuse at top nightclubs, and her antics—some of them—received national press. For a quarter-century, she lived openly as a lesbian woman. "Sweet-dispositioned" columnist Louis Sobol recalled Gladys coming over to his table one night and whispering, "I'm getting married tomorrow."
When he inquired who the lucky man was, Gladys giggled. "*Man?* Why, boy, you're crazy."

Later, she lived with a white lesbian lover whom she wed in a highly publicized ceremony. Indulgent columnists like Beebe and Sobol pictured Bentley and other black singers as newsworthy but harmless eccentrics. Columnists like Winchell, Hedda and Louella wouldn't give such women news space.

As the book *When Harlem Was in Vogue* pointed out, musical androgyny was being flaunted by "Harlem hussies" long before the Brits tried their hand at it. Bessie Smith mock-puzzled over "mannish-actin' women" in her "Foolish Man Blues" and Ma Rainey confessed in her "Prove It On Me Blues" that she liked to "wear a collar and a tie." So-called "bulldaggers" like Gladys Bentley figured as characters in popular novels of the time, like Claude McKay's *Home to Harlem,* Gilmore Millen's *Sweet Man* and Blair Nile's *Strange Brother*.

An article about Bentley in the 1988 premiere issue of the gay quarterly *Out/Look* charted her checkered career. The "hot honey of Harlem" was a regular headliner at the mafia-run Ubangi Nightclub on 133rd Street, where she shared the bill with Moms Mabley and a chorus line of female impersonators. "She was simultaneously commanding and lovable," wrote Louis Sobol.

But, as with Billie Holiday, trouble dogged her footsteps. She was too sexually honest for her era. As a black woman, she was too sexual. As a black lesbian, she was pursued by police. During her 1940 run at Joaquin's El Rancho in L.A., police stopped the show until the club obtained a costly permit to "allow Gladys Bentley, 250-pound colored entertainer, to wear trousers instead of skirts during her act."

During the war, as before the '29 crash, gay bars and clubs mushroomed. Gladys, billed as "the brown bomber of sophisticated songs," often performed at Mona's, the famed San Francisco lesbian bar. But bad times for Gladys and gay people in general accelerated with the witchhunts of the late '40s and early '50s; though purportedly political, the witch-hunts also targeted minorities like Jews and homosexuals.

Gladys wrote or had ghostwritten an apologist autobiography titled *I Am A Woman Again,* then in 1952, contractually wed a cook sixteen years her junior. After the inevitable divorce, she spent the rest of her life living with her mother and consumed by religiously induced guilt. In 1960, shortly before becoming an ordained minister, Gladys Bentley died from a flu epidemic at 52.

"The biggest tragedy," said Eric Garber, "is that the lesbian and gay movement, which could have supported her through the difficult times and saved her from her ultimate co-optation, just did not come soon enough."

The last great black blues star was Alberta Hunter, who died in 1984 and performed until the end. In later years she was candid about her lesbianism and particularly the great love of her life, Lottie Tyler, whom she met in 1919 and with whom she had a lengthy relationship. Hunter performed with Louis Armstrong, Billie Holiday, Bessie Smith, Ethel Waters and many more. After the blues waned, she became a nurse for 20 years, then resumed singing when she lost her job because of her age.

She was often invited to the Carter White House and was among the first batch of artists to receive the Kennedy Center Honors, in 1978. Frank Sinatra has said that he learned more from Hunter than any other singer in his life.

La *D* Da

D was never quite as big a singing star as O, and her sales decline began before O's did. Unlike O, D was a wife and mother before her stardom. Like O, she is foreign-born and -bred. Quite unlike O, D had a feminist image, and still does, somewhat.

In spite of the feminism—which turned many music critics against her—there were even fewer rumors about D's sexual orientation than about O's.

H: How are things for you today, professionally and personally?

D: Professionally, I'm now used to it. I tour a lot. I always did, even when I had hits—I'm the restless sort. Personally, I'm content—the toughest times are behind me.

H: What do you think of O's marriage, etc?

D: I honestly never thought she was the marrying kind. But it's an old game, isn't it?

H: I suppose you know that, at one point, you and O were rumored to be having an affair?

D: That may be so. But now let's try and shed some light on this subject we're pursuing, and not on my past.

H: Who are some of your favorite female singers?

D: Let's see . . . without mentioning anyone's sexual proclivity or politics . . . Hildegard. Don't ask me why. Grace Jones, I like visually. The woman has no voice, though. I like all types of singers. Anyone with a good, clear voice, even if they don't enunciate like Julie Andrews, which isn't popular anymore.

H: What about female groups?

d: Like the Go-Go's? I think they were more of a marketing gimmick than anything else. . . . I will tell you who I enjoyed and really admired, and that was a trio called Deadly Nightshade. All committed feminists.

H: Sure! I saw them perform at the Bottom Line in New York, in 1975. They were great.

D: You did? You're lucky. They didn't last too long. They didn't have the, um, requisite outer trappings.

H: A charge that sexist critics also leveled at you.

D: Let's talk about Deadly Nightshade a bit.

H: Well, they put out an eponymous album. I still have it. It's a wonderful blend of melodies and themes.

D: The great thing about them, I thought, apart from their feminist politics, was that all three were excellent musicians. They did their own material, and it was hummable, not just significant. I was sorry when they split up. I wonder what's happened to them since.

H: I remember when *Ms.* magazine gave them quite a build-up. But, apparently, their album went nowhere.

D: That's not surprising. They looked and dressed like farm hands, which is no criticism, as far as I'm concerned. But in this business, men decree that a singer has to look like a tart and act compliant. You know, "like a lady." Or, if she's aggressively inclined, she has to drip with glamour.

H: Like Shirley Bassey.

D: Yeah. . . . I used to be criticized, even by my peers, for not employing a hairdresser!

H: At that time . . .

D: (sighs) At that time.

H: Your look is, if you'll pardon my saying so, a little more matronly now.

D: That's just age, dear. Or the earrings.

H: You were married, a mother, yet in your feminist days there were still rumors, weren't there?

D: "Dyke, dyke, dyke." Is she, isn't she? It was worse, in one sense, at that time—you couldn't say "feminist" without people thinking or implying "lesbian."

H: Do you consider yourself lesbian?

D: I have been exclusively lesbian a few times in my life, but I've primarily had a heterosexual lifestyle. And sometimes girlfriends along the way. So to do myself justice, I'd have to use the bisexual label.

H: So your marriage wasn't for the image?

D: Oh, dear. . . . That's rather complicated. But no, not for the most part. . . . What I did earlier on wasn't for my career's sake. I had other motives, plus I have loved a few men in my time. But nowadays, yes, I can admit to doing things for my image and marketability. I've earned it.

H: Who do you think has done the most for women in song?

D: *Me,* for one! I was a pioneer, and I've bloody well paid for it. My career may never be the same again, 'specially now with the market so youth-flooded. Excepting of course Tina Turner. . . . Who else? I'd have to name the obvious names, like Joan Baez and . . . actually, very few others. Few singers have challenged the system. As a feminist, I tried to, for *all* women.

But most of the dykes still keep it quiet, though I can't blame them much, since I'm looking at it from the inside. You can be honest and successful, but I doubt you can be honest and a superstar. Maybe someday. . . .

H: Why do you think there are still so many fewer female singers than male ones?

D: Well, it's not like a movie, is it? There, even in an action or a gangster movie, there has to be some kind of leading lady or at least a romantic interest.

H: Glenda Jackson once said that in most male-oriented films, the actress is only there to prove the hero isn't gay.

D: Yeah, in a nutshell. It works in the reverse, too. Even in a vehicle for Streisand or Fonda, there's got to be some kind of guy who's there just to show her character's not a lezzie. . . . At least in movies, women are indispensable, even if second-class. In music, women *are* dispensable! On every level, from lounge singers to members of bands and solo singers to superstars— there are so many fewer of us.

And, again, our sales success is so wrapped up in how we look, so that by age 40 our marketable days are mostly past, while Tony Bennett or Sinatra or several other guys I could mention can go on and on, regardless of age or wrinkles. But, as Joan told Christina, "Nobody ever said life was fair, sweetie."

H: Is it getting any fairer?

D: Life's getting better in many ways, but the situation for lesbians in music is scarcely any better. The few open ones, like Holly Near, are on very minor labels and they don't get played on radio and hardly get heard anywhere. At best, they have a small cult following.

H: What about newer, star singers who are lesbian but hide it? Is it so imperative they hide it, these days?

D: No. It's still a question of greed. When you get in this business and start going places, you sign a pact with some devil. . . . So, even if you're E (a superstar young singer), you keep denying it to the press. But I do feel that the press even bringing it up, and even though in a negative or salacious way, is definitely progress.

H: Better some visibility or doubt than invisibility, right?

D: Of course right! Of course. Just don't pin the label on *me*; at my age (past 40), as a mother, as a feminist, as not quite a raving beauty, the last thing I need to further depress things professionally is that kind of label in public.

H: Do you think a star-calibre singer will come out, in the forseeable future?

D: Futures are never forseeable. . . . Thing is, they call America a melting pot. Now, I love America. I love the good things about it, and I'd like to help change the not so good things. But this is definitely not a melting pot. What it is, is this (fingers interlaced). And the fingers are right up against each other, living in this cramped yet separate proximity, and sometimes it's like a rash, with each finger pressing upward, creating friction, one against the other. It's not easy.

But I want to end on a positive note. There's already an openly lesbian singer, and she may never be mainstream, but mark my word, she will be a star, not too far from now. K. d. lang.

H: I didn't know she was on record about it.

D: She is. And if you read the *Advocate* (Aug. 16, 1988 issue), you saw the review where the critic calls her a "lesbian with a lariat." I must say, I was surprised that, in a gay publication, it was a negative review (of lang's *Shadowland* album). But she's getting a lot of attention, it's increasing, and sooner or later her private life will be raised, and even if she keeps it quiet, her example is important. . . . She's kind of a female Boy George, and her time will come. Wait and see.

H: Do you think in his way Boy George helped gays in music?

D: Frankly, I don't. If he'd not done the drag bit, it would have been a lot better. The talent's there, but the packaging was all wrong.

H: By another token, do you think without that packaging, he would have risen to stardom as quickly?

D: I couldn't really tell you.

H: Do you think drag of any kind is more offputting than it is revolutionary?

D: On *men*. On women, semi-drag—like k. d. lang does—is something else again. Pants aren't even drag anymore. . . . On Dietrich, it was stunning. On lang, it's a statement, a way of underlining what may or may not be so obvious.

See, there are singers like E, who go for the gold, and singers like k. d. lang, who have more integrity, though on the other hand it's easier for them to have more, because their potential isn't as obvious. But I think it's the younger generation who's going to make the difference—*some* of them, a few of them—finally. We're rolling along a little faster than we were; it's like a stalled vehicle now and then, but we definitely are rolling forward, and there's no stopping us, unless we allow ourselves to be stopped.

"Pepsi Cola Hits the Spot"

"Self-esteem has so much to do with everything," says A, a superstar singer whose professional and media peak occurred when she was habitually linked with a gay or asexual (depends which source) politician several years ago. "We chose to play with the press," she nonchalantly explains during a session not quite long enough to be considered an interview.

"Everyone saw us as a high-profile chic couple, which did us both a world of good. . . . I loved that, back then; I didn't begin taking myself seriously as a human being or a performer until I received all that coverage. But I did get over it. Like I say, it really boils down to self-esteem." Out of the political limelight, the male of the "couple" has gone on his own, very private way, while A continues to turn out albums.

"My heroine," she adds, "has to be Josephine Baker. She transcended such an incredible amount of shit. Against all the odds, she rose like a phoenix. . . . Josephine felt respect for herself because that was how she was finally treated, in France.

"Showgirls and singers in the old days had to slog through so much shit, but my God, they developed character! More than today, when everything's deals and percentages, and an unquestioned allegiance to the closet. . . . I'm sure when they transcended their crummy circumstances, those women felt an even bigger sense of accomplishment than we do today."

The twin worlds of the Gaiety Girls in London and the "glorified" Ziegfeld Girls in New York were indeed tough and sexist, with the casting couch often the sole means of auditioning for a coveted job that might end with marriage to a millionaire. In her autobiography *The Glamorous World of Helen Rose*,

Hollywood costume designer Rose harked back to her early days with Ernie Young, "the Ziegfeld of the Middle West," who produced musical shows for Chicago and environs:

"His extramarital affairs with beautiful young chorus girls were notorious, but wife Pearl Young went along because they were so short-lived. His attachment for one girl had lasted a few weeks longer than the rest, and Pearl hated her. She said the girl was tough, too fat, a lousy dancer and a tramp with illusions of grandeur." Lucille LeSueur bolted the show without giving her notice, then resurfaced months later in Hollywood where she began a new career in 1925 as Joan Crawford.

Promoted by gay actor friends like William Haines and gay directors like Edmund "Grand Hotel" Goulding, Crawford earned fame in dance vehicles like *Dancing Daughters* and *Dancing Lady*. She also, at first, sang, and was introduced in one film musical segment as "Joan Crawford, that symbol of youth and beauty, of joy and laughter." (At one point, Joan had illusions of becoming an opera singer!) Like her older brother Hal, she was bisexual. But, unusually for a former chorus girl, she didn't indulge her sexual duality until well after she arrived in tinseltown, and then only cautiously.

Small wonder. Central Casting, later a clearinghouse for job information, was originally set up by Will Hays, the movies' chief censor, to scrutinize the moral conduct of actors. (A Presbyterian elder, Hays had been Postmaster General under Harding and was known to have accepted bribes in Washington and Hollywood.) MGM, Crawford's studio, had a "moral turpitude" clause in all its employee contracts, and both non-marital pregnancies and "homosexual conduct" were grounds for instant dismissal.

In the book *Conversations With Joan Crawford*, the elderly star remembered, "Louis B. Mayer told me once—it was when the studio was trying to decide how 'bad' a woman to make me in *Rain*—that, 'Families go to the movies, and I'm not going to put anybody on the screen who isn't a fit subject for families to watch.'"

Ironically, it was only after Crawford had passed her musical phase and constructed a mask from her drama-based self-esteem that she was known around Hollywood as bisexual. Publicly, she often admitted she didn't like women. As friends. One friend was Betty Grable, whose biographer Spero Pastos declared,

145

"Grable, like Crawford, shared a peculiar and distorted view of sex. They seemed to find sex unwholesome and repugnant despite the fact that both women spent their lifetimes in secret and not-so-secret premarital and extramarital affairs.

"Both Joan and Betty had been abused by their parents and in turn victimized their young children."

Daughter Christina noted after her mother's death that Joan had "lesbian tendencies," and biographers like Charles Higham have detailed Crawford's mostly unrequited passions for stars as diverse as Greta Garbo, Bette Davis and Marilyn Monroe. Most of the legend's lesbian affairs were carried out with starlets and devoted fans who were also pressed into housekeeping and secretarial duties, as described in *Mommie Dearest.*

But with four husbands and as many adopted children, Crawford considered herself thoroughly heterosexual. After viewing Ingmar Bergman's *Cries and Whispers,* a story of three sisters, she told journalist Carl Johnes, "I still say it's about a bunch of dykers [*sic*]."

In the showgirl milieu from which Lucille/Joan emerged, occasional bisexuality was quite common, as various chorus girls had affairs with each other, in between sugar daddies or stagedoor johnnies. Crawford recalled, "There were always a few girls in the line who went exclusively after other girls, or tried to! Of course, they hit the jackpot when they landed a wealthy patroness. But most of the girls preferred something in pants, even if we were willing now and then to experiment, for fun."

"You and the Night and the Music"

The 1968 book *Ladies Bountiful* told the stories of several patronesses of the arts, some of whom favored *les* girls. One such was Polish-born Wanda Landowska, who single-handedly restored the harpsichord to popularity in this century. Gay composers like Manuel de Falla and Francis Poulenc composed especially for her, and Landowska performed and taught in Berlin, Paris, New York and Lakeville, Connecticut.

Though legally married, Landowska was a lifelong lesbian,

as illustrated in *Ladies Bountiful*. She so took the homosexuality prevalent in the music world for granted that, upon meeting a new and celebrated pupil, an American musician, she casually inquired, "Et vous êtes un pédéraste, naturellement?" (And naturally you are a pederast?)

One of Landowska's friends and a sometime pupil was actor and former dancer Clifton "Laura" Webb. The waspish alter ego of Waldo Lydecker and Mr. Belvedere was also friends with torch singer Libby Holman, with whom he'd starred on Broadway in 1929's *The Little Show*, which featured the infamous number "Moanin' Low." In it, Webb portrayed a pimp or "sweetback," and Holman his whore. While Webb performed his "snake-hip" movements on her, Libby crooned the soon-to-be-banned-and-a-hit tune.

That same year, Holman, one of the most spotlighted singers in the "paragraphs," or columns, was escorted all over town by gay story editor and future producer Richard Halliday, who was reputed to be Webb's on-again, off-again lover. Though close to Libby, Webb couldn't escort her, because his constant "date" was his clinging mother Maybelle, who also served as his manager and secretary. The pair lived together until Maybelle died in her 90s. Clifton was so disconsolate over his loss that he kept crying in public, until Noel Coward caustically remarked, "It must be tough, being orphaned at 72. . . ."

Née Holzman, the dark-skinned, Jewish Holman was self-conscious about her looks and socially insecure. By nature lesbian, Libby coveted social acceptance, and passed herself off as gentile, while painting Manhattan with flashy show biz males, usually gay. This didn't prevent local tabloids from hinting that Libby sought the intimate favors of actresses like Jeanne Eagles and singers like Josephine Baker. Libby was also rumored to be infatuated with singing comic Bea Lillie, whose routines at the Sutton Club she attended almost nightly.

She had a brief "pash" for Tallulah Bankhead, who shunned her, believing her to be jinxed, on account of the many people in her life who had died violently. One night, Libby unexpectedly appeared at Tallulah's home while a party game was in progress. As she walked in, the hostess announced, "Dahling, we're playing Murder in the Dark. Do join us. We could use a professional."

Bankhead once addressed a letter to her bisexual rival, "Dear Libido . . ." and turned green with envy and outrage when Holman announced that she had bedded their favorite actress, Greta Garbo.

In the late '20s and early '30s, Holman introduced standards like "You and the Night and the Music" and "Body and Soul." The latter was banned on radio: it used the provocative word "body" and the then-obscene world "hell."

The love of Libby's life was a lesbian member of the house of DuPont, a strawberry blonde named Louisa d'Andelot Carpenter Jenny. The mannish, outdoorsy Louisa had briefly married—for her inheritance's sake—then adopted a daughter, Sunny. Libby lived with them several years, including after her much-publicized marriage to Camel cigarette heir Smith Reynolds, with whom she had a son, Topper. He later died prematurely, as did Smith, whose mysterious death by shooting implicated Libby, thereafter known to the media as The Scarlet Woman.

Holman was acquitted after the publicity-shy Reynoldses cut short the trial and settled millions upon her and Smith's son.

Luxuriating with Louisa in a succession of sumptuous estates, Libby was restless nonetheless, and attempted several comebacks, none of them successful. It was said her voice had "turned" on her, after the shock of losing Reynolds and the agony of the prolonged pre-trial hearings, during which she was accused by the prosecution of secretly being a "Jewess." Audiences stayed away from her shows, which were sometimes backed with her money. Her publicity had backfired. Audiences evidently preferred a torch singer whose life was less "scarlet" than her lyrics.

According to the biography *Dreams That Money Can Buy,* Libby was tragically misguided except when singing. Her private life was a storm of conflicting charges and lightning-like personal tragedies. Unwisely, she eventually left the faithful Louisa and undertook experimental, unfulfilling marriages and love affairs with a parade of men and women, among them bisexual actor Montgomery Clift. Director Billy Wilder has stated that Clift turned down *Sunset Boulevard* because he feared real-life comparisons would be drawn with his older-woman benefactress, Libby Holman.

"Apart from the time spent with my son," Libby later said, "I was happiest when on a stage singing. . . . I never got from any relationship the jolt of exuberant confidence that I felt whenever I was up there singing my heart out."

"Illusions"

The following item, in "The Clothes Make the Man Department," appeared in January, 1988 in the *Hollywood Kids' Newsletter:*

"Rumor around town deals with a top-secret T.V. club in Hollywood. It's at this undisclosed location that some of Hollywood's top luminaries meet every few weeks in drag! There's no hanky-panky, mind you, just good old-fashioned socializing and dancing, according to one source who says, 'It's the best kept secret in tinseltown. You'd flip out if you saw the list of big names who belong!' After much prying we did discover that some of the regulars include that top Hollywood director and his actress wife who just love to cross-dress, and that famous male TV comic."

Said director's wife, once a top musical superstar, years ago found her name in the gay magazine *In Touch,* among a list of actresses and singers reportedly lesbian or bisexual. Rumors have long circulated in Hollywood that the sweet-throated diva and her husband are busy bisexuals in their private life, as well as frequent professional collaborators. The singer-actress originally consented to be interviewed for this book, then changed her mind most politely and firmly.

I was later informed, without seeking the information, that she'd requested her friends and associates not to divulge anything about her or, particularly, her husband (who may personally have K.O.ed the interview). But I never sought any further facts on the woman, whose career peaked—literally —in the mid-1960s.

Though firmly entrenched as part of the Hollywood scene, the actress-singer, her director and their marriage have a certain pertinence to the world of music. Says Cher, an avowed heterosexual who played an Oscar-calibre, naturalistic lesbian in *Silk-*

wood, "Music is about freedom. For some people I know, bisexuality is the only sexual freedom. . . . Singers and musicians still don't want to be thought of as gay, but so long as it's kept low-key, they don't mind a reputation within the business as kind of enlightened, progressive bisexuals."

B is a former Broadway singing star, now ensconced in a second hit TV sitcom. A divorced lesbian who doesn't play footsie with the press, she allows that "Acting is about pretending. Music is even more fun—it's pretending *and* playing dress-up. Look at the rock world, if you want proof. . . . This whole thing of men wearing studs and earrings that's now so accepted by all types of men, really began with the boys in rock 'n 'roll, not all of them straight. . . . The only time I wear a dress is on the set, or sometimes at an industry function. For me, a dress is drag, it's a part of the playing pretend."

K, a sapphic comedian and singer, feels, "We're caught in a web. As performers, we like to use our imaginations—but only up to a point! It's not true what they say about you eventually believing your own publicity and becoming what you pretend to be. That does not happen." Unlike B, K is a mother. "For me, motherhood is part and parcel of the lesbian experience. . . . A far bigger percentage of homosexual women than men choose to parent.

"The other side of this sticky web we're caught in is that you *can* bend the rules. If you're pretty. . . . You can go the Dietrich route, where she kissed women on the lips in her movies and looked ravishing in top hat and tails. But I'm not a beauty. So I had to go into musical comedy, and what that genre of comedy means for a non-beauty is always playing the madcap, man-hungry dame. . . . No, I have *not* become what I always portray."

Marlene Dietrich, who often sang in her films and eventually became solely a cabaret *artiste,* had her cake and ate it, too. Before and after her Hollywood daze, she was married to a man who inhabited a chicken ranch in the San Fernando Valley, near L.A. The unflappable Dietrich was on good terms with his mistresses, and the couple had one child, a daughter who's prepared a tell-all tome about her mythic mother's affairs with everyone from Joe and Jack Kennedy, Frank Sinatra and bisexual Michael Wilding (Liz Taylor's second husband) to Claudette Colbert (already noted in *Hollywood Babylon*) and the former actress wife of a Top Politician, to the late British telejournalist Nancy Spain, and many, many others, possibly including Edith Piaf.

Marlene's musical legacy appears slim, but numbers film ditties like *The Boys in the Backroom, Illusions* and Cole Porter's *The Laziest Gal in Town.* Also un-reel *chansons* of silky-khaki longing like *Lili Marlene* and *Don't Ask Me Why I Cry,* plus a platoon of huskily-intoned anti-war songs from her fabled cabaret act.

But her visual aesthetic and her impact upon moviegoers of that era, and on fans today, is substantial. Dietrich was the first star to popularize pants for women, starting when she moved to America in 1930. More than any screen performer before or since, she made androgyny elegant, acceptable and sexy.

Suits, pants, ties and men's hats were acceptable in Dietrich's private life, because she didn't give a damn what the neighbors or her peers thought. They were acceptable to mass movie audiences because whenever she wore male drag on-screen, she also sang, thus undercutting the pants' politics and transferring her sartorial iconoclasm into the realm of musical fantasy.

Later, she took this ambivalence a step further, and daringly sang love songs—on stage and in albums—which she didn't bother to re-gender, as in "I've Grown Accustomed to Her Face" on her *Dietrich in Rio* album, whose cover features Marlene in a white suit and heel-less white flats.

The prickly question of pronouns caused Columbia Records momentary pause. An executive was quoted in the '60s: "With any other singer, the use of 'she' sung by a lady might be extremely confusing, even sensationalistic. But Miss Dietrich is more than a singer . . . and she's been doing this sort of thing for years now."

Lesbian Mercedes de Acosta's 1960 memoir *Here Lies the Heart* was the first book to shed light on the Teutonic temptress' flexible libido. The late playwright and screenwriter—who also described her "nature getaways" with Garbo—opined, "Marlene is more effective singing than acting, because she *chooses* her own songs." Presumably, an actress' lines, written by somebody else, can never be as emotionally revealing or privately insightful as a singer's repertoire of songs from the heart.

More on the ultimate glamourpuss appeared in Leslie Frewin's *Dietrich,* Charles Higham's *Marlene* and Sheridan Morley's *Marlene Dietrich.* Only recently have the personal revelations been tempered by an assessment of the actress and the singer. In her heyday, the million dollar legs often overshadowed the actress, whose fanzine nickname was Morelegs Sweet-trick. In 1985, *In Style* magazine declared, "She began on the screen singing (in *The Blue Angel*), and in her final picture, *Just a Gigolo* (1978, with David Bowie), she ends singing.

"Like so many musically astute actresses, Dietrich has turned in older age to what she did in her youth, and did best: sing. . . . Her voice may be quirky, at times as low as a female impersonator's, but it is the material which matters. She lovingly and convincingly puts across lyrics depicting the horrors of war, the folly of first impressions, and the toughness of a woman who, even in a crowd, is fundamentally alone, but doesn't seem to mind."

"I Only Want a Buddy, Not a Sweetheart"

There is a school of thinking which holds that song lyrics are often "coded" for hidden meanings, especially gay meaning. But as previously pointed out, most songs then and now are deliberately shorn of any gay significance, and coding usually—at most—involves a change of gender. Even so, "It's tough to prove that a gay lyricist wrote a song with gay intent," said Johnnie Ray. "You may be seeking for something that isn't there," as occurred with hostile straight critics who accused Edward Albee of basing an unhappy heterosexual marriage on a gay one in *Who's Afraid of Virginia Woolf?*

Albee's response: "If I'd wanted to write a play about a gay couple, I would have." The difference: he could have, but with 99 percent-plus of songs, one can't.

Even with well known expressions, it's difficult to establish that a particular song is gay-coded. An instance in point was 1982's biggest hit, "Bette Davis Eyes," written by Jackie De Shannon and Donna Weiss and sung by Kim Carnes. Whitney Stine, author of two books on Davis, noted, "'Spy,' has often been used for a lesbian trying to pass.

"I met Jackie when Anais Nin brought her to my party—she was houseguesting with Anais. We discussed our obsessions with Bette Davis, and years later she did that song! What struck me most was the lyric 'All the boys think she's a spy,' because a lot of people over the years have wondered about Bette. . . ."

The song also mentioned super-divas Jean Harlow ("hair of Harlow gold") and Garbo ("Greta Garbo stand-out size"), but although dissected by much of the media, only gay music critics knew or divulged "spy's" double definition, which seems to give the lyric more sense and meaning. Stine opined, "It could be about a stunning lesbian with some of the attributes of Davis, Garbo and Harlow, who's trying to pass via an exaggerated sense of glamour—as happens so often in Hollywood."

If de-coding is difficult, even fairly obvious lyrics sometimes aren't consciously heard or believed, as with Elvis Presley's "Jailhouse Rock." Likewise, cross vocals (CVs) say one thing but indicate another, seldom taken at face value. In CVs, a vocalist of the "wrong" gender sings a lyric which hasn't been re-pronounced to fit the heterosexual standard. Most CVs have been sung by female artists, with little or no lesbian implication—another case of audiences conveniently not believing their ears.

A typical CV is Dietrich's "I've Grown Accustomed To Her Face" (a majority of the few women who've interpreted this song sang it about his face). Another—filmed as well as recorded, in *Funny Lady*—is Streisand's "I Found a Million Dollar Baby," the grownup baby doll being female. Streisand even sang it in a white top hat and tux, shades of Marlene! Unlike male CVs, feminine ones aren't intended to tacitly appeal to the gay marketplace; a woman singing lovingly about another woman somehow isn't meant to mean anything, and failed to arouse mass suspicions.

Today there are more suspicions, hence fewer female CVs. (One of the more recent was Joan Jett's "Crimson and Clover.") Nor were female CVs meant to be funny, the way a man singing a love song to another man was to most audiences (who therefore didn't have to take it seriously). In his memoirs, *A Book,* Desi Arnaz described how Richard Kollmar, the romantic lead in the Broadway musical *Too Many Girls,* sang "the girl's part" one night during a performance. "He started his verse with 'Once I was young, yesterday perhaps, danced with Jim and Paul and kissed some other chaps.'" In Arnaz's book, it was a page's worth of hilarity.

The Cuban co-star of *Too Many Girls* wondered in print what Kollmar's female singing partner thought of during his accidental CV of "I Didn't Know What Time It Was," but didn't think to question what was in Kollmar's mind, or subconscious. The singer later wed journalist Dorothy Kilgallen, and following his death stories of his bisexuality emerged from the rumor stage into the light.

The first male CV was probably Jon Terrell's "He Certainly Was Good to Me" in 1898. More recent ones include "The Best of Everything," sung in 1959 by Johnny Mathis over the titles of the film of the same name (with Joan Crawford), and the man-to-man love ballad "Wind Beneath My Wings" by country-flavored Gary Morris. Bette Midler appropriated the song for her *Beaches* soundtrack, imbuing it with pop flavor and the sweet smell of success—the platonic paean to girl-friendship earned a Grammy and flew to the top of the charts. *Billboard* headlined, "Bette Midler Breaks 'Wind' . . . Into No. 1 Position!"

Male CVs may be as rare as $3 bills, but so are female buddy songs. By contrast, the friendship and even—purportedly platonic (though Plato was gay and preached homosexual love!)—love between men has been celebrated in more than a few songs over the years. 1922 saw the bow of "My Buddy," probably inspired by World War I and ostensibly about military mates, even though the singer longs for the sound of his buddy's voice and the touch of his hand, and hopes the guy will "understand."

Gay critic Rudy Grillo felt "My Buddy" was about more than male bonding. "The romantic waltz tempo, sentimental intimacy and tenderness of the words suggests something more." He wondered, "Was it a joke that misfired?" On her *The Way We Were* album—not the movie soundtrack—Barbra Streisand brilliantly rendered "My Buddy," but ironically, in spite of her singing a man's song and technically doing a CV, by so doing she automatically heterosexualized the lyrics.

"My Buddy" was re-recorded in swing time in 1940 by Frank

Sinatra and other male vocalists, and released to an America inevitably moving toward WWII. Bing Crosby's record of "My Buddy" was backed by the similar "I Only Want a Buddy, Not a Sweetheart." Its final line makes clear that he desires a "buddy, not a gal." Such songs were the closest the Crooner or Old Blue Eyes ever came to doing a CV.

In the "Gay '90s," it's still hard to imagine Don Ho at the Hilton Dome in Honolulu singing "I've Grown Accustomed To His Face" . . .

"I Enjoy Being a Girl"

"I have the voice and face of a frog, but when I sing I'm beautiful. Such," proclaimed Lotte Lenya, "is the power and the magic of music!" Most of her life, Lenya the singer was overshadowed. First by her husband of 24 years, composer Kurt Weill, then by her celluloid gallery of grotesques. These included such sapphic figures as Col. Rosa Klebb in the second 007 opus, *From Russia With Love,* and the Contessa Terribili-Gonzalez, who peddles gigolo Warren Beatty to Vivien Leigh in Tennessee Williams' *The Roman Spring of Mrs. Stone.*

In 1930 Lenya appeared in a film of Weill's *Threepenny Opera,* her career high mark until after his death in 1950. She'd already survived a sexually abusive father and child prostitution, and during her celebrated marriage was unfaithful with both men and women. Post-Weill, her last three husbands were all gay. She survived them all, then underwent cosmetic surgery on her breasts at the optimistic age of 82.

Threepenny Opera was revived in 1953, and Lenya became a star in her own right. She worked on stage and in the recording studio, aided by her first gay husband, who according to biographer Donald Spoto "arranged for Lenya's international recording contracts, helped her to overcome her stage fright, and even showed her how to dress."

Apart from her interpretations of Weill, Lenya's greatest musical triumph was the long-running Broadway musical *Cabaret.* "My numbers are more wonderful than the charming young actress' who plays Sally Bowles," she noted. Yet her character didn't survive the film version, which she grumbled was "just a vehicle for that daughter of Miss Garland who stole Louise Brooks' hairstyle!" The unbeautiful Lotte believed "A woman can express herself better through music if she has no face. If she is Garbo, then she acts, and her face, not her voice, reflects her anguish."

The plight of the unlovely isn't unknown to but has been energetically spoofed by comedian-chanteuse Sandra Bernhard, who titled her 1988 mock-memoirs *Confessions of a Pretty Lady*. Via book, album, stage, screen, etc., Bernhard has achieved a cult status typically reserved for the non-Marilyns and -Madonnas. Labeled "an artist on the razor-sharpest of cutting edges," Bernhard is a master, or mistress, of tease.

Rolling Stone admitted, "Her sexual orientation is the subject of constant debate. She encourages this." On Robin Byrd's TV show, she took viewers' calls. One man asked, "Sandra, what's a guy gotta do to get a date with you?" Said Sandra, "Get a sex change!" A woman asked, "What's a girl gotta do to get a date with you?" Sandra—"Get a sex change!"

Bernhard's off-Broadway show *Without You, I'm Nothing*—the title a reference to the archetypal movie "good woman"—was transferred to film. Her monologues on modern living are pro-gay and more anti-homophobic than anything attempted by some-time monologist Midler. A recurring motif is the beautiful black female who may symbolize Sandra's alter ego?

But if a black was Sandra's parallel self, bottle-blonde Madonna represented another kettle of fish entirely. The woman born Madonna Louise Veronica Ciccone once stated, "I'm a sexual threat." But her relationship with Bernhard threatened the even larger audience that doesn't buy her albums or attend her concerts. On David Letterman's show in 1988, Sandra facetiously confessed to having slept with both Sean Penn (then Mr. Madonna) and Madonna, while Madonna revealed that the twosome hung out at a lesbian bar in Greenwich Village called the Cubby Hole.

The affair (or not) seized the media's timid imagination and inspired Mr. Blackwell to join Madonna and Bernhard in tenth place on his Worst Dressed list, describing them as "the Mutt and Jeff of MTV—vampy, trampy and campy." The *National Enquirer* decided, "Madonna's Sleazy Show Shocks Audience," illustrating with word and photo the scantily-clad pair "rubbing against each other and fondling themselves as they performed the song 'I Got You, Babe.' When their torrid number was over, the bizarre pair walked offstage holding hands!" Ye gods.

The fun-scandal of 1989 was ultimately denied not by Madonna, but Bernhard. She told *Interview*, "We're kind of tired of the whole thing. . . . We're just girlfriends—silly, juvenile girlfriends." Sandra was more forthcoming about her own life. In 1990 *Glamour* magazine asked what problems she'd encountered as a "gay woman in Hollywood," and *Vanity Fair* stated, "Bernhard is open about her own lesbian affairs." She said of her audiences, "Men and women can relate to both the man and the woman in me. Everybody lets go of his/her preordained disposition."

Like Lenya, Bernhard is at least as much a Personality as a singer. In her nightclub act, she would sometimes choose a man in the audience and come on to him, then instantly turn violently angry at him, retreating into on-stage narcissism by fondling her own breast. Sexual symbolism?

Madonna is more than a sex symbol. Her 1990 world concert tour, *Blond [sic] Ambition,* featured mimed masturbation, topless men in 12-inch pointy brassieres, and a hint of discipline—"You may not know the song, but you all know the pleasures of a good spanking." Unlike Bette Midler, who performed with mermaids, Madonna employed hunky mermen who smilingly writhed against each other. She also showcased female wrestlers, and promoted safe-sex by telling her male dancers (six dudes who open their yellow Dick Tracy trenchcoats to reveal G-strings), "Don't be silly, put a rubber on your willy."

Her choreographer Vince Paterson explained, "Madonna said, 'Let's break every rule.' She wanted to make statements about sexuality, cross-sexuality, the church and the like."

Initially labeled a pop-stitute by music critics and media moralists, Madonna has emerged as one of the strongest, most indefatigable—and pro-gay—entertainers of the '90s. If her image isn't quite feminist, *she* tends to be. During a Tokyo concert sound check, when a male technician questioned one of her decisions, she snapped back, "Listen, everyone is entitled to my opinion."

An MTV icon and a platinum singer, Madonna has overlooked the string of movie flops she began in 1986 with *Shanghai Surprise*. She is prepared for a multi-media future: her music company is named Boy-Toy, her film company is Siren, and her video organization is Slutco. Via hot videos and her hotly discussed relationship with Sandra Bernhard, Madonna has become a sex goddess for all generations and genders. (*Vanity Fair* acknowledged rumors of an alleged affair with Jennifer "Dirty Dancing" Grey during filming of the musical *Bloodhounds of Broadway,* whose writer-director Howard Brookner died of AIDS in 1989.)

Interestingly, Madonna and her image are more mature than her typically disposable songs. Most, e.g., "Like A Virgin" and "Like A Prayer," offended the expected targets, but others, like "Papa Don't Preach," dismayed feminists, pro-choice advocates and Planned Parenthood. Overall, however, Madonna's social consciousness dwarfs those of most singers. Her *Like A Prayer* album included an educational fact sheet about AIDS, for which she's done numerous benefits. "AIDS is the No. 2 evil in the 20th century, after Hitler."

Madonna plans to return to her Latin and brunette roots by starring on screen as bisexual Frida Kahlo—a 180-degree switch from Breathless Mahoney in *Dick Tracy*. It remains to be seen if Hollywood will approve the golden vamp as a dark-haired painter, and whether even Madonna would include the woman's dual sexuality, or go the thorny way of *The Rose* (which brings to mind the anonymous sentiment "Life is a bed of roses—except for the pricks!").

In 1990 media-mistress Madonna went too far for the supposedly liberal MTV. The music network banned the video of her song "Justify My Love," without giving the real and indisputable reason—homophobia. The video features elegant homoeroticism, most spectacularly Madonna exchanging a passionate kiss with another woman, something that pop-rock's closet kings wouldn't dream of doing. . . . Madonna told the *New York Times,* "Why is it that people are willing to go to a movie and watch someone get blown to bits for no reason, but not to see two girls kissing or two men snuggling?"

(Ironically, an MTV poll found that 92 percent of viewers would not stop buying the records or CDs of a singer they liked if they found out said singer was gay or lesbian.)

Alluding to the boy-beauty of the actor and the macha of the actress, the *Advocate* described Phranc as "the grown-up tomboy daughter of Bea Arthur and Tom Cruise." The self-described "all-American Jewish lesbian folksinger" became the first openly lesbian singer-songwriter on a major label when she signed with Island (Grace Jones' former label), which released her 1989 LP, "I Enjoy Being a Girl."

As with k. d. lang, much of Phranc's media publicity, of which she has considerably less than lang, centers on her minimal hair. But there's plenty more to the ex-Susie Gottlieb than an eye-catching flattop, a white shirt, blue jeans or black combat boots. Phranc has wowed audiences as an opening act for the Smiths, Huesker Du, the Pogues and others.

Her songs run the gamut from "Martina," a love/lust song about tennis champ Navratilova, to "Myriam [*sic*] and Esther," about Phranc's supportive grandmothers. She also sings against neo-Nazis and about her collection of G.I. Joe dolls, and sings/talks about being lesbian:

"My sexuality is no more a big deal than the color of my hair. It's definitely not the main focus. But people have said, 'Okay, enough—you've said you're a lesbian, and you keep saying it. Why don't you shut up already and just sing?' Well, I don't think homophobia has changed or stopped in this world, and until it goes away, I'm not going to shut up about it."

To an extent unique in the music world, Phranc is committed to visibility and progress. "When I was coming out (at 17), there were very few people in the big world who were out as lesbians, setting a positive example. . . . It's important to be out, because if we hide in the closet, it's like saying that there's something wrong with us."

Phranc's debut album, the 1985 *Folksinger,* established her as a novelty and a talent. Four years later, she released the eagerly awaited LP boasting "I Enjoy Being a Girl," a Broadway tune blindly celebrating traditional femininity. As sung by Phranc, especially live, it becomes a radical statement: with her hands on her denimed hips, she belts lyrics like "I'm strictly a female female!" expanding the limits of "girl"-hood and self-enjoyment.

At the Cubby Hole in Manhattan, Phranc explained, "I hated growing up as a girl, only because there was such a big barrier. I couldn't be on the Little League like my brother, couldn't wear my hair up like I wanted, had to wear a dress to school every day. I had almost no choices. Now, I enjoy being a girl, and thought it would be fun and ironic to do that song."

Because her identity is so intrinsic to her music, Phranc receives scant commercial radioplay. Her first notable video exposure derived from *Bloodbath,* included in MTV's *120 Minutes* and in regional airplay. "You sell so many more albums because of a video than you ever did from the radio, it's spooky." Further videos widely aired should bring Phranc to the masses and illustrate her musical messages of tolerance and human diversity.

"You'd Be Surprised"

When I asked George Cukor why he thought his movie about three showgirls, *Les Blondes,* had become a cult classic after flopping at the box office, he replied that it probably had to do with the title! "I don't know why it should be," says a friend at Capitol Records in Hollywood, "but almost all the lesbian singers or the AC/DC ones are brunettes. Unlike in the movies," where blondes frequently have more fun, off the screen.

The stereotype lingers. Think, quickly, of a lesbian, any lesbian. Chances are you pictured an athlete, possibly an intense yet slinky European actress, or a stoutish woman past 50. And most likely she was dark-haired. Subconsciously, we still think of blondes as too light and feminine to be otherwise. And what's more feminine than your typical blonde singer? No matter that her hair may be a wig—like Dolly's—or have dark roots—like Olivia or Madonna's. On screen and in song, blondes have become the archetypal female sex symbols.

The *ne plus ultra* of them all was of course Marilyn—Monroe, not Boy George's male singing companion. A singing actress, today her albums sell throughout the world in a volume never attained during her lifetime. Not just the soundtracks of *Gentlemen Prefer Blondes* and *There's No Business Like Show Business* (dominated by Ethel Merman), but standards of the period like Cole Porter's "My Heart Belongs to Daddy," "You'd

Be Surprised" and "She Acts Like a Woman Should."

Again, the woman's talents, as actress, comedian and singer, were overlooked in favor of her physical attributes and venusian status within the celluloid pantheon. Posthumous books have explored the "real" Marilyn, but predictably, it wasn't until a woman finally wrote a Marilyn book (Lena Pepitone's 1979 *Marilyn Monroe Confidential*) that her bisexuality was uncovered. Or, if you like, her sexual experiments, for Marilyn had a long-standing fear that she might be lesbian; in his Marilyn book, Norman Mailer reported that Elizabeth Taylor once allegedly called MM a "dyke."

"Poor Norma Jean," reads *The Gay Book of Days*. "Packaged and sold around the globe as a male wet dream, exploited even after death by necrophilic writers great and small, vilified in a gross and pompous play by her former husband, is it any wonder that she once found a rare moment of comfort in an affair with a female drama coach?"

That affair was with the late Natasha Lytess, with whom Marilyn lived for a while and from whom she was virtually inseparable on several movie sets. The relationship was impartially chronicled in 1985 by veteran columnist Sheilah Graham in *Hollywood Revisited*. On that book's heels came a feminist summing-up of the woman behind the front, *Norma Jean*, by Gloria Steinem. During and after her lifetime, Marilyn was more sympathetically treated by women, although L.A. talk show host Woody McBreairty reconfirms that "Joan Crawford was downright venomous toward Marilyn in the early part of her career."

The animosity was sparked by Marilyn's spurning Joan's advances at a cocktail party, when Crawford offered to give the starlet some of her cast-off gowns, so long as Marilyn would try them on in Joan's bedroom. Later, when Marilyn accepted an award as Most Promising Newcomer at the *Photoplay* awards banquet, Crawford was in the audience, seething. She feigned to be offended down to her fuck-me pumps by MM's spectacularly revealing gold lamé gown.

The following day, in an exclusive interview syndicated nationwide, Crawford gave Monroe a piece of her mind and took her to task for being vulgar and unlady-like. The American public, Joan felt, liked sex, but they didn't want it flaunted in their impressionable faces.

Male directors and co-stars were often as ungallant. Billy Wilder said Marilyn had "breasts of granite and a mind like a Gruyere cheese." Tony Curtis professed that kissing Marilyn in a love scene was "like kissing Hitler." Marilyn got her revenge when she held up production on *Some Like It Hot.* She informed the press, "I'm not going back into that film until Wilder reshoots my opening. When Marilyn Monroe comes into a room, nobody's going to be looking at Tony Curtis playing Joan Crawford. They're going to be looking at Marilyn Monroe." The cross-dressing comedy became her biggest movie hit.

George Cukor, who directed both stars more than once, told the author, "Both Marilyn and Judy Holliday were proud of their singing, which was quickly dismissed. . . . Marilyn was a fine actress, praised for *Bus Stop* but underrated as a comedienne, while Judy was Oscared (in his *Born Yesterday*) as a comedienne but underrated as an actress."

Los Angeles-born, Norma Jean Baker was named after two reigning actresses, Norma Shearer and Jean Harlow. Early on, she sought work as a singer or dancer, but wound up stripping at Hollywood's Mayan Theatre. Through most of her career, she kept up her voice with singing lessons. But she didn't dwell on her vocal talent. Thus, when signed for the musical *Gentlemen Prefer Blondes,* she was to have been dubbed by a professional singer. The gay choreographer Jack Cole aided Marilyn in recording her songs, which were then played for Fox honcho Darryl Zanuck, who at first refused to believe that the voice really belonged to "that dumb blonde," who received about one-fifteenth the salary that her brunette co-star, Jane Russell, did.

"I Had the Craziest Dream"

Judy Holliday (née Tuvim, meaning holiday in Hebrew) verifiably had what some now claim Marilyn had: a near-genius IQ. Like Marilyn, she was saddled with a very specific image through her too-brief career, ended by cancer at age 44. Though a bubbly blonde, Judy's looks initially almost did her in. After a small role in Cukor's *Adam's Rib,* the director recommended her to Columbia head Harry Cohn for the lead in the film *Born*

Yesterday (Judy had starred, on Broadway).

The mogul also know as Genghis Cohn flatly refused. First off, Holliday wasn't a Name. Second, she was a "fat, Jewish broad!" But eventually, with much coaxing from Cukor and "Adam's Rib" co-star Katharine Hepburn, talent won out, and Judy got her first vehicle and an Academy Award—beating out Bette Davis as Margo Channing and Gloria Swanson as Norma Desmond.

Originally, Holliday intended to write. In school, she'd appeared in, written and directed plays. At 16, she tried to enter Yale's School of Drama as a playwright, but was a year too young for admission. Instead, she headed for New York, immersing herself in the demimonde of music and theatre, in which many of her friends and lovers were gay. In her *Bernstein* biography, Joan Peyser asserted:

"During the early 1940s . . . Judy Holliday was a lesbian. . . . At the time of her entrance into show business, she and her lover, a police woman, shared an apartment that contained a pool table and was generally crowded with their lesbian friends. Once, when the police woman entered the living room, she found Bernstein at the piano with tears running down his face. Asked what had happened, he answered that everyone in the room was homosexual."

Peyser insisted that the beloved comedian, who later married, "became" heterosexual, while the problematic composer-conductor, even though he later married, remained stubbornly attracted to men. More on Judy's bisexual love life may be gleaned from Gary Carey's *Judy Holliday.*

The undisputedly great love of her life was musician Gerry Mulligan, with whom she recorded a couple of albums. She also co-wrote with him. Her singing was laughed off by critics, and the albums faded into obscurity, returning in the 1980s as valued and sought-after "collections by a sensitive and unique song-stylist." In Judy's words, most of her songs and all classical love songs put forth the sentiment that "Love is eternal as long as it lasts."

Holliday's last movie was a musical, *Bells Are Ringing,* in 1960. The Broadway version had enjoyed a lengthy run thanks to Judy's unflagging warmth and charm. The film, co-starring a leaden Dean Martin and featuring a mostly mediocre score, was one of musical specialist Vincente Minnelli's lesser pictures.

Today, *Bells* resonates only through Judy's personality, a golden humanity which also delineates her interpretations of semi-biographical songs like "Trouble Is a Man," "What I Was Warned About," "What'll I Do," "Am I Blue," "Confession," "An Occasional Man," and "I'm One of God's Children."

Holliday was one of the few stars with whom George Cukor became close. He declined to discuss her sexual orientation. I explained, "I mention it because her latest biographers seem willing to deal with it, and one of them has said she suffered greatly for it, and that it may have been part of what she drew on to give more subtle, affecting performances. . . . "

Cukor responded, "I imagine that most performers use their private emotions and struggles to a greater extent than we ever realize."

It was another Hollywood blonde, Betty Grable, who once said, "In the words of Mrs. Eleanor Roosevelt, you can only be made to feel less than you are if you give other people permission to do so. . . . Problem is, in this business, you've got guys all around you, telling you how dumb or phony you are, telling you what to do, what to say, and how to behave."

Grable made this statement when asked why, as the 1940s' top box office star, she'd never had a recording career, despite having introduced hit after hit in her Fox musicals (one was the gay cult favorite "I Had the Craziest Dream"). Zanuck hadn't permitted Grable to do records of her hit movie songs, and she'd never tried to challenge him in court.

Most singers agree that singing is a very private place. It has been likened to a fire which needs constant emotional stoking. But sometimes, the consuming flames may require dousing. . . .

Joan Baez has said, "I was not confused about what I was feeling, which seemed very clear to me, but rather about what to do about what I was feeling. . . . My confusion came mainly from what everybody else would think."

Leonard Bernstein: maestro, gay activist, friend

Beethoven: in silhouette
at 16, and a later portrait

Tchaikovsky in 1875
(at right) and actor
Kenneth Colley as
his also gay brother
Modeste (above)

Rudolf Nureyev: as Rudolph Valentino, dancing with Nijinsky (Anthony Dowell)

Carmen
Miranda:
the queer
lady in the
tutti frutti hat

Noel Coward: dry wit in the Nevada desert

Cary Grant (bi) as Cole Porter (gay) in hetero movie bio *Night & Day*

Marlene Dietrich: the lady is a (bisexual) vamp

Liberace: roses on your piano or tulips on your organ?

Janis Joplin:
bi-bi rock diva

Mick Jagger and David Bowie: once upon a mattress

Boy George: mad about
the cross-dressing boy

Julie Andrews in *Victor/Victoria*:
declares herself egregiously not gay!

Ryuichi Sakamoto: Oscar-winning sexual enigma

Madonna and her stamps
(Grenada, above; St. Vincent, at right)

Bette Midler:
straight
woman,
gay humor

Barbra Streisand: better pro-gay late than never!

LESBIANS ON THE LOOSE

NOVEMBER 1995 • ISSUE 71 • VOL 6 NO 11

FREE

the
secret's
out

melissa etheridge

Melissa Etheridge: *Yes I Am* (Used with permission of *Lesbians on the Loose*)

LESBIANS ON THE LOOSE

APRIL 1997 • ISSUE 88 • VOL 8 NO 4   FREE

Ellen's out!

Ellen DeGeneres: *first* she came out *singing!*
(Used with permission of *Lesbians on the Loose*)

The British Are Coming!

"An artist cannot change society; all that he can do is to express that it is sick." —Kierkegaard

"Gay's The Word"

Ladies first. Beatrice Lillie (née Constance Munston, 1894-1989) became one when she wed Sir Robert Peel, an asexual gentlemen of leisure who didn't know what to do with his. The pseudo-couple lived apart, and at 36 he died. "The funniest woman in the world," Lady Banana Peel's trademark was her boyish bob. Early on, the comic/singer had played in drag on stage and in film. Long before "camp" gained popular coinage, the self-described mezzanine soprano was a high-camp favorite.

Queen Bea's most famous song was "There Are Fairies At the Bottom of Our Garden." Pal Noel Coward told a friend, "I should love to perform that, but I don't dare. It might come out 'There Are Fairies in the Garden of My Bottom.'"

Because celluloid never carved a niche for the androgynous Lillie, she became famous via live performances, records and Broadway. Also through her wit. Once, asked if she were really a lady, she loudly replied, "You're goddamned right!" During a Manhattan reception for Josephine Baker, the American singer was acting very grand and employing a French accent. Introduced to Lillie, she extended a velvet-gloved hand. "Eet ees a great plaisir, Lady Peel." Said Bea, "Ah likes you too, honey."

An associate informed Noel Coward about a new singer: "He's a masculine Beatrice Lillie." Coward advised, "Don't be redundant." Another time, Noel informed "Beattie" that in her severely tailored suit, "You look almost like a man." She hissed back, "So do you!" In a Paris hotel room, Bea coyly inquired of Noel, "Do you have a gentleman in your room?"

"Just a minute——I'll go ask him."

In her youth, Bea befriended certain butch comediennes with whom she worked. Some became lifelong friends. During WWI she customarily dressed as a soldier while singing to same. She did a specialty number, "My River Girl," on a bike dressed as an Eton boy with bicycle clips on white trousers, a coat and a cap. Many thought her a male, until she commenced singing. She recalled, "Two amorous nurses kissed my hand one night and pinched my cheek. They must have imagined I was a dyke on a bike!"

Although she had a wide circle of renowned lesbian friends— among them Elsa Maxwell, Katharine Cornell and Tallulah Bankhead——Bea reportedly kept her same-sex relationships hush-hush and limited them to non-celebs (the easier to impress?). Her closest friend, with whom she often lived and clowned, was actress Gertrude Lawrence. "I knew her better than a husband would," Bea once affirmed, without elaboration.

Her last film, in 1967, was *Thoroughly Modern Millie*, a Julie Andrews musical in which she impersonated a comical white-slaver. To her chagrin, the movie was a hit without a single Lillie tune. In 1972 she published her memoirs, *Every Other Inch a Lady*, but was soon after forcibly retired due to senility. At a MOMA screening in New York, she'd exposed a 70ish breast to her horrified audience. Eventually forgotten by the celluloid generation, she dwelled at Henley-on-Thames in the misty climate of her mind. She died at 94.

Her pal Ivor Novello had explained, "At heart, she's an anarchist. She's much too funny to have been just a singer. Whenever Beatrice opens her mouth, it's mutiny on the high C's."

Like Lillie's, Novello's legacy hasn't stood up to be counted, again because he's seldom seen on the screen. Yet he did have a flourishing film career from 1919 to 1934, including the intriguingly titled *Call of the Blood* and *Why Boys Leave Home*. David Ivor Davies (1893-1951) was also a screenwriter whose greatest Hollywood contribution was the immortal MGM line, "Me-Tarzan, you-Jane."

For a time, Novello was Coward's chief rival as king of the London musical stage. Noel envied him his matinee idol looks and cameo-like profile: "The man's too irritating for words. Like me, he does everything well. But to top it, he *looks* it . . . He's every mother's dream." Ivor's was a singing teacher who encouraged him to cultivate the fine soprano which eventually won him a scholarship at Magdalen College choir school.

In his teens, "the Welsh prodigy" began writing songs, and was proudly introduced to one and all by Clara Novello Davies as "my composer son." Mr. Davies, a tax collector, consented to the family's move to London, where Clara became an in-demand singing coach. She arranged for Ivor to meet several influential musical luminaries, and in 1914 he published his most successful song, "Keep the Home Fires Burning." The WWI anthem earned him a fortune and made him famous.

In 1916 Ivor met Bobby Andrews, a 21-year-old actor. It was "love at first sight . . . much more than friends, far more than lovers." The lifemates were together thirty-five years and often worked together in Ivor's plays and musicals. Novello branched into writing and starring in long-running West End musicals like *Glamorous Night*, *The Dancing Years*, *Perchance to Dream*, *King's Rhapsody* and his last, *Gay's The Word* (also the name of Britain's leading gay bookstore).

During WWII he toured throughout the UK, but was charged in 1944 with misuse of petrol ration coupons. He pleaded that he'd needed the petrol to drive from the theatre to Redroofs, his country home near Maidenhead. Nonetheless he was sent to prison for one month, a sentence so severe that it was universally supposed he was being made an example of or being punished for another type of "offense." After emerging from Wormwood Scrubs prison, he and Bobby entertained troops on the continent, and Ivor had another huge hit with his song "We'll Gather Lilacs."

Though his reputation would ultimately be eclipsed by the longer-lived Coward, Novello was celebrated in his day as the personification of glamour and romance. "The British Adonis" was married to Bobby Andrews, but the media denigrated the relationship to invisibility; a "romance" with co-star Gladys Cooper was cooked up by a press agent and perpetuated by a one-track press. Ivor and Bobby's flat atop the Strand Theatre was the uninhibited site of endless parties attracting guests as diverse as Edward VIII, Paul Robeson, Tyrone Power and the crème de la crème of the West End thespians.

Novello had proclaimed, "I want glamour with a capital G. I want great crystal chandeliers, and satin trains fourteen feet long, and footmen in velvet liveries. I want grace, dignity, curtsies and royal salutes." He attained all of that, and an enduring love relationship as well. No wonder Coward, who had less luck with men, was always jealous! And although the British government did Novello assorted honors after he died at 58 of a coronary thrombosis—hours after appearing on the stage—not a single newspaper account of the star's death mentioned that Bobby had been with him at the end.

Two of the British institution's hit plays were titled *The Truth Game* and *I Lived With You*. . . .

"Mad About the Boy"

At 70, Noel Coward (1899-1973) was finally knighted. He'd done more for the British stage than anyone since Shaw —who was Irish—yet Sir-dom was a long time coming. This, it was generally believed, was due to his sexual orientation. He told the author, "I was a late bloomer by my standards. I expected success and wholeheartedly pursued it as soon as I stepped out of the womb. But it eluded my grasp until the ripe age of 25."

From then on, things happened fast. Coward shined as a playwright, composer, lyricist, actor, singer and the most quoted wit since Oscar Wilde, whose more talented spiritual successor he was. (Unlike Oscar, Noel didn't wed or father; he once sniffed, "I've never been able to fathom what is convenient about a 'marriage of convenience.'") He wrote *Hay Fever* in a weekend and *Private Lives*, his biggest hit, in four days. It all came so easily that he had hordes of detractors who derided his manicured, silk-dressing-gowned image and typically perfect poise with or without a cigarette in hand.

After WWII, he fell vertiginously out of favor. His sophisticated plays were eschewed in favor of the "angry young man" school of realistic theatre, and his songs—like "Mad About the

Boy" and "Mad Dogs and Englishmen"—were considered *outré* and hopelessly camp. (The former was inspired by Noel's early lover Cary Grant, whom he addressed privately and publicly as "dear boy" and who once admiringly introduced him to Mae West, with whom Grant twice co-starred until she discovered—via his lengthy affair with Randolph Scott—that he was gay.)

In the '60s, however, Coward was rediscovered and deemed a national treasure. The composer of "The Stately Homes of England" was now one of England's stateliest homos. Through motion pictures, he became known to the non-theatre-going masses, and even played a gay character, the Witch of Capri, in Tennessee Williams' 1968 *Boom!* opposite Elizabeth Taylor. But his songs were less frequently revived than his plays. They included "Don't Put Your Daughter On the Stage, Mrs. Worthington," "London Pride," "Matelot" and "Marvelous Party."

Like Cole Porter, Coward all but came out in his lyrics, which were more gay-informed than any other British composer's. In "Green Carnation," he daringly satirized Oscar Wilde and the Aesthetic Movement. The song's closing punch-line used "gay" in both senses of the word. In the early 1950s, Coward trailblazed the concept of Name stars playing Las Vegas. He later noted, "The good people in the desert appreciated my wit, which is as dry as gin. But I knew in advance that most of my own songs," sung in his "voice of a baritone dove," "would leave them puzzled or hostile." His one-man show was a mixture of songs old and new, racy jokes and elegant patter.

"Audiences would rather hear me speak than sing. Can't think why!" Coward's veddy clipped manner of speaking was primarily a response to his mother's deafness, the result of her falling out of a porthole in Madeira and landing on her head. Also, she was a lousy lip-reader, but her dutiful son's mannered speech became his trademark.

Homophobe Rex Harrison announced that Coward "sounded like a cunt." Despite all his contracted marriages, Harrison was himself taken by much of Hollywood for "an English queer," to quote Hedda Hopper. His biggest film comedy hit was Coward's *Blithe Spirit*, which Noel had performed on the stage with at least as much brittle macho as Rex could muster.

Assessing his legacy, Coward guessed, "Of course my plays

will survive. . . . Musically, a handful of songs may survive, and I shall be remembered for my personality and for living life to its fullest." Asked to define the perfect life, he once answered, "Mine!"

During and after his lifetime, Coward anecdotes poured forth by the hundreds, insuring his place as British wit of the century. For example: apprised that a dim-witted actor friend had killed himself, he inquired, "How?"

"He shot his brains out."

Said Noel, "He must have been a marvelous shot."

Another time, the composer of "I'll Follow My Secret Heart" decided to leave a party early. His hostess implored, "But it's not even late yet!" He demurred, "I really must think of my youth."

"Well, next time bring him along."

Benjamin Britten (1913-1976), aka Lord Britten of Aldeburgh, was the outstanding British composer of the modern period. Like Coward, he bypassed contractual marriage and was in fact semi-famous—in a post-Novello era—for his life partnership with tenor (later Sir) Peter Pears. Queen Elizabeth II treated Pears as Britten's mate, and six months before his death Britten became the first musician to be created a life peer. His 1945 *Peter Grimes* had been almost unanimously acclaimed as the first great English opera since Purcell's *Dido and Aeneas*.

Britten was significantly stuffier and less flamboyant than Coward, who opined, "Ben is a very major talent, but all of his talent goes into his career." The opposite of Oscar Wilde, of whom it was said he put all his genius into his lifestyle. Throughout his life, Britten avoided speaking of his gayness. He was however a role model for monogamous gays, with two consecutive fully-committed relationships. In 1937 Britten began his union with Pears (1910-86), whom he'd met three years before; they joined up after the plane crash death of his mate Peter Burra. Coward once quipped, "Lucky Benjy—he went from Peter to Peter!" He added cattily, "Who could ask for less?"

Britten's mother was an amateur singer from a musical family. A junior tennis champ, Ben took up piano and composing, and began his career in 1935 by composing incidental music for documentary films. In 1939 he and Pears moved to America, but missing their homeland, soon returned. Back in the UK, the pacifists were ordered to appear before a conscientious objectors' tribunal. They were exempted from military service, and several of Britten's works reflected his pacifism.

His works also reflect his admiration of and yearning for rebellious male heroes. Musicologist Hans Keller cited "the enormous creative advantage of Britten's homosexuality." This is particularly evident in his major operas, e.g., *Peter Grimes*, *The Turn of the Screw*, *Billy Budd* (from Melville's homoerotic novel) and *Death in Venice*. Also in his songs, especially the Michelangelo sonnets and the canticles.

Ned Rorem summed up the great Britten: "For two centuries after the death of Henry Purcell in 1695, England produced no music of great consequence. With Benjamin Britten's birth in 1913, the land awoke like Sleeping Beauty and picked up where she had left off. As though reincarnated, Purcell himself was Britten's main influence and love."

Britten's 1962 oratorio *War Requiem*, performed at the dedication of the new Coventry Cathedral, was a mass for the world war dead. In 1989 openly gay director Derek Jarman turned it into a 92-minute classical-music video. "Complex, beautiful, harrowing," said the *Los Angeles Times'* Kevin Thomas. (The pacifist film included Laurence Olivier's final performance.)

Hans Keller concluded that Britten's difference from the majority "placed him in the privileged position of discovering and musically defining new truths which otherwise might not have been accessible to him at all" were he not gay. Question: Does gayness make for better composers? Noel Coward believed, "A great composer who's heterosexual is no less great than one who isn't. But there are more of us in the great category. . . ."

"Sticky Fingers"

Britain's post-'50s musical contributions were far removed from the fey or glamorous, once white Brits took over leadership of rock 'n roll from black Americans and Elvis. From the outset, the Rolling Stones were much more sexually revolutionary than the more mainstream Beatles. Mick Jagger (born 1944) was easily more androgynous than any of the Fab Four, also more apparently sexual. Mick the Stick, aka Jumping Jack Flash and Super-Lips, stood out from the Stones in a way that no individual Beatle overshadowed his fellow Liverpuddlians. Ego was mother's milk to him, and when he did wed, he married a much-publicized look-alike named Bianca. The Nicaraguan claimed he chose her because "He wanted to achieve the ultimate by making love to himself."

When Jagger made the transition to film, his 1969 *Performance* was termed obscene and bisexually provocative because of group sex scenes and Mick's mascara. He was the first rock star to flaunt makeup in performance, further inflaming parents and media guardians with many of his songs, whose subjects ranged from interracial love and sexual "Satisfaction" to fellatio.

"Mick's as famous for the contraband *Cocksucker Blues* as Auden was for his poem on the same subject," said one critic. The "ambisexual" singer's appeal was immortalized in the epochal rock musical *Hair*. The 1968 phenomenon was probably the first piece of theatre to depict non-gay acceptance of gays (up until 1967, New York state law prohibited onstage portrayal of gay characters). *Hair* featured a bisexual character who sang about his passion for Mick Jagger, who was more than once called a sex symbol for both genders!

A December 16, 1988, showing of *Cocksucker Blues* at the Anthology Film Archives on 2nd Avenue in Manhattan was an SRO event despite its not being advertised by name in the *New York Times* or other mass market papers. CB was a 1972 documentary by Robert Frank, made with the Stones' then full cooperation. It contained scenes of their American tour, but after the fact, the group tried to suppress it, allegedly because Frank didn't focus on their music-making. The drug footage may have depressed the band's morale, for Keith Richards was experiencing drug-related legal problems in Toronto at the time.

The lawsuit's result was that Frank could publicly screen the film only four times annually, and not for profit. Because of the hassles involved, he reportedly chose to take CB off the market after the 12/88 NYC showings. *New York Native* reviewer Peter Miller described "the naughty bits:"

"A shot of Jagger filming himself in a mirror with one hand while simultaneously playing with himself with the other. . . .

Sequences of male and female members of the Stones' entourage . . ." and an airplane sex act viewed by the encouraging Stones who accompany the male-female coupling on percussion instruments.

Is Mick bi or isn't he? I asked his mentor and photographer Cecil Beaton, who felt that Jagger, even though hetero, preferred to create an impression of bisexuality. In the '70s, that was chic, and even in his 1985 video *Dancing in the Streets* with David Bowie, Jagger postured campily and flirted with his less outgoing, crucified co-singer.

In an early-'80s *High Society* interview, Jagger was queried about gays. "It's like the old line about different strokes for different folks. . . . If we're going to worry about any form of sexuality, it should be the prissy, repressed people who never enjoy any form of sex. I have just as many gay friends as straights. I don't worry about being seen with either.

"And let's not be unfair to the bi's. Bisexuals are probably the fastest-growing population in the world. . . . In Europe, bisexuality is practically an accepted lifestyle." Asked about his own sexuality, he stated, "People always want to know, but they usually don't have the balls to ask." Then he explained two things: he doesn't fellate men or screw them. . . .

"Does that answer the question?"

However, the girlie magazine interviewer couldn't seem to let go of the subject, and wondered, "Does the inference bother you?" Said the Stick (does any erection have a conscience?), "The reason I don't care if people think I'm gay is simply because being gay just isn't bad. . . . I appeal to them the same way I appeal to heterosexuals."

Rumor in rock circles had it that Jagger and Bowie used to be *thisclose*. In spring, 1990, Bowie's look-alike ex-wife Angela appeared on Joan Rivers' daytime talk show and divulged that she'd once caught her husband in bed naked with Mick Jagger. Her reaction? "I made breakfast." British tabloids had a field day with the item, and the *National Enquirer* screamed, "Mick Jagger's Gay Affair With David Bowie!" Angela was free to publicly dish because a divorce-settlement gag order had expired on April 1 (she'd received some $750,000 when she divorced him in 1980 on condition that she not talk about Bowie for a 10-year period). Angela gave a series of "graphic" interviews.

175

According to the *Star*, "She and Bowie fought about it (the alleged affair) afterward. 'He was really angry that I fancied Mick,' she recalled." The paper added, "Jagger has admitted in the past experimenting with gay sex, saying, 'I have to confess that I've slept with men. I'm a passionate person. I love living life and being hungry for all kinds of new experiences. I went through a phase where lots of men were attracted to me and I was quite turned on by it all.'"

The tabs ran photos of the two men in a semi-recumbent position, Bowie embracing Mick with one languid hand. If the news didn't generate much of a stir in rock circles, it did receive international coverage and undercut the men's more staid and non-bi late-'80s image. One early summer, 1990, tabloid item titled "Jaggerwacky" reported that Bowie was in Rome seated at a sidewalk cafe with his latest girlfriend, Gloria, whom he leaned over and smooched. "Just then somebody driving by on a motorbike yelled in English, 'Does she kiss better than Mick?' Bowie freaked. He threw money on the table and knocked chairs over pulling Gloria to his waiting limo." Sic (rapid) transit Gloria.

As one rock journalist put it, during the '60s and '70s Jagger "gave lots of teenage boys confusing hard-ons." Perhaps they arose in "Sympathy For the Devil" they wished to priapicly emulate. After all, Mick's legend was nothing if not phallic, and to this day, the most famous Stones record cover is *Sticky Fingers*, the one with the denimed crotch (of which Springsteen's *Born in the USA* was literally the back side) and the working zipper which launched a thousand hips.

From the day of its release, the album, as opposed to the record inside it, became a collector's item and—where not banned!—a global best-seller, thanks partly to Mick-maniacs who'd never before (and never again?) purchased a Stones LP.

"Aladdin Sane"

Bowie was born David Jones in 1947, and in the '60s changed his name to avoid confusion with another British singer, Davey Jones of the Monkees. As if they could have been confused! Jones was an even perkier, squeakier Paul McCartney.

And where Mick Jagger was every *inch* a star, Bowie became famous for his androgyny and pansexuality. Rock encyclopedist Irwin Stambler wrote, "For many, Bowie's talent tends to be overshadowed by his private life, particularly his avowed bisexuality."

In 1972 in the British mag *Melody Maker*, Bowie "avowed" his sexuality. And reiterated it in *Playboy* in 1976, stating that he and Angie were both bi. "Angela and I knew each other because we were both going out with the same man." The British version was a bit rawer: "We were both laying the same bloke." Angie admitted, "David had scores of men and women when we were married, and so did I," adding, "Often there would be three of us in bed—usually another girl . . . "

Then there were his songs, some gay, some anti-gay ("Cracked Actor"), some bi, some bitchy, and one about lesbians in the army. There was "Queen Bitch," about a youth who "dresses like a queen but . . . can kick like a mule." One song celebrated a stud who "came on so loaded, man, well-hung, and snow-white tan." Plus "All the Young Dudes," "Aladdin Sane," the convincing drag in his video *Boys Keep Swinging*, and the avant-garb he affected on unisexual record covers, TV, stage and video appearances.

"Bowie was the first major rock star to claim that he slept with other guys and to make it part of his act, his persona and his music," said *The Advocate*. *Esquire* marveled that Bowie was widely publicized "for having been photographed wearing a dress," which he soon after traded in for "hot pants, dyed red hair, high boots, earrings—the full panoply of what would become the Glitter Rock Movement."

His 1972 incarnation as Ziggy Stardust was cited by *Esquire* as No. 3 of the Top Ten events which helped homosexualize American pop culture. On stage, Bowie carried out a virtual revolution. Martin Greif remembered, "In the early '70s he was fond of staging a mock blow-job of his guitarist Mike Ronson before a delighted audience of shrieking 14-year-olds." *Esquire* observed that "He adopted the posture of a pederast when onstage with his lead guitarist Mick [sic] Ronson."

The singer's film appearances were at first similarly offbeat, if nowhere as daring (for, such is the nature of film). His 1976 debut, *The Man Who Fell to Earth*, was helmed by Nicholas

Roeg (who'd co-directed *Performance*). In it, Bowie was an alien from outer space who eventually unpeels his earthly guise to reveal a glaring lack of genitalia. Pauline Kael called his iconographic performance a "leering lesbian Christ." Two years later he was *Just a Gigolo*, most significant as Marlene Dietrich's movie swansong.

In the '80s, it was Catherine Deneuve who was bi, a vampire in *The Hunger* who traded lover Bowie for new love Susan Sarandon. And in *Merry Christmas, Mr. Lawrence*, Bowie primly rebuffed the ardent kiss of a young Japanese military officer! (pop star Ryuichi Sakamoto).

Bowie's sexual frankness didn't hurt his career. On the contrary. But *Newsweek* later described his "promoting a new and more conservative style in sync with frightened and reactionary times." In the AIDS-infested '80s (it attacked *minds* more than anything else), he launched his 1983 U.S. tour by telling *Time* he'd never been bi, let alone gay. His *Rolling Stone* cover caption read "David Bowie, Straight." But whatever his sexual and/or marketing stance, Bowie seemed more asexual than anything else. *Esquire* may have hit the nail on the head: ". . . like an updated Liberace, and just about as sexless."

It therefore came as a shock to some when in 1987 newspapers reported that Bowie had been charged with rape by a Dallas woman. He denied it. The woman also alleged that the rock star had infected her with AIDS, and demanded he take the test. A local grand jury found there had been no rape (Bowie appeared in court to testify, which recalls the fact that in the Middle Ages a male appearing in court had to swear to tell the truth or else forfeit his testicles—hence the term "testifying"!).

Back in the '70s, Bowie had been up for a flashy supporting film role in the Who's rock opera *Tommy* (rival Elton John essayed the platform-shoed Pinball Wizard). But it was Tina Turner who got to play the Acid Queen. Who drummer Keith Moon explained, "David has more images than any singer, ever! He can be anybody, because at heart he's nobody. Or nobody that he'd recognize." Bowie's post-Ziggy avatars included Hard-Hearted Harlequin, the Thin White Duke and a would-be movie star (in flops like . . . *Lawrence*, *Labyrinth* and *Absolute Beginners*).

Andy Warhol considered Bowie "mythological. He lives for

what he'll next appear to be, and he's loved for what he appears to be—only. He's not a legend, but a myth."

Funny. Rowan & Martin once defined a *myth* as an effeminate moth.

"The Bitch Is Back!"

Elton John (born Reginald Dwight in Middlesex in 1947) differed in various ways from Mick and David. Neither as pale nor as thin as his almost-anorexic competitors, the ex-Reggie remained pink and pudgy, and dieting became his weigh of life. He also started to bald early, and took to a flamboyant array of hats which complemented his vast collection of gaudy, glittery eyewear. Like Bowie, he clothed his stage persona in spectacular costumes, from Tina Turner drag to chicken outfits, Mozart pompadours and Bowie-esque space-oddity suits.

In 1976 designer Mr. Blackwell included Elton on his Worst Dressed Women of the Year list (Bowie also made the list), and one critic opined, "When Elton breathes his last, it undoubtedly won't be his life that flashes before his eyes, but a parade of past outfits."

Unlike Bowie, whose '80s wardrobe featured ostentatious restraint, John kept having fun and maintained the courage of his indiscretions. (Unlike Jagger and Bowie, he never movie-starred, and kept postponing the soccer-themed film he hoped to do with Rod Stewart.) Like Bowie, John came out at the height of his popularity; of the famed *Rolling Stone* interview, he half-joked, "Ever since I said I was bisexual, it seems twice as many people wave at me in the streets." The fallow period which followed was due, he later noted, more to exhaustion and lack of creativity than to negative fan reaction. A relative slump had been bound to occur after so long in the stratosphere:

In 1972 and '73, Elton's Top Five singles included "Rocket Man," "Honky Cat," "Crocodile Rock" and "Daniel," followed by his smash album *Goodbye, Yellow Brick Road*. He formed his own company, Rocket Records, and went on to bigger hits, like "Benny and the Jets," "Don't Let the Sun Go Down On Me" and "The Bitch Is Back!" He made the cover of *Time*, got a star on the

Hollywood Walk of Fame, and filled the L.A. Dodgers' baseball stadium——the first rocker to do so since the Beatles. Like no other music star, Elton dominated the 1970s.

But in '76 the tide turned. Primarily, many felt, because he broke up with handsome lyricist Bernie Taupin, who left to create a solo career. For eight years the pair had been the Rodgers & Hammerstein of rock, and close friends. Said Elton, "I can't remember too much from 1970 to 1976 because there was so much stuff going on." Slowing down, he became more candid. He teased in *After Dark*, "The towel bills that David Bowie must run up dyeing his hair . . . " and he posed for pictures with Cary Grant and chum Andy Warhol.

In 1979 Rod Stewart revealed a bit about their friendship to *Rolling Stone*. "I've always been known as 'Phyllis,' and she's 'Sharon,' and we've had a few ups and downs, but he's still one of my best friends." By contrast, there was no love lost between Elton and Bowie, who inaugurated gender-bending rock but lived to see John's success outstrip his. When *Circus* magazine asked how John felt about Bowie's statement that he was "rock's token queen," he replied:

"I try not to be bitchy, even though at times we're all bitchy in conversation. Saying it in print is another thing. . . . I didn't retaliate when Bowie said I was a token queen, even though he's had a couple of go's since. Because I know what's happened to him. I'll always remember going out for dinner with him and Angie when he was Ziggy Stardust. It was a fabulous evening, and over dinner he admitted to me that he always wanted to be Judy Garland, and that's the God's honest truth."

In 1979 *Creem* wondered "whatever prompted" Elton to lay open "such a personal subject like your sexuality" (heteros' sexuality must somehow be less "personal"!).

"The only reason I made that statement about being gay was because nobody had actually asked me before. I don't think it was some startling revelation——a lot of people already knew. I felt that I'd rather be totally honest about it than try to cover it up . . . get married for the sake of appearances and lash it to a toothbrush."

His 1984 Australian marriage to the German Renate yielded assorted rumors and allegations in the British press. In 1987 the *Sun* prematurely wrote of a marital "dissolution." "Many said it was the perfect marriage of convenience. *He* preferred the company of men. *She* preferred the company of women."

Also in '87, the *Union Jack* headlined, "Mock Wedding Claim By Elton's Friend. . . . Gary Clarke, a handsome 30-year-old Australian, revealed how he and Elton John went through a mock wedding in Australia in 1980. Clarke claims he and the star exchanged vows and signed a document to seal a friendship that began during Elton's tour of Australia that year. Following the ceremony the two spent five weeks in the West Indies and then Clarke stayed with Elton in his mansion in Windsor."

Elton never explained his contractual marriage which so dismayed fans who'd admired his honesty. In the late '70s he'd admitted—and revealed—"The only artists who have openly ever said anything concrete about being gay or bisexual have been David Bowie, Marc Bolan, Tom Robinson and myself — and Robinson has been the only one who has come out and admitted to being 100 percent homosexual, which is a very brave step.

"But then he's got nothing to lose. . . . "

Elton didn't wed for kids, as numerous gay stars have, nor did he entirely shun a non-hetero image. His messages have been mixed. He told *Creem*, pre-Renate, "I've not had one bitter thing aimed against me. No hate mail . . . I don't think people care. . . . In America, it's slightly different. I've had more people insult me in the streets in America . . . and yet America's supposed to be the great liberated free-minded society—which of course it isn't. . . . I couldn't ever live there."

In 1982 he produced *Elton John's Visions*, a 13 ½ minute video featuring three songs, including "Elton's Song," described in a gay video brochure as "a lyrical, dreamlike homage to adolescent gay love. This obscure piece is a glowing moment in gay film history." There were subsequent sexist hits like "Wrap Her Up" and "Nikita," with their corresponding videos. Yet overall, his video image is neither straight nor gay, but celibate, or at times voyeuristic. Elton has written for Tom Robinson, but the anticipated duet never happened. Asked if he'd ever write a song like Robinson's "Glad To Be Gay," he answered:

"I don't know. . . . There's a lot of things I want to say, but it's a question of collecting my thoughts. I'm just disgusted that people build up preconceived ideas about things, and it's their parents' faults because from a very early age they're inbred with a bias or a hatred against something or somebody."

That was also pre-Renate, but in 1986 Elton joined Dionne Warwick, Gladys Knight and Stevie Wonder to sing "That's What Friends Are For," which raised over $1 million against AIDS. And in 1990 he canceled his appearance on the International Rock Awards show on TV when he learned that hate-comic and professional homophobe Sam Kinison was co-hosting. (Bowie and Adam Ant did not cancel.) He then relented, and used the occasion to publicly voice his pretaped opinion of Kinison:

"I do this under protest. Sam Kinison is the first pig to ever host a rock 'n roll show . . . I hope in the future the producers will get someone decent, instead of an (bleeped)."

It would seem that Elton John is a rock star for all reasons. But he's still standing, and for better and worse, he still fascinates. Recently, when Sir John Gielgud received a Variety Club award, he mused, "I thought about what I contributed towards variety—and the only important thing is I danced with Elton John." O lucky man—and vice versa.

"Glad To Be Gay"

How come British singers and thespians tend to come out more routinely than their Hollywood counterparts?

Cyril Ritchard is best remembered as *Peter Pan*'s Captain Hook. ("My singing isn't really as bad as it sounds.") His least typical role was a rapist in Hitchcock's "Blackmail," Britain's first talkie. He once apprised Cole Porter, "You Americans always assume Englishmen are queer anyway—the way we talk, our good manners, . . . So we can get away with more. And do. . . . "

George Rose appeared in several Broadway musicals, among them *Peter Pan*, *My Fair Lady*, *Coco* and *Drood*. He told *Gay Times* magazine, "Bravery is an individual thing which crops up here and there . . . I just read *Private Domain* by Paul Taylor (American dancer-choreographer). It's amazingly frank about his sundry bisexual affairs! On the other hand, Winston Churchill long ago went to bed with Ivor Novello just to see what it was like. How many men would dare satisfy their curiosity like that?"

The British Are Coming!

(In Churchill's case, it probably wasn't the first time. His mother used to tell friends that young Winston had had affairs with older men. In older age, Churchill denied this. But he did admit the Novello fling to W. Somerset Maugham. According to Maugham's biographer Ted Morgan, when Maugham asked Churchill what it was like bedding the handsome musical star, Sir Winston succinctly replied, "Musical!")

Influential gay theatre critic James Agate once wrote, "We British behave differently on our own island than overseas. There, we often behave outrageously—or rather, outlandishly . . . !" True enough, many eccentric Englishmen were better tolerated—precisely because so alien and not reflective of their host country—on Broadway or even in Hollywood. Ritchard, Rose and Jack Buchanan never publicly came out, but Buchanan admitted, "I was frequently challenged to prove my manhood in my own country, particularly as a trembling youth."

Past middle-age, Buchanan—who'd worked with Bea Lillie in the famed Charlot revues—found that his florid manner fit him like a glove. As in the role of campy Jeffrey Cordova, whose fruitiness in 1953's *The Band Wagon* makes Fred Astaire look butch by comparison. "I could not have played Cordova twenty years ago," said Buchanan, with double meaning behind his words.

Until his death by drugs in 1978, the Who's Keith Moon was the world's most famous drummer after Ringo Starr. Upon enacting a "bent" costume designer in Mae West's *Sextette*, he daringly told *Motion Picture*, "I like film roles which reflect different aspects of me personality. . . . I got into rock because it's a lot like playing dress-up." Back in Blighty he was less bold. In print anyway. The posthumous bio *Full Moon* depicted him not as gay or bi, but a lovable transvestite and rabble-rouser.

He was both those things, but also gay, as insiders readily conceded. In the 1975 *Tommy* he played "dirty" Uncle Ernie who reads *The Gay News*. As per *Full Moon*, Pete Townshend of the Who would playfully call him "you cunt," while Moon affected Noel Coward's "dear boy" when addressing dear boys. The British press relished illustrating articles about Moon's adventures on the road with a pal named Barry the Poof and Barry's boyfriend, a transvestite, but laid special emphasis on Moon's penchant for trashing hotel rooms.

183

Full Moon recounted how Keith supposedly decided on certain days "that today he is a poof. . . . He frequently takes it into his head to act the ginger beer (Cockney rhyming slang for queer), especially if he can get hold of a dress or two." For the benefit of non-Cockneys, the bio appended a glossary of names for the male member like "mutton javelin" and "pork sword," and the sex euphemism "third-leg exercise."

Marc Bolan (né Feld) died one year before Moon, in a car crash. In 1968 the former '50s child star founded T. (originally Tyrannosaurus) Rex. With partner Steve Took, Bolan's folk-flavored rock duo achieved a cult following in England. In 1969 Took was replaced by Mickey Finn, and in the '70s T. Rex became Bolan backed by various musicians.

"For a long time, I was afraid of success," said Bolan in the mid-'70s, "because I thought it might amplify my personality too much and bring my secrets to the fore." The singer-guitarist-composer-poet handled his success and fear of exposure by making himself known as bi (he wed twice). With hits like "Hot Love," "Ride a White Swan," "Get It On" and "20th Century Boy," T. Rex conquered America too and grew more rock-oriented.

Like Bowie, Bolan was as renowned, or "notorious," for his Look and Persona as for his LPs. "I know I'm too 'off' to be 'in' with the squares, even most kids. . . . But with the future running in all directions, ya never know." Nor did potential Bolan fans, for in 1977 he was killed while being driven by wife No. 2, American singer Gloria Jones. Sic transit Marc.

Rock group Queen's original gimmick, as proclaimed on album jacket sleeves, was "no synthesizers!" There was also the name, which gave many critics pause. The lead singer was Freddie Mercury, who'd run an antique clothes stall in London and was noted for his shrill vocals. Songs like "Killer Queen" and "Bohemian Rhapsody" rejected traditional rock formulas yet became international hits. Mercury bragged, "Nothing is typical of my work." An atypical Queen hit was "Another One Bites the Dust," because it wasn't written by Mercury; friend Michael Jackson had urged Freddie to release the future hit single.

Queen's heyday was the '70s, when they could often claim "We Are the Champions." In 1981 a collaboration with David Bowie, "Under Pressure," cracked the Top 30—just—and band members began trying their own solo projects, including Mercury's album *Mr. Bad Guy*. Freddie also created a distinct video persona by donning a leather skirt in *I Want To Break Free!* and a black leather bra and drag in *The Great Pretender*.

Tom Robinson came right out and sang "Glad To Be Gay." Naturally, the song didn't get radio play, and his forthrightness and lack of coy libertinage got him grounded off the musical mainstream. Gay pride undergirded his compositions, and Robinson refused to divert his fans' minds from his affectional and sexual orientation. Far into the '80s, he declared in song, "It isn't the bride that I want to kiss!" when his former drummer-boyfriend chose to take a wife.

In 1989 "the original earnest gay rocker" reformed his band, TRB, a decade after their last hit, and toured Britain with a new song, "Hostage," about AIDS, while preparing for a new album. The dawn of the '90s found Robinson living with a woman, but to his credit he didn't recant—and he would have been universally and gladly believed by the mainstream if he had. He asserted in Ireland's *Hot Press* while trying for his big comeback, "I continue to count myself as gay."

Great Scott

"Scott" is a rock star, now past 40, "really actually heterosexual" in his own strictly-off-the-record label words. He's had more than his share of gay liaisons, but these have been hidden from view by himself and the press, which dotes on his not-so-bad-guy image, since he's had blondes, marriage, blondes, kids and more blondes.

In a borrowed posh flat in London's Knightsbridge, Scott — —half-stoned but "in full control of me thoughts"—shares a few anonymous answers to my questions.

H: Would you have come out as bi, pre-AIDS?
S: No! Because . . . no.
H: Because you're more straight than gay?
S: (nods hesitantly) What they think is, bi means you do it one night with a bloke, next night with a bird, then with a bloke

again. Nobody's 50-50, though——I bloody defy you, Boze, to find one.

H: Everyone has an inherent predisposition?

S: You know it.

H: And many people also think "bi" is a codeword for gay?

S: That's even more like it.

H: Do you think Tom Robinson didn't make the big-time because he said he's gay?

S: It didn't bloody 'elp 'im, did it?

H: Bowie's and Elton's bi admissions didn't hurt their sales much, did they?

S: They didn't?

H: I heard Elton lost some sales in America, but not much. I doubt his paying fans felt they'd been duped. Unlike Rock Hudson, say, he wasn't selling hetero fantasies.

S: . . . Me, I got kids to think of, and it's not really me——the escapades with the lads. It *happens*, but I don't pre-plan it. I don't go out cruising, and when I do feel a sexual urge, there's always a bird around, handy.

H: Americans seem to expect more visual flamboyance from British rockers. I always thought Tom Robinson came across more like an English Springsteen.

S: Is that a question, mate?

H: No, an observation. Sorry. But am I right in assuming that visual flamboyance, while it attracts attention, also creates sexual rumors?

S: There's been little whispers 'bout me right from the start. The very start, Boze. That's why, even if I was Tom Robinson, I'd have the birds gather 'round me.

H: So you feel a bi image would have hurt your career?

S: (fidgets) Wouldn't be true, either. An' I 'ave this sex symbol reputation——I'm what everyone, all the working-class blokes on both sides of the pond, wants ta be like.

H: And you need to be liked by everyone?

S: I bloody don't want to be hated!

H: Of course by "everyone" you mean straights?

S: Yeah. Didn't mean to leave out the gays, but ya do go for the biggest numbers.

H: Like a politician. . . .

S: (stunned, then:) Oy 'ope not!

H: Do you still have the odd gay affair?

S: What 'appens is, it's mostly three-o's now. Once in a while it's me and me bird and some bloke—nothin' heavy-duty. Safe, like the posters say. I'm not against doin' it wif men, but I like birds better. . . . I just wouldn't want someone to tell me, 'ere, ya can't have but one or the other, mate. That's fer me to decide, and it's like wif anyone else —I 'ave me moods and me varying tastes. Everyone does. Only wif me, bein' free and creative, I don't try and stifle meself.

H: So you honestly are basically hetero?

S: Honestly. Why would I lie in a situation like this 'ere?

H: In your opinion, are American singers more uptight about exploring the full range of their sexuality?

S: Boze, you should know! Even if yer not a singer. Yeh, eye think so.

H: Why?

S: Why? Dunno . . . I think we're closer to our mates 'ere. Men 'ang about wif other men. It's the lads—we like each other better. We 'ave wives and girlfriends, but in this country we 'ang around wif our mates and drink and get inta mischief. Over in the States, it's the guy what sits 'ome with the wife, right? The women got more power over there. Which is okay if ya wanna live that way.

H: Do you think it's good for the public to know which gay stars are gay?

S: . . . Think so. *Sure.* I'm not ashamed o' bein' bleedin' 'eterosexual. Why not?

H: Have the rumors of your bisexuality bothered you?

S: I don't like it if they think I don't like birds. That bothers me. But if they think I like blokes too, where's the 'arm? Why not? Anyway, I can't prevent it.

H: Who do you think has more suspicions about you— your male or female fans?

S: The birds! But . . . lemme get this right: (slowly) Blokes don't think about it. Don't want to. Birds is always wondrin'— 'bout everything. (giggles) But they won't always 'fess up, and the truth is, s' long as they don't think you're real poofy, birds get excited when a bloke ain't all macho-full-of-it. The women what fantasize about me most write in about me 'air and earrings, an' I'm still gettin' mail where birds send me their undies to wear on and off o' the stage. "Wear it in bed," some of 'em tells me! Birds don't really mind if a man's a bit fancy, s' long as they 'ave a chance at goin' t' bed with ya.

H: Sort of like straight men who don't mind if an actress or singer is bi, so long as she's also amenable to men?

S: Wha' it is, Boze, is nobody really cares that much what the opposite sex does, s' long as they come across in the end. But everyone gets antsy-like if their own sex don't act like they're supposed ta.

H: I suppose there's something to that.

S: It's all true, mate. I got the ruddy letters ta prove it—only, no one's ever gonna read 'em but me!

"It's Not Unusual"

Rumors traditionally abound about the sexuality of beautiful actors (Rock, Tyrone, etc.), English actors (regardless what they look like!) and most male singers. I had a friend in Santa Barbara, Calif., who swore up and down that Tom Jones "must" be gay. Jim had two reasons. "He's so masculine, and nobody's completely masculine or feminine. They're both acts." And "He's the world's biggest sex symbol (at the time), but you never see him paired up with bimbos or starlets."

Knowing how most gay actors deliberately pair with b. or s., I knew the latter wasn't much of a reason, and didn't necessarily believe then or now that Jones is gay or bi, though as his big hit song said, "It's Not Unusual."

There were a few scattered rumors about Engelbert Humperdinck, Jones' principal rival. Probably because "The Hump" was English, sexy and romantic—although born Arnold George Dorsey in India. In 1988 he rehashed for *Beverly Hills (213)* the days in the 1960s and '70s when bras and underwear were thrown at him as he performed on stage. "I didn't care for that too much. It kind of annoyed me." Pause. "Because they never fit me . . . Such a waste."

The same year, the *Hollywood Kids*' "'After the Loving' Dept." rued, "Oh, the pitfalls of being a Vegas ballad singer . . . Take poor Engelbert Humperdinck. Seems he fired a sexy dancer in his show because she was just too tall. 'No way,' claims the dancer. She's suing, claiming sexual harassment. In fact, making a lurid story even more so, when the dancer took the witness stand she told the court that Engelbert was AC/DC and was having a torrid affair with the man who has been blow-drying his hair for the past seven years!" (The hairdresser denied it.)

Jones and Humperdinck were managed by promoter Gordon Mills, whose third superstar "creation" was Gilbert O'Sullivan. The Irishman debuted in 1970 and ensorcelled legions of fans with songs like "Alone Again, Naturally" and "Clair," and his Lancelot-like beauty and frequently exposed hairy chest. Five-foot-seven, brown-haired with eyes of blue, Gilbert idolized Cole Porter and was born Raymond O'Sullivan. Reportedly, the name change was designed to evoke the classy Gilbert & Sullivan—of whom Sir Arthur was of course gay.

A 1973 *After Dark* interview indicated how in demand and closely guarded O'Sullivan was. "Not only do you have to have your credentials verified, you also have to prove your faith, your belief and your good intentions. Then, audience granted, you are told how long you can stay in the revered presence and of course he will be chaperoned. Photographs must be taken by his photographer—in private."

After a few top albums, notably *Back To Front*, rumors began swirling 'round the world that Gilbert was gay. He avoided stage and concert appearances and informed journalists, "It is all an act, really," about his cool. "I am very nervous, and people keep telling me I'll become an ulcer case." Whether because of his management or otherwise, O'Sullivan kept changing his look; unlike Jones and Humperdinck, his fans weren't mostly women over 30. The singer-composer appealed to fickle teenyboppers, among others, and seemed surprised that people would write "saying they want hairs" from his chest "and offer other interesting ideas that he is too bashful to mention."

He disclosed, "I like to wear clothes that can't be bought everywhere. I want clothes that are original and unusual," e.g., suede suits, boutique sportswear and "girls' duffel coats, because the men's don't come in such bright colors." In interviews, he divulged little about himself, more about his wardrobe. "My biggest buzz was buying an army surplus Hussar's suit for five pounds. I thought I looked fantastic in it——very proud of it I was."

Then he vanished from the music scene, a beautifully dressed memory still laced with speculation.

Another singer with a gentle, flower-powered image was Donovan, the "Mellow Yellow" folksinger who crooned the quietly defiant "To Try For the Sun," his own composition about sleeping with "the Gypsy boy." As a child, he ran away from home a few times. Later, "I would spend my time in the record stores——hanging out, reading Buddhism, hunting for rare albums." At 14 he formed his own group, and then was tagged "the British Dylan." Shaking that label, he became the thinking person's sex symbol and chief conveyor of musical peace and love.

In a 1976 *Playgirl* he explicated, "The most important thing I've communicated to people is the feminine principle. Early in my career I made musical statements containing words that were regarded as feminine. The word 'beauty' coming from a male singer in 1964 was considered less than masculine.

"My big appeal to women was never totally sexual. It was because the way I looked at life, both musically and spiritually, was from the point of view of the female."

More soporific was Cliff Richard, who never won the U.S. market but made an impact in pre-rock Britain, with much the same G-rated relationship to the Beatles as Pat Boone had to Elvis in America. As *The Advocate* put it, Richard "became a 'born-again' Christian at about the time that the Beatles stole the pop charts out from under him." The singer born Harold Webb was quoted in 1989 in *Nostalgia* magazine re the persistent "silly rumors" about homosexuality, due to his remaining single and living with his manager. Said Richard, "Look at the Pope . . . !" Ah, but he doesn't live with *his* manager.

Brian Epstein was gay. Brian Epstein's favorite Beatle was John Lennon. Ergo, there have long been rumors about Lennon's bi-ness. However, bisexuality is too subtle a distinction for a mass media which has yet to discover that "heterosexual" and "homosexual" are adjectives and not nouns. Biographer Albert "Elvis" Goldman was pilloried from coast to coast to British coast for remarking that Epstein fellated Lennon. True, Goldman has a skin as thick as hospital custard and can be mean-spirited

190

(even, surprisingly, homophobic), plus he suffers from faulty logic—he reasoned that the term "queer" would be more readily applied to Lennon via his being orally serviced than meatily javelined, which Lennon was prepared to let Epstein try.

Lennonites took more umbrage at Goldman's revelation of occasional bisexuality—which in their minds turned Lennon potentially gay—than at the star's detailed bigotries, i.e., anti-Semitism. Paul McCartney was furious; said Ed Sikov of the *New York Native*, "Goldman's allegation and the resulting scandal have taught me that Lennon in the middle-'60s was probably hipper and less homophobic than McCartney in the late-'80s."

Girlfriend May Pang, who entered Lennon's life after Epstein's death, was widely quoted by anti-Goldmanites as a definitive source on Lennon's sexuality. She admitted Goldman's material about her was "pretty much" accurate, but insisted Lennon was "as heterosexual as they come." Sikov:

"We've heard that line before. It's an exact repetition of Tammy Faye Bakker's laughable defense of her husband Jim. . . . Like Tammy, *Rolling Stone* isn't hip enough to see the difference between 'a homosexual,' someone who engages almost exclusively in homosexual acts because he or she prefers to do so, and 'homosexual acts,' which can be and are enjoyed by anyone regardless of overall sexual orientation."

'Nuff said?

Rod Stewart sang about gay-bashing way back when, in "The Killing of Georgie." But he was better known for fondling "Hot Legs" and wondering "Do Ya Think I'm Sexy?" However, the British tabs ran a far-out '80s story—barely repeated in America—that Stewart had blown so many rods during one alleged Wilde night that he subsequently had to have his stomach pumped for semen! Of course he sued.

The comelier the singer, the more persistent the rumors. And what was Duran Duran—named after a character in Jane Fonda's *Barbarella*—if not beautiful? At one point the world's leading band, DD was the *Charlie's Angels* of rock, with emphasis on hair and mascara. Their looks were as crucial as their music and videos to their global success, and when individual members contracted matrimony, the groom was invariably prettier than the bride. 'Twas said that DD's record sales began to plunge when singer Simon Le Bon's sleek looks were lost to too many bonbons. Sic transit anorexia.

Adam and the Ants weren't an insect avatar of the Beatles, but a vehicle for the mostly UK success of beautiful Adam Ant. In 1980 he didn't leave the group; rather, the group sort of left him. Sartorially taking up where Bowie had left off—though resembling a cute pirate more than a martian—Ant was reviled by reactionary critics. Pete Scott carped that "Adam himself was a lovely mover, albeit as faggy as hell." His material was varied, in albums like "Dirk Wears White Sox" and sado-glamour singles such as "Whip In My Valise."

One album's liner notes explained the visual impact Ant hoped to make in his self-designed Prince Charming Revue. "I wanted to make people feel the way I did when I saw the New York Dolls. . . . I'd gone about as far as I could with that makeup. It's a bit like Bowie after 'Aladdin Sane.'" Ant's greatest exposure wasn't via record but TV commercial, when he teamed with Grace Jones for a Honda ad—a stunning, and very odd couple.

Sadly, Britain supplies more than gender-benders and harmless rock trends to the world. Example: rock robots Dire Straits are noted for their pioneering anti-gay lyrics, specifically Mark Knopfler's homophobia in the 1985 megahit and award-winner "Money For Nothing," but also "Les Boys" and similar tunes. While these hate-supportive songs flooded British airwaves, the BBC—radio and TV—banned Pete Shelley's tame but pro-gay "Homosapien." The Beeb also refused to show the video of Olivia Newton-John's *Physical*, which ends with hand-holding hunks heading for the gym showers—no doubt a dangerous revelation, that men who work out are often or usually gay!

"Church of the Poison Mind"

In 1983 Culture Club exploded onto the American scene. The quartet's singer and mascot Boy George (George O'Dowd) quickly found that "Censure is the tax one pays for being famous." As was censorship, in some cases; Brigham Young (Mormon) University bookstores banned CC's records because they were mad about the Boy's drag. Yet was it really drag?

Unlike priests, say, BG always wore pants beneath the non-dresses. . . .

He also wore the pants in CC, which he formed with boyfriend Jon Moss, whom *RPM* magazine called "the second-best Jewish drummer in the biz," presumably after Ringo Starr. Rounding out CC were blond guitarist Roy Hay and black bassist Michael Craig. The group recorded two of their compositions in 1982, "White Boy" and "I'm Afraid of Me." Both flopped, but George pressed Virgin Records to let them release one more single, the reggae-flavored "Do You Really Want to Hurt Me?" A local reviewer called it "rather pathetic" and predicted that CC was doomed to failure because "listening to them is like being an embarrassed outsider at a lavender party."

Third-time lucky: "Hurt" zoomed to No. 1 across Europe, and the two "flops" were also incorporated into CC's debut album, *Kissing To Be Clever*, which bore more hit singles than any debut album since the Beatles. Its follow up *Colour By Numbers* was a bigger hit, with chart-busters like "Karma Chameleon," "Church of the Poison Mind," "It's a Miracle" and "Miss Me Blind." Whatever one thought of BG's eclectic and makeup-fueled Look, there was no denying his talent and charisma.

Thanks almost as much to his *haute couture* face as the hits he spun, BG became a star and a controversy, popping up everywhere—on TV, awards shows and magazine covers. Highly articulate, he was reticent only on the topic of his sexuality. When he guested on her nighttime talk show, Joan Rivers demanded, "Which do you like, boys or girls?" George grinned, "You, darling!"

"No, really," she pursued.

"Well, either one. . . . I don't really have time to think about that these days." Like Andy Warhol, he tried to curry favor not by denying the obvious, but claiming Work came First—and last.

Time considered him for their cover (they'd profiled several less successful singers) but decided he might queer newsstand sales. *Newsweek* put him on the cover, but not solo; he was "neutralized" by Eurhythmic Annie Lennox. Ironically, even though it was a hetero pairing, it was he who resembled a female, she a male. The gender-benders had arrived!

When *People* put BG on their cover, a record number of

defacings were reported in drugstores and supermarkets. Early articles on both sides of the Atlantic were moronic as well as malicious, with headlines like "Is It a Her? A Him—Or Neither?" and "I Don't Care If People Think I'm a Girl, Says Boy George." London's naive *Daily Express* deemed him "the most outrageous character since Elton John and Liberace."

Despite the slimelight, once BG's success was firmly established, he became more outspoken than ever. He talked back to hostile audience members on the Phil Donahue show and upbraided Barbara Walters when she misguidedly put him on the spot for not conforming to "Moral Majority"-ite Jerry Falwell's standards. "I wear makeup and I dress this way because it makes me look better. I'm not doing it to get people to stare at me. It's easy just to get attention."

Accused of cross-dressing, he snapped, "I wear Y-fronts! I'm a man. I'm quite manly, actually." And "Nobody's perfectly straight, you know. What a boring way to be if you're perfectly straight!" As a celebrity, he was asked his opinions of fellow celebs. On Marilyn Monroe: "She was a glorified transvestite." Andy Warhol: "He's an idiot, like a big cheesecake on legs." Prince: "He looks like a dwarf that fell into a vat of pubic hair." In 1987, amid escalating rumors of CC's imminent breakup, he told *Us* about his personal split with Jon Moss, "I'm not embarrassed about it. If he was ugly it might have embarrassed me, but he's cute."

(After the Fall, BG alleged that Moss, like all his prior lovers, was semi-closeted. He related to *The Advocate* that Michael Dunn, his beau of four years, was "the first I've had who says, 'I don't fancy women.' There isn't much you can say about me that hasn't been said already, so I figure I've gotten to the stage where honesty is the best policy. . . . I learned a lot from Jon, a so-called straight man. Like never to fall in love with someone who says he's heterosexual —ever.")

Predictably, Culture Club's third album wasn't as big a hit as its predecessors, though it did well. Its chief song and video was "The War Song," which promoted peace. "All war is stupid . . . and love means nothing in some strange quarters." On TV, George had to defend himself against "trying to entertain and impart a moral at the same time. But as a responsible individual on this planet, I feel I should speak out against the wrongs and injustices I see."

194

Increasingly politicized, he was willing to speak out against homophobia (reportedly alienating other CC members by doing so). "There's this illusion that homosexuals only have sex and heterosexuals fall in love." This and other indictments of the mass media were seldom reproduced there; most of BG's serious statements wound up solely in the gay press. He could easily have uttered Madonna's declaration, "I am a sexual threat," for he was, very much so, and his success worried millions. The general media tolerated him only so long as he was self-deprecating, sexually and politically neutral, and a trendy joke whom macho men could use to prove their evanescent masculinity.

Then came the drug arrest which often seems inevitable in the music world. But unlike for instance Paul McCartney's in Japan, which made him a hero/martyr in the West, George's drug bust was used against him like a lethal, career-killing weapon. Media and moralists manipulated it to invalidate his statements, his music, his band and the man himself. After his heroin conviction he was legally banned from the USA and thus unable to enter the country and promote his 1987 solo LP, *Sold*. It was a hit in Britain, where the single hit No. 1 (in the U.S. it peaked at 145 on *Billboard's* chart).

It would be a while before George was *persona grata* in America again, and to date—despite good material—record stores, radio stations, MTV and other media have minimized his chances of resurfacing as a popular solo star. Asked in Los Angeles during a 1990 concert appearance if he's bitter about his cultural banishment from the U.S., BG smiled and rhetorically asked, "Do you really want to hurt me?"

Back in England, he was off drugs, had taken up Buddhist chanting "to feel good about myself," and had toned down the makeup. He also shed twenty pounds and his dressy robes. "I was very conscious of being a blimp, and used to think I was everybody's fat friend. Especially when I got friendly with (transvestite singer) Marilyn, who was so beautiful." He explained, "The makeup and frocks were a way of hiding myself and sexually attracting straight men—that somehow made it okay for them."

George became more politically involved than ever, and in 1988 protested recent homophobic British legislation with his agit-rap song "Stop Clause 28." It opened with a denunciation of

195

Prime Minister Margaret Thatcher's "frump" frustrations and prejudices. UK radio stations refused to play it, and Virgin Records cut it from the U.S. version of BG's newest LP. Rock critic Adam Block stated, "There are rumors that George is being urged to curb his recent candor about being gay."

Speaking out at anti-28 rallies, BG repeated his comment about the illusion that gay people only have sex and then added, "People who aren't viewed as loving and whole are considered less than fully human, therefore more expendable. . . ."

Asked by American rock magazine *Spin* what he'd like to be reborn as, he replied, "Matt Dillon's underwear!" In late '88 he gave Briton Kris Kirk his most candid interview yet, revealing intimate sex habits and recalling his heyday between 1982-87, after which "the depraved-junkie headlines sparked off a media witch-hunt to rival that of Fatty Arbuckle."

George admitted to being influenced by boyfriend Michael Dunn, an "extremely hunky blond" who stood by him during his drug trials and urged him to "be completely open about my sexuality. . . . I was mentally closeted in a way, and I've decided I can't live like that anymore. I was never lying when I said I had affairs with women, but the main thing is that it's men I fall in love with and men I have serious relationships with."

Having synthesized his music and messages in solo LPs like *High Hat* and hit Euro-singles like "Everything I Own," Boy George attests, "Being a pop star used to be my lifestyle. Now it's my job. . . . I'm in this for the long haul, and if it takes time to work my way back to the top, so be it." Let's hear it for the Boy!

"I Want Your Sex"

Outside of Duran Duran, Wham!'s George Michael and Andrew Ridgeley were rock's most beautiful stars in the early '80s. Close chums George and Andrew had spent much of their growing-up time at Andrew's home near North London, where their record faves included Chic and Sylvester and their preferred musical genre was disco. Unlike many would-be singers who quit school early, the pair remained in school "so we'd have an excuse to stay at home and wouldn't have to go out to work, being lazy. We both knew that all we wanted to be was pop stars."

In 1982 their goal drew nearer via a hit called "Young Guns (Go For It)," about the foibles of early marriage. In '83 came "Bad Boys," and in '84 stardom was at hand with "Wake Me Up Before You Go-Go" from their enormously successful album *Make It Big*. Since inquiring teenyboppers wanted to know, the two were probed about their love lives. Critics wanted to know why George hung on to Andrew, since the former was not only the singer, but played most of the instruments, wrote most of the songs and produced almost all of them.

He retorted that there could be no Wham! without Andrew, but a year after vanquishing the U.S. market he chose to go solo. Fans and medians speculated about the reasons for the breakup and whether it was as amicable as represented. George Michael went on to single superstardom, while Ridgeley maintained a very low profile and became interested in car racing.

Michael's first single was 1987's"I Want Your Sex"— "terribly inappropriate in this time of AIDS!" Thirty percent of U.S. radio stations banned it, but the red-hot video amply displayed Michael's adonisian inheritance (he was born Georgios Panayiotou). There was much talk of Hollywood in his future, but so far Hollywood lies in the future, tense.

As his fame intensified, so did media scrutiny. First there were hints. One magazine noted that Wham!'s management company had been called No Miss. Another observed that the couple had been greatly inspired by Elton John; George assented, "I'm surprised his influence hasn't shown up more in my writing." *The Rolling Stone* asked point-blank, "Are you gay?"

"I've always thought that people speculated so much because I was so quiet about my private life, and secondly because I've always had a very ambiguous-sounding voice—I'm not exactly Springsteen. To listen to, you know . . . I've never been concerned with who was doing what with who in bed, you know? I've always thought that people ought to get on with what they're doing in their own beds." A far more courageous response than those proffered by the Hollywood contingent!

In June, '88, *Paris Match* reminded, "The English press said you're homosexual. If you were, would you say so?"

"I'd be crazy to say so, don't you think? But I won't contradict that further. Because to defend oneself signifies that one's ashamed of that if it's true. I have many bi and gay friends, and I believe in free choice in that area. But above all, I don't believe these interrogations should be, that they're an invasion of privacy. That's why I neither confirm nor deny any rumor concerning my private life."

Months later, Fox TV's *The Reporters* achieved its highest U.S. ratings of the year to date via an interview segment that led off with the question, "George, are you gay?" Michael had allegedly been informed that the tabloid-format show would air only in Australia, and was not forewarned about the Question (Fox belongs to Rupert Murdoch, who owns the *Sun* and other homophobic tabs). George acceded:

"Um, I've never said 'No.' I've never said, 'Yes, no I'm not.' In other words, I don't think it benefits anyone listening to music to know whether or not I was in bed with a dog or a man or a woman last night." Atta boy, George! He also told the breathless Aussie reporter that he'd used a "bottom-double" in his sizzling "I Want Your Sex" video.

Weeks later, the *Los Angeles Herald Examiner* reviewed a George Michael concert. "Michael dressed in tight-fitting black, stripping down as the evening went on to vest and pants and—no surprise—finally baring his (hairy) chest. . . . Still, one (dance) routine with a male member of his band does nothing . . . to support rumors that he might be heterosexual." The paper automatically assumed that pop stars without exception desire to be considered hetero.

Most of the press at one time or another linked Michael with a female, including some of his video co-stars (in 1991, *Us* assumed his heterosexuality and that he'd denied being gay, but Michael replied, "No, you'll have to find the place where I've denied it. . . . I've never denied it."). The newly totally candid Boy George must have objected to such coverage, for he publicly stated that George Michael was gay. Michael instructed the press, "I've always kind of liked him. I've always admired his strength of character. But I don't really call what he's been doing 'strength of character.'"

It may have started when Boy George commented that "Sleeping with Michael would be like having sex with a groundhog." He non-apologized, "It's just a joke, and if he can't see that, it's his problem." Or when he explained, "I got a message from

Aretha Franklin saying she'd love to do a song with me. Later, after she'd done the (duet) with George Michael, the *London Evening Standard* asked me if I thought she'd called the wrong George. I said, 'I think she banged on the wrong closet.' George got very upset about that."

BG told *The Advocate*, "If you go around covering up your tail so heavily, people are going to start wondering . . . what it is you've got to hide. That girl Pat Hernandez whom he's with was my fag hag for three years, and when I read the newspaper story 'How Pat Broke My Heart,' I was tempted to write one called 'How Pat Broke My Hoover.' Because the idea of her and George having a relationship is about as likely as my having sex with a door."

Now, now. Boys will be boys. Or as the late gay nutritionist Gaylord Hauser once said, "You are what you eat. . . . "

"I Want Your Love"

Throughout the '80s and after, Britain produced a steady stream of openly gay and crypto-gay acts. Alas, most of them— even those seemingly entrenched in the mainstream —thrived briefly before dissolving or regrouping. "The pressure of being so visible as an artist and persecuted by the press for being yourself is damned tough to bear," said an anonymous musician in *RPM*. Still, at least it was possible to become famous there and not have to engage in fool-the-public relations.

After Boy George, the most successful gay music act was Frankie Goes To Hollywood, which took its name from the title of a '40s fanzine article about singing sensation Frank Sinatra, who was Hollywood-bound. In 1984 FGTH became famous overnight with their smash debut double-disc *Welcome to the Pleasure Dome*. Its megahit single was "Relax," dubbed "the first love song ever addressed to an anus." The song stayed on the UK charts longer than any since the '60s, and in the U.S.— where its video was tamely reshot—it activated Congressional wives who tried to censor rock lyrics ("Relax . . . when you want to come") and to lump homosexuality with drugs, prostitution, rape and bestiality.

Frankie's lead singers were Paul Rutherford, the musta-chioed "clone in chaps," and Holly Johnson, "the goofy one." In their album's liner notes, Johnson wrote, "I enjoy certain things, no one else has to enjoy them. . . . Then again, no one has the right to tell me it's immoral or selfish or wrong to do what I do." Rutherford admitted, "I'm not cuddly all the time. I'm just myself. . . . I don't have an instrument, I don't have a great voice, I just have some nice clothes maybe."

When "Relax" became the fourth-biggest-selling single in history, Frankie was recognized as a marketing phenomenon and criticized not just for homoeroticism, but commercialism. *The Pleasure Dome* record sleeves boasted not only personal philosophy but an artful array of gay-oriented products for sale —Jean Genet Boxer Shorts, the Sophisticated Virginia Woolf Vest, Andre Gide Socks, the Sophisticated Charles Baude-laire Sweat Shirt and the Edith Sitwell Bag. FGTH t-shirts became the latest fad among rebellious British youth, gay and straight.

Paul and Holly, "leather boys from Liverpool," were the spokesmen for FGTH (whose three non-singers didn't identify as gay). As such, they were sought out for endless official state-ments in the Year of Big Brother. Their heroes? Paul credited Gene Kelly with inspiring him, while Holly lauded gay role mo-dels Andy Warhol, Greta Garbo, Montgomery Clift and James Dean.

The pair's politics were analyzed because of Frankie's hits "War" and "Two Tribes." The latter ("When two tribes go to war . . . ") pitted the USA against the USSR and blasted the Cold War's arms build-up. "War" featured a Reagan imitator yammer-ing to a disco beat about his revolutionary sympathies and admiration for Che Guevara, etc. FGTH were scrutinized more closely and given much more press in Britain than the U.S., where "Relax" was more of a controversy than a record-breaker. American gay activists lambasted Paul and Holly for downplay-ing their orientation in the American market. Debatably, Paul explained, "There's a lot more teenage girl fans than gay fans. . . . "

Frankie retreated from the impregnable U.S. market and eventually went their separate ways. Paul Rutherford subdued his act if not his sexiness and worked with Frye & White on singles like "Get Real" and "I Want Your Love." Holly Johnson, managed by his Austrian art-collector lover Wolfgang, came back with a yuppie image. His hit singles included "Love Train" and "Americanos," and his LP *Blast* entered British charts at Numero Uno. A gay fan described Holly's voice as "a blend of Elvis Costello and Connie Francis," while a detractor compared it to "Ethel Merman gargling a pink lady."

Britain's other top-mid-'80s gay band was Bronski Beat, a trio ignited by the Bee Gee-type falsetto of Glaswegian Jimmy Somerville and by his impish energy. The group's debut album in 1984 was titled *Age of Consent* because of Jimmy's ire over the unequal ages of sexual consent in the UK for straights (16) and gays (21). (In 1989 a Labour politician reintroduced a bill to equalize the ages of consent, but it was aborted by the Conservative-dominated Parliament.)

Consent's top single was "Why?", about gay-bashing, reportedly inspired by the violent death of a playwright friend of Jimmy's. Another song was "Smalltown Boy," about a gay lad who must leave home thanks to unloving, bigoted parents. And "Ain't Necessarily So," about "the things that you're liable to read in the Bible. . . " BB's videos, which also played MTV, were eye-openers for general audiences, depicting the illness called homophobia and nearly impossible to shrug off.

Unlike Culture Club or Frankie, Bronski Beat was neither glittery nor flamboyant, and all of its members were out— Jimmy, Larry Steinbachek and Steve Bronski. Top of the pops at home, they were scheduled to open on Madonna's American tour until Jimmy was arrested in London's Hyde Park for, as one American paper delicately phrased it, "lending an undercover officer the use of his throat" in a public lavatory. Jimmy departed BB in 1985 over creative and philosophical differences—a committed socialist, he was personally and professionally more politically active than Larry and Steve cared to be.

He joined with gay Richard Coles. The duo's first LP—as the Communards—sold 1.5 million copies in Europe. Their second was titled *Red* and dedicated to Mark Ashton, a politically active young socialist—one of its songs was inspired by Mark. MCA omitted the dedication on the American version's inner sleeve. Likewise, the U.S. *Age of Consent* had lacked the ages of consent chart for European countries, concerning gay sex, which was included on British sleeves. Said Coles, "I've found that such 'mistakes' cover a multitude of sins." (Another of *Red's* songs was composed by Somerville to a homoerotic poem by W.H. Auden titled "If I Could Tell You.")

Then Jimmy and Richard split, and Jimmy went solo, releasing occasional singles (e.g., a cover of Sylvester's classic "Mighty Real") and devoting himself to protests via ACT-UP (AIDS Coalition To Unleash Power). The star's involvement with ACT-UP helped move it into British headlines, for example after the obstruction of traffic in front of the Australian embassy because of that nation's unfair policy on HIV and immigration.

Jimmy, who once tried to commit suicide out of desperation over being an outcast, released his first solo LP in late '89. "Read My Lips" took its title from "the ACT-UP graphics that wed George Bush's punchline to photos of gay couples kissing." One of its singles, "Adieu," was a duet with Somerville's long-time drummer, June Miles-Kingston. Upon its release, he went to Paris to do a benefit concert for the new French chapter of ACT-UP. Another single's proceeds were earmarked for gay activist groups in smaller towns throughout England. Clearly, this singer puts his heart where his voice is.

Meanwhile, Bronski Beat went through various permutations, finally emerging—as of this writing—as a duo with Steve Bronski and gay vocalist Jonathan Hellyer, whom the L.A. *Times* rated as "campily charismatic" and "an exceptional singer." BB's latest collaboration was with Eartha "Cat Woman" Kitt on the campy "Cha Cha Heels." The single was backed with the "Peggy Lee-on-Thorazine ballad" "My Discarded Men."

"You Blow Me——Away"

Then there's the cool-as-peppermint Morrissey, whose voice often sounds as if he's profoundly moved to hear it there. "The poet laureate of the awkward, the outcasts and the terminally sensitive" became more famous for his self-proclaimedly drug-free, meat-free and sex-free lifestyle than for his output, which included an album frankly titled "Meat Is Murder."

But thanks to celibacy, he overlooked the important issue of AIDS, and in 1987 the Communards called him on it. Morrissey responded publicly in 1988. "I think that was Jimmy

Tattyhead, not Richard Coles. Richard is a very well-brought-up young man, but I'm not sure about Cilla Somerville. I really don't know what they mean."

Though allegedly gay—when not celibate—Morrissey disdained to ally himself with gay British groups or indeed any of his peers. In 1989 when the *New Musical Express* inquired, "Are there any contemporary acts that you feel at one with?" he quipped, "Not a living sausage." Asked about the importance of sex, he ejaculated, "Sex is humor to me!"

Even Boy George was puzzled. "I met Morrissey, and I don't understand his stand. I had lunch with him in Paris, and I still don't know if he's just another gabbling Oscar Wilde clone or if he really has something to say."

In early 1990 Morrissey was in America shooting a video in Death Valley—doesn't everyone? During an L.A. radio interview he reassured an "anxious" fan that he was still celibate after all these years, then congratulated his listeners on their "intelligence and good taste." He disappointed many by saying there definitely was no Smiths reunion in the works. Morrissey and The Smiths had emerged in 1983, instantly becoming known for their but mostly his uniqueness. And contradictions. Even Morrissey's visual messages were mixed.

On stage he wore plain-joe National Health Service glasses and a hearing aid. "He cultivates an interest in symbols of disability," wrote critic John Huston, "and his lyrics are riddled with references to illness . . . Irony exists in his presentation of himself as misunderstood and unlovable, since he is a strikingly handsome pop star adored by legions."

Early Smiths songs, as well as Morrissey's debut solo LP "Viva Hate," dealt repeatedly with unrequited love; the mournful "I Know It's Over" on the '86 LP *The Queen Is Dead* was vintage Morr. After The Smiths' breakup, he stressed celibacy to such a degree that sex became the focus of his act. Said *Christopher Street*, "He uses asexuality to be in fact hypersexual," warbling about chastity "while removing his shirt strip-tease fashion and indulging in Presley-esque hip swivels."

Lyrically, Morrissey's also ambiguous. Most of his love songs can be sung to either gender. However, titles like "Sweet and Tender Hooligan," "Suedehead," "Last of the International Playboys," "Lucky Lisp" and "Michael's Bone" indicate an orientation stronger than mere ambiguity or disinterest. During his concerts he permits dozens of handsome youths—what he calls "natural specimens"—to leap one at a time onto the stage and kiss their plaintive idol or drape themselves across his shoulders.

Nonetheless, Morrissey has denied gay influences in his work and even denies that he has a gay following! (It certainly exists, but perhaps said following is itself closeted and therefore hard to find. . . .) *Christopher Street* pointed out, "One mustn't lose sight of the fact that his protestations against gay associations help him sell more records. Yet there's simply no denying that the furtive themes of many Morrissey lyrics and the beautiful male figures that grace many Smiths albums evoke a distinctly gay sensibility."

For all his caution, which seems primarily directed at the U.S. market, Morrissey is much more popular in Britain, where he has a hardcore cult following and where the press bemusedly but faithfully covered his "platonic but romantic friendship" with singer Pete Burns. In the late-'80s their androgynous courtship was hailed by some as a should-be role model for young gay men, as the singers exchanged flowers, candy and poetry, but no more—except mutually profitable headlines. Morrissey also garnered publicity for vegetarianism and himself by sending the Queen Mother a bouquet of vegetables on her birthday.

Pete Burns, lead singer of Dead Or Alive, was called "a bargain-basement Boy George" and was more notable for his startlingly girlish videos than the monotonous tunes he intoned. One adamant TV viewer in Bug Tussle, Texas, wrote his local paper to excoriate music video programs for airing "the likes of Death [sic] Or Alive and other anti-man rock sissies who corrupt our children's minds." The town father declared that he was "old-fashioned and proud of it. . . . I firmly believe women should be put on a pederast." Is that a Freudian slip or what?

Dead Or Alive's last video of the '80s, "Come Home With Me, Baby," was banned by the BBC for "homoerotic content and frank sexuality." Same with their song "I Don't Want To Be Your Boyfriend." A UK critic complained that their *Nude* LP was "an open celebration of a promiscuous gay lifestyle." Pete Burns flamed back, "If I say, 'Stick A Condom On It, Baby,' they still won't play it on the radio because you can't say 'condom'!

The British Are Coming!

"So what can you do?"

A song title like "You Blow Me——Away" would likely pass the BBC review board if the male singer aimed it at a theoretical female listener. For, as Kitchens of Distinctions's gay feminist singer Patrick Fitzgerald said, "Eighty percent of rock is either cock-thrusting or its female opposite cock-receiving." But when "You Blow Me——Away" is sung by openly gay Paul Lekakis, problems of perception and censorship arise more quickly than a celibate sex symbol's erection.

(Most banned songs have only a half-life, but one which was born again was 1982's "Homosapien," "the best gay dance 12-inch ever," according to Adam Block. Seven years later it came back as "Homosapien II" via Pete Shelley, who with ex-boyfriend Steve Diggle had headed the seminal pop-punk band The Buzzcocks. The group, which released its final LP in 1979, decided to re-form in time for the Gay '90s. Their old record company promised reissues of their complete catalogue.)

After three distinctive, well-received singles, the South London trio Kitchens of Distinction came out (in their lyrics too) with a 1989 debut LP, *Love Is Hell*. KoD looks to have an impact on both gay and straight fans, for their material isn't exclusively gay but neither do they avoid gay themes. "In A Cave" is a love-sex fantasy set in a cave on the moon where the planets are seen orbiting 'round. The haunting fantasy is available to either sexuality and to thin, fat or in-between——"Forget your fat/it's a pillow soft for my head."

"Four Men" has Patrick musically noting, "It's too much——strong men are too enticing/ . . . Here I lie between his thighs/ looking up into his eyes, wondering if this is allowed/ . . . It takes my lust and strength to say/'I want you. I need you!'" The LP's "Hammer" is simultaneously exhilarating and frightening and deals with gay sex and the possibility of AIDS——an emotional, educational experience for straight listeners too.

But again, public access to this young and auspicious band is limited by a mass-only media which bans the lovestyles of ten percent of its recipients. Naked sexual honesty in hetero lyrics is more tolerated than ever, but when Kitchens of Distinction cantillate "I want to melt inside you," those in charge——straight and closeted alike——censor away the gay reality. And are allowed to do so. Thus far.

"A Little Respect"

Neil Tennant and Chris Lowe, the Pet Shop Boys, became Britain's leading synth duo in the mid-'80s. Against the odds, too, for neither was pop star material—great-looking, glamorous, funny, articulate or even cheerful. Plus Tennant's voice was described by one UK mag as "thin, colorless and characterized by a boyish lisp." Supposedly, the PSB don't perform live because of his voice.

Yet between 1985 and '88 they spawned nine consecutive Top 20 hits, becoming MTV staples with their hypnotic brand of Euro-pop. Their dour but memorable songs include "West End Girls," "You Were Always On My Mind," "Get Away With It," ... The hooks are typically strong, the lyrics weak. Said "RPM," "They don't write songs so much as eat alphabet soup, spit out a few words, then requote them over and over."

In their videos, the wan twosome mostly watch others, with Tennant expressionlessly sing-commenting his single thought about the proceedings. During a concert stay in Los Angeles, Neil and Chris visited Studio One, the West Coast's leading gay disco, and were reported to have "stood meekly on the sidelines, amid their own kind but observing like visitors from Mars."

Their 1987 debut film, *It Couldn't Happen Here*, similarly cast them as "casual observers of events past and present as they travel through England in search of their destiny." Re *Films & Filming*, "The movie's target audience is anyone's guess. PSB fans will last about twenty minutes before walking out. Practically everyone else will not be interested in seeing a film starring them." F&F predicted the picture would go the way of the Beatles' '60s *Magical Mystery Tour*—"vilification and failure followed by rediscovery in 20 years' time and instant attainment of cult classic status."

The ambitious pair also branched out into comebacks for songbirds with sizeable gay followings. i.e., they collaborated with Dusty Springfield on a razzmatazz song and video, wrote for Liza Minnelli and were rumored to be prepping a song for diva *emeritus* Petula Clark.

In early '88 Erasure's openly gay singer Andy Bell recalled "running into" the PSB and "asking them things about being gay, and Neil said he thought the reason Erasure hadn't made it in America yet was because of my being out." He continued, "It was at a gay club in Munich. We were both in town for a TV show. I hitched a ride back in their limo, and they were joking about the gay pop establishment in Britain, casting it as a private girls' school. They had Elton John as headmistress, Freddie Mercury as head-girl, and all of us—Jimmy Somerville, me, them, Boy George, etc.—as the pupils."

Bell was asked if the duo had "loosened up" a bit about their sexuality?

"Well I *hope* they have. Perhaps they're realizing that you don't have to be as uptight as they've been, that you can say things and no one is going to lock you away for it."

Pre-'80s, there was no gay pop establishment in Britain, only a few stars whose headlines bannered bisexuality but whose lyrics and subsequent actions supported the sexual status quo. During the '80s a generation of gay singers born, like the gay rights movement, during the '60s came onto the stage and out of closets which most hadn't inhabited for long. They and the now-emerging gay artists of British pop-rock will be the unambiguous stars of international '90s hits which will remind gay and mass audiences that gays exist and are people, not pariahs.

Of course there'll always be the push and pull between gay stereotypes and the greater number of unflamboyant and so less visible gay men. "But between us we represent the diversity and strength of gay life," says gender-bender Marc Almond, who can resemble the boy next door or a sailor more into eyeliner than ocean liners. Almond's material ranges from emotionally deep to physically high, from "A Lover Spurned" to "Mother Fist." Andy Bell found him to be "an inspiration:"

"I feel strongly about some gay lyrics, like 'Smalltown Boy,' but also seeing Almond on *Top of the Pops*. He was so camp. I thought, What nerve! I remember him taking these dark glasses off and having all this mascara and eyeliner on, and I thought, This is so amazing—in front of all these people, on TV. Things like that I find intense and affecting."

Newer acts include the blond trio Big Fun, whose gayness is strictly interior and whose handsome looks eased their ascension into teenybopper hit-heaven and shocked the general media into graceless headlines. In September, '89, *The People* trumpeted, "Gay Shame of Teeny Heartthrob Jason," about the group's lead singer. The shame was entirely the tacky tabloid's, which darkly admitted that the other two boys in the band, Mark Gillespie and Phil Creswick, are lovers.

Six weeks later, Big Fun—flush with the success of their LP *Handful of Promises*—sashayed onto the nationally televised *Smash Hits* Readers' Poll Awards Show wearing James Dean black leather jackets. They performed "Blame It On the Boogie" and accepted their award for Best New Act. A majority of Big Fun's record buyers may be teenaged girls, but thanks to *The People* and *anal*ogous periodicals most of them probably knew that the three hunks were glad to be gay.

Adam Block watched Big Fun at the awards ceremony and deplored the mostly non-UK music scene in which gays and lesbians all too often deny their affectional identities. "It's guys like Almond, Somerville and Bell, and gals like Phranc and Williamson, who stand as singing shock troops in the war against pop invisibility. Theirs are the faces and voices I want to find on the Grammy awards show—while Michael Jackson with Chastity Bono on his arm gazes uncomprehending from the balcony. Yeah, we can dream."

Andy Bell grew up in a small town in England where "I used to fear getting beaten up for my sexuality. Now I use it as a weapon. I haven't done enough, but I'm still coming out in my music." At 19 Bell beat out forty-hopefuls auditioning to sing with famous musician-songwriter Vince Clarke, the avowed heterosexual who'd founded Depeche Mode, Yaz, and The Associates. Four years later, Erasure produced two of 1988's outstanding pop(ular) songs, "A Little Respect" and "Chains of Love."

They won the BPI Award (Britain's Grammy) for Best Group of 1988, and "Respect" was nominated for Best Contemporary Song via the lofty Ivor Novello Awards. The songs also penetrated the Top 20 on U.S. charts. In November, they headlined a sold-out show for 30,000 in London, later telecast throughout Europe.

In 1989 the blond duo's LP "Wild" entered UK charts at No. 1, and their triumphant European tour was choreographed by Michael Clark, the "gay bad boy of British dance." Later in the year they became the first openly gay act to sell out California's 18,000-seat Great Western Forum. "Frontiers" called it "one mixed marriage that works—gay vocalist Andy Bell and straight keyboardist Vince Clarke."

"I told Vince at the outset that I was gay, that I wouldn't hide being gay." Clarke became Bell's "ally," and they performed at several gay benefits in the UK. Thanks to Bell's electric and playful presence and costumes, their concerts were campy, even homoerotic. Andy admitted, "There's a lot of Erasure's popularity that's built around not just the gay thing, but the camp elements in the show."

Their LPs, starting in '86 with *Wonderland,* are more mainstream, non-controversial. In 1987, when they opened for Duran Duran, they were told DD was "worried about what our act was like. There was talk that Vince and I are too close. Since it's a 'gay act'—since I'm flamboyant—they assume Vince and I are lovers." Many Erasure fans jump from assuming that both members are straight to assuming they're lovers.

Andy clarifies, "He lives with his girlfriend and I live with my boyfriend." There's also been pressure to tone down the act "for TV, in videos. That's why I'm usually in t-shirts and jeans, unlike live concerts . . . But record companies are realizing more that it really is a powerful marketing force to have something that's unusual."

Edge magazine asked Bell to what he attributes his considerable following among young Americans? "I don't know if a lot of people do know I'm gay. I'm sure they know because I say things about it in interviews. But there's not been much information about Erasure in the States yet. They know in England that I'm gay—it's all they talk about."

Andy revealed that Jimmy Somerville had come up to him, "took me aside and said, 'You're the one carrying the flag at the moment,' which I thought was really good. I've always felt that of all the contemporary gays, even though I'm the person who's not really shouting about it, I'm gonna have the most effect on everyday people. I've always believed that, and still do.

"I want to make things easier for other gay artists . . . It's always important to let people know you're gay. I wish people could just wake up . . . I've seen programs on TV where a guy of 80 is coming out, and crying—because he's wasted 80 years of

209

his life. I don't want to be the kind of person that has to go around conducting his life in secret."

Erasure's songs present a less gay image than Bell would eventually like. "We compromise, but sometimes Vince objects to a certain lyric if it's leading to a gay love song, though he doesn't say *that's* why he doesn't like it . . . We've done benefits to fight AIDS and Clause 28, and played gay clubs and plan to do an American Gay Pride Parade. So we're both still evolving, and I'm challenging people's preconceptions on the stage.

"I want to shatter that silly rule that says you can be openly gay or a pop star but not both . . . Right now, because times are tough in Britain, it's time to come out and say in our own strong voices, 'That's enough! We're not going to take this anymore.'

"Like I tell our audience, 'All it needs is "A Little Respect."'"

Bring On the Dancing Boys

"What is success? A toy balloon among children armed with pins." —Charlie Chaplin

Games

Dancing. So basic, it's what one does when there's nothing else to do. No matter where, no matter who. Example: Michael Caine told *European Travel & Leisure* magazine about the 1975 filming of *The Man Who Would Be King*, with Sean Connery. "We were in this little town on the edge of the Sahara, and there was nothing to do at night except go to this disco.

"But it was all men dancing with men because women weren't allowed out at night. So we're standing at the bar, watching all these guys dancing, when Sean leans over and says to me, 'Do you mind if I dance with your driver? Mine's too ugly.'"

But there's dancing, and there's dancing. Men who do it for a living are suspected of being actually non-heterosexual! Even nowadays. When Ronald Reagan ran for national office in 1980, he had to divest himself of his son's career. Ron Reagan Jr. gave up the ballet and, to complete the turnabout of public image, took up a wife (no children as of this writing; more later about The President's Son—which was also the title of a late-1980s gay *roman à clef*).

Edward Villella, former principal dancer with the New York City ballet, once boasted, "It takes more strength to get through a six minute *pas de deux* than four rounds of boxing."

213

On TV, the admittedly heterosexual *danseur* described his lectures to urban school kids, manually illustrating how a fist unclenching "resembles a flower, blossoming."

Dancer-choreographer Bob Fosse explained, "I'm not sure who does more apologizing for being a dancer—straights or gays ... I stopped making excuses when I became a film director. That's a really paternalistic image, a director. It helped me feel really comfortable about my whole dance background. And don't think I don't know that's dumb!"

Because of dance's rigid sex roles, it's frequently a case of homosexual artists presenting heterosexual views of life and thus, in the words of *Dance Magazine* editor William Como, "supporting the sexual status quo. To put it another way, most gay dancers work for 'the enemy.'" Or "the heterosexual dictatorship," as Christopher Isherwood called it—"that 90 percent of society which demands and usually gets 100 percent of the credit, influence and say-so."

Then as now, this practice is fostered almost as much by gay creative and interpretive artists as heterosexual ones. "We bow to the status quo sometimes without even realizing it," said Como, pointing to the celebrated ballet *Jeux:*

Shortly after the 1911 coronation of George V (who believed gay men ought "to shoot themselves"), Vaslav Nijinsky appeared in London with Sergei Diaghilev's Ballets Russes de Monte Carlo. The pair were the toast of Mayfair, invited by one hostess after another to luncheons and soirées. At her Bedford Square digs, Lady Ottoline Morrell discreetly inquired after the young dancer's sexuality by asking, *"Aimez-vous Platon?"*

Also at Morrell's that day was painter Duncan Grant, a charter member of the Bloomsbury Group and the lover of economist John Maynard Keynes (who eventually wed a ballerina; no kids. . . .). Nijinsky raptly watched Duncan and fellow artist Leon Bakst playing tennis in the hostess' garden. Poet William Plomer wrote, "Nijinsky, seeing the ballet/of tennis players in white/darting between the tall, theatrical/and sepia-mottled columns of the vaulting trees,/threw out a dancer's arm, and called/in a faun's warm voice/'*Ah, quel décor!*'"

The game inspired Nijinsky's ballet *Jeux* (Games), with music by the gay French composer Debussy, and decor by Bakst of "dreaming garden trees" masking the facade of Bedford

Square. That wasn't all that was masked; in his diary Nijinsky recorded what was altered to suit mass tastes. "*Jeux* is the life of which Diaghilev dreamed. He wanted to have two boys as lovers. In the ballet, the two girls represent the boys, and the young man (danced by Nijinsky) is Diaghilev." That was 1913. However, for the most part it's also 1963, 1973, 1983, . . .

What *had* changed was that a dancer of Nijinsky's calibre, audaciously spotlighted by Diaghilev, had taken center stage. Diaghilev, whose sexual bent caused him to showcase male dancers, effectively broke the ballerina's monopoly of ballet. "In this part of the century," Bill Como told me, "it's hard to remember, especially for you younger people, how thoroughly female a domain ballet used to be."

So was all of dance, but particularly that form born in Italy over 500 years ago, named and nourished in France and matured in Russia. Today's ballet stars are as apt to be male as female, and Nijinsky has in fact been superceded, though the century's greatest ballerina is still widely considered to be Pavlova. "Since the '70s, a lot of straight men have gotten into dance," allowed Como, "even ballet. Often for monetary reasons, and because the onus of dancing for a man isn't so repressive now. . . . (But) ballet is still thought of as the most refined and intrinsically feminine form of dance, and the average American public is still uncomfortable with it." *Tant pis.*

It was Michel Fokine, Diaghilev's protegé, who changed the emphasis of modern ballet, creating works in which the male could be centerpiece, not just a literally supporting partner. His ballets didn't push ballerinas toward one side, but allowed each gender a chance to shine, sometimes apart, sometimes together. Yet even Fokine's brilliant choreography mightn't have taken off without a star sensation like Nijinsky, who exploded out of the danseur's lowly rut.

A century before, French novelist Théophile Gautier had written, "For us, a male dancer is something monstrous and indecent of which we cannot conceive." Hypocritically, Gautier was best known for *Mademoiselle de Maupin,* a novel in which a female singer masquerades as a man!

Everything changed in 1909, when Diaghilev's premiere season of the Ballets Russes introduced Nijinsky to the West, in Paris. Despite Russia's emergence as the dominant force in ballet, Paris was yet the capital of ballet. In 1672 Louis XIV established a school for music and dance in which ballet thrived for centuries to come. His nickname, the Sun King, derived from a role he danced at 15 in *Le Ballet Royal de la Nuit* (Royal Ballet of the Night). The court ballet in four parts had forty-three scenes and lasted thirteen hours, with Louis as the Sun, emitting golden rays from his head, shoulders, wrists, knees and shoes.

During Louis' reign, male courtiers danced the women's roles *en travesti*, "in disguise." Louis' gay brother, the Duke of Orléans, was a patron of the ballet and dared argue for women to be permitted in any female role. When women did achieve the stage, their movements and virtuosity were hemmed in by the long, full garments male modesty made them wear.

Women came into their own in 1832, when *La Sylphide* made a star of Marie Taglioni, *the* prima ballerina until Pavlova. Much of Taglioni's mystique was her approximation of toe dancing, which became possible in the late 19th century, with technically improved toe shoes. By then, the male in ballet had been relegated to the background, and toe dancing was deemed for-women-only, although in 1924 Anton Dolin surprised French audiences by dancing *en pointe*. But in 1909 Nijinsky forcefully and lastingly reminded audiences that men in ballet were also capable of creating beauty on the stage. He continued to redefine and upgrade the term "danseur" until he was institutionalized for schizophrenia, at 29.

Sergei's Boys

The Polish-Russian Nijinsky is today almost as renowned for his insanity as for his role in modern ballet. In his youth, he was noted for his modest brainpower. As Edgar Allan Poe put it, "The question is not yet settled, whether much that is glorious does not spring . . . from moods of mind exalted at the expense of the general intellect."

Would Nijinsky have become *Nijinsky* without the drive and molding of his lover/benefactor Diaghilev? Would he have remained *the* danseur of his time had he not jettisoned Diaghilev to wed a plain, manipulative Hungarian? And had he not snapped, would he have evolved into a choreographer at least the equal of the celebratedly heterosexual George Balanchine? *Qui sait?* (Balanchine himself came from the Ballets Russes.)

The dimming of Nijinsky's reputation has as much to do with out-of-sight-out-of-mind as with subsequent danseurs like Nureyev and Baryshnikov, who've eclipsed his memory and feats. (We are told by anatomical experts that these men's terpsichorean capabilities out-strip those of the generations-ago Nijinsky, whose photos disclose a squattish physique with thick lower limbs, and a bland visage.) There exists no film of Nijinsky dancing, and he had time to compose only four ballets—*L'Après-midi d'un Faune, Le Sacre du Printemps, Jeux* and *Til Eulenspiegel.* Fortunately, photographs chronicle his life, from before his admission to the Imperial Ballet School in Russia to the dismal years in Swiss confinement.

John Singer Sargent, who sketched him in London in 1913, said: "He was lucky. His timing, or rather Diaghilev's, was perfection." In strai(gh)t-laced biographies and even the 1980 film *Nijinsky* it has become fashionable to analyze Vaslav as an independent force. *The Gay Book of Days'* Martin Greif wrote, "One cannot underestimate the influence of Diaghilev's Ballets Russes on the development of 20th-century art. The importance of his homosexuality to creative art is sometimes overlooked.

"Had he not been gay, had he not attracted to his cause the great homosexual writers and artists of his day, the stream of 20th-century art might have flowed in a different direction."

In *Children of the Sun,* Martin Green declared, "He made the dancer Nijinsky first his lover and then his choreographer, inspiring him to become the company's chief ballet-creator. Diaghilev's superb taste was made manifest in this new Nijinsky and in the ballets he created. These works of art were the children of Diaghilev's sexual passion."

After Nijinsky's defection, Diaghilev worked the same sexual/creative spell on Leonide Massine, Anton Dolin and Sergei Lifar. His genius was recruiting wildly individualistic and differing temperaments to work together, for him. His ballet *Parade,* for instance, was co-created by Cocteau, Picasso and Erik Satie. Diaghilev made household names of Bakst, Fokine, Stravinsky and the dancers to whom he played Svengali. His intimates included Proust, Rodin, Cocteau, Manuel De Falla,

Reynaldo Hahn, Lucien Daudet, etc. That lavender côterie, based in Paris, engendered the greatest cultural ferment since the Florence-based Renaissance—also largely gay, with artists like Da Vinci, Michelangelo, Botticelli, Raphael, etc.

It was Jean Cocteau who discerned "the contrast between the Nijinsky of *Le Spectre de la Rose*, bowing and smiling to thunderous cheers as he took his fifty curtain calls, and . . . backstage between bows, gasping and leaning against any support he could find, half-fainting, clutching his side, being given his shower and massage and rubdown by his attendant and the rest of us. On one side of the curtain he was a marvel of grace, on the other an extraordinary example of strength and weakness."

Nijinsky's star plummeted after the break with Diaghilev, who wouldn't take him back. His remaining efforts centered on obsessive drawings. Critic Marsden Hartley called them "essentially psychopathic in their value, romantic charts of the closing down of his mind." The drawer's most recurring theme was a huge, staring eye, which some called the Eye of God. Others wondered if it didn't represent a pursuing demon?

Upon his desertion by the 18-years-younger Nijinsky, Diaghilev turned his sights on Leonide Massine (24 years his junior). The sloe-eyed hunk succeeded Vaslav in Diaghilev's bed and as dancer and choreographer. Handsomer than his predecessor, Massine was the toast of Gay Paree, pursued by both men and women. History repeated itself:

After performing in De Falla's *The Three-Cornered Hat,* Massine announced his engagement to the ballet's female star, and was immediately dismissed by Diaghilev from the Ballets Russes. Three years later, the precipitate marriage was annulled. Again, the impresario refused all entreaties to take back his ex, personally or professionally. Post-Diaghilev, Massine's career peak was the fifth-billed role of Ljubov in the ballet movie classic, *The Red Shoes.*

Anton Dolin was discovered by Diaghilev in 1921, an Englishman born Sydney Francis Patrick Chippendall Healey-Kay. He took a Russian name in honor of his patron, who encouraged him to choreograph enduringly popular ballets. Dolin also became the first great English danseur of the modern era and headed up several ballet companies. In 1986, a year before his death, he recalled, "I was launched by a legend, a man for whom great art was even more important than good sex." Dolin's lengthy career was depicted in several colorful autobiographies.

In 1925 Sergei Lifar replaced Dolin as Diaghilev's premier danseur. Thirty-three years the impresario's junior, he was said to be completely asexual, but ambitious. He knew what to do to get and keep his namesake's attention. And he was pliable in other ways: he had talent, a fine body and a handsome face— except for the nose. Diaghilev suggested a rhinoplasty, at the time a new and risky operation. Cocteau counseled, "A blemish in the soul cannot be corrected in the face. But a blemish in the face, if corrected, can refresh the soul."

Afterward, Lifar's colleagues teased, "Don't sit in the sun, the paraffin will melt." But the new nose healed nicely, and at 20 Lifar became No. 1 in the company and in Diaghilev's private life.

In 1929, Diaghilev died in Venice, it having been prophesied he would die on water (ergo, he'd avoided travel by ship). The funeral on San Michele island drew a galaxy of famous mourners, from Coco Chanel to Lifar and company. At the service's conclusion, Lifar dramatically leapt into Sergei's open grave, and had to be drawn out by attendants. Post-Diaghilev, he devoted himself to French ballet, and after WWII was accused of having collaborated with the occupying Nazis. *Too* pliable.

Another ex-member of the Ballets Russes, dancer-choreographer Wakefield Poole, became best known as the director of the first gay porno hit, 1971's *The Boys in the Sand,* with Casey Donovan (it had a 1984 sequel). The legendary Ballets Russes de Monte Carlo also inspired the farcical yet highly polished Ballets Trockadero de Monte Carlo, a troupe of male dancers cum prima donna ballerinas. Said Anton Dolin, "Diaghilev might not have approved of Trockadero's gender-bending, but he would have praised their style and elegance, and their brazenness!"

Rudi, Robert and Co.

Nijinsky's greatest successor was Rudolf Nureyev, who defected from the USSR and the Kirov Opera Ballet of Leningrad in Paris in 1961, at 23. Bill Como believed, "Rudi became a superstar solely on merit. Baryshnikov also has talent, but much of his media status comes from his heterosexual appeal. . . . With Rudi, who is my friend, the media studiously avoided his private life——or else fabricated straight romances for him."

The charismatic if occasionally glacial Nureyev was born in 1938 in Siberia. His 1962 memoirs revealed that his family wasn't Russian, but Tartar, and Moslem. With an appeal which transcended gender, he was a sought-after party guest, night-clubber, interviewee and lover throughout the '60s and '70s. His friend Cecil Beaton proposed co-habitation to him. "Rudi is the best at what he does," said Sir Cecil, "but he's much more than a dancer. His beauty and persona have made him a pop star to millions who may never attend the ballet in a lifetime."

Nureyev's gayness was common knowledge, though never mentioned in the press. In the late '70s he was "outed" by Dave Kopay, a gay athlete of another sort, who casually noted in his autobiography that Rudi visited gay bars. There was no ensuing fuss, no Hollywood-style denials by a publicist. Italian director Luchino Visconti publicly stated his passion for the danseur, calling him "a beautiful cat, as sexy as a tiger."

Early on, dance critic Alexander Bland also classified Nureyev as feline. "To describe a dancer to somebody who has never seen him perform is almost impossible. A rough way of putting him into a category is to divide all dancers into two groups—dogs and cats. Dogs are strong, active, . . . extroverted. There is nothing strange about them. . . . If they are (women) they will shine in bravura roles; the men will be virile and bouncy. Cat men are sinuous and outsiderish. They arouse adoration, and sometimes acute dislike. In dancing, these are the potential stars."

A so-called friend was Marlene Dietrich, who in her 1988 memoirs meowed, "I've never known a vainer man. . . . He constantly complained about his legs, which he considered too short. . . . Baryshnikov didn't have any inferiority complex. I think he owes this remarkable balance to the fact that he loves women. He's not a loner, not even in his art. He's healthy, thank God!"

Natalie Wood got to speak Russian with Rudi at a party at Rupert Allen and Frank McCarthy's house in the Hollywood Hills. She enthused, "He's a wonderful ambassador for Russian culture and for ballet as such an athletic form of self-expression!

He's also very sexy—I think he should be in movies, though I'm sure he'd never 'go Hollywood.'"

He did, however, go to English director Ken Russell, who starred him as a heterosexual version of Rudy Valentino in *Valentino.* Russell dealt peremptorily with Valentino's homo- or bisexuality by making the character shrug off the "rumors." The R-rated film's homoeroticism was limited to a tuxedoed tango between Valentino/Nureyev and Nijinsky/Anthony Dowell. Despite the sexual alteration, the film flopped big, and Rudi's subsequent movie career didn't outdo it.

Based in Paris, Nureyev successfully extended his dancing career well beyond his late 30s, combining dance, choreography and the cult of personality. If his slow-aging looks have outlasted the American media's interest in him, he remains fascinating to many, a sex symbol as much as a dance legend past his prime. In the '60s and '70s, audiences would chant, "We want Rudi/in the nudi!" Today, they still want Rudi, period. Semi-lewd stories abound; most will never see print. . . .

But in 1990 an anonymous waiter at Manhattan's Ginger Man restaurant was quoted in *7 Days,* "Whenever Nureyev ordered a Coke, he'd say, 'I'll have a big cock.' He didn't even want the Coke—he just liked to say that."

Sir Robert Helpmann didn't have quite Nureyev's talent, certainly not his looks. He called his "a face halfway between Margaret Hamilton and Quentin Crisp." However, unlike Rudi, he had a thriving film career as a supporting actor. His celluloid images have partly blotted out the memory of Helpmann the dancer, choreographer and director. He also worked tirelessly on and before the stage. His close friends included Noel Coward, Tennessee Williams, Katharine Hepburn and Vivien Leigh, whom he championed when she was divorced by Laurence Olivier, whom Helpmann nicknamed Old Sourpuss.

Critic Alexander Walker: "He was a homosexual with a sting, a mimic, a gossip, a wit, a man of transfiguring ambitiousness who had trained himself up to leading roles on the ballet stage but, being unsuited by temperament and looks for *jeune premier* roles, made the rare transition to the theatre and ultimately director."

Walker added, "Vivien found his bitchiness amusing, Olivier less so."

In 1938 Olivier played Iago in *Othello*, and based his characterization on Helpmann's "homosexual jealousy" rather than the conventional heterosexual jealousy in which Iago envies Othello his Desdemona. Helpmann himself did Shakespeare a decade later, alternating as Hamlet with Paul Scofield at Stratford.

Also in 1948, Helpmann co-starred (fourth-billed, above Massine) in the cult classic *The Red Shoes,* whose title ballet he choreographed. (The film ran for over two years in New York City.) He danced memorably opposite star Moira Shearer as Ivan Boleslawsky, though today it is disconcerting to watch him do so in full makeup and lipstick!

Future film roles found Helpmann portraying everything from a Chinese eunuch in *55 Days at Peking* to a waspish child-catcher in *Chitty-Chitty, Bang-Bang*. At 75 he concluded, "My sole regret was having chosen an art which so favors youth, and where handsomeness is as important as for picture stars. Even so, the purest joy in all my careers was, simply, dancing."

More than a few ballet dancers, with age, became better known as choreographers. In 1939 Antony Tudor emigrated to the U.S. with his lover Hugh Laing, who danced in most of Tudor's works. The two met when the native of Barbados came to London to study art but instead converted to the dance. A successful danseur, Laing became most closely associated with Tudor's ballets, including *Lilac Garden,* in which he typically played a heterosexual lover in a straight triangle.

Sir Frederick Ashton was inspired to take up ballet after seeing Pavlova perform. His family was horrified, so he secretly took lessons from Leonide Massine and deliberately botched his job at a London business firm. Like Helpmann, Ashton came to the dance too late to become a danseur of the first rank, and in middle and older age both men happily accepted comic ballet roles, sometimes playing *en travesti*——Ashton was one of the Ugly Sisters in his own version of *Cinderella*——and sometimes not——Helpmann was Don Quixote in Nureyev's production of *Don Quixote* for the Australian Ballet.

Jerome Robbins' first ballet cast him as a sailor in *Fancy Free*. It was also his first association with Leonard Bernstein, his eventual partner in *West Side Story*. Robbins (né Rabinowitz) was apotheosized in the late '80s in the Tony-winning musical revue *Jerome Robbins' Broadway.* Such was not the case 30-odd years before. In *Naming Names,* a history of the Hollywood Blacklist, Victor Navasky wrote:

"The choreographer Jerome Robbins was rumored to have turned informer to keep the House Un-American Activities Committee's investigators from publicizing evidence that he was a homosexual, at a time when our society attached a cruel stigma to such sexual preferences. Robbins denies that this was his motive, although his demeanor before HUAC was so compliant that his appearance had about it the aura of social blackmail."

The founder of Alvin Ailey's City Center Dance Theater, who died in 1989 of AIDS, first worked as an actor and dancer off-Broadway. His all-black dance companies were influenced by choreographers like Ted Shawn and Martha Graham, and integrated styles as diverse as calypso, jazz, African, ballet and modern. When he revived Shawn's 1935 "Kinetic Molpai," Ailey offered, "There are traditionalists who believe that ballet should remain untouched by modern dance. Others say that dance must be naturalistic and free of the past.

"I believe in dance for dance's sake. If it should be anything at all, I think it should have a Dionysian approach, celebrating life for life's sake."

From the sublime to the . . . Reagan, junior. On second thought, skip it. Suffice it to say that the very senior Reagan once tried to reassure the press (and probably succeeded!), "We brought him up to be all-man." Doesn't everyone? (And did Nancy know that her godmother, legendary Alla Nazimova, was both Russian and lesbian?)

Roaring '20s, Swinging '60s?

An anonymous non-actor was once quoted as saying, "An actress must be something more than a woman, and an actor something less than a man." If this is so, it's ironic, for acting is a field still dominated by old-fashioned sex roles, and female actors are still, persistently, called actresses—as opposed to the now-archaic use of poetess, sculptress, authoress, etc. Likewise, dance, which according to all indications attracts an even higher percentage of gay men, remains bound to me-Tarzan, you-Jane stereotypes, particularly in ballet.

Said Bill Como, "To the best of my knowledge, there are few lesbians in the world of dance. . . . If tennis is an arena crowded with lesbians, then dance must be the opposite."

Of course as creative artists many female dancers have no doubt experimented bisexually, and probably with less apprehension, terror or denial than heterosexual male dancers. By another token, "If a man dancer is homophobic about gay men dancers, then he's stupidly picked the wrong profession," asserted Robert Helpmann. "For he'll be miserable every working day of his life and under constant suspicion of being what he hates."

As Anne Bancroft said in *The Turning Point,* a male ballet dancer in "those days" meant "queer," hence Shirley MacLaine's character hastily wed the dancer she'd fallen in love with, to prove to herself he wasn't. Most likely, the husband sought to "prove" it to himself too. *(Point* was written by Arthur Laurents, who later called it inane to do a ballet story without including male homosexuality, noting that MacLaine vigorously opposed a gay subplot and that the film was a vehicle for its actress-stars and for Baryshnikov, whose Heterosexual Character was to ballet danseurs what Warren Beatty was to hairdressers in the homophobic hit *Shampoo.)*

Although bisexual, Isadora Duncan's reiterated ideal of beauty was the female form. In her Greek togas and draperies, she revealed more of the feminine body on the legitimate stage than anyone during or since the recent Victorian era, with whose morality she jousted all her life. During one American performance, she bared a breast and informed her audience, "This is what beauty is!" The outraged press blared that the "hussy" had stripped naked and displayed her "unfeminine lack of shame"——gulp!

Isadora's mother was a devout music teacher, "my greatest influence." Despite well-publicized marriages and liaisons with variegated men, Isadora relied throughout her life on strong relationships with women. Elsa Lanchester, aka gay actor Charles Laughton's wife, trained with Duncan and was for a time a "dance instructress." She told the author, "Isadora was by no means a lithe or lovely woman! She was plump and 'handsome.' Yet when people think of her now, they see Vanessa Redgrave (who portrayed her on screen). And no one remembers that she flirted with everyone, both sexes alike.

"I was a mere slip of a girl at the time, yet she made a pass at me. I was sophisticated enough to recognize it for what it was but young enough to decline! . . . Later I heard rumors about some of her lady friends in Gay Paree." These probably referred to the sapphic circle of rich, intellectual American émigrées who helped make Paris the capital of salon culture in the opening decades of this century.

Perhaps Isadora's best-loved friend—Platonic?—was Italian thespian Eleanora Duse. One biographer wrote, "She was so good a friend to her, so great a comfort upon the death of her children, that a miniature photo Duse gave Duncan was always kept at her bedside." One lone woman publicly bragged of her affair with Isadora, Spanish playwright Mercedes De Acosta, whose remarkable 1960 memoir *Here Lies the Heart* wove passionate circles around her relationships with Duncan, Dietrich, Garbo, Eva Le Gallienne and others.

It has been said of Isadora that she was born too soon. Her concepts of naturalism in dance, of freedom and holistic health for the body, and free dance instruction for the masses—children too—were viewed as crackpot or even dangerous by most of the press. It pained her that as a celebrity, she inspired more sensationalism and gossip than sincere interest in the dance. So, early on, she turned to Europe—including Russia—for artistic affirmation.

Back in the USA, the '20s roared at her impudence, and she was banned from several cities' public halls during her tours. When she performed in a red gown, headlines screamed, "Red Dancer Shocks Boston!" and "Duncan in Flaming Scarf Says She's Red!" She was eventually hounded from the U.S., having alienated America and its media with her love of not only classical Greece but contemporary Europe.

She flamboyantly informed detracting journalists, "You know nothing of Food, of Love, of Art, . . . So goodbye, America! I shall never see you again." She died on the French Riviera, via a legendary if not mythical freak accident, when her flowing scarf caught in the spokes of her car's wheels and strangled her. Her last words, while flinging back the scarf, were *Je vais à la gloire!* (I go to glory!).

Perky British dancer Judy Carne went to Hollywood in the '60s and became better known for teleseries like *The Baileys of Balboa*, *Love On a Rooftop* and *Rowan & Martin's Laugh-In* ("Sock it to me!") than for hoofing. Lessons had begun at age three. Her family had hoped she would become an English Shirley Temple. Instead, after enduring numerous beatings from a dance instructress named Bush, Judy tapped her way to the West End and then Broadway, most notably in *The Boyfriend.*

Three thousand miles west of 42nd Street, her leggy abilities were completely overlooked, and she was typecast as a Limey ingenue on TV. But "Sock it to me!" fame didn't translate into a stellar acting or dancing career. Rather, she became known as Burt Reynolds' only ex-wife, before being written up in the papers for various drug busts, detailed in her candid 1985 autobiography, *Laughing On the Outside, Crying On the Inside.* The book also elaborated on her some-time lesbianism. Reynolds, she said, was indirectly responsible, after "he threw me against our fireplace and cracked my skull."

On a friend's dare, Carne went to a lesbian bar in Hollywood where she met a beauty who happened to be "the daughter of one of the most famous screen actors of all time. I can't tell you who!" There was another affair with Aussie singer Lana Cantrell, which Judy describes in her nightclub act. "Lana wasn't beautiful, but stunningly handsome, and she attracted men without ever trying at all. . . . Johnny Carson had such a thing for her; she was on the show at first once a month.

"But despite his best-laid plans, he could never get alone with her. At one point, Lana, Johnny, Doc Severinsen and I had dinner. Then Lana and I went off together. It was obvious we were together. Johnny never spoke to me after that."

In a 1990 *Advocate* interview, Carne stated, "I was the first female celebrity ever to address bisexuality openly. Even a few years ago, it was still taboo."

More readily than most male ones, female dancers tend to give it up when acting jobs become available. S is a statuesque blonde actress-dancer: "We have shorter career spans than the guys, because of the premium placed on girlish looks. Not only that, we don't have the same opportunities to become choreographers, let alone switch to directing, like Michael Bennett and several men did."

S performed in a few big-budget movie musicals and had an affair with O (see *Songbirds*) when she danced in a film starring O. "It was a fast, hot, unforgettably passionate experience. After, we stayed friends a while, but friendships with people on that superstar level don't really last. . . . The funny thing is— like in funny-weird—that she met another gay dancer, her future husband, on the same set."

Early Stages

Like Josephine Baker, Barbette went to Paris an entertainer and there unexpectedly became a star. It couldn't have happened in Round Rock, Texas, where Vander Clyde was born in 1904. "My dreams were full of estrogen, and my love for beautiful clothes and dancing and prancing made me a misfit in what I called Drowned Rock." So it was goodbye Texas and hello *le tout Paris*, before whom Barbette appeared on stage in a metallic dress and feathers, stripped nearly nude, then mounted the trapeze and performed graceful and daring acrobatic feats.

Virgin audiences thought they were watching a woman. But after taking "her" bows, Barbette doffed his wig and broke records at top venues like the Café de Paris. *La grande Barbette* was all the rage in the late '20s, and became an intimate of Cocteau, who cast him as a lady in a theatre box in his surrealistic film masterpiece, *Blood of a Poet.*

Not coincidentally, the man with the patrician nose and cleancut profile resembled Julie Andrews, which is who Julie Andrews resembled when she played a man impersonating a woman in *Victor/Victoria*, the musical whose title character was inspired by Barbette.

Friendly rival Maurice Chevalier remembered it well. "Barbette was unique. What he did was not unique. *He* was unique. . . . Poetry in motion." Alas, his only film appearance was sitting, not leaping through the air with the greatest of ease and sequinned outfits.

Far better known in America were two gay men dominated by female partners of sorts. Both were born in 1891, though in Clifton Webb's case alternative dates of 1889 and '93 have been cited. From childhood through the 1930s, before attaining movie stardom in middle age, Webb sang and danced his way through Broadway and parts lesser known. His mother Maybelle had guided him into musical comedy, and even left her husband for show biz. Queried about the man's whereabouts, she once replied, "We never speak of him. He didn't care for the theatuh."

Clifton was born Webb Parmalee Hollenbeck in Indianapolis. After Maybelle shed her businessman husband, she took her son to the Big Apple and enrolled him in dancing school and the Children's Theatre. Young Webb aimed for a career in opera, and later said, "I wasn't fat enough. I've always been cursed with perfect slimness." At 18, Webb had a one-man show of his portraits and still-lifes in New York, having already done provincial grand opera and honed his English-type speaking accent. Close friends included Noel Coward, Libby Holman and some-time lover Alan Campbell, who eventually wed Dorothy Parker.

In 1929 he and Holman had a hit and a scandal in *The Little Show*. In the already mentioned "Moanin' Low" number he played Libby's pimp, who was supposed to be black, she white. Libby was coached in her "snake-hip" dance by black dancing instructor Buddy Bradley. Webb boasted that he'd made a bed buddy, if briefly, of Bradley. When Holman and Webb pre-viewed the provocative song/dance number for the show's backers, they found it too blatantly sexual. Coward informed Webb, "If even a soupçon is changed, the producers would be quite, quite mad." Webb told them that, and they gave in.

Webb had done silent movies in the '20s. He returned to the screen in 1944's smash hit *Laura*, as the crypto-gay villain Waldo Lydecker. He stayed at Fox and played with everyone from Tyrone Power and Robert Wagner to Barbara Stanwyck—whom he dubbed "my favorite American lesbian"—and starred as Mr. Belvedere, the Remarkable Mr. Pennypacker and others. His box office success and longevity caused his Broadway career to fade from popular memory. Rather, he was famous as the screen's most pompous and scathing character-star. To wit:

In *Three Coins in a Fountain*, in a party scene, a rich matron with literary aspirations insists, "If anyone just took a pencil and followed me around, they'd have a novel." To which Webb ripostes, "My dear lady, I would be delighted to get behind you with a pencil. . . . "

He told *Coronet* in the '50s, "People comment about my poise. I was of course born with most of it, but I perfected it as a 'ancer. . . . All that perspiration finally paid off."

Webb's private life was dominated by mama Maybelle. Thus, he never had a live-in lover for long. The jealous Maybelle was also her son's business manager and invariable public date. At 65, Clifton confessed to a friend that he'd been living with his mother so long, it was like "a womb with a view." But after she died, in her 90s, he was disconsolate, crying and carrying on so, that Noel Coward drily sympathized, "It must be tough, being orphaned at 72."

Ted Shawn was female-dominated by his in-name-only wife, Ruth St. Denis, the principal co-founder of the Denishawn School of Dance, from which graduated Martha Graham, Doris Humphrey, Charles Weidman, etc. Fourteen years Shawn's senior, she lived into *her* 90s, and once wrote Ted, "When you reach that point when you realize that your destiny is to serve me and my career, subordinate to me at all times and in all ways, you will finally reach some happiness."

Shawn's struggle wasn't so much with Ruth as with his dominant sexuality, to which he fully admitted late in life (he died in 1972). Anxiously, he'd attempted to make male dancing respectable, in a time and place where it was thought disgraceful. Seeking to *prove* men dancers could be masculine, he formed an all-male dance troupe. But Ted Shawn and His Men Dancers—who last performed in 1940—were considered freakish, almost a circus act, in the same vein as that other 1930s novelty act, Evelyn and Her All Girl Orchestra.

The fraternal troupe, a self-reliant commune, was headquartered at Jacob's Pillow in Lee, Massachusetts. They adopted the Denishawn Creed, which held, "The body ought to be freed from the bonds of tradition and allowed to respond to the natural rhythms. . . . " This may have been Shawn's way of urging sexual freedom. He already practiced occasional freedom from clothes; the premiere of his *Death of Adonis* was delayed due to "obscenity," namely semi-nudity, and his year-end newsletters to friends around the world featured an illustrated flyer with Shawn posing in the nude. These poses continued into his 70s!

Louise Brooks studied with Denishawn. "I thought he was

'of the brotherhood' the moment I saw him. . . . Miss Denis, who was not born a Saint, was an egomaniacal iceberg. It flattered her ego to have a pretty, younger husband." Shawn's publicity called him The Most Beautiful Man in the World, however his looks were in his body, not his face. When St. Denis and Shawn wed, he read aloud from Plato's *Symposium:* "Our kind of love . . . must be lived on a higher plane. . . . " Insiders said it was a sexless marriage, struck for professional purposes. One '80s critic argued that Shawn and his men's troupe only gained "respectability and acceptance" via the connection to the more famous, and female, Ruth. (Ruth-less people?)

In *The Advocate,* Shawnite Barton Mumaw reminisced, "We were the Chippendales of the '30s," and recounted how he and Shawn had become lovers. Another Shawnite was Jack Cole, who felt, "Ted had faults galore and poor judgment. On stage he liked the rest to play second-fiddle to his star turn. But he did for male dancers in America what Nijinsky did for them in Europe."

Like St. Denis, Shawn had sought to free dance from classical rigidity. He also infused it with international color. A travel devotee, he loved costumes and performed as a whirling dervish, Mayan, Japanese, Cretan, Egyptian, Greek, Native American, Valentino-style sheik and tango dancer, and tried his hand—and feet—at Spanish flamenco. "It didn't become me," he joked. "My fandango was too big for tight black pants!"

If Shawn's name and reputation never became as big or lasted as long as Nijinsky's, his influence was considerable, via male Shawnites whose dancing and choreography moved on to Broadway and Hollywood, and from there, the world.

Yet in his 1960 memoirs, he was still apologizing for his chosen field. The book—intriguingly titled *1001 Night Stands* —included a chapter whose title proclaimed, "Men Do Dance!" When Shawn had left college a dancer, he'd been told, "But Ted, *men* don't dance." In the book he admitted he'd been preoccupied with presenting his Men Dancers as warriors, laborers, athletes and so on (sort of a dancing Village People). In 1969, the year of Stonewall, he averred, "I wasted too much time and energy worrying what people might think."

A 1976 Shawn biography's title capsulized his legacy: *Father of American Dance.*

Broadway Babies

"I'm not talking the 1980s. I hate the Aching '80s. But *before* that, I'd be willing to bet at least half the masculine dancers and choreographers on Broadway and in Hollywood were gay. At *least!*" That's the experienced opinion of "Ice" Tucker Smith, an actor-singer-dancer—"not necessarily in that order"—who was second-in-command of the Jets in the classic "Cool" number from *West Side Story*.

"Sometimes, you see a number in a musical or film, and you *know* the choreographer was gay." For instance, Jack Cole's avant-garde "Ain't There Anyone Here For Love?" number in 1953's *Gentlemen Prefer Blondes*, with Jane Russell and a bevy of semi-dancing athlete-hunks in trunks. "That was my libido, spilling all over the screen," Cole later confessed.

Cole was Marilyn Monroe's choreographer of choice, responsible for *Gentlemen's* much-aped (by Madonna, etc.) "Diamonds Are a Girl's Best Friend" number, which had in its chorus line George Chakiris—later called "a forerunner of John Travolta"—who would go on to win a *West Side Story* Oscar. Glenn Loney's Cole bio, *Unsung Genius*, revealed that it was Jack who "developed the real Marilyn, teaching her to move and deliver her lines and songs." He would often be within three feet of her, beyond camera range but creating the movements and even expressions which she would imitate for the camera, including the breathless, open-mouthed pout that became her trademark.

It was Cole who convinced Columbia's Harry Cohn to start a dance unit at the studio, headed by himself, rather than importing dancers from Broadway. He choreographed several Rita Hayworth movies (Fred Astaire once broke down and admitted she was his favorite dance partner) and helped polish the classic *Gilda:*

"In *Gilda*, one of the things I did was at the beginning, when she came up, with her hair—you see Rita for the first time, and all the hair goes up. I did a lot of things on the picture that were like that."

On Broadway, he devised dances for, and sometimes danced in, *Something For the Boys, Kismet, Jamaica, A Funny Thing Happened on the Way to the Forum, Man of La Mancha,*

... Carol Haney (*Pajama Game*) and Bambi Linn (*Oklahoma*) trained with Cole, and Broadway dance whiz Gwen Verdon was Cole's pupil, then his assistant. During their seven years they had several fistfights. "Sweetheart, I would punch out anybody who didn't put dance first, ahead of their vanity. . . . Too many gals want to look divoon while they're dancing, so they come off dull and mannequin-like, like Ginger whatsername. Old Fred had an advantage there—he just *danced;* he *knew* he had no looks!"

Asked which he preferred, film or stage, Cole laughed, "Broadway, baby! You can correct your mistakes the following night. In Hollywood, mistakes are forever. The nature of dancing is that each new step is an improvisation and, hopefully, an improvement."

Michael Bennett, who left the biggest-ever bequest to AIDS research, in 1987, told *Talk* magazine, "For me, dance is an improvement on everyday movements, and as a gypsy your nightly dancing moves you ever closer to utopia. I chose what I did for love, not for money. Not at first. . . . "

Cecil Beaton collaborated with Bennett on *Coco,* starring Kate Hepburn as Chanel. "The most driven man I've ever known, but he doesn't enjoy it. He's half-Italian, half-Jewish, you know, and he vacillates between being defiant about his homosexuality and hiding it. I've the impression he's unhappy without fame and fortune, that he's always trying to prove himself—wanting to fit in, yet wanting to stand out."

Privately, Bennett's "type" was WASPy blond, and his tendency was promiscuity. But after he hit the heights with *A Chorus Line,* he married dancer Donna McKechnie. Friends speculated that he was "going Hollywood," some said he was using McKechnie as a "beard," and Studio 54's Steve Rubell claimed, "Michael's trying for the impossible conversion." The marriage was short-lived, but a smug Bennett later told an associate, "Now I have matrimony in my resumé." Success was his resumé.

Though he never made Hollywood fame, the ex-gypsy experienced another triumph, *Dreamgirls,* before his time began running out. Bill Como opined, "*A Chorus Line* was a revolutionary concept. Michael created it from a dancer's heart and guts. He took a group of people who were always in the background, and shoved them out front at the audience. He exposed dancers as individuals, among them of course gay ones.

That show did more for dancers and dance on Broadway than anything in eons.

"It was also Michael's undoing. It drenched him with so much pressure and success, as did *Dreamgirls*, that the real Michael, the happy young dancer, was washed away. He started trying to be what he wasn't, including straight, a tyrant and a mogul. . . . I think his super-career ravaged his nervous and immune systems and left him open to a devastating illness."

A Chorus Line survived Bennett. Broadway's longest-running show ended its 15-year run on April 28, 1990, after 6,137 performances. It greatly overshadowed the dismal flop film version, which was stripped of much gay content because director Richard Attenborough believed, "You cannot present a gay character today without discussing AIDS." (The film was turned down by John Travolta and Michael Jackson, reportedly because of the lavender taste which male dancers leave in the public's mouth—as Jackson subsequently confirmed.)

Original cast member Sammy Williams won a Tony as Paul San Marco, the gay Puerto Rican dancer. He recalled, "Michael came up to me after a rehearsal and said, 'You're not playing the part right, you're way off.' He kept pushing my buttons until I started to cry. Then he put his arm around me and said, '*That's* the way I want you to do it.' He just badgered me until I got to the point where I needed to be for him." Paul was based on openly gay dancer and *Chorus Line* co-creator Nicholas Dante.

After his tour de force as Paul, Williams went to Hollywood, but found little work there, certainly no big roles. Most likely because he'd played gay. Prior to *Chorus Line,* Williams was a chorus boy, appearing in *The Happy Time* and *Applause,* the latter with Dante. At first, he was hesitant about playing gay in *Chorus Line,* though not for the usual reason. He apprised *After Dark,* "It's a heavy trip—one false accent, and you have a caricature."

Like all the *Chorus Line* alumnae, Williams never found another role or show to equal it, and as of 1988, he was in the business of "creating floral arrangements."

Pixie-ish six-foot-six Tommy Tune didn't take Hollywood by storm, either. One of his two films was *Hello, Dolly.* Its director Gene Kelly advised, "I understand it's your real name, but change it. It's just *too* theatrical." Like Tucker Smith, Cole,

Bennett and Williams, Tune began in the chorus. He explained in *Interview,* "I love that team thing. I was never interested in sports because I don't like that kind of competitiveness. I don't like to see people lose. . . . A chorus is a team working together to give."

Like Bennett, Tune won a shelf-full of Tonys. His first was for the supporting gay role in Bennett's musical *Seesaw.* As a Broadway director, he had a hit with *The Best Little Whorehouse in Texas,* but Hollywood deemed him "too light" to helm the screen version. Ironically, the chore fell to gay writer-director Colin Higgins, who succumbed to AIDS in 1988.

In between Broadway hits, Tune took time off-Broadway to tackle "cross-gender characters and sex role confusion" in *The Club,* a 1976 musical revue, and 1981's similar *Cloud 9* (in which Glenn Close played a man). Like Bennett, Tune eventually chose to keep busy mostly behind the scenes of his singing-and-dancing Broadway spectacles. In spite of his age-less looks and androgynous appeal.

Bennett once declared, and presumably he was talking about shows, "When you're young, you put yourself on display. When you're not, you choose the display. . . . "

Fred & Ginger, Fred & Minnie

"I don't know what it is about them, but movie musicals do attract participation by some very talented homosexuals," mused publicist Harry Brand, who worked at Fox from 1935 —its birth year—to 1963. "I'm not plugging anybody's way of life, but I will say that at Fox, without question, our musicals would have been a lesser product without the homosexuals who shaped the way they looked and sounded."

Brand, who helped mold the public images of Power, Stanwyck, Fonda, Lorre, Romero, Carmen Miranda and Dan Dailey, was speaking of gay men and women behind the camera. But gay performers have also been magnetized toward musicals. In fact, the leading men in two *top* screen musicals were (and still are, of course!) gay. One, a non-singer, was dubbed; the other sang only at the beginning of his career.

234

Of course, gay *characters* didn't enter musicals until the 1970s, typically in a pejorative way, reflecting the bias of writers and directors, frequently despite the presence of gay leading men or women. In one of the two above musical hits, a minor gay character serves as a joke and a scapegoat —in spite of the two gay stars, a reportedly gay director, and gay producers and writers! Who was it said Hollywood integrity is harder to discern than a butterfly's fart?

Cabaret in 1972 allowed Michael York's character, based on gay Christopher Isherwood, to be bisexual. The non-musical version, *I Am a Camera,* in the 1950s starred gay Laurence Harvey as a hetero Isherwood. In 1976 *The Rocky Horror Picture Show* featured a bisexual, transvestite "sweet transsexual from Transylvania" (Tim Curry) as hero. But by fadeout he had to be "destroyed" for "the good" of the planet. 1980's *Fame* took place in Manhattan's High School of the Performing Arts, but included *one*—ridiculously lonely —gay character! (It was worse in Cuba, where TV showings of *Fame* edited out Paul McCrane's character Montgomery, named after gay legend Montgomery Clift.)

It isn't always so bad. In Travolta's 1983 *Staying Alive,* his hetero character replaces a gay dancer to star in a Broadway show, but the gay character is treated with dignity *(Alive* was a sequel to *Saturday Night Fever,* 1977, which along with its anti-gay epithets made fun of David Bowie for being "bisexual"). The 1984 dance musical *Footloose* had no gay characters (though at least one of its producers was gay), but its hero puts a homophobic teen firmly in his place. When the bigot taunts the hero, "I thought only pansies wore neckties," he answers, "I thought only assholes used words like 'pansy.'"

However, for *performers* who specialized in movie musicals, the medium's message was marriage, and in real life they usually also spread that word. Notwithstanding, a whiff of lavender accrued to virtually every male musical performer, no matter what his marital or procreative resumé. Fred Astaire, in Harry Brand's terminology, "was plagued" by those rumors. "He was a dancer's dancer from the word 'go.' But he wasn't viewed by any of the studios as picture-worthy."

Why? Because in his 20s, Astaire was already balding (he made his screen bow in his 30s), "he was slight, had no sex appeal, and after all, he was a dancer, and dancers . . . weren't thought of as romantic figures."

Kate Hepburn noted about Astaire and Rogers, "He gives her class, and she gives him sex." The implication is clear: without a woman, Astaire seemed sexless, or "worse."

It appears he wasn't highly sexed in real life. Daughter Ava was quoted in the book *Fred Astaire: His Friends Talk,* "Daddy wasn't a romantic, not at all. He was very enigmatic about that sort of thing. . . . He once asked my husband, 'What is the story of *Romeo and Juliet?'* Richard explained that it was like *West Side Story."*

Because Astaire was far from macho, he was drawn, at least on screen, to extremely feminine women. Screenwriter Leonard Gershe revealed, "The only dancing partner he didn't cotton to was Kay Thompson. . . . Kay has a mannish, direct approach to things, almost masculine. . . . He was more attracted to the femininity of Audrey Hepburn, say." (Hepburn, Astaire and Thompson co-starred in Gershe's *Funny Face.)* Only once did Astaire exchange a passionate screen kiss—in 1960's *The Pleasure of His Company,* with Lilli Palmer, who offered, "Fred's a marvelous dancer. That goes without saying. But he's a good actor too. . . . "

Astaire's first wife was a rich New York socialite—he had a keen yearning to join the aristocracy—who according to friends was jealous, humorless and "kept him on a tight leash." His second marriage occurred in 1980, to a jockey forty-six years his junior. For years, the main woman in Fred's life had been his sister and dancing partner Adele, considered the star of the family and the greater talent. She retired to wed an English aristocrat. Like brother, like sister? In some ways, but it was Adele who had the mouth of a sailor, Fred who abhorred naughty words. Her pet name for him was Moaning Minnie.

Astaire was also close to his mother, who lived with him all her life. She died at 96.

Despite his paucity of looks, Astaire was consumingly vain. His platonic friend actress Carol Lynley said his lifelong obsession was "getting the right toupee." Director Stanley Donen said, "Fred would have given anything to have had hair." And Ava said, "He loved to potter around the 5-&-dime in Beverly Hills and look for chains that he could sew onto his shoes and diamond earrings that he could clip on his slippers—just a little glittery something."

Co-star Leslie Caron noted, "He used to tell us how Judy Garland was overeating, and how it was no wonder she became so huge. Oh, he was a gossip!" Douglas Fairbanks Jr.: "I always heard from the girls that he was not such a hot dance partner at parties." And, "He was very shy, and much preferred the company of men."

Choreographer Hermes Pan: "Fred taught the Prince of Wales to dance" (the future Edward VIII was a closet bisexual who had an affair with Woolworth heir Jimmy Donohue and was once arrested at a gay sex party; he gave up the throne of England partly for the woman he loved, and veddy little so far has been printed about the men he may have loved).

Friend Jean Howard explained that first wife Phyllis, a "little tiny woman" who'd been married before and already had a child, "was insanely jealous of Fred. He wasn't allowed to kiss Ginger Rogers (on the screen, either!). I don't think Phyllis needed to worry, because I don't think Fred wanted to kiss Ginger anyhow, or anybody else."

Whatever his sexuality, Astaire the married gossip seemed quite aware of the gay performers around him. Sometimes more than the men themselves. In 1935 he wrote Adele a letter about his co-star Edward Everett Horton. "I believe old Ed is a little bit of a pansy . . . Doesn't quite know himself—however—do not camp with him—he is apt not to understand. . . ." Funny, that "Minnie" would have had to explain "camping" to Ed.

Horton played Astaire's companion with definite gay undertones in *Top Hat, The Gay Divorcee* and so on. This was no coincidence. RKO paired Astaire with asexual or nellie older sidekicks like Horton, Victor Moore and Eric Blore to make him appear sexier, manlier and younger by comparison. Up through WWII, conventional Hollywood wisdom held that Astaire wasn't a star solo, that his success rested on Ginger's legs and blonde hair.

When she successfully struck out on her own (somehow even winning an Oscar, as Astaire never did!), he was joined with other actresses but flopped big, and in 1946 decided to retire. He did, for two years, until an MGM executive talked him out of it. Privately, Fred worried that he'd been overtaken by the younger, handsomer and sexier Gene Kelly. He admitted to Vincente Minnelli, "Kelly looks like an athlete. He could make it without dance. My stuff's more balletic."

On Their Toes!

Leonard Gershe said about Astaire, "He was truly modest, as opposed to Gene, who thinks he's hot stuff, and he is, but he knows it."

Yves Montand said Kelly "put the dance on the street" by appearing as a dancer in trousers and regular street clothes. Kelly felt, "The joy of my kind of dancing is that you never forget it's an eternal fertility rite." As opposed to Astaire's?

Louise Brooks remembered in *People Will Talk*, "I heard (Kelly) in an interview, a very interesting interview, and I thought it was a dead giveaway. He said, 'You know, it's a shame that a guy can't dance without being called a homosexual,' and then went into this long routine defending himself —you know, 'I'm married and have kids.' Now, look at Fred Astaire . . . I don't think he had any sex life. . . . I didn't care for Ginger Rogers. He didn't care for Ginger Rogers either."

Kelly explained, "I hated dancing. . . . I thought it was sissy. I bless my mother now for making me go."

Judy Garland must have doubted whether a dancer could be 100 percent heterosexual. As noted in *Conversations With My Elders,* during filming of *The Pirate* in 1948 she suspected Kelly of having an affair with their director, her husband Vincente Minnelli. Kelly certainly had a gay following; he became a sailor-suited icon in films like *Anchors Aweigh* and *On the Town,* and favored buttocks-clinging pants which favored him in *An American in Paris* and elsewhere.

Jack Cole danced with Kelly on Broadway in *Pal Joey.* "Every chorus boy had a crush on him, and Gene had several gay friends in New York. . . . Once he became a star, he slaved like Hercules to make his dancing as butch and athletic as possible, and then he worked at becoming a movie director and changing his image once again. . . . Far more than Astaire, he has a love-hate relationship with dancing."

Gossip columnist Joyce Haber was on TV promoting her Hollywood-exposed novel *The Users.* Her host asked her to dish some "titillating Hollywood gossip," and she let fly that one of filmdom's top dancer-actors was a closet transvestite with a costly and beautiful wardrobe that would be the envy of any actress. The host gasped, as he and everyone watching probably thought of The Two Top Movie Dancers and then wondered, Which One? But chances are Haber was referring to Dan Dailey, who died shortly afterward, in 1978.

Not really handsome, and nowhere as sexy as Gene Kelly — with whom he worked—Dailey was one of Fox's top male leads in the '40s and '50s (along with Clifton Webb and Tyrone Power). Initially, this was due to his being Betty Grable's favorite co-star. Grable was Hollywood's No. 1 box office champ of the 1940s, and Dailey's big break was teaming with her in *Mother Wore Tights,* her biggest-ever hit. Grable was willing to share the spotlight, and actively helped promote Dailey.

She also helped save his career after *Confidential* magazine published photos of him in drag in the '50s. Vocally and publicly, she came to his defense, and pointed to his wife and family. Privately, she knew that gay dancer-actors well up on their toes acquired nuclear family units as a matter of course. Having been around chorus boys most of her life, Betty realized what was ailing the repressed Dan (who underwent mental therapy), and encouraged him to have therapeutic gay affairs with some of the dancers and actors he was pining for.

She also lent him some of her screen wardrobe, accustoming him to the best *couture* Hollywood had to offer. Fox wardrobe supervisor Charles LeMaire declared that Dailey had "a penchant" for Linda Darnell's gowns. He had to warn fellow costume designers when Dailey was making midnight raids on the wardrobe department, borrowing costumes which often had to be discreetly taken in again.

Three failed marriages and the suicide of his only son left Dailey an embittered alcoholic who was nonetheless a good enough actor to play the cheerful father figure in the '60s sitcom *The Governor and J.J.* By that time, Dailey was minimally associated with dance. He'd also long since come to terms with his sexuality. "Many people based in Hollywood or New York during the late '40s and '50s remember his visits to local gay bars, the polite whispers without pointing, and the path that parted like the Red Sea when he walked by," said Martin Greif.

"One wonders whether anyone ever so much as talked to him."

George Cukor directed Dailey in *Susan and God* (1940), with Joan Crawford. "Dan was a loner. He was lonely in his marriages, but would not give up on marriage. He thought it a crucial part of his public personality. In private, he couldn't commit to another man, or trust one. He shouldn't have trusted his wives . . . nearly all his private disappointments stemmed from his public relationships." For Dailey, film and marriage went together like a horse and carriage.

Likewise, marriage didn't halt the rumors about Ray Bolger, whose screen apex was the Scarecrow in *The Wizard of Oz* (1939; the role was reprised after a fashion by Michael Jackson in *The Wiz*, 40 years later). Bolger had earlier achieved Broadway stardom in 1936 in *On Your Toes*. Post-Emerald City, he appeared in asexual roles in films like *Where's Charley?* (a musical *Charley's Aunt*) and *Four Jacks and a Jill*. His *Jacks* co-star Desi Arnaz had this to say:

"Ray does it all. He acts, dances, sings, is a great comedian, and he's president of the Ray Bolger Fan Club. About the only thin' he doesn't do is ball chicks. He says dancin' and exercise take care of all those needs, but I heard some pretty perversive [*sic*] rumors about that guy's love life!"

Rumors swirl around a majority of actors, especially those who dance, and probably always will. When John Travolta became the late-'70s' dance king in *Saturday Night Fever* and *Grease,* everyone wondered. *Rolling Stone* asked point-blank, "Are you gay?" (No medals for correctly guessing his and everybody's answer who works in Hollywood!) In 1990, the 36-year-old bachelor made the *National Enquirer.* The cover story: "I Was John Travolta's Gay Lover," by a some-time porn star who had a small role—on screen—in Travolta's *Perfect.*

Today there are no dancing movie stars of either gender, and dancing alone isn't enough to cause rumors. Even though there are more rumors about more people than ever before — a semi-acknowledgment that gay individuals aren't one in a million, as Louis B. Mayer believed, but closer to one in ten. And matrimony is a less common antidote to gossip, whether for dancing men or those who keep their legs together. That old antidote seldom worked anyway. Not in the long run.

Bill Como pointed out, "Even with sacrosanct romantic symbols like Cary Grant, who wed for cosmetic reasons and whose heterosexuality was skin-deep, the truth will out."

George Cukor disclosed that during the 1950s he was passed over to direct the lavender-tinged *Tea and Sympathy*. The film was helmed by Vincente Minnelli, Hollywood's top director of musicals, which T&S decidedly was not. A 1989 biographer marveled that Minnelli was "fond of dressing in flamboyant yellow jackets which were not exactly seen in the '50s as macho," and that his films contained "mixed messages about manliness."

Cukor said, "Vincente began as a costume and set designer in New York. He knew that he had to marry, or do different things. . . . He married, all right, more than once. So he did all those musicals, and often had some provocative things to say about masculinity, homosexuality and sex roles" in *Lust For Life, Tea and Sympathy, Home From the Hill, Designing Woman* and *Goodbye, Charlie.*

"I did not marry. But both of us were workaholics. We had to be . . . *then*. I shot some retakes on *Lust For Life* because Vincente was already shooting *Tea and Sympathy*. Don't think that Hollywood didn't know about both of us. Hollywood is small, and not so easily fooled as the public. . . . But knowing about us, and knowing the public, they assigned that sensitive and rather daring picture to the man who had one more requirement for the job than the other —to the one who had married." The one with a visible marital resumé.

Dancing in the Closet

M is the contractual husband of O. He was interviewed separately from her, without either's knowledge—till now—that their mate was being interviewed. M was a dancer, as was S, when both had non-speaking parts in O's movie musical.

H: Why did you take a wife?

M: (shrugs) . . . Something different.

H: You are gay?

M: Of course.

H: And you still have sex with men?

M: Yeah, but that's only a part of being gay. It's an affectional thing too. Also cultural and political.

H: You sound like an activist, strangely enough.

M: I do contribute money . . .

H: Secretly?

M: Anonymously. I have to, for the marriage's sake.

H: Then why the marriage, if you're gay?

M: (laughs) It was an offer I couldn't refuse.

H: Money?

M: That's just part of it. The career too.

H: Has it helped yours?

M: (laughs bitterly) Not so far, not much.

H: Was it to help change your image as a dancer?

M: At first, yeah. But whatever the reasons, it is a wonderful friendship. And loving, also. To me, a marriage is any two people together, both for each other. Period.

H: What I find ironic is that Hollywood, not the public, does the casting. You'll admit that Hollywood knows you and she are each homosexual?

M: Yeah, they know. Even if they can't prove it.

H: So?

M: To tell the truth, I'd have moved in without tying the knot. But that wasn't part of her deal.

H: Do you think a lot of dancing men have married for their image?

M: In Hollywood? Sure.

H: Not on Broadway?

M: Not so much. Only, it's not just dancers, it's all kinds of ambitious actors who meet important women, and it's also boys who sing.

H: You said "boys."

M: . . . In my case, I married young.

H: Not to give offense, but did you figure that O was your best or only hope of becoming a star yourself?

M: But that is offensive.

H: I'm sorry, but it's realistic. You're extremely attractive.

But so are 10,000 other guys in this town, in this business. In the long run, a Dustin Hoffman usually has a better chance. You'll get hired quicker than a young Hoffman, but you must admit, he'll stand out.

M: (sighs; laughs) Yeah, right. I'm talented enough, but I know I'm not exceptional.

H: Except in your marriage?

M: Not in Hollywood. Most of the gays who work here are married.

H: If you hadn't been a dancer, would you have contractually married?

M: I don't know. But I knew so many gays who were dancers, and dancers don't really get anywhere. You hear about Astaire or Gene Kelly, but they're the only ones.

H: And Dan Dailey.

M: I never heard of him.

H: Are you as ambitious today as when you wed?

M: Not quite. But that's the years, you see. Like, I always had discipline about my dancing, but that was it. I didn't want to have to *age* into success.

H: You wanted it right away.

M: My Grandma had a proverb. I always thought it was nutty, till I met O. She used to say, "There's more than one way to climb to the top of the tree than sitting on an acorn." (grins) Get it?

H: You mean, sitting on an acorn is the slow way, and marriage to a woman speeds it up?

M: Not just any woman! Marriage only helps you into the club, but marriage to a *star* . . .

H: But you said it hasn't really helped.

M: Did I know that then?

H: Is that sort of a marriage, as they say, "convenient?"

M: It's hard work!

H: The sex?

M: There's a reason we do it.

H: Breeding?

M: We won't talk about that.

H: Do you have a beau, or beaux?

M: (smiles; sighs) Well, because of all *that* (AIDS), I have to keep it down to a few guys. A special few. So it's plural, but it'd be a lot more plural if everything was okay.

H: Back to dancing—do you miss it?

M: As you get older, you're not quite as good at it. So it doesn't miss *you*. Why should I miss the old days?

H: Astaire, Kelly and others danced into middle-age and beyond. It's not as demanding as ballet.

M: It's still real hard work. Marriage—I mean, *acting*—is a lot easier.

H: So much of life boils down to what's easier, doesn't it?

M: (nods)

H: A personal question: How does sex with the wife differ from with boyfriends?

M: I won't talk about the first, but with a guy I like, it's not just sex. It's making love. 'Cause it's from my own free choice, and from within *me*. It's like loving who I am, and it's not forced, it's . . . it's just great!

H: I'm surprised you and she are still together.

M: She gives me plenty of space, but . . . so am I!

H: Did she want you to give up dance?

M: She didn't ask me to give up anything.

H: Not even your identity?

M: Oh, come on! . . . Not all of the time.

H: Is dancing considered more manly these days?

M: That all depends on the man!

...Sing Out!

"It is immoral not to tell."—Camus

As a famous song once noted, time goes by. With it, we learn more about figures past and present, and about ourselves and our true place in our world. When we think of public figures, we seldom consider the mechanics of their private lives. Even with gay celebrities. The parallels between composers Cole Porter and Noel Coward were so numerous, they've inspired two joint biographies. One book was largely negative and drearily analytical, trying to "explain" the gayness of the two artists. Why does no one question what "causes" heterosexuality? Why are there, say, left-handed people? Answer: because there are.

This needless and inaccurate approach is one of two negative ways of dealing with homo- or bisexuality. The other is denial, as for instance in a recent bio of Cary Grant—who played Porter in the bio-myth-ographical film *Night and Day* (it can now be said: Alexis Smith, who played Cole's asexual or possibly sapphic wife, Linda, was lesbian)—via a university press who should know better.

The better bio is *Genius & Lust*, whose authors examine the men's sexuality and its impact on their work, and also the price both men paid for living in a closet. Despite his surname, Coward never hid behind a trophy wife as did Porter. For decades Coward was denied a knighthood because he was gay, despite his friendships with the royal family (of whom he bedded at least one member). The honor was withheld by homo-

247

phobic press lords and conservative politicians, as the records show (no pun intended). But when he finally went to receive that greatest of Britannic honors, Coward attended not with his male life-partner of a quarter-century, but with two female friends....

As one struggling thespian put it, "If ever I chance to win an Oscar, an Emmy, or a Tony, you can bet I'll thank my significant other. If I didn't, how could I honestly consider myself a success?"

Of course, times change, but only to the extent that we actively change them. Howard Ashman was the Oscar-winning lyricist of Disney animated films like *The Little Mermaid* and *Beauty and the Beast*. He died of AIDS in 1991, whereafter his posthumous Academy Award was publicly accepted by his male partner in life. About half a decade later, the studio decided to offer domestic partner benefits to its gay and lesbian employees. For this reason, and because of the acknowledged gayness of Ellens DeGeneres (real) and Morgan (reel), Disney is the object of a 1997 boycott by fundamentalist Christians—zealots whose bumper stickers would never read "*Family Valued*: We Love Our Gay Son ... or Our Lesbian Daughter."

In a more positive updating from the early '90's, diva-*auteure* Barbra Streisand may since then have all but given up music—in terms of regularly issuing records or CDs—but she has discovered that her son is gay and embraced gay rights (her 1993 *Back to Broadway* sequel album featured a *West Side Story* duet with Johnny Mathis, but they're either singing to each other or to absent heterosexual partners, for Mathis croons his love to a "her." And off-mike he does not make things clearer. He and/or his handlers decline to let him do interviews that include any mention of his own life and love. Though he came out in 1982, the word since then has been mum....)

And remember the censorious Washington Wives, led by Tipper Gore, at the time possibly better known than her husband? The late Frank Zappa was quoted, "The Wives see sex and violence everywhere. They need to sort out their priorities.... They're categorizing gay love lyrics with songs from antigay rockers and rappers that treat gays, lesbians, and straight women like fifth-class citizens."

By the mid-'90s, the tune had changed:

"This Administration will continue to fight for the rights and needs of lesbians and gay men in our nation. During the past four years, much progress has been made, but there is more to do." So said the vice president's wife in a letter to the Lesbian Women's Inaugural Gala in Washington, D.C., on January 20, 1997. Vice President Al Gore told the audience at the AIDS Action Foundation's National Leadership Awards, held April 9, 1997, in Washington, DC, "There is no room in American medicine or American life for discriminating against people because of their sexual orientation. Gays and lesbians are part of the American family."

Acknowledging and including one's gay relatives is certainly more common in music than in movies and TV. k.d. lang recently stated, "I feel very fortunate in that I grew up in a family with three out of four children being gay." Talk about an in-house support group! The songs of country music superstar Garth Brooks have now and again focused on social issues, often alienating the traditional country crowd. "The Chase" "talks about prejudice against color or sexual preference. That's real life for me today." Brooks has acknowledged his lesbian sister publicly and lovingly. His 1992, "We Shall Be Free" received less radio play than it would have, as the song was about freedom to love and supported gay rights.

Also unusual for country music, Brooks's songs occasionally deal with issues of sexism, such as domestic violence and date rape. Garth puts his money where his mouth is; sister Betsy Smittle plays bass in his band. In 1994, singer Cyndi Lauper shared a float with her big sister in New York City's gay pride parade. Three years later, Cyndi's album *Sisters Of Avalon* boasted a song called "Brimstone & Fire," which she wrote to "give my sister a giggle," explaining, "How many years when I was growing up did I hear guys saying that all lesbians need is a good lay? I'd tell them, 'Don't you freakin' understand? Are you fuckin' dense?'"

Madonna outed her brother Christopher Ciccone at the height of her pro-gay, openly bisexual period, which was followed by her reheterized period comprising a backlog of flop movies, but-I-really-love-men, playing a fascist dictator's wife (in *Evita*), fading youth (her own, not a tired stud), and motherhood. Ciccone *frère's* latest project is directing Dolly Parton—who admits she has a husband—in a dance remix of the 1970s hit *Peace Train*. The effort is aimed at gay audiences, but the ditzy pair left off their thinking caps while choosing a song. *Peace Train's* royalties will go to its composer, the former Cat Stevens, latterly known as Yusuf Islam and a convert to Islamic fundamentalism.

The ex-Cat has broken his reclusion to make such comments as "Homosexuality is a sexual perversion, a sickness," and AIDS is a punishment from Allah. Frank Zappa once asked, "Where's the fun in fundamentalism?" One might also query why religious fundamentalists of all ilks try to recreate a god in their own small-minded, small-hearted images?

The often-daring *SPY* magazine, in its August, 1993, issue, ran a photo of fellow blonds Cyndi Lauper and Dolly Parton out on the town. The caption: "Girls Just Want to Have Fun with girls who just want to have fun with girls."

Gay composers. For some reason, it still comes as a surprise to most people that any pre-modern composer was gay, except perhaps Tchaikovsky. A big reason is probably the movies. We've rarely seen Tchaikovsky on the screen, but—outside of Russia—when we have, he's usually allowed to be what he was: gay. As Christopher Isherwood put it, "It's like they permit us *one* great gay guy per field, preferably tortured, like Tchaikovsky, or prematurely deceased, like Rock Hudson. . . . *One* gay artist, one gay composer, one gay movie star, etc." In the old days, movie biographies often spotlighted composers, classical and not. (Usually heterosexual composers, like Mozart.) Ironically the film *Amadeus* starred now openly gay (though reticent) Tom Hulce as Wolfgang Amadeus Mozart and, fourth-billed, openly gay Simon Callow as Wolf's hetero pal. And openly gay Sir Ian McKellen won a Broadway Tony as Salieri in *Amadeus*. The movie Salieri was Oscar-winning F. Murray Abraham (sexuality unknown to this author), who brilliantly portrayed a gay bathhouse patron in the hilarious cult movie *The Ritz* (1976, detailed in author's *The Lavender Screen*).

Or, when gay or bisexual composers are spotlighted, they are, even now, heterized for maximum screen profit. An example was *Immortal Beloved*, produced by alleged homophobe

Mel Gibson's company. The script, commissioned by Gibson, re-sexualized Ludwig; not the first time Gibson was responsible for heterizing a *character (The Man Without a Face)* or distorting history for homophobia's sake *(Braveheart)*. *Films in Review* magazine noted:

"Failing an interesting portrayal of events, one may hope for historical accuracy. But even that's not forthcoming in this movie." One distortion: Beethoven did *not* will his estate to Ms. Immortal Beloved. The movie's narrator-"friend" was no friend to Beethoven; for one thing, he destroyed 260 of Ludwig's approximately 400 conversation notebooks. Et cetera. It's worth bearing in mind that most of what we know about the man Beethoven comes from contemporary accounts of two of his friends and associates. In a time when non-heterosexuality was punishable by death and governments were church dictatorships, the truth about an uncommon man's love life would rarely surface. Then, as now, friends of a deceased celebrity might paint him as "straight," so their own sexuality isn't called into question.

Was Beethoven a practising bisexual? A repressed homosexual? Who can know for sure? But heterosexual he was not, and those claiming he was are more interested in representation and propaganda than in the facts. *F.I.R.* concluded, "Beethoven never married ... (he had) a lifelong indecision over intimate relationships with women. ... Beethoven was the first composer to raise orchestral music to the status of choral or operatic music. In other words, his greatest achievement was realized in the absence of language and of lyrics; his hearing loss eventually precluded him from engaging in conversation.

"Beethoven left only one letter expressing physical passion, a letter which probably never reached its intended reader. These facts lead us to wonder whether his exquisite music was composed from a well of frustration, suppressed passion, unexpressed emotion, and unrequited love—the stuff of great movies, but not *this* movie."

Just as virtually everyone in the western world has heard Beethoven's "Fifth," so virtually every American has sung the words of "America the Beautiful," beginning, "Oh, beautiful, for spacious skies. . . ." Far more singable—in melody *and* lyrics— than the official anthem "The Star-Spangled Banner," it is arguably America's most famous song. Its words are by a lesbian, though more former students with retentive memories will recall that Samuel A. Ward composed the music. In 1893, poet and Wellesley instructor Katharine Lee Bates accepted a summer teaching job in, ironically, Colorado. En route, the scenery she saw from her train window impressed her deeply and poetically. She wrote a paean to what she saw, and "America the Beautiful" was published on July 4, 1895.

When a Massachusetts paper reported on July 4, 1994, that Bates was gay, several readers (not thinkers) wrote in to say that: a) it couldn't be true; or b) saying so made the song "less respectable." Au contraire; Bates had a 30-year relationship with Wellesley history and political economy professor Katharine Coman. It was of course a partnership formed and maintained through love, not pressure, social expectations, filial sacrifice, a rut, or the law. Bates once wrote to Coman, "Your love is a proof of God."

Oh, say, "The Star-Spangled Banner" also has a same-sex, though more tenuous, connection. Anacreon was a Greek poet born circa 570 B.C.E.. who penned several poems about his male lovers. Their structure's popularity endured into modern European times, and when the English rediscovered his work, they called their imitative efforts Anacreontics, which resulted in the popular song "Anacreon In Heaven." The music was eventually borrowed for the American national anthem, to which Francis Scott Key affixed his own lyrics—words more militaristic and less inspiring than those by the awestruck Katharine Lee Bates.

A song which gay audiences shouldn't be surprised was written by a gay man for his lover is "I Left My Heart in San Francisco" (hetero audiences mostly assume that all love songs are by and about heterosexuals). The 1995 gay/lesbian almanac entitled *Out In All Directions* also disclosed as gay the composer of "Over The Rainbow," Harold Arlen. However, he had a wife and may or may not have been bisexual. The point is, if a man had a wife, he is officially counted as "straight." If, like George Gershwin, there was no contractual mate and not enough evidence to say he was homo or hetero, then he is still tenaciously labeled as heterosexual; particularly if he was famous, successful, and admired.

Then there are those composers/lyricists whom one might well guess at, but who decline to clarify matters (aka set the record straight). Friends-of-Liza John Kander and Fred Ebb are the rarely publicized team—more than once described by the print mainstream as "flamboyant"—behind *Cabaret, Chicago*, and several brilliant successes up until the recent, lackluster *Steel Pier* (dance marathons were definitively done in the non-musical drama *They Shoot Horses, Don't They?*—detailed in author's *The Films Of Jane Fonda*). Their musicalization of *Kiss of the Spider Woman* was initially a flop, despite the relative success of the film of the novel by Argentine Manuel Puig, whose official bio falsely claimed he was a husband and a father.

The movie *Kiss* is probably best remembered for somehow (chutzpah?) winning William Hurt the first Best Actor Academy Award for a gay role, despite his not playing gay *or* Hispanic very well. But an improved *Kiss* went back to Broadway, became a hit and won the 1993 Tony for Best Musical (or vice versa). *Kiss'* book was written by openly gay Broadway stalwart Terrence McNally (*The Ritz, Lisbon Traviata*, and *Master Class* featuring "Maria Callas"). McNally has said that some gays criticize him for not labeling himself "a gay playwright....I *am* saying I'm a gay man who is a playwright." McNally also wrote the book for the '97 musical hit *Ragtime* which has no gay characters, for which he received yet more criticism from certain quarters. But he feels, "I do my bit for the cause if *Ragtime* is a big hit and a good show and people say, 'You know, the book writer's gay.'"

The playwright's openness is the thing: "I think the most important thing we do in our lives is to be out, and then, simply or not, live one's life." McNally didn't have to come out; when he surfaced in the theatre world, he was already known as the love of now-openly gay playwright Edward Albee, with whom he lived for six years. Creators of plays and musicals have long had no excuse to hide their sexual and affectional natures, except self-loathing. Says openly gay Jerry Herman, "I tell people who I am, what I am, not what I do. There's a difference."

In 1997 the somewhat publicity-shy Kander and Ebb were profiled and interviewed—per *Steel Pier* and the *Chicago* revival—by such deft mainstream outlets as *CBS Sunday Morning* which conveniently (quote-unquote!) omit a lesbian celeb's private life (or her public appearances with her female partner) or which instead show a gay male at a public function next to a female friend and/or actress. In 1993 Kander and Ebb were reportedly interviewed by the gay magazine *The Advocate*, which killed the piece when the two men refused to discuss their sexuality and non-professional lives.

Says Jerry Herman, "If somebody would not want to come and see a show of mine because I'm a gay man, then I would love for that person not to buy a ticket for my show." Herman did admit in a 1993 *Advocate* interview that he'd been appalled that the 1992 Republican Convention cynically and without permission used his song "The Best of Times Is Now"—from the gay-themed *La Cage Aux Folles*—at that most virulently homophobic of all presidential nominating conventions. In 1996 Herman composed the Clinton re-election campaign theme and published his very frank yet upbeat and entertaining memoirs, *Showtune*. The book also described Jerry's relationship with Marty:

"Finally, I'd found a soul mate who loved me as I loved him. He was adorable, only thirty-six when he died" of AIDS. The author also disclosed his own HIV-positive status.

Oscar-winner Paul Jabara, composer of "Last Dance" and "Enough Is Enough," once allowed, "I love music, and somewhere I read that music is the art that has the biggest concentration of gays. But if I had the looks, I'd be an actor....The one advantage of being in music is I can be who I am, which is quite an advantage as the years go by." Among those who've officially gone bi, or come out as such, is pianist-singer Michael Feinstein. He long avoided the topic and did say in one gay periodical that by not pretending he was hetero he'd been in some ways professionally hurt. As a singer and as an attractive man peddling song standards to a non-rock-oriented crowd, it's understandable. Gay *Roseanne* writer William Lucas Walker told *Los Angeles* magazine in 1996, "I was surprised how conservative a town (Hollywood) is in practice, even though they'll say the right things in public." A friend of Walker's had just appeared on *The Tonight Show* on TV: "He was talking about what a 'fag' Feinstein (another guest on the show) was, and all the writers were joining in.

"I felt my whole insides imploding in slow motion. It was like walking in on a Ku Klux Klan rally."

In the mid-'90s, Feinstein came out with a CD and a book each titled *Nice Work If You Can Get It*. Of the former, music critic Barry Walters explained, "Nearly every song celebrates the joys of heterosexuality—which should come as no surprise to followers of a singer who hedges his bets when it comes to sexual orientation." Regarding the latter, gay historian Michael Willhoite pointed out that Feinstein was discovered and "nurtured" by gay actor Richard Deacon (interviewed in this author's *Hollywood Gays*), but that the book was unforthcoming about the off-stage, off-TV Michael. The autobio, clearly aimed at a hetero readership, defends homophobes like Ira Gershwin, who saw nothing wrong with a lyric like "On western prairies/we shoot the fairies," and dismisses "rumors" of George Gershwin's gayness—not dismissing the rumors of his royal hetero-ness—also semi-apologizing for Cole Porter's relative openness (Michael's pleased he was at least "discreet"), etc.

Still, Feinstein came out further than most actors or singers do. Asked, "When did you first realize you were attracted to men?" he replied, "I had those feelings of desire when I was about five or six." Indeed, pre-puberty, most gay men's feelings for other boys is nonsexual but *there* . . .just as with most heterosexuals pre-puberty.

Paul Jabara, who died of AIDS in 1992, apprised *Melody* magazine in 1989, "I was in a movie and so was a good-looking actor who was gay and extremely troubled. Years later, I hear he's calling himself an 'ex-gay.' Which is the biggest crock of crap! Like someone saying 'ex-heterosexual,' you know?" The difference is, heteros aren't constantly encouraged to renounce or lie about their sexuality. Jabara's point in the interview was to differentiate the levels of closeting among musical and especially movie celebs.

By actors' standards, composer/lyricist Stephen Sondheim is nearly out. But gay fans have long puzzled at the homophobic lyrics in some of his work. Some fans of *Company* have wondered at protagonist Bobby, the allegedly hetero hero who, one gay critic says, "just can't find the girl of his dreams. Maybe it's time for Bobby to come out of the closet—and bring the composer with him." Ironically, the '95 revival of the 1970 *Company*

255

was directed by openly gay Scott Ellis. Larry Kert played Bobby in the original *Company*:

"True, Bobby's thirty-eight and a bachelor. That gets funny looks. That's the conundrum at the heart of the story.... Is Bobby gay? Nowadays [1983] you might think he's experimented, just to be sure .... I think as conceived by [Sondheim], you're safe in assuming Bobby's 100 percent straight." Thus, 100 percent commercial. Sondheim's work hasn't always aimed at the sure commercial thing, but at the excluding mainstream, yes. The son of a dress manufacturer, he began with scripts for *Topper*, much later penning that anti-gay flick with secretly gay but posthumously "hetero" Tony Perkins (like bisexual Brad Davis, who since AIDS is officially "straight").

Sondheim has not done the girlfriend or fiancée or wife act that is so remarkably unremarked in show biz. But unlike Herman, he avoids gay content and gay comments. Music critic Barry Walters: "Sometimes one wishes Sondheim would get over himself and write another pop tune. If his morals mean so much to him, why, after all these years, hasn't he come out?" Friend and activist Larry Kramer asked in print, "Why doesn't Steve write a gay musical? ... Steve is in love now and is having a happy relationship. Why does he write something like that *Passion* and not something about him and Peter, who is very much younger?" Or if not something based on his own life—an unrealistic expectation—then a work at least including gay characters?

Tim Flack, vice president of creative affairs at CBS, was uniquely outspoken for television when he explained in 1994:

As far as I'm concerned, the term "gay community" is an ideal. So far, it's just a concept. The paranoia about being stigmatized or out of work for being gay is so widespread in entertainment, that even people who wouldn't lose work go by it.... Being out hasn't hurt singers like lang or Etheridge or Elton John, but who's followed in their brave footsteps? And where's the men singers? The black singers? There's no backup system for gay artists who come out, and everything's so fragmented into groups, and that's apart from all the usual show biz back-stabbing and the petty jealousies of so many gay men I've worked with or come across.

Human nature being what it is, most members of a

minority group that can pass, *will* pass. The easiest way out . . . particularly in a business that cultivates pretense and illusions, one where the stakes are probably the highest of any business."

Flack's words remind one that it is above all a business, and that money corrupts—the more money, the more temptation, and more giving in.

Jacques Morali was a co-creator of the Village People. Once they hit the heights, he ensconced them in the closet—that is, those members who were gay; the two successive lead singers were apparently not, and the first—dismissed before the VP's movie/epitaph *Can't Stop The Music*—has made minor headlines for drug-related arrests. Morali was quoted in *Télé Sept Jours* that "Bisexuality is a lure for Americans if the woman in question is beautiful, young, and also likes men" (redundant). Bisexual (quote-unquote!) men in the States, he warned, were a no-no. "The Americans do not accept men's little frailties. After so many centuries, they are still like the Puritans." As gay UK music critic Paul Burston put it, "In the mad, bad, and dangerous world of pop, a little queerness has always gone a long way—but don't make too strong a case of it or you'll never be Big in America."

Several Village Persons complained on and off the record that Morali grew more and more restrictive and erratic, and that even after the homophobically proclaimed "death of disco" and myriad comeback attempts, he refused to back-pedal on the straight-jacketing of the group's newer but unsuccessful image. Either Morali was genuinely bisexual or himself unable to accept his own "little frailties," for he was reportedly contractually married when he died of AIDS in 1991. (True enough, in Chicago, USA, the Village People were pelted in concert with pink marshmallows, a latter-day equivalent of the 1920's pink powder puffs used against Rudolph Valentino.)

Some areas of music have been traditionally more homophobic than others. Classical institution Aaron Copland was urged by his friend of some fifty years, Leonard Bernstein, to come out of the closet. Copland, in his eighties by then, was said to have declined not so much because of his career as his age. On the other baton-ed hand, classical and even Broadway music are still leery of non-heterosexual and non-male conductors.

257

(How phallic is that baton?) Broadway producer Saint Subber felt, "Audiences want to feel the conductor is in charge . . . the conductor is a father figure." Who decided these silly sentiments? Subber, himself gay, insisted, "People enjoy speculating about performers, of course, but the position of a conductor must be above reproach." Blah-blah.

The busiest conductor of Broadway musicals in the 1940s and '50s was Lehman Engel. Posthumously outed, he also composed, wrote books, and was a friend of Monty Clift. Leonard Bernstein himself confessed, "There was a time when a wife or at the least a brief marriage was an unspoken requirement for an aspiring conductor." Things are slowly changing for gay male conductors, although reticence (aka being "discreet") still seems part of the bargain (when would Bernstein have come out if he hadn't been outed in Joan Peyser's 1987 biography which *New York* magazine deemed "biased and homophobic"?). San Francisco Symphony conductor Michael Tilson Thomas doesn't discuss his life outside his work.

The August 6, 1995, *San Francisco Examiner* wrote that MTT lived with his "longtime partner and production manager, Joshua Robison." MTT's friend John Corigliano, a gay composer, offered, "I don't think it's Michael's preference not to discuss his private life. I suspect that the symphony's board has made some strong suggestions about what he shouldn't say. He's dealing with very rich people who don't want to have to deal with things like homosexuality. So they win." And gay people lose, for homosexuality isn't a "thing," it is people.

Corigliano also said he'd heard of gay composers being paid less "because they didn't have a family to support, as if that should matter," especially as having a family (aka kids) and how large are matters of choice. An anonymous because lesbian conductor profiled—or silhouetted—in OUTRAGE magazine had found, "A conductor has no private life. She or he should, but does not.

"It's ridiculous that who you live with is a measure of your fitness for the podium. . . . A woman has it ten times as hard. Whatever her home life is, she's a woman. So she has no orchestral mystique . . . (or) magisterial presence, in the view of those who could hire her." Thus, a would-be "conductress" is double-whammied by the patriarchy, via its non-democratic insistence on only-heterosexuality and only-males. In '96, American classical composer Robert Maggic opined that composers can now be out, but "It's the conductors and performers the audiences see. The re-creative artist, rather than the creator, is focused on. In that way, the work is removed from the personality of the composer." Such will remain the case as long as non-heterosexuality is considered something worth hiding, and as long as most gay people hide.

The nearly all-male domain of jazz has long been primarily very anti-gay. Also because of and despite the large presence of blacks in jazz; a 1997 poll of 1,000 Californians by the *San Jose Mercury News* found that whereas 36 percent of whites found homosexuality "morally wrong," 58 percent of blacks did so. Ironic, in view of one minority disparaging another, and tragic for black gay people . . . like the late and very underrated Billy Strayhorn, an accomplished jazz composer and the man behind Duke Ellington. In 1938 the renowned heterosexual took the twenty-three-year-old talent under his wing. Strayhorn's contributions to Ellington's success remained mostly hidden, long after his death from cancer at fifty-one.

Billy was showcased and given his due in the recent biography *Lush Life* (the title of one of his compositions). He wrote, uncredited, several of the songs that the Ellington orchestra made famous—among them "Take the A-Train"—and he arranged countless others. Ellington tolerated Billy's gayness ("I'm not going to change for anybody," he'd announced), but never signed a contract with Strayhorn or gave him a regular salary. Billy came up from poverty and had studied Debussy and Ravel. His talent and ambition (the latter not as big as the former) would have taken him high, if not to the top, but for the combination of his color and sexuality.

In the jazz world, Billy Strayhorn was esteemed and liked. He had a generous and likable personality. But with time, the lack of recognition and the restrictions against his personality and private life created a growing rage that he drowned in an eventually debilitating alcoholism. Gay writer-composer Paul Bowles, in a celebrity round-up on Billy Strayhorn, summed up the situation: "He wasn't allowed to be himself away from work, and he wasn't given credit for most of his work." (An accurate if ironic summation; Bowles is the widower of the short-lived writer Jane Bowles, a self-hating Jewish lesbian who married a man . . . in a church. . . .)

Things are changing. In 1996 black jazz singer Thomas Shipley was awarded Best Male Jazz Vocalist by the Manhattan Association of Cabarets and Clubs. He thanks especially "my partner Jeff" and declared, "I just refuse to live half of my life."

A number of jazz greats have been deeply closeted bisexuals (or gay men). Rumors have long swirled around the purported sexual flexibility of cornettist Bix Beiderbecke. Rumors are the sole level on which the establishment (formerly the Establishment . . .) will deal with non-heterosexuality. Jazz critics, historians, and biographers elide the gayness of leading musical creators and influences (jazz is, unsurprisingly, also very anti-female). Another jazz great, Miles Davis, was too often publicized for the umpteen (a clue?) women in his life, but is widely believed to have been bisexual. His friend and host, openly bi writer James Baldwin, said as much to several people.

Gay UK music writer John Gill pointed out that Davis officially died of pneumonia, stroke, and heart failure, not unusual for many people with AIDS. Some UK mainstream newspapers reported that he died of AIDS. Not so in the U.S., where a lack of comprehension of the term "political correctness" means that white reporters are terrified of labeling a black bisexual or gay man as black *and* bisexual or gay. Gill of course added that the initial closeting came from Davis himself, who was very discriminating about his reputation, "putting the women in the foreground and keeping the young male lovers strictly in the background."

The late Sun Ra feigned to have ancient Egyptian ancestors and also pretended he was not gay or bisexual, which he was. Cecil Taylor *is* out, but the jazz establishment doesn't refer to this at all when writing of the influential pianist-composer. Bassist Larry Gales told *The Reader*, "How does it mesh if music is about expressing yourself, and you're in that stuffy closet depressing and repressing yourself? . . . I couldn't say how much a jazz musician's personal life's got to do with his music. I do know the guys' girlfriends get mentioned a lot and even written up. But if a guy's got another guy in his life, there's a big, nervous silence over that."

When a figure is deceased, his estate can try and hush up

the truth, as with the black relatives and white entrepreneurs attached to, say, trumpeter-composer Miles Davis and poet Langston Hughes. Silence in death, silence in life. John Gill wrote of the ultra-conformist dealmakers in a performer's life who "demand and get something vastly more expensive than money—silence." Late saxophonist-composer Gerry Mulligan was by numerous accounts bisexual. In 1947 he presided over the birth of "cool" jazz with Miles Davis, and he conceived the "pianoless quartet." He also became prominently publicized as heterosexual via relationships with two female celebs who were lesbian or bi (there were even misreports of marriage to both women): screen comedienne Judy Holliday and Oscar- and Tony-winning actress Sandy Dennis (interviewed for this author's *Hollywood Lesbians*).

In point of fact, Mulligan may have been a lover of a young Johnny Mathis, who in his 1982 coming-out interview in *US* magazine namelessly noted his affair with a "baritone sax player" in his twenties when Johnny was sixteen, and how awful it was leaving his love in San Francisco to go work in New York City. Larry Gales believed "Mulligan's for the guys and the gals. From what I've gathered, with the guys it's an emotional and sexual thing, but the ladies are for his emotional and professional well-being.... But Mulligan's very private. He can get very distant if you get close to where he lives."

A growing number of jazz artists won't hide their sexual category or categorize themselves as strictly jazz. Singer-songwriter Steven Kowalczyk, thirty-three, had his debut album, *Moods and Grooves*, coproduced by jazz impresario and Atlantic Records founder Ahmet Ertegun. A promising star was born, but Kowalczyk insists, "One style I write in is swing- and jazz-influenced." In 1996 he spoke in *Out* magazine of his partner Peter, and celebrating their ten years together. His songs aim to "say modern things in a more traditional way," and his openness is part of the package:

Bill Leopold, who's my manager now, came to see me play, and afterwards he asked me if I was gay. I said yes, and he asked if I had any problems with that, and I said no; so Bill—who's straight—said, 'Good, the girls are gonna love you, and the guys are gonna love you.'

Another non-jazzy approach is followed by the jazz duo Theo & Kirk. The gay duo is a six-year partnership (the first year of it romantic, both now single) comprising German-born singer Theo Bleckmann and pianist-composer Kirk Nurock. After the death of his writing partner, C. J. Ellis, Nurock began setting the words of Emily Dickinson and Shakespeare to music "because I couldn't face searching for someone to work with." Their output thus combines jazz, Shakespeare, the Beatles, and Gershwin, as in their '96 CD, *Looking-Glass River*. (An ex child prodigy, Nurock has played with jazz greats like Dizzy Gillespie, who, however, foolishly declared that "There are no homosexuals in jazz.") After their affair ended, the men kept working together because "The music was too good and valuable for both of us."

Of course when one is young and the closeting lies haven't yet congealed into an opaque or solid wall, coming out is less difficult. Gary Burton, now fifty-four, was by the 1970s the country's leading vibraphone artist. The Grammy-winning jazz musician has yielded more than fifty albums, has been a composer, a bandleader, and a music instructor at the Berklee College of Music in Boston for over two decades. His past also includes two wives and two children. Burton's second wife, divorced from him in 1984, kept suggesting he come out. But Burton, now a dean at Berklee, kept waiting....

Jazz pianist Fred Hersch came out in 1984, probably the first openly gay jazz musician (he also revealed his HIV-positive status). Hersch had been waiting too, for someone major in jazz, or at least the music world, to come out. "No one did," said Hersch, "and I couldn't wait forever." Five years after Hersch, Burton came out. "Fred was one of the first people I talked to when I finally decided I wasn't going to avoid talking about it. I wasn't going to start announcing it to everybody, but I'd no longer evade the subject, and I knew it wouldn't take long before the word would be out, given the grapevine in the musician community."

Burton told the *Village Voice* in 1994, "The climate socially has continued to improve ... with how much more informed the public is, particularly in the entertainment industry." Besides, time was pressing: "I said to myself, This is midlife now, time to make up my mind. Either live what's left of my life honestly or face the fact that I'm not going to deal with this." Burton worked on k.d. lang's *Ingenue* album; like Fred Hersch, she expressed disappointment that more musicians hadn't followed her lead and come out.

"One of the problems in the performing arts," explains Burton, "is that if you get hired, it doesn't mean you have a job for life. It's not like working for the phone company. You're constantly being hired over and over. It's one of the challenges for a gay person in the arts, because even if coming out only costs you one job, it could be the one that would have had a big impact on your career."

Like lang and Hersch, Burton hasn't experienced career damage, but acknowledges, "If I had been in classical music or other areas of the performing arts, I would have long since felt there was no problem being accepted as gay. . . . But jazz has always had this macho connotation—the idea was that a gay person couldn't play hard. That was why women weren't welcomed in the jazz world." As a longtime jazz insider, Gary Burton has seen the waste and the lies closeup:

> We're all the worse off because of the closeted lives through the decades. The historians have absolutely avoided the issue, of course. They're all suck-ups to the history of the art and don't want to raise issues that might, in their eyes, denigrate the art form. Too bad. It makes them lousy historians.

One of the more unusual musical projects of recent years has been the opera *Harvey Milk* (though perhaps less strange than the opera about Nixon in Beijing). Not a *rock* opera like *Evita*—sadly, *Harvey* would not be viewed as a commercial/average enough subject—but a *real* opera, which had its world premiere in 1995 in Houston (strange venue for such a work). Its director, Christopher Alden, forty-seven, explains, "My sexuality is part of me, and so it is a major part of everything I create. Opera, like no other art form, delves deeply into treasure troves of sexuality in its lightest and darkest forms.

"It experiments with sexuality and confronts it in a way that gay people do a lot more openly than the straight world does." Alden tries to broaden audiences' perspectives by "slipping homoerotic elements into a lot of operas . . . not hard to do since they're already there. A lot of the composers were gay, and a lot of the relationships in opera have plenty of homoeroticism just under the surface." (Alden's partner Peter McClintock is a staff stage director at New York's Metropolitan Opera; his identical twin, David Alden, directs opera in Europe.) But not until *Harvey Milk* was Chris Alden "dealing with the real thing on stage," a "wonderfully freeing" experience.

Time will tell how frequently *Harvey Milk* is revived outside the slain city supervisor's political hometown of San Francisco. The opera's creators, Stuart Wallace and Michael Korrie, followed it up with the music for the opera *Hopper's Wife*, a bizarre fantasy in which painter Edward Hopper's meek wife Josephine metamorphoses into ambitious non-housewife Hedda Hopper, who heads for Hollywood and a career of her own. (Ironically, the reactionary and homophobic Hedda's only offspring was William Hopper, who fell in love with gay costar Raymond Burr on TV's *Perry Mason*.)

Gay classical composer David Del Tredici's pet project for several years was an opera titled *Dum Dee Tweedle*, inspired by a chapter in *Alice in Wonderland*. The Juilliard instructor broke through in 1976 at age thirty-nine with his composition *Final Alice*, one of several works based on that best-selling children's classic penned by an alleged heterosexual pederast (who may have been celibate). Another Del Tredici opus is *An Alice Symphony*, composed in 1969. Interestingly, DDT was beneficially mentored by Aaron Copland, who though he never came out to the media, "showed me that it was OK to be making music and be gay. And he had a true interest in young composers. He wasn't the type to use sex as a tool of power—he never put the make on me."

DDT has confessed to "sexual addiction," now in the past thanks to a sympathetic and pro-gay psychiatrist. Originally, David's mother had sent him to a Catholic shrink. "She wanted me to stop being queer and go back to the church," he recalls. *That* was when he became sexually active. Decades later, the more insightful shrink led him to the realization that being forced to constantly perform (music) as a child and teen was linked to an excessive, impersonal sexuality—"I met a million men, but I didn't want to get to know them." Peace of mind and happiness, he feels, are the keys to personal success.

Gay French pianist and international celeb Jean-Yves

Thibaudet agrees. "I have to enjoy my life, because it will reflect in my playing," says the bi-continental thirty-six-year-old who in a recent season played 120 concerts around the world. "Some people say that you should have a miserable life to be a great artist, but I don't agree. I think pleasure and being an artist go better together." Thibaudet enjoys a love relationship of over a dozen years with a certain New Yorker; J-YT also resides in Paris (one of his recordings comprises the complete solo piano music of Ravel).

Comfortably, openly gay, J-YT wishes more classical musicians were out of the closet (aka a vertical coffin). "I don't think it has so much to do with the classical world as the way these people deal with themselves. They are just not comfortable with it. Because if you're happy with it and you have no problem with it to start with, then it can easily relate to your professional life as well." Music historians have often distorted gay musicians—those they even admit are—as being "miserable homosexuals," when in reality what would make anyone miserable is their environment's unceasing homphobia. As pianist-wit Oscar Levant once said, "I'm not an unhappy Jew, but I am pretty unhappy about anti-Semitism." Paradoxically, Levant was homophobic—and possibly latently gay or bi. As recent studies confirm, so often the obsessively homophobic man is secretly homo- or bisexual (or hires the services of male prostitutes in dresses . . . on or off a *Murphy* bed . . .).

Another happy and gay musician is composer Marc Shaiman, who has been Oscar-nominated for scoring the films *Sleepless in Seattle* and *The American President*. Away from the studio, he has served as a judge at the Gay Erotic Video Awards along with movie directors John Schlesinger and John Waters. And he is proud of his eighteen-year relationship with theatre director Scott Wittman, with whom he attended the Academy Awards. Had he won, he'd planned to acknowledge Wittman—as most winners now acknowledge their wives, husbands, children, girlfriends, etc., etc. (aka saying *I'm-heterosexual* in code).

Remembering Bill Lauch's moving acceptance speech on behalf of his late life partner Howard Ashman when he received the Oscar for the song *Beauty and the Beast*, Shaiman states, "What I would have said is, 'All you people out there who love *Beauty and the Beast*, just remember that the movie you cherish was created by a gay man.' Obviously that point comes across anyway, but maybe there are still some people for whom it does need to be spelled out."

Not only the freedom to love, but the freedom to have (other) gay friends is a relatively new one. Gay screen actor Farley Granger informed journalist Robert L. Pela that Aaron Copland was composing the score of *The North Star* (1943), in which Granger (*Rope, Strangers on a Train*) made his screen bow, when the men became friends. Producer Samuel Goldwyn warned Granger against the friendship because, "He's suspected of being a homosexual." Goldwyn later warned Granger—who had publicity dates with Shelley Winters—against writer (and later a Broadway director) Arthur Laurents (*Gypsy, La Cage Aux Folles*) for the same reason, plus Laurents' leftist politics (virtually all the Tinseltown moguls were extreme rightists). But Granger maintained his friendship with Copland and became Laurents' lover for four years. (One assumes Goldwyn eventually found out about Granger.)

Not only employers, but biographers of homophobic bent try to rearrange a man's love life and friendships. Pianist Van Cliburn came to fame in 1958 when he won the Tchaikovsky International Music Competition in Moscow. Another irony was his later being described as "the Van Johnson of the piano." Born in 1934, Cliburn hailed from Kilgore, Texas, the hometown of openly gay, underrated playwright Robert Patrick (who contributed a foreword to the first edition of this author's *The Lavender Screen*). Because he wasn't Jewish, was blond, and, uh, didn't act like Liberace, VC was vigorously promoted by the then-Establishment, especially in the South.

However it's often been said his career fizzled within a few years of the 1958 victory, which was as highly touted for ideological reasons in the USA as for artistic ones. By the late 1970s he had begun an "eleven-year retreat into privacy." In 1996 a Texas judge dismissed a palimony suit against VC by his alleged lover of seventeen years, aged forty-eight. The reason the suit was thrown out was that the state of Texas does not recognize same-sex relationships. . . .

Likewise, a 1993 bio-gap-ography of Cliburn by a Nashville-based Christian publisher totally omitted the pianist's private life, relationships, friendships, loves, yearnings, and emotional makeup. Only a few stereotypical clues surfaced: that as a kid, VC read *The Opera News,* and in high school the basketball coaches despaired of him since he was tall but disinclined to balls . . . that go through hoops. The alleged biography did make sure to note that while in Russia, VC made a donation to the local Baptist church—which brings one back to 1997 and a realistic Disney empire that would indeed have the talented but multi-bigoted Walt Disney spinning in his grave (or in his special case, refrigerator).

"When I was growing up in the middle of nowhere in Australia," said Peter Allen, "I had rather a dull life but lots of marvelous musical influences. They were what lifted me up out of my small world . . . an eclectic mix: Judy Garland of course (she arranged Peter's marrying Liza Minnelli, who now admits her first husband was gay but not that her father was gay or bi), American musicals, Argentine tangos, cowboy songs—although my favorite one was "Don't Fence Me In," by Cole Porter, so that was already a hint. . . ." Michael Callen of the Flirtations numbered among his musical faves "Lerner and Loewe, who weren't as cutesy as Rodgers and Hammerstein. . . . What really knocked me out was learning that John Williams is gay! We can always be surprised. Thank goodness! Yet what saddens me is that while John Williams is up-front about it, the whole informational structure isn't. So the mass public doesn't know what they owe him, just a few gay men reading a few gay papers." Williams, conductor of the Boston Pops, is best known for his epic scores for such megahit films as *Star Wars, Superman, Raiders of the Lost Ark,* their assorted sequels, and so forth.

More than any man except MGM mogul Louis B. Mayer who signed her—and then consistently denigrated her—composer/arranger Roger Edens was responsible for the musical stardom of Judy Garland. Edens, who had a crush on hunky but anti-gay Clark Gable (he allowed himself to be serviced by pre-talkies movie star William Haines; see *Hollywood Gays.* . .), penned "You Made Me Love You, Dear Mr. Gable" for Garland, and it launched her. He became an MGM musical supervisor and also a producer, but always kept a hand in Judy's career and life, mentoring her as well as Angela Lansbury, who has recently admitted Edens was gay (as was Hollywood's ace hairdresser,

Sydney Guilaroff, whose largely fictional memoirs featured a foreword by Lansbury; SG died in 1997, still firmly in the closet and terrified of exposure, having allegedly signed over his home to a lover rather than be accurately categorized).

Edens had begun his illustrious but low-key career arranging special material for would-be movie star Ethel Merman at Paramount in the early 1930s. His final assignment was teaching Kate Hepburn to sing as the (also, yes!) bisexual designer Gabrielle "Coco" Chanel in *Coco*. When the musical opened in late 1969 it marked the first time on Broadway that a star uttered the word "shit." (Hepburn, whose friendship or romance with (impotent) alcoholic Spencer Tracy has been increasingly media-sexualized over the years, once declared, "There are things in my life which I would never discuss with anyone. I would never even discuss them with myself.")

Carlos Gardel (1890 – 1935) was as prominent and esteemed in Argentina as, say, Katharine Hepburn in the USA. He was the Argentine's most famous singer and the composer of many of its leading tangos. He *was* tango, they used to say. In 1993 he was posthumously outed—apparently the persistent rumor had never seen the light of print—by seventy-eight-year-old musician Virgilio Exposito in a Buenos Aires newspaper. And it was charged that Gardel stole the authorship of some tangos, but what outraged much of the nation wasn't the claim of plagiarism, but the "challenge to his manhood" (aka heterosexuality, real or imagined) of the man who symbolizes Buenos Aires. Yep, outcast sexuality is still reserved by the powers that be for outcast citizens, south and north of the border.

They say one is judged by the company one keeps, by no one more so than the media. Rodgers and Hammerstein were both hetero, both staid, unlike their incredible output (and despite many of the latter's words). Alan Jay Lerner was a flamboyant heterosexual, media-publicized for his umpteen wives and staunchly sexist views. Frederick Loewe, the son of a tenor, was an occasionally flamboyant gay or bisexual man; he was media-publicized for his association with the unquestionably "straight" Lerner. At fifteen, Loewe had written the Euro-pop hit "Katrina," which sold over a million copies. His music, which unlike Lerner's lyrics can stand on its own, gloriously, is among the best ever written for Broadway or elsewhere. (Incredibly, the deep-closeted Mary Martin, who also had a gay second husband, after hearing the music and lyrics for *My Fair Lady*, sighed, "Oh, those boys have lost their talent!")

Frederick Loewe was, in composer Burton Lane's phrasing, "a composer's composer, talented to talented men." Yet the public spotlight was almost inevitably on Lerner—who also wrote the books for their fabled musicals—a publicity-hog in today's language. The Viennese Loewe preferred to do his own thing in relative privacy. One of his escapades, remarked in the book *Palm Springs Babylon*, was passing off his pal Allan Keller as "Anna Maria von Steiner, world-famous pianist and inspiration of *My Fair Lady*." The Palm Springs press bought the impersonation. Once the cat was out of the bag, though, there was no print coverage of the man behind la Steiner or about Frederick and Allan's relationship or interests. . . .

When people are not open, they can be misrepresented in any number of ways, and hurt. Like a minor 1940s film actor falsely accused of raping a female starlet who chose to go to jail as a presumed heterosexual (and lose his screen career) rather than declare himself homosexual, and *not* go to jail (but lose his screen career anyway). And again, when someone can pass, even now, they generally do, though it's changing faster in some musical spheres than others. Television composer Laura Karpman had hesitated to come out "because there are so few women in this field. That's generally a strike against you as it is, so I had concerns." Karpman has scored non-fiction series like *A Century Of Women*, TV movies like *Doing Time on Maple Drive* and miniseries like NBC's *A Woman of Independent Means*.

A musician "since age seven, basically," Laura grew up "hearing Beethoven concertos, Miles Davis, Hebrew folk songs, flamenco, you name it." After her first same-sex love affair at twenty-one, she came out to her family "and everyone was fine with it. I was lucky to have grown up in an environment where there were always gay people around"—gay people known as such, not invisible and unhelpful. At work, she came out in part "because of the way I work, with producers and directors coming over to the house.

"It's completely obvious to anyone who wants to see. I began to care less and think, If they don't like it, that's their problem. With more success, I became more open about it."

Versus actors' success, which increasingly embeds them in the closet.

As to why fewer women in music—apart from singers—come out, Karpman makes two strong points. She brings up a woman with whom she had a five-year relationship in New York, who is racked by doubts and needless guilt. "This woman was *born* a dyke, came out of the *womb* a dyke, and she now thinks traumatic situations brought her to this and that she can work it out in therapy. I'd love to get her therapist disbarred ... but this is what happens with many women I know of.

"It's easier for women to move back and forth than men. To be sexual as a woman requires a different kind of activity—you can just lie there!—so it's a lot easier to vacillate. Men settle into it and accept" being gay. "For women it's different. I know women who have been lesbians for years, and all of a sudden when they hit thirty or thirty-one, they start thinking they want to go out with guys again.

"It's partly because men and women are socialized differently. Women—gay or straight—are socialized like women, so they still half expect a guy to come along and rescue them. Men don't have that." Karpman is fully open and articulate, but her female mate of several years—an actress—is still struggling with the residue of homophobia. Karpman partly attributes this to her partner's un-artistic, non-intellectual childhood milieu. "She was a total outsider as a child. The fact that she was artistic was viewed as 'different.'" Time and again it's been said that gay kids who grow up around books and music, in a more intelligent and culturally diverse background have a head-start in self-confidence and dealing with the non-gay world.

Among the many who have died from AIDS since the first edition of this book are Peter Allen (in 1992) and Michael Callen (1993), both out, and Michael a sweet-hearted AIDS activist to the very end. "I can't imagine why there hasn't been a book about gay music-makers before this," Michael wrote me in 1991, "but you're going to have to do an updating in a few years, what with tragic or inspiring events affecting the music world." He referred to the AIDS deaths and to the comings out which both seemed to be accelerating.

After k.d. lang and Melissa Etheridge came out, I asked

Michael his theory of why, except for Britisher Elton John, it seemed to be women only exiting the closets? "Well, men rule. And men think they can control women and women's sexuality. But a man's sexuality, that scares other men. Being less individualistic than women, (hetero) men think that anything another man does, at least sexually, reflects on them." More so in some cultures and sub-cultures. Michael explained:

"My Latino friends who are gay have acclimatized to this country. So they all wonder why Juan Gabriel (a leading Mexican singer and composer reminiscent in manner and girth of Liberace) won't come out? It's one of those situations, like Liberace, where everybody really *knows*, but since the guy won't say *yes*, the people who'd prefer him not to be gay have an excuse to say he isn't."

Such, then, is the problem with outing. If one declares that a gay VIP is gay and the VIP denies it, that's what the media and most of the public go by. Outing *per se* does not work; at most, it can hasten a VIP's coming out once the silence on the topic has been broken. A small constellation of stars, and a handful of politicians, admit they made the decision to come out after being outed in the media, usually tabloids.

Michael continued, "There's this country singing star. He's gay. The country people know he's gay. His fans know he's gay. *He* knows he's gay. But what he did is marry his female manager. It's platonic between them, but it's enough of a cover to fool most of his fans." Or at least stifle the Topic. "That part of the country is so in need of positive gay role models, of *any* openly gay person. He could do so much good by being honest. . . . But it's a background where being non-gay or non-Christian's like being sinful or something."

Peter Allen flirted with a bisexual image, and would tease fans, "Yes, I am—bicoastal!" Or tell his audiences, "Yes, what you've heard is true! I am—Australian!" At one concert he announced, "I was in Sydney recently—Sydney loved it!" He told the *New York Native* in 1991, "I was *out* on stage years before anyone else." Not quite true; after they're out, a number of gay celebs say they've been out all along (one music VIP was repeatedly outed, then claimed to be bi, then came out as gay, now says he was always openly gay . . . anyway, better late than never).

Allen admitted, "It's (being gay) just less of a fuss in

Australia." Indeed, Australia has many more pro-gay laws than the USA—though its celebrity exports are stubbornly closeted (aka desperately ambitious). "But when I made a name for myself in America, I knew I had to tone it all down." Peter began as half of the Allen Brothers, though his partner Chris Bell was not his brother. He then opened for Judy Garland, earned minor fame as Liza's husband (the 1992 bio *Liza* states that the union was never consummated, though how could an outsider know that?), and broke through as a songwriter when Olivia Newton-John (a fellow Aussie) recorded a hit version of "I Honestly Love You." A Sydney comedian-singer once informed his audience:

"I just finished my latest album. It's called *Music to Listen to Olivia Newton-John By.*"

Peter Allen's career as both a flamboyant singer and a successful songwriter was "less vulnerable to the stud syndrome than with many of the handsomer, more middle-of-the-road local (American) singers." When Peter and three others won the Academy Award for the theme song for *Arthur* he told the audience the group had wanted to divide the Oscar statue into quarters if they won, but they couldn't agree: "Carole Bayer Sager and I wanted the same part. . . ."

Singer-dancer Larry Kert, also a victim of AIDS, was perhaps best known as the male lead in Broadway's *West Side Story*. Never a popular singer or concert attraction, he nonetheless always enacted heterosexuals on the stage. Leonard Bernstein commented, "Larry is exceptionally private, for a number of reasons. . . . He wants to ensure a long stage career, certainly a commendable though sometimes naïve aspiration." Which puts one in mind of the AIDS-era lament, Hope I get old before I die.

Kurt Cobain died a suicide, and just as he was getting closer to confessing the bisexuality that seemed to fascinate him. He was undoubtedly pro-gay. The note on the sleeve of Nirvana's *Insecticide* album read, "If any of you in any way hate homosexuals, people of different color, or women, please do this one favor for us—leave us the fuck alone!" Earlier, Cobain used to write the graffito God Is Gay, and told the *Advocate* that he thought he was too. His best friend was gay and got gay-bashed, as Kurt did for having a gay friend. Was Kurt gay? He answered, "In spirit." Bisexual? "Probably."

Nirvana, which formed in 1986, wore drag on video, kissed

each other on *Saturday Night Live*, and in the song "All Apologies" stated, "What else should I say? Everyone is gay." No previous superstar rock band had taken such an openly pro-gay stance. Before he died, Cobain had been seeing much of semi-open Michael Stipe (more anon . . .). Insiders said their possible collaboration was all Kurt could get excited about. Stipe then wrote the song "Let Me In" about the deaths of Cobain and of gay or bi (but closeted) actor River Phoenix. So what combination of fear, disillusion, and drugs drove Kurt Cobain to suicide? In any case, it was a true loss for music and humanity.

By contrast there was Tiny Tim, né Herbert Khaury, who trilled, "You can call me Lebanese or even lesbian, but please don't call me a homosexual. I have feelings, you know." The wrong kind. Gay or not—the one homosexual experience he admitted to is standard procedure for curious male heterosexual teenagers—he was a fundamentalist Christian with more than one wife (at a time, thanks to the law) who in his heyday admitted he spent about $200 a day on cosmetics (to what effect?). The gay media noted that whenever the subject of same-sex came up, Tiny uttered biblical preachments against it. The *LA Weekly* noticed, "If he is what he insists he is, he spends an awful lot of time agitating against the gay community and their bedroom habits."

TT hailed from Minneapolis, like the more free-wheeling Prince (when Oprah asked Prince, "People thought you were weird or gay—did that bother you?" in 1996, the name-challenged singer-musician replied, "Hey, whatever floats your boat."). Tiny Tim died there in 1996, on stage cooing his one semi-hit, "Tiptoe Through the Tulips."

A less publicized and less trivial career was that of black singer Jimmie Daniels (1907 – 1984), born in Laredo, Texas. He went to Paris in the late 1920s to sing. Later in New York City he had a bit part in a Katharine Cornell play (she and husband-producer Guthrie McClintic were both gay, though he was far more active sexually than she). Daniels gave up the stage to be a cabaret singer, describing his singing as "a bit of a bluff." In the mid-'30s he met Scottish Kenneth MacPherson, with whom he was lovers for years. The Scot was wedded to rich lesbian author Winnefred Bryher. When the "couple" divorced in 1949, she settled considerable money on MacPherson, who gave a generous amount to Daniels, who had an eponymous nightclub in Harlem and by the 1960s had become a host at assorted New York City and Fire Island nightclubs.

A well-liked entertainer and host, with a bigger talent than he believed in, Jimmie Daniels died all but forgotten. Unlike Tiny Tim, he hadn't experienced the luck of landing on a popular TV show that conferred more than the proverbial fifteen minutes of fame, since TV is an endless rerun and its spotlight is recyclable, not to mention impervious to good taste or graceful aging (many were surprised to learn that TT was in his 70s when he died).

Since the first edition of this book, a number of allegedly/rumoredly diverse singers have taken steps that more closely align them with the masses, specifically, Michael Jackson, Whitney Houston, and Prince. All have become parents, at least two of them presumably the usual, non-laboratory way. The first two contractually wed without much delay; the latter is less concerned with man-made legalities than with his moniker. A funny coincidence that Jackson named his child Prince, now that that's what The Artist (Prince) is formerly known as.

Publicist Alison Carreon states the not always obvious: "In show business, a baby" may or may not be a wish fulfillment. Before and since Joan Crawford, a star often has a baby"—adopted, natural, or artificial insemination—"as an image-enhancer. To tone down a wild heterosexual image or do away with a homosexual one." Rarely, she says, does the public consider the motive, or the method. And sometimes a baby is a publicity-booster. Babies always make the news when a parent is a celebrity, invariably creating some measure of warm feelings toward the celeb.

Time magazine called (Prince) The Artist Formerly Known as Hot. His *Purple Rain* album (1984) sold 13 million copies, but his '96 album *Chaos & Disorder* sold fewer than 100,000. The 'zine also cited (Prince's) "eye-lined eyes" and soft voice, and his comparing his *late*-1996 opus to *Citizen Kane*! And yes, he did eventually marry. An insider at Paisley Park (the singer's recording complex) affirmed, "He doesn't like contracts, he's had the most terrible experience with his label (Warner Bros.). . . . I think he did it 'cause of the baby and the bride . . . she

274

worked for him (as a dancer). She just demanded it."

Prince, now sans movie career, still makes demands himself. Namely, that he be treated as musical royalty. In the words of *Time*, "But pretentious quirkiness without the platinum popularity to back it up can begin to feel a little Norma Desmondish. . . ."

As for the self-proclaimed king of pop, la Jackson—who unrealistically yearned for a movie career—can out-manipulate Prince any day. After the boy-child molestation charges, Jacko settled mega-millions on the boy's father. Elton John assured Barbara Walters that had he been in Jackson's place, he—a lover of adult men—would never, if innocent, have conceded a penny. The next step was marrying the daughter of the late king of pop, Elvis Presley, whose title recalls the saying that the secret of praising is to let others do it for one. The alleged marriage didn't take—even if it did, it wouldn't have proven anything; Tinseltown was/is be-glittered with long-lasting official pairs of all descriptions.

The megalomaniacal album *HIStory* was notoriously anti-Semitic (columnist James Bacon suggested it might have been deliberately so, garnering despicable publicity for its bigotry and then more, supposedly positive, publicity for erasing the mindless hate-lyrics). It also sold far short of expectations. The Michael Jackson jokes continued—about his alleged propensities, via *Tonight Show* host Jay Leno and countless others, and about his racial and gender incongruities. At a Friars roast of Burt Reynolds, Red Buttons quipped, "Only in America can a poor black boy like Michael Jackson grow up to become a rich white woman."

The *LA Village View* asked, "Why does Michael Jackson want to be white? The answer is as clear as the nose on Elizabeth Taylor's face." As a child performer, wrote the *LAVV*, "he knew he needed to learn to dance like James Brown, but he didn't dream of being James Brown. He dreamed of being Fred Astaire."

With age, the well-mannered image gave way to open arrogance and an obsessive need for control and adulation. Nor did the constant craving for conformity abate. The news broke that a female associate was pregnant by him, and then news of a second wedding ceremony. Columnist Jack Martin called it

"Addams Family Territory" and wrote, "The daddy (in the widely publicized photos) looks like the mother, the mother looks like the grandmother, and the baby . . . Prince (which makes him sound like an Alsatian) looks a damned sight smarter than the pair of them put together."

In '97, Jacko's new CD arrived on store shelves with a fraction the publicity of *HIStory*, grossly titled *Blood on the Dance Floor*. *Frontiers* magazine reviewed: "The five new songs he drummed up are surprisingly bloodless. . . . What inspires these wacky stories about psychopathic women running around with knives? Did Brooke Shields refuse to lend her hair gel? Did Lisa Marie forget to comb the llama? On 'Morphine,' Jackson tries to act tough . . . the image overhaul fails abysmally. Loosen up, Michael, before your career becomes *HIStory*."

The new album aims for an image re-do, but memories aren't that short. The *LAVV* remembered, "*HIStory*'s dedication, 'to all the children of the world,' may read a little creepy these days (nobody, not even a zillionaire like Michael Jackson, forks over 20 million bucks on an unfounded charge). . . ." The *New York Daily News* quoted a female British columnist re Jackson's new video, "Ghosts," "I thought it was just sick! There was enough there to put him away for twenty years. All these little kids who love him? What a pervert!"

Italian journalist Christiana Peterno felt, "Michael Jackson is telling his story (in "Ghosts") in such a self-celebratory way. He spent so much money and used so many special effects—all this just to defend himself." But while "Ghosts" set tongues wagging in '97, one pathetic and revealing bit of news almost got away. Jay Leno noted that Jackson had given away his once widely publicized pet chimp, Bubbles. The animal had grown older, less "cute" (publicly presentable), and was consigned to a minimal care facility, out of the lap of luxury and the limelight. Yes, publicity and photo ops are one thing, feelings another.

In December, 1994, Jodie Foster chose to share with *Los Angeles Times Magazine* readers some of her most intimate feelings (no, not those).

She confessed that she abhorred "weakness" (does she deem openly gay performers as weak, one wonders?), and were she to find a wounded bird on the sidewalk, her instinct would be not to aid it, but to "kick it." The following month, the *LATM* ran reader responses:"Hey, weakness really, really bugs me too.. .. If I were to find Foster flopping on the Hollywood Walk of Fame, wounded by one of her psychotic admirers, I'd have no choice but to kick her." "She comes off as not only cold but cruel as well.""If Foster is so fearless, why did she dodge [a question about her sexuality]? ...If she is, why doesn't she simply set the matter to rest by saying, 'Yes, I am, and what of it?'"

And, "Perhaps Foster's attitude defines, in one sad sentence (about the hypothetical wounded bird), the state of mind that one must have to succeed in the entertainment industry." They do call it a jungle ....

Many performers who don't wish to be perceived as gay feel that way because of an aversion to camp. Camp is but one aspect of gay culture and/or behavior. Unfortunately, when a minority is mostly silent and invisible, it is defined—and therefore limited—by the majority. Ian Shaw, touring the States in '97 with another gay jazz vocalist, Steven Kowalczyk, asserts, "We are singing some songs connected with Peggy Lee, Billie Holiday, and Judy Garland. But it's *not* a camp thing." American Kowalczyk agrees:"Some people think if you're going to express yourself as a gay artist, it has to be campy. But expression is very personal, and it doesn't necessarily include stereotypes."

Briton Shaw explains,"Singing involves wearing your heart on your sleeve. That's considered okay for a woman, however in jazz it's not very acceptable for a straight man."

Shaw is a bigger celebrity in the UK than Kowalczyk is in the USA. London's *Time Out* magazine dubbed him "the vocal find of the decade." The thirty-four-year-old feels that jazz, an alien musical form, is better appreciated in Britain. "Europe has a long tradition of art. We also tend to appreciate a piece of art regardless of who created it. You lot tend to like or dislike a work depending on who made it and what he stood for." He points to composer Harry ("I Only Have Eyes for You") Warren as a man whose output is liked and who is thus posthumously closeted in nearly all American books mentioning him.

Steven Kowalczyk agrees with the sentiment that if one wastes time and energy hiding in the closet, there's less of it for making music. Alas, the singer was dropped in 1996 by Atlantic Records—along with other gay acts like the band Extra Fancy—

despite his popular, already noted album *Moods and Grooves* (1995). Homophobia was the rumored reason, and a clear explanation has not been issued. Kowalczyk cautiously offers, "I'm not sure what it was." The singer-composer mostly avoids gay content in his songs and has a debatable take on the dilemma of a gay man singing "he" or "she."

"When you sing 'he' instead of 'she,' the statement becomes bigger than the song. Your art becomes a kind of propaganda." In other words, what the majority does is okay, "normal," uncontroversial; what the minority does is political, confrontational, "propaganda." That will only change when being openly different is accepted—by most people, including the different ones—as natural rather than deliberately provocative.

The late Johnnie Ray mused, "If I could sing all my hits and the standards the usual way (to a "she"), but just do one song singing 'he.' That would be my contribution. It *could* be, if it wouldn't upset most everyone listening to me." Christopher Isherwood, who coined the phrase "the heterosexual dictatorship," once urged, "If they're 90 percent, for their own reasons they'll insist on 100 percent, but for our own, more logical reasons, we mustn't let them have 100 percent." Activist-prophet Larry Kramer points out, "If we're not included, it's not a democracy. And we're not included."

Still, even with the wrong pronouns, gay and lesbian singers find some degree of emotional release or expression in their work. Ian Shaw said, "It's essential that we find this release somewhere. There's nothing more comforting—for me, anyway—than going into a gay bar and seeing men express themselves. It's something that many of us are denied in our jobs and relationships with parents, sisters, brothers. And I feel absolutely privileged that I, for one, can go onstage and sing it away."

In *Elvis* and *John Lennon* author Albert Goldman's opinion, "Country music is mostly formula. . . . The new trend in the early '90s is for a handsome guy to plug into the formula and make himself a fortune. But he has to go by the formula and follow all the rules." In 1995 it was reported as "the juiciest country scandal in years, and certainly the gayest." Rising country singer/stud Ty Herndon was arrested for allegedly exposing himself to a male undercover cop in a Texas park. (Those guys don't have better things to do?) Ironically, he was due ninety minutes later to perform at a Texas Police Association convention. Talk about bad timing!

Also, the thirty-three-year-old conventionally married rising star had a #1 hit on *Billboard*'s country charts and was embarking on his first cross-country tour. Herndon's manager Johnny Slate professed, "I honestly don't know what Ty's sexual preference is, but it shouldn't matter. I hope this will change the way people think of being gay in country music. I don't know how the fans will react, but I feel that they are ready for a major country star to come out." Slate was uniquely honest and sadly naïve. It so happened that Herndon had on him methamphetamines, and so he promptly checked into a drug rehab center in Arizona (another state where homosexuality is "illegal").

Herndon announced that the drugs' influence was responsible for his "erratic" behavior. He got the charges dropped, and said that the clinic had helped him to turn his life around. So, welcome back, Ty. As the *Advocate* cracked, Herndon "made the news by waving his weenie at an undercover cop." But hardly—excuse the expression—the sort of news an aspiring country star would seek to make, regardless of where the truth lies. . . .

French-born Robert Clary is best known for TV's *Hogan's Heroes* but since age twelve has been acting, singing, and dancing—with a three-year interruption as a teenager in Auschwitz and other concentration camps. "I never knew from day to day if I was going to be killed," as all his relatives were. Pre-*Hogan*, he released several LPs. During *Hogan*, he was one of the quartet on the 1967 LP *Hogan's Heroes Sing the Best Of World War II*. After *Hogan*, Clary essayed a nightclub singer in the soap opera *Days of Our Lives*.

In late 1994 Clary was arrested in a Beverly Hills park via a "vice sting operation." The *Beverly Hills Courier* obnoxiously trumpeted, "He may have continually slipped through the fingers of Colonel Klink and Sergeant Schultz, but he couldn't escape the Beverly Hills police." Thereafter, the Jewish Television Network dropped Clary's talk show. Efforts by this writer to ascertain whether the reason was homophobia met with excuses or silence. Legally, homophobia is rarely provable, and police entrapment for victimless crimes is as prevalent as ever.

Clary met his eventual wife via Merv Griffin (no comment . . .), who introduced them. For fifteen years Clary was friends with Natalie Cantor, the daughter of multi-media star Eddie Cantor. As soon as *Hogan's Heroes* debuted, Clary proposed marriage (is that timing?). Marjorie Cantor was the eldest of Eddie's five daughters. By all accounts gay, she died in her early 40s and had not wed a man. Hollywood busybody George Jessel tried lamely to explain the situation, writing that she "never fell in love with anybody because she so looked up to her father. (Other men) all suffered so by comparison!" Really! As for she "never fell in love with anybody (*male*)," that's the way lesbian and gay love relationships were and are hidden from view.

For example, our library system has no classification for same-sex partners and relationships. Gertrude Stein and Alice B. Toklas were inseparable from 1907 until Stein's death in 1946, yet *The Autobiography of Alice B. Toklas* by Gertrude Stein— how much closer can you get?!—is filed by the Library of Congress under "friends and associates," not partners, lovers, gay couples, etc. By comparison, a Hollywood-style marriage of, say, four months (like Ethel Merman and Ernest Borgnine) or a few years (Michael Jackson and female) *is*. Larry Kramer bears repeating: "If we're not included, it's not a democracy. And we're not included."

In other words, it's still not liberty and justice for all . . . .

Of course the closets hardest to crack or exit are those self-made by ignorance and/or self-contempt. Most astonishing are the stereotypical closet cases, the Liberaces. Boy George has since said, "The first go-round in the United States, I was ordered to deny this, deny that. I told the record people I wasn't going to go out there and say I was straight . . . who'd have believed that?" The point being that most people believe what they want to believe, facts aside.

Kurt Cobain said, "Liberace was such a sad case. His gullibility . . . the whole situation of his not liking who he was, his whole not caring a damn about other people like him." In interviews, Cobain admitted he sometimes wore "a comfy" smock or dress around the house, and his rock group's wearing drag on video ("In Bloom") and he on the cover of *The Face* and sometimes on stage did encourage other bands to experiment with drag. Ironically, such groups weren't necessarily gay or pro-gay.

And Kurt clarified, "Drag is just something I'm kind of interested in. It's not to make a gay statement, 'cause most gays don't even wear drag."

He also tried to explain to Nirvana fans, "I don't mind being called politically correct. All it means is not using hurt-words like 'nigger' or 'faggot.' . . . It's not so hard, saying 'gay' instead of a hurtful word. . . . Yeah, Nirvana is politically correct." Unlike most music superstars, Kurt wasn't self-obsessed; he interrupted one music interview to share, "A pretty good friend of mine, one time he said ballet was baseball for fairies. 'You mean like X?' I said, and then we had a conversation about that." The singer had named a retired but living, contractually married baseball legend who in the '60s never hid being Jewish but continues to hide being gay (in Tinseltown, a number of older performers still hide both; in Hollywood it was often said that Dinah Shore— who was heterosexual, female golfers and Palm Springs notwithstanding—was "a closet Jew").

Singer Little Richard has occasionally been nicknamed the bronze Liberace. While he was never as accepted by the mainstream, and cut his own career short, he still makes with the denials. He shouted at one gay fan, "I don't go that way, no, no, it's completely the other way. Now, shut up!" (The *other* way??) And in 1995, performing live at Dollywood (Dolly Parton's taste-free theme park), he chastized another fan, "I am not like that. Don't say that about me."

By contrast, RuPaul is one crossover drag success (unlike, say, the UK's Danny LaRue, remember him?) who doesn't deny his sexuality. Obviously, a number of openly gay celebs or demi-celebs—like Clive Barker and Roseanne's sister, respectively— will say they're gay in *Out*, *Genre*, and other homophile periodicals. But on television (almost as if living rooms have been defined as heterosexual), the same celebs will say nil about being gay—Barker on *Tom Snyder*, Geraldine on *Phil Donahue*—and thus only the readers of gay publications *know*.

RuPaul has proclaimed that "We're born naked, and the rest is drag." More importantly, he's stressed the need for openness and positive gay role models for kids and teens of all backgrounds, citing the tragic statistic that three times as many lesbian and gay teenagers are apt to commit suicide as are heterosexual ones. Some humane musicians, gay or hetero or bi, have rallied to the call. Beastie Boys' Mike D told *Alternative Press* magazine, "It's not even enough to say we're not homophobic, you have to go the next step and say we're anti-homophobic and pro-gay."

Still waffling last one heard, Michael Stipe of R.E.M. once stated, "Labels are for canned food. . . . I am what I am, and I know what I am." Would a heterosexual say that? Why isn't "heterosexual" considered a label? Stipe was in the '96 movie *Color of a Brisk and Leaping Day*, which had gay undertones, but he was too shy (that's one label) to discuss those with gay journalists at the Sundance Film Festival. In '96 he did attend the AIDS-Dance-A-Thon in Los Angeles, as did the latest recycling of the Village People (whose comments to mainstream periodicals say one thing, their comments to gay ones another. . .). Regarding his preference for the label of bisexual in *Rolling Stone* in '96, Stipe guessed, "There's probably a minority percentage of the gay community who still feel like I'm cowardly and copping out." Not if he's bi. . . .

In *Out* magazine, Stipe let down his guard a bit but still wouldn't come out, though clearly flirting with the notion. Some readers applauded his saying as much as he had, especially "if one happens to be the lead singer of the world's greatest band." Others wondered why there's been so little progress since "David Bowie treaded on similar ground twenty years ago?" Another wrote, "'Nobody's business' and 'Don't label me' are such petty, tired, worn-out, lame excuses when gays and lesbians are out there still being discriminated against, beaten, and killed for who they love."

Another major leaguer, the B-52's' Fred Schneider, was urged by journalist Lance Loud to come out, but wouldn't. Lance tried getting him to come out via fax, and he did, obliquely. Lance asked, "Why do you feel so guarded about discussing your sexual orientation?" Fred said, "I'm on the same side of the fence as k.d., Elton, and Frederick the Great. I just don't like to share my personal life with the public." Half a *bravo* to Fred; but Robert Redford doesn't like sharing his personal life either, and doesn't—nor does he shy away from his correct label of heterosexual.

As Boy George put it, "Stop asking permission from the straight world to be who we are. It has nothing to do with them."

In 1993 Roddy Bottum (no cracks, please), keyboardist of Faith No More, came out to Lance Loud and said he'd formed his own band, Star 69—for which he turned singer—so he could do some specifically gay songs. A year later, Lance asked how coming out had affected him? "There were no repercussions career-wise. It was a positive and uplifting experience. I guess I expected some of the fans to burn crosses or throw panties at me, but nothing like that ever happened."

By contrast, actor-singer Nathan Lane's screen career comprises gay and/or drag roles almost exclusively. He almost stole the show as the lusty, life-affirming gay priest in the '95 movie of the gay play *Jeffrey*, at which time openly gay playwright Paul Rudnick said on tape that Lane was openly gay too. Then came 1996's first $100 million movie, *The Birdcage*—another gay *and* drag role for Nathan—and the actor suddenly and officially had no personal life. Previously best known outside Manhattan as the voice of the queer-like and queer-likeable meerkat in *The Lion King* (see Elton John. . .), Lane then went into the Broadway musical *A Funny Thing Happened on the Way to the Forum* rather than repeat his gay (and partly drag) stage role in Terrence Rattigan's *Love! Valour! Compassion!*'s screen version. Despite his celluloid opus (opi?) Lane was rumoredly through with gay roles and hoping for a hetero movie role, perhaps in the big-screen *The Honeymooners* (the Jackie Gleason role; the real Jackie was openly anti-gay).

In time-honored—that is, "honored"—Hollywood fashion, a non-gay TV star (as with *Jeffrey*) got the plum gay role. *Seinfeld*'s Jason Alexander enthused to *Entertainment Weekly* magazine, "I'm the only straight actor that I know of who has played this role." (Isn't that special?) In spring, '97, Lane was spotted hanging out in West Hollywood's famous gay bar the Motherlode—wearing a mustache. Eventually he was spotted, and *4Front* magazine reported:

"*Passion of Carmen* super-dancer Marco de la Cruz—sporting a beautiful diamond and sapphire ring given to him by one of his fans—moved in on Lane and bent his ear for a while about mutual friends and dancers. By the time Lane left the Motherlode, fourteen musical theatre queens were belting out hits from *Forum* and he was literally running across Santa Monica Boulevard in terror. Just remember, stardom can have its drawbacks!"

It's the younger generation that's less uptight, less saturatedly propagandized. The Williams Brothers are an acoustic music duo and nephews of pop singer Andy Williams. David, formerly a *Tiger Beat* pinup boy, is openly gay. Twin Andrew is not. Naturally, they began in show biz at age six, on *The Andy Williams Show*. One of their songs, "Don't Cry Now," is a tribute to friends dead from AIDS. David explains, "I just couldn't sit by and be quiet. We live in a world where being gay is considered morally subordinate to being straight, and I don't believe sexuality is about morality. Morality is about how we choose to behave, regardless of whether we are gay or straight. The most important thing is how we love, not who we love."

Being honestly gay is one thing. Performing gay material is another. Again, the powers that belittle deny playing time to gay, lesbian, and bi songs. And record labels discourage them. Openly gay pop/rock singer Paul Delph: "It's a question of gimmicks. George Michael is semi-out, but most people don't know it. . . . RuPaul is open, but he appears as a blond woman and puts aside being a gay man, and he's said he's 'transcended' the gay community, whatever that means. Has he also transcended being black or a man?" True enough, when RuPaul sings, the effect is a non-racial, presumably hetero female, but he's said the general public's not ready (were they ready for *Ellen*?) for him to sing to a man. And the general public is Ru's aim.

Delph continues, "Fred Schneider's solo album, *Just Fred*, is devoid of openly gay creativity, although it's good that Fred's fairly open now and he says he supports gay causes, not just AIDS but the legal rights organizations and such. . . . Luther Vandross has at least said he doesn't like the women in his audience to throw their underwear at him—that takes *some* guts." Vandross also appeared on *Rosie O'Donnell* (. . . !) in late-'96 with Roberta Flack and dueted on her "Killing Me Softly With His Song," and Luther did *not* change the masculine pronoun. Which takes more guts.

Younger musicians who may or may not be bi or gay are also less uptight, sometimes making declarations that closeted gay celebs of any generation wouldn't dream of uttering. Metallica's lead guitarist Kirk Hammett said of drummer Lars Ulrich in *Details* magazine, "We'd sleep together. And we both sleep naked. . . . It's not a big issue. I've known the guy going on fourteen years. We're very open with each other." Also in '96, singer-actor-writer Henry Rollins, thirty-five and a bachelor with a cat, chose to "come out" . . . as heterosexual, due to rumors to the contrary. (One is hard-pressed to think of anyone who came out as gay because they were rumored to be heterosexual.)

Rollins did add that he is anti-homophobic and "I take it as a compliment when some guy approaches me or thinks I'm attractive. I don't understand why a compliment makes some guys angry."

Red Hot Chili Peppers' guitarist Dave Navarro apprised *Spin* magazine, "Perry Farrell (ex-Jane's Addiction front man) and I used to kiss all the time." Navarro appeared on the cover of *Guitar* magazine in a lip-lock with RHCP bassist Flea and he kissed lead singer Anthony Kiedis in the video of their "Warped," which played MTV and elicited little complaint. Unlike the *Guitar* smooch, perhaps because a picture lasts longer? Retailers and wholesalers complained, calling it "porn" and "smut." The magazine was taken aback—"It's kind of like Welcome to the 1950s"—and Flea, via Warner Bros. Records, called the cover "a couple of heterosexual friends joking . . . with their affection for one another." Navarro added, "I don't have a problem with playful affection between friends. I only have a problem with those who do."

Hüsker Dü, the Nirvana of the '80s, was two-thirds gay. They split in 1988. Drummer Grant Hart quietly came out, and in the mid-'90s guitarist Bob Mould started noting his sexuality in the songs and videos of his band Sugar, which disbanded in 1996. On his own, with an eponymous CD, Mould later explained to the gay press, "I'm sorry if anybody was offended (in the gay community) by my reluctant stand" of a few years back, when reacting defensively about being gay and repeating, "I'm not going to be paraded around like a freak."

The reaction was understandable. Mould grew up in Malone, New York, where "a high school acquaintance of mine who was gay got taken out in the woods and killed." And when Bob's parents first learned of his true sexuality, it was in *Spin*; the reconciliation is ongoing. "I spent fourteen years not talking about something that was pretty central. I see where that got me." He admits, "I'm trying to overcome a warped perspective of what the gay community is about. I think I have a lot to offer people, but man, I don't like going to gay bars, because I'm not looking for that."

Mould underlines the two pillars of his life, "my work and Kevin," his partner of over seven years. "I work on it every day . . . my two loves. I try to give my full attention to both of them."

Pansy Division is the most successful "queercore" punk band, a San Francisco-based trio comprising singer/guitarist Jon Ginoli, bassist/singer Chris Freeman, and drummer Dustin Donaldson. Their aim is to make good music and shatter some homophobic myths. Also to lighten and enliven the sometimes moribund gay image; Ginoli states, "AIDS shouldn't be the only subject in gay art." Unlike some such bands, PD sounds fun and upbeat, not whiny. Increasingly, their subject matter has traded in sex and shock value for relationships, and the same-sound-ingness of many of their earlier songs graduated to a very well-reviewed fourth album, *Wish I'd Taken Pictures*, in 1996.

Prior to *Pictures*, PD was introduced to a whole new live audience when they toured with mainstream band Green Day. GD singer Billie Joe Armstrong admitted in *Out* magazine that he hoped listening to Pansy Division would defuse the intoler-ance of much of GD's audience. Echoing Kurt Cobain a few years before, Armstrong confessed, "The kind of people I've hated all of my life come to my shows." Regarding the disre-spectful, even brutal macho jocks who abuse women before his eyes, "One time I just stopped during the song and I said, 'If you grab another woman's breasts like that, I'm going to take you up on stage, grab you by the balls, and squeeze as hard as I can.'"

What prompted Armstrong to back Pansy Division? He told *Interview* associate editor Ray Rogers he'd learned to discuss "issues that matter" to him, among them his bisexual feelings. "I think I've learned to accept a male body for what it is and the beauty of it, instead of thinking (homosexuality) is this anti-reli-gious or antisocial behavior." His pro-gay influences included Bob Mould and other prominent gay musicians. Another reason was his eleven-month-old son Joe: "I want my son to have space to breathe and to be whatever he wants to be, and I'll accept him for whatever he is."

MTV displayed a double standard when it aired the video, just once, in June, '96, "Sinner Man" with its man-to-man kiss via

Los Angeles-based Extra Fancy. That other same-sex kiss was via the better known and self-proclaimedly hetero Red Hot Chili Peppers. (Censorship places a lot of emphasis on how much censors think the participants *enjoy* what they're doing; sexual or erotic enjoyment remains a Judeo-Christian no-no unless the result is more over-population.)

Buzz magazine opined in '95, "Judging by its latest album, *Sinner Man*, the four-man Extra Fancy has all the makings of a great rock 'n roll band. So why doesn't it have a major record deal?" Lead singer Brian Grillo was succinct: "It's because I'm a fag. Our music is better than most of the stuff out there. . . . So what else could it be?" Some gay fans have said EF isn't "gay enough," but the group's lyrics are often about being gay—unlike most of, say, Elton John or Melissa Etheridge's. *Buzz* quoted a radio "insider" who believed a song simply wouldn't get on the radio if it had gay content.

EF was later signed by Atlantic Records. To what degree would Grillo compromise his integrity? "I get letters from kids all over who are getting beat up every day and don't know why, or want to kill themselves because none of their friends are like them. When I hear they look up to me, it makes me realize the struggle and pain I've gone through is all worth it." Atlantic was the first major record label to create a department targeting gay/lesbian audiences and promoting gay/lesbian acts. But the following year, in '96, Extra Fancy and other acts were dropped.

The usual corporate veil of reticence has obscured what really happened. Some said there hadn't been enough time to judge EF's long-range potential, for this first of the hardcore homo bands to be signed by a famous label was let go mere weeks after their first album came out. Paul V., Extra Fancy's manager, told the gay press, "No record company is ever going to say, 'We dropped you because of your queerness.' They can't say that. It's illegal." (For the most part, it isn't illegal, just bad public relations among CD-buyers.)

The gay *Edge* magazine ventured another explanation, stressing the difference in EF's "hardcore sounds" and the "dance music gay music fans have been spoon-fed since birth." Atlantic had announced theirs as "a business decision," and *Edge* wondered, "Where were gay music fans when [EF] played countless concerts throughout Greater L.A.? Had they been there, the band would have received better support, more records would have been sold, Extra Fancy would still be signed, Atlantic would be counting their profits, and everybody would be happy."

In view of the other gay acts dropped, and the brief time span involved, the explanation might not be as simple as that. On the other hand, gay people tend to be significant moviegoers and yet the vast majority of gay-themed films fail to attract gay viewers who are elsewise occupied paying ($) homage to mainstream films and stars. Patronage, like charity, should begin at home. Post-Atlantic, Grillo, who is HIV-positive, got a job painting houses. But didn't give up: "Extra Fancy has done something for the world. We are enlightening people, and that's important. . . . People are starving for bands like us." And Paul V. promised, "Extra Fancy is so passionate, real and strong, that the band is unstoppable. No record company will stop this band." Music to the ears.

On the so-called distaff side, the biggest news post-first edition has been the comings out of k.d. lang and Melissa Etheridge. With lang it was only a matter of time. She was repeatedly outed, most of her publicity stressed her tomboyish or boyish manner and appearance, and she played a lesbian Eskimo in the haunting German (English language) film *Salmonberries*, which also features her haunting song "I'd Walk Through the Snow Barefoot (If You'd Open Up Your Door)." A girlfriend of k.d.'s said on TV that lang came out in order to save time on The Big Question and to end the constant speculation.

Interestingly, after she made music history, lang's publicity and press stressed her talent and the work in question more than the artist's surface. That increasingly became a given, and once admiration for lang's courage in coming totally out receded into the background, there was enough talent to sustain interest and a presumably long-lived career (with hopefully more than the one movie). Of course, few followed k.d.'s example, though many were inspired and/or came out in real life. Again, those better able to "pass" than k.d. lang tend to do so.

Melissa Etheridge debuted platinum in 1988. As with lang, another undeniably great singing-composing talent was born. There was less speculation about Etheridge. She came out spontaneously at the Gay & Lesbian Inaugural Ball for President Clinton in January, 1993: "It was an amazing time full of pride and joy. I stood up there with k.d., and I just said, 'I'm proud to have been a lesbian all my life.' I heard everybody going 'Yippee,' and I said to myself, 'I guess I just did it.'" The success has since grown, and Melissa is now also famous for her successful marriage to Julie Cypher, with whom she had a baby in 1997.

In 1996 *Girlfriends* magazine put Dionne Warwick's niece on the cover, which read "Houston—We Have a Problem: Ten Tips for Whitney on Playing It Straight." They may have been redundant. The following year, a Connecticut reader wrote, "I really enjoyed the interview with Boze Hadleigh ('Hollywood Lesbians Revisited')" and cited "Whoopi Goldberg, Whitney Houston, or the other three black Hollywood (alleged) lesbians I can count on my hand," noting that "Hollywood homosexuality (particularly lesbianism) is mostly a white thing" (see Janis Ian. . .). Post-first edition, Houston wed and had a kid, a movie career, and image problems relating to her temperament and her husband's episodic peccadillos.

A producer at E! Television in Los Angeles observes, "With show biz, you just can't expect the whole picture, though it filters out privately. . . . A guy might be bisexual, but you'll only hear about the ladies in his life. His wife, you might just hear old rumors, wonder why she puts up with him, but meanwhile she has her own thing going, only she's either not very sexual any more or she's got this one girlfriend and meantime he's got enough girlfriends and boyfriends for a Roman orgy, only Roman's the wrong shade, you dig?" Sometimes gay rumors refer to a bisexual reality, but in most such contractual unions the husband is more active than the wife.

After k.d. lang posed intimately with Cindy Crawford on the cover of *Vanity Fair*, rumors linked the two women and swirled around the super-model. Husband Richard Gere was not linked with any specific male, and had said all along that he didn't mind being thought gay. Then came the ad in the British paper saying Gere and Crawford were happily married, heterosexual and monogamous. The marriage went bust within weeks, and Crawford later revealed the whole thing was Gere's idea, one which certainly alienated a mass of gay fans.

After this book first came out, one reviewer asked why certain names weren't included, like Dolly Parton and Jane Olivor? The book's purpose was and is to make points about the music game and its players, not merely to list names. And the author had never heard the rumors (no one can hear all of them. . .) about Olivor. A fact: the cult singer took several years off from her career to be with her husband who eventually died of cancer; by 1995 she was touring, singing Rob Stein's "Unknown Soldier": "They gave him a medal for killing ten men and took it away for loving one."

Another reviewer noted in passing that there've been surprisingly few rumors about Whitney's aunt Dionne, in view of her not having married and her now-smiling-but-always-boss demeanor. A far younger Neneh Cherry cooed to the gay press, "I have, I have, I have. I've slept with women, and I loved it. It was lovely." Such are the statements which males—singers or actors and even off-stage and off-camera men—feel they don't dare to make, even now.

It bears repeating that the *whole* truth has always been a *rara avis*, almost an endangered species, in show biz. Most of what is declared in public is career-motivated, even when it seems frank—that is, aside from plain and simple statements of "I am gay" or "I'm lesbian" (or the justly celebrated "Yep, I'm gay!"). Example: *an* actress recently confused many a heterosexual and a few gays when she averred that she'd never been gay until she met a certain female someone. And true, she may well be bi. But the Someone is *not* her first female, and the basic reason behind her pretense of former heterosexuality—it doesn't work that way—is her protecting the tinseled reps of the men she has previously been linked with, one of whom is a comic movie star who is very privately bi or gay. *Voilà*.

Of course any acknowledgment of sexual diversity is welcome, and in the cases of some less stereotypically attractive women, one puzzles over the source of hesitation. Openly feminist Lily Tomlin did make gay media headlines (the mainstream ignoring it altogether) in 1996 when she attended the supersapphic Dinah Shore (golf) weekend in Palm Springs; she came out—of her blouse anyway—while the band Betty was performing. "Tomlin jumped onstage and flashed the delighted all-lesbian audience." Not coincidentally, Lily was appearing in Betty's new music video.

Betty's Elizabeth Ziff declared, "Ms. Tomlin is a terrific supporter of the arts. She has impeccable taste in music, and a lovely set of coconuts."

Then there's Tracy Chapman, who made her folksy bow in 1988 with "Fast Car." Thereafter, said the *Advocate*, "Chapman stayed in the closet and nobody cared." Sales slumped, and she finally returned with a CD titled *New Beginning*, which the *Advocate* deemed "another closety bore." *Time* took Tracy to task for being aloof to her fans, who in turn were aloof to her. In '96 *Girlfriends* reported, "Everyone's betting on whether Chapman's new single "Turn it Right Around" is about rumored love interest [author] Alice Walker." In '97 Chapman was in the audience during the taping of the historic *Ellen* episode, as was, separately—but already *out*—Chastity Bono. Time will tell. . . .

In 1996 the *Advocate* put it to Liza Minnelli, "The only woman (we've) ever heard that you were lovers with was one-time New York cabaret singer Lana Cantrell." Liza: "No, no, no." (Though she did speak of same-sex kissing in her past, more than the male of the show biz species will do.) During a '96 interview with this author, the Australian magazine *Lesbians on the Loose* explained its disappointment in former singer Lana (see prior comments from Judy Carne on how Johnny Carson couldn't come between them), who agreed to come out to Sydney's gay-and-lesbian Mardi Gras, the world's biggest gay event. But only to appear, not to talk.

Cantrell spoke with *LOTL*, but on condition she not discuss her life or loving. "I never have before." Fellow Aussie Peter Allen had said, "Now in the '90s it doesn't verifiably hurt singers to come out. But some of us more 'mature' singers remember a time when a rumor or a bit of misplaced honesty *cost* us. So then some of us don't try it again. Not with the media, which always seems ready to devour you with sensationalism." Again, if being gay stops being "sensationalistic" in the media's and public's definition—when there are enough gay people admitting to same—then that one aspect of a person won't devour or dominate the other facts about a famous or non-famous person.

Plus, there are different degrees of outness. One lesbian editor says about one lesbian performer that today's more accepting climate and the peer pressure to come out did "inspire her to come out to her family. Can you believe it? As if they wouldn't have known! I suppose we should be grateful for all small miracles, but pardon me while I hop back into the closet and reveal my terrible, dark secret to my teddy bear only!"

Times change, thank goodness. Things were changing in the late '60s and early '70s, but only up to a point. In 1997 singer/songwriter Laura Nyro died of cancer at 49. She was survived by her son and her companion, Maria Desiderio. Perhaps best known for the song "And When I Die," she penned several songs which became hits for others, e.g., "And When I Die" (Blood, Sweat and Tears), "Stoney End" (Barbra Streisand) and "Wedding Bell Blues" (the Fifth Dimension). An anonymous and "sort of bisexual" longtime friend of Nyro's offered: "She wanted to be judged on her work, not her life." Did the promiscuous Picasso's life cause his work to be underrated? "I think Laura did want to be more open . . . she admired the girls who are out in the open, she believed in full equality. . . . Laura's been associated with so many important people in her career, I think she felt if she was more open about herself, it might somehow reflect on those people, you know, cast doubts. . . ." *If* that's how she felt, then it's gay shame, which is induced from the outside but perpetuated inwardly.

The Andrews Sisters' Maxene Andrews died in 1995. How many people outside show biz ever knew that one-third of *the* most successful sister group ever was lesbian or bisexual? The well-liked Maxene was very pro-gay, also motherly; the point being that feminine gender and motherliness so often cover up any hint of other-sexuality—a pro-gay female celeb is almost a show biz given, but when a man actually says he's pro-gay, immediately there's The Question. . . . An associate who worked with Andrews and John Travolta (. . .) in the musical *Over Here!* revealed, "I knew. Lots of us did. But she was older and she'd been famous, so no one asked."

For a long time, singers' private lives weren't much covered by the press (unless they made movies, of course). Then the press . . . covered up for them. The late Carmen McRae's sexuality was common knowledge among coworkers. Sylvester told one reporter, "One of my diva icons was Carmen McRae. . . . I wanted to be like her—slim, mahogany, an icicle with a ready-made voice. Only, I didn't want to have to turn on to women, honey!" The quote was published minus the last sentence. McRae was very private, even for a singer of a certain generation, and it was felt by some insiders that had her sizeable talent melded with greater publicity, she could have been a bigger star. Perhaps her not playing the PR game was her way of maintaining professional and personal integrity.

Some female singers avoid coming out, even as "bisexual," due to the public knowledge's reflection on past male relationships—the legal husbands whom most lesbian and bi actresses have consented to along the way—or current female partners not ready to come out yet (if ever). Muffin Spencer-Devlin, pro golfer, became the first—and so far only—LPGA player to come out in *Sports Illustrated*. Her significant other is composer Lynda Roth. "When you're single, you come out, it's one thing. When you're not a solo, it's a whole other thing." And some women feel defensive about the female-male relationships they chose or were pressured to undertake.

Holly Near, now fully out, described her brief hetero interlude, "He asked if I was bisexual. I said I didn't feel like a bisexual. I felt like a lesbian when I was with a woman and a lesbian making love to a man when I was with a man." Near and Cris Williamson (a cofounder of Olivia Records) are occasionally and understandably peeved by the far greater emphasis given more recently out singers for whom they helped pave the way back when it was definitely not profitable to do so.

Janis Ian was a "bisexual" pioneer who came out as lesbian in 1993, seventeen years after she was outed. One reason she finally 'fessed up was, "It's hard to justify having worked for black civil rights in the '60s and not work for my own civil rights in the '90s." For a long time, Ian, who tasted real success in her teens, hid all her differences—gay, Jewish, pro-feminist—for career's sake . . . and husband's sake. "I knew that I was gay when I was nine." But she spent seven years in a physically abusive "marriage." (*That's* the kind—unkind—that should be illegal in over half of the fifty states. . . .) When hubby declared he wanted a ménage-à-trois, meaning another woman for him, Ian proposed that they could later have another trio, with a second man. Husband: "Never! I'm no faggot!"

Toward the end of her seven-year sentence, Ian's husband threatened to kill her and pulled a gun on her. He kept it on her for six hours. . . .Astounding what so many women will put up with from men, be the women gay, bi (remember Judy Carne and hubby Burt Reynolds?) or hetero (Nicole Simpson, for one). The '94 biography *Wishing on the Moon* about bisexual Billie Holiday threw some light on her friendship with bi legend Tallulah Bankhead and revealed that Billie's female intimates called her Bill or William. The "Lady Day" moniker was for public consumption. And after her estranged husband tried to read to her from the Bible, Holiday was quoted, "I've always been a religious bitch. But if that evil motherfucker believes in God, I'm thinking it over."

(Then there was the late, sweet-voiced, heterosexual singer who took a quantity and quality of abuse from her brother, with whom she collaborated, which has never been made public. A friend of this writer was a lover of the brother, while the famous pair toured Japan. The sister died uniquely and prematurely, the brother still lives off her voice, and he hides his gayness while publicizing himself as a "conservative Republican" and a "family values" father. Yes, he still fools around with the lads, and he could use a bumper sticker reading "*Family Valued*: We Love Our Gay Dad . . . Even If He Doesn't.")

In 1994 Janis Ian began her *Advocate* column "Breaking Silence." One of her more incisive pieces was about an encounter with a closeted black songwriter in Nashville, where Janis lives with Pat, her lover of eight years (aka "my wife" or "Mr. Lesbian"). The songwriter had given a speech to a mostly white audience on being black in a white industry. Mr. L. asked her, "Why not talk about being gay in a homophobic industry?"

The songwriter replied, "The black community has a very low tolerance for gays." Effect and cause, cause and effect. . . .

The songwriter added, "I'd lose my base if I came out," to which Mr. L. pointed out, "Your audience base is white."

"Why me? Being famous doesn't mean I have any obligation." Mr. L.: "People take courage from the folks at the top of the publicity machine, like us." (Celebrities often speak of their rights, seldom of their responsibilities as privileged people, public figures, and role models.)

Then the songwriter said, "It's hard enough being black—" and Mr. L. interrupted, "Enough of that excuse. It's hard being black, it's hard being gay, it's hard being in a wheelchair—*life is hard.*" The coffee-house was temporarily silent, one imagines.

The songwriter said, "I don't want people to say, 'There goes so-and-so, the famous gay writer.'" Mr. L. countered, "But you see nothing wrong with people saying, 'There goes so-and-so, the famous black writer.'" "Being black is a fact I can't escape." "And being gay is fiction?" Janis' wife concluded, "The convenient thing about being gay is that you *can* hide it. You were outed as black when you were born. But maybe underneath it all you're a coward. Maybe you would change your skin color if you could. Which is worse, (being called) *faggot* or *nigger?*"

Ian, whose godchildren are black and were "difficult to place," eventually adopted by a lesbian couple, was illustrating in black and white the indefensibility of the closet for any group of people. As activist-author Vito Russo said (far) more than once, "I've heard all the excuses for staying in the closet, and they're all bullshit."

Ian's long ago, once-controversial interracial song "Society's Child" was taken up and promoted by Leonard Bernstein. "One artist helps another," notes Janis. "I think k.d. lang coming out helped a lot of artists. She came out and nothing bad happened." Ian's decision to come fully out was prompted by the gay teen suicide statistic, and the comings out of lang and Ian were a big factor in Chastity Bono coming out. As were her having been outed by the tabloids—at first she denied it, when the press asked if it was really true (fact: heterosexuals almost never get outed)—and "watching the slow death of my lover [which] taught me that life is far too precious to be lived as a lie." As Cher's daughter, Chastity had her own band, Ceremony, and her record company—despite gays at the top—urged her to stay *in*.

"I became disillusioned with the recording business and started to question my career choices," wrote the columnist and eventual activist. "I thought I might want to work within the gay community, and I knew I had to come out to do that." Chas had already given her mother an "I Love My Lesbian Daughter" button. It took time for Cher to adjust, but she eventually joined P-FLAG (Parents and Friends of Lesbians And Gays), a group that she has publicly spoken to and to which Jason Gould's mother Barbra Streisand has donated money. (By contrast, father Elliott Gould "explains" away Jason's homosexuality by saying it was caused by growing up with an ambitious, busy mother—who however made about one movie to every four of Gould's. And semi-singer Sonny Bono entered Republican politics, emerging as a Congressman against gay rights and pro the ban on same-sex marriage despite his daughter's attempt at enlightening him on gay issues and in spite of her loving and devoted marriage to Joan, who died of cancer.)

By happy and fair-minded contrast, Sweden's top female rock star was able to legally wed—and receive the various benefits therefrom—her girlfriend in 1996. Eva Dahlgren wed Eva Attling on January 25th. Dahlgren outed herself the day before, when she applied for the marriage license; she had previously refused to discuss her life, but the rumors had been rife. After the civil ceremony, Dahlgren stated, "It is wonderful to be married." One out of seventeen Swedes owns Dahlgren's 1991 album *The Heart of a Faded Blonde*, and a gay newspaper in Stockholm suggested that January 25th become Sweden's annual coming out day (which in the USA is October 11th).

Back in the land of the free heterosexuals, Joan Jett warned gay *Genre* magazine in '94 that "she keeps her personal life private." But she explained that her new CD, *Pure and Simple* (Oscar Wilde quipped, "The truth is rarely pure and never simple"), included a song called "As I Am" which she cowrote "in the wake of the extremely hateful Republican Convention (of '92). They were just up there saying that if you weren't exactly like them, they wanted you wiped off the face of the earth. It was just a complete horror show. So I wanted to write a song that would be all-encompassing, not just for gay people, but for strong women or any minority."

For a time, Courtney Love flirted with a bisexual image, then told the press that after sampling lesbian sex she wondered, "Where's the main course?" Love had been photographed tumbling out of a limo in the middle of a French kiss with Sandra Bernhard, arriving at a post-Oscars party (in '96 Love played the bisexual wife of pornographer and anti-gay-male homophobe Larry Flynt in *The People Vs. Larry Flynt*). Sandra, who lives in the Valley with her longtime girlfriend, has described herself as not lesbian, as "bisexual," says it's very important to her that men find her attractive, has said all her real relationships are with women, that she could never wed a man, that she strongly identifies as a Jew but not with the gay community, etc., etc.

Bernhard was a paid entertainer on a gay RSVP cruise during which she was so rude to the audience that two men threw drinks at her. She stormed off stage "as the 800-plus crowd chanted, 'Leave, leave!'" When one gay paper reviewed Bernhard's new CD, *Excuses for Bad Behavior*, a reader wrote to urge, "Please stop reviewing this unfriendly closet king." Her last movie appearance to speak of was in the interesting flop *Dallas Doll*, as a "pansexual" golf pro! Reviewing Sandra Bernhard and Her Band in '96, the *New Times* stated she seems "intent on trivializing herself," that no fading star so often appears in others' vehicles (those of Madonna, Mizrahi, Roseanne, etc.), and she has "become the counter-culture equivalent of a *Hollywood Squares* guest," is experiencing "premature irrelevance" which seems due to a "lack of focus or sheer self-destructiveness."

A clearly more caring heterosexual artist is the one-of-a-kind Diamanda Galas, whose playwright brother Philip-Dimitri Galas died of AIDS in 1986. Reviewer Mr. Damon wrote in *4Front*, "Although her music is totally unique, she is sort of a compilation of Maria Callas, Yma Sumac, Tina Turner, Edith Piaf, Janis Joplin, and at times Annie Lennox and Nina Hagen." Across her left hand, Diamanda bears a tattoo: "WE ARE ALL HIV+." Meaning that not everyone is infected, but everyone is affected. Or will be.

More problematic is Me'Shell NdegeOcello, who was signed onto Madonna's Maverick record label. A self-proclaimed bisexual, she appeared in a Gap print ad that partly defines her as a mother but makes no mention of her sexual/affectional orientation. Born Michelle Johnson, MN is often edgy and needlessly defensive. *Out* wrote that she was "unwilling to fill in the gaps" about her background or her life (she lives with her girlfriend and son, and is now a Muslim) or motivations. In 1996 she gained new notoriety from both sides with her single titled "Leviticus: Faggot." Some called it homophobic, some said it denounced homophobia. The lyrics were ambiguous; several critics felt it could simultaneously confirm the opinions of gays and homophobes alike. The song had little chance of radio play due to its subject matter, but it doesn't seem too much to ask that if a song is sincerely making a pro-gay statement, it shouldn't be so unclear—and with hateful language which can easily boomerang—that listeners have to debate whether or not it is pro-gay.

The '96 memoirs of R&B diva Patti LaBelle included her links to the gay community and friendships with such gay musicians as Elton John, Sylvester, and Luther Vandross. Of musical collaborator Nona Hendryx, LaBelle wrote, "She's been out as long as she's been gay."

Melissa Ferrick's big break was as Morrissey's opening act for his 1990 tour. At Atlantic Records she met her lover Nancy Bennett, a staff video producer. Ferrick's '93 bow was the CD *Massive Blur*, but Chastity Bono noted that though Ferrick's never denied being gay, her second CD, *Willing to Wait*, does deal with lesbian life and love. Ani DiFranco founded Righteous Babe Records; the singer-songwriter came out lyrically on *her* second album, *Not So Soft*. As bisexual: "Dykes say I waffle, but I can only be myself."

What happens with *some* bisexuals is they play it gay or bi for the gay media and hetero for the general media. To some degree that's been the case with perky blond Canadian Jill Sobule, the singer/songwriter behind the breakthrough hit "I Kissed a Girl." Radio and MTV did *not* shy away from her sapphic song and video (as they would have regarding a male-male song and might have regarding a black or Asian or butch sapphic song). That set off an Is-she-or-isn't-she? guessing game in the media. Gay periodicals contacting Atlantic Records were told, "She's straight." At first, Sobule wouldn't clarify, giving an impression of bewildered hetero-ness. She eventually affirmed her bisexuality.

"I've had experiences with women and men, but I didn't say anything about it at first because the point was that 'I Kissed a Girl' should be a song for everyone. Also, I have problems with the word 'bisexual' . . . that sounds like, I'll fuck anybody," she told *Entertainment Weekly*. Promoting subsequent material, Sobule still says she doesn't like saying, "I'm bisexual," but admits that she is. True, *bisexual* is a word loaded with connotations—"Both gays and straights are prejudiced against us," she says—including promiscuity.

For that matter, "lesbian" can over-sexualize a woman in a

way that heterosexual women, let alone "ladies," don't have to deal with. While promoting *Hollywood Lesbians* on radio, I was told breathlessly by one male host, "You know what really scares me? Lesbian *grandmothers*!" After the commercial break, humble guest replied, "But most grandmothers, including heterosexual ones, aren't necessarily sexually active." The host realized, "I guess I think of lesbians as being sex maniacs or preying on young girls" (*TV Guide* often uses "young girls," which is redundant). One TV talk show host asked me—like there are no lesbians to ask?—"Do you think lesbians are that way because a woman's had a bad experience with a man?" I said, "If that were the case, all women would be lesbians."

Sometime musical comedy star Rosie O'Donnell (*Grease*) has a few known singing connections. The *Globe* revealed in September, '96, that ROD was allegedly in a loving lesbian relationship with singer-dancer Michelle Blakely, living together in a Miami condo and riding motorbikes together. Same year, *Lesbians on the Loose* reported that ROD "was at one time the gal pal of singer Sophie B. Hawkins . . . confirmed by several sources." In '95, the blond Hawkins appeared on an MTV special titled *Duets*. *LOTL*: "As the two of them sang 'Damn, I Wish I Was Your Lover,' Sophie crawled, prowled, and knelt before Melissa Etheridge, generating quite a bit of, ahem, heat!"

Melissa, who in more mainstream eyes was confirmed a rock superstar when Bruce Springsteen draped his metaphoric mantle around her, in turn used her star power to help introduce Joan Osborne to average audiences. In '96 Osborne made the front page of the *New York Post*—"Furor Over Grammy Star!"—regarding her *Relish* CD's song "One of Us'" lyrics questioning the nature of the anthropomorphic Judeo-Christian God. Joan informed *Out* magazine:

"Maybe I address spirituality in non-traditional ways, but I don't make music in order to pick fights with the Catholic Church. Besides, the church's stands on homosexuality and women make the pope look far more ridiculous than any pop song could." She added, "The *Post* headline was much better than winning any Grammy." Some big-circulation periodicals which don't address Osborne's sexuality do focus on her "long-standing work with abortion rights groups." Before her very mainstream TV chat show, Rosie O'Donnell told the mostly lesbian group at a 1992 pro-choice fundraiser, "The only person who has anything to say about what happens to my body is me. And Michelle Pfeiffer."

(The first season of her TV show, O'Donnell hired openly gay comic Kate Clinton as a writer. Since then, she has reportedly tried to *in* Richard Simmons the exercise maven, among others. That's one effect of monetary and numbers success on a national scale. . . .)

Until insiders and the public force change, it's worth remembering that the mass media are hetero-friendly only. Fem 2 Fem—comprising two lesbians, two hetero women and one bisexual—had their video banned on MTV because of lesbian content. They did make it in *Playboy* (guess why . . .), were interviewed regarding "lesbian chic" on *Joan Rivers* and *Geraldo*, and their album *Woman to Woman* was rare in that it musicalized about all the women's sexuality, not just one portion. Originally Fem 2 Fem was said to be all-lesbian; by 1996 when the group was starring in *Voyeurz* in London's West End, it numbered just one lesbian and one bisexual. Sometimes the problem is that a non-het group member feels frozen out (or more likely, in) or may have separate, more personal artistic goals.

Bigger, Better, Faster, More! was the debut album of the group 4 Non Blondes. The 1992 CD sold more than 3 million copies internationally. But Non Blonde Linda Perry didn't want to make "poppy" music; even with fewer sales, she "wanted to play weird atmospheric music." And so she went solo, which also meant being able to be openly gay. "All my life I've loved women, and that's it. I've never been any other way," she told Chastity Bono. She also launched her own label, Rockstar Records, and signed two bands to it.

One of Perry's goals is "to cut through all the corporate bullshit." She recalls when 4 Non Blondes was riding high with a Top Twenty hit, "What's Up," and "certain business associates thought honesty wasn't always the best policy." As the group began playing bigger mixed or hetero outlets, it lost much of its lesbian following. As a solo act, Perry can be as honest as she wishes. She started early: at fifteen her mother asked her if she was homosexual. "When I told her I was, she thought about it for a second and said, 'Just look good at it.' You see, there was this total biker dyke who lived across the street from us who dressed really butch. My mom did not want me to be like her. My mom is cool about it now. My whole family is. They're pretty open-minded."

Corporate homophobia reared its head again—but illogically, in view of the Indigo Girls being openly lesbian—when Epic Records vetoed (reportedly) an interview the duo was planning with the *Lesbian News* in 1994. (In fairness, one should state that certain large and small corporations are way ahead of government in providing varying measures of recognition and benefits to gay employees and their domestic partners.) A lesbian writer was to interview Amy Ray and Emily Saliers for both the *LN* and the *Philadelphia Inquirer*. The story goes that Epic okayed the *PI* interview but not the *LN*, later denying any bigotry was involved. The story finally wound up in the late lesbian magazine *Deneuve*, which French actress Catherine alleged was named after her, to her commercial displeasure.

The dynamic duo of folk-rock hasn't had a radio or video hit since their 1989 debut but has built a growing cult following based on consistency and quality. Since coming out in *Out* in 1994 they have increasingly bonded with their audience. Around 1991, says Amy Ray, a male reporter asked them if they were gay, then chose not to use their positive response. Indigo Girls are *the* lesbian group of choice today, but for some time both members resisted coming out, lest they be known as lesbians rather than musicians; their being out proves women can be both (in some quarters, that actually needs proving!). Apart from professional concerns, Saliers admits, "Part of it was fear too. Then there just came a point where it was like, 'What's the big deal? I've been out in my private life forever.' But until you get to that point, nobody can push you there. And it takes some people longer than others." Not just celebrities—one misconception about outing is that it reveals private citizens, not just public figures. The appalling truth is that in more than forty American states, people can be legally fired from their work for being homosexual (including bi).

President Clinton did side with his gay and lesbian constituents in supporting national legislation to end homophobic workplace discrimination, but in 1996 the Republican-controlled Congress defeated ENDA (Employment Non-Discrimination Act). It has been re-introduced in '97, again with Clinton's backing—which could be a little more vigorous or outspoken—but it's almost a foregone conclusion that such a Congress will keep defeating it.

For the record, Indigo Girls has never been a romantic duo. The work comes first. Says Saliers, "Our personalities are different, but we believe in a lot of the same things—the important things—so that's the glue." Ray, whose two older sisters are also lesbian, says of Indigo Girls' increasingly outspoken and political songs, "I feel louder about everything now....I never want to be quiet again—or subtle."

In the quiet/subtle department: Dame Joan Hammond (1912 - 1996) was the first operatic diva to sell a million records. She was also a champion athlete (golf!), a New Zealand-born Australian—the first two nations to give women the vote. Hammond began as a violinist, was three years with the Sydney Philharmonic Orchestra, left Oz in 1936 to study with the Vienna Boys' Choir, then made her operatic debut in 1938 in London. During WWII she made numerous recordings and drove an ambulance. Post-war, she toured the world and earned many prizes. In 1974 she was created Dame of the British Empire. In 1932 she'd met Lolita Marriott; the friends shared a common interest in golf and later became lovers. They were together for sixty-two years, constant companions who lived and traveled and worked together.

After Marriott died in 1993, Hammond's health declined irreversibly. At her own eightieth birthday party, Dame Joan had publicly acknowledged her lifelong friendship with Lolita Marriott but never came out. When Hammond died, the conservative Aussie papers such as Rupert Murdoch's *The Australian* summed up her personal life in three words: "She never married."

"I'm well aware that there are a lot of people who are curious to know if I'm lesbian or not. I think that that is of no importance to anybody but the people I sleep with," said '60s icon Dusty Springfield in 1994. A British TV special on Springfield, hosted by the absolutely fabulous Jennifer Saunders and Dawn French, was glaringly devoid of any focus on her personal (aka "private," even if the person's famous) life. Rather, Dusty laughingly recalled, "My brother was in love with Carmen Miranda. He loved her platform shoes. I don't know if he still wears them."

When Princess Diana's brother had a night out at a gay club, the tabs had a field day, speculating about whether that might "influence" Diana's son, an heir to the throne. (Somebody once defined royalty as "people whose ancestors killed far more people en route to the top than yours or mine ever did.") What the UK press keeps mostly hush-hush is the real orientation of one of the Queen's sons; especially since he vigorously, and many said hypocritically, denied the, uh, allegations.

UK-based Aussie drag icon "Dame Edna Everage" has a "gay son, Kenneth." Regarding her TV series, Dame Edna gushed, "Some of my guests are actually staying with me. Dusty Springfield is going to be on the show. Which will be very good news to my son Kenny's friends. It was at Kenny's request that I invited Dusty. She's over there in Amsterdam, of course. I don't know much about Holland except the story about the kiddie with his finger in the dyke. I'll be asking Dusty if she knows that story. . . ."

(Dame Edna, who is outspoken—by bloody few—once referred to Jodie Foster, who speaks French, as "that cunning little linguist.")

Pete Townshend, guitarist and chief songwriter for The Who, came out as bisexual, but the general media kept the news very low-key. Years later, the '96 bio *Behind Blue Eyes: The Life of Pete Townshend*, dismissed this aspect of his life in a few paragraphs. . . .

David Bowie, repeatedly distancing himself from the bi-flavored past that helped make him a star, has been labeled a "so-called former bisexual and current Laura Ashley wallpaper designer." It's been revealed in more than one book that Bowie was all along adamantly against gay rights. He also called Hitler the first rock star and suggested at one point that the UK might benefit from a dictatorship. At one London concert for Rock Against Racism, Bowie's photo was next to those of Hitler and ultra-rightist/racist Enoch Powell. In the '70s Bowie had an alleged flirtation with fascism, and at a 1988 UK concert some fans gave him the Nazi salute.

"Yes, of course I'm gay and always have been," said Bowie

to reporter Michael Watts, then told *Rolling Stone*, "I'm an awful liar," and came out as heterosexual. *Sic transit* truthfulness.

Is one of Japan's leading rock stars gay? Bi? In that eastern—"eastern" from the western viewpoint—land, homosexuality is not a "sin," but non-conformity (marriage/offspring) is a major *shame*. Ryuichi Sakamoto played gay to David Bowie's hetero war hero on screen (see prior Bowie...). He collected an Academy Award for the score of *The Last Emperor* and then scored *Little Buddha*—about a child monk—for Bernardo Bertolucci, Italy's leading movie director, whom David Ehrenstein listed as gay or bi in the *Advocate*.

Sakamoto's father, a book editor, worked on the first book by gay but maritally contracted bodybuilder/suicide Yukio Mishima (see *The Lavender Screen*). In 1994 Ryuichi collaborated on the album *Sweet Revenge* with Holly Johnson, formerly of Frankie Goes To Hollywood. Sakamoto was composing in the USA, but because Johnson is HIV-positive and the USA bans such people from its shores (remember Emma Lazarus? and what she wrote on the Statue of Liberty?), "I couldn't enter the States. So I had to send the tapes to him, and he'd send them to me, back and forth. In London I'd add my vocals, word by word to song by song, and back to him, back to me, and it took quite a while to finish the project, which left me emotionally exhausted."

Marianne Faithfull began as an actress and worked with (now-Member of Parliament) Glenda Jackson. She put her musical success on hold for a man, Mick Jagger, and her '94 autobiography was most notable, media-wise, for its homoerotic revelations about Mick—who she said yearned for Keith Richards, aloud, while having sex with her. In the '60s, Joe Dallesandro was famously quoted that he "wouldn't throw Mick Jagger out of bed" if he had a chance. (Dallesandro was a screen hunk for Andy Warhol, who was played—more or less—by David Bowie in a recent movie.) In 1993 Dallesandro changed his mind about tossing Mick, because he's now "so fucking ugly."

A '93 bio of Jagger by Christopher Anderson claimed Jagger was bedmates with Bowie. At a '94 press conference for the Rolling Stones' summer tour, Mick was asked, "Did you really sleep with David Bowie?" He answered, "Yeah. Of course." Jagger's screen career began in 1969 in a bi-rock role in

Performance. Its bisexual co-director, Donald Cammell, committed suicide in 1996, having helmed but four films, the last of which, *Wild Side*, costarred Anne Heche (Ellen DeGeneres' girlfriend) in a homoerotic role. In 1997 Jagger's movie odyssey came full circle when he played a drag queen named Greta in the long awaited film of Martin Sherman's gay-themed concentration camp drama, *Bent*.

The Broadway version of *Bent* had starred a pre-Hollywood Richard Gere as one of the two lovers murdered by the Nazis. Gere informed *Rolling Stone*, "Yes, I'm gay—when I'm on that stage. If the role required me to suck off Horst, I'd do it. But I didn't consider it a bold move." Obviously, he'd consider it so now, especially in light of that misjudged and ill-fated newspaper ad he took out in London. *Sic transit* boldness.

The memoir *Faithfull* did discuss Marianne's bisexuality and same-sex affairs. "I was very European," she told *Details* magazine. "You didn't have to make a choice about your sexuality." As for the future, "I can't bear using condoms, so I'd rather not have sex. Maybe I will have a girlfriend again someday." But a *Vanity Fair* profile/interview with Faithfull made no reference whatever to the lesbian affairs and bisexuality that she herself was willing to discuss. *Sic transit* journalistic integrity.

The Swinging Sixties saw the flourishing of four gay entrepreneurs who were instrumental in the birth of the Brit-beat with its bright, trebly and internationally accessible sound. They were: the aforementioned Brian Epstein of the Beatles; producer Joe Meek; Kit Lambert, who managed The Who during their peak; and Larry Parnes, who managed Elvis clone Billy Fury, who was gay and had nineteen chart hits; Parnes was also affiliated with Joe Brown, Marty Wilde and Georgie Fame. It was long after Brian Epstein (see prior Lennon) that John Lennon became secure enough to shed his homophobia.

In 1994 Yoko Ono, John's widow, signed over her royalties from the original cast recording on Capitol/EMI of the off-Broadway musical *New York Rock* to AmFAR (American Foundation for AIDS Research). Ono had made previous large donations to AmFar, and in 1995 said of the '93 movie *The Hours and Times*, "I haven't seen it, though I was told it was very good." It depicted the rumored affair between Lennon and Epstein. Ono was not with John at that period of his life—they wed in 1969—but later mused, "I don't think he had an affair with Brian. I'm not denying it in the sense of 'Oh, dear, *no*, he didn't!' But John wasn't the kind of person who would have an affair with Brian and then hide about it. And ultimately it doesn't matter whether he did. It's more important that he was a person who was sympathetic to the gay community."

Veteran blues singer and bandleader Long John Baldry was openly gay and six foot seven—Mae West would've said, "Never mind the six feet, let's talk about the seven inches, big boy." He was a father of the British blues boom of the early '60s and led the group Hoochie Coochie Men. He introduced Rod Stewart as a second singer in the band. When he formed Steampacket, Long John took Stewart with him. Later he hired a young pianist named Reg Dwight who asked saxophonist Elton Dean if he could use his name. Elton said no, so Reg created a new name for himself by borrowing Elton's and John's first names. . . . In '67 Baldry had a rare chart hit with "Let the Heartaches Begin;" as of the mid-90s he was still touring the UK and fronting his own rock/blues band.

In the USA Baldry is almost unknown, and remains little-publicized in the UK, though, according to Brit journalist John Gill, he "begat the whole hard rock/heavy metal scene, that fount of everything macho in pop and rock today." What *else* could the lack of publicity be? But Elton John, now fifty, is finally out as gay, with his own Elton John AIDS Foundation, consistent hits and acclaim, and an ongoing boyfriend, David Furnish, who created a 1997 documentary about the hair-challenged music *divo* titled *Tantrums and Tiaras*. Elton had reached his unexpectedly widest audience via the musical soundtrack of the 1994 mega-success *The Lion King*, from Disney. Despite the participation of the singer-composer, openly gay executive producer Tom Schumacher, etc., *The Lion King* presented some of the usual tinsel anti-gay stereotypes, particularly the gay-implied evil uncle, Scar.

Notice how often the movies further villainize a character by coding him as gay (see *The Lavender Screen*). Heroes in films invariably have a female partner and usually kids; villains often have neither. Disney's '97 animated product, *Hercules*, employed another Tinseltown trick: re-sexualizing its hero. In

Greek mythology, the demi-god Hercules was bisexual. Disney made him blond, but so was Alexander the Great, who was gay and Greek—that is, Macedonian. Mythical or historical, aiming for juvenile or adult audiences, Hollywood still prefers to invisibilize or villainize gay people (bi's included).

Unlike Elton, Freddie Mercury (né Frederick Bulsara) never came out, even as bi. Singer Paul Delph, in a tribute to the late AIDS victim, averred, "He was brilliant at combining diverse elements that appealed to audiences everywhere. . . . Drag was about as far as he dared, in one sense. Much of his life was a fleeing from his identity, sexually but also ethnically . . . he tried to seem English or universal rather than Mideastern . . . sexual without boundaries rather than gay." A few insiders felt that as Mercury's (note he named himself after a god) and Queen's popularity rose, the singer's resolve to be honest about his love life diminished.

Queen put out their first, eponymous album in 1973. Two years later they hit the top with *A Night at the Opera*, the most expensive LP produced in Britain since the Beatles' *Sergeant Pepper*. Its single "Bohemian Rhapsody" became the longest-running number one hit in the UK in decades (peaking in the USA at number nine). Mercury and Queen rode high for about a decade, eventually declining in the '80s, Freddie still ensconced in a cocoon of privacy and avoidance. Ironically, as his and the group's fortunes waned, Mercury was no more able—so he felt—to come out, due to fears that being known as gay or bi might cost him his remaining (hetero) fans.

He never did come out, and only disclosed what was already known—that he had AIDS—the day before he died. As with Rock Hudson, his death and the resultant AIDS benefits were nevertheless used to raise public awareness of the disease and funds to combat it. A semi-halo of loss and martyrdom accrued to each man for a while, despite neither having addressed in their well-heeled lifetimes the issues of AIDS, discrimination and government indifference, gay identity, homophobia, gay rights, etc.

There was a time when the Pet Shop Boys were so paranoid of the truth that they required interviewers to sign a document stating they would not ask Neil Tennant or Chris Lowe about their private lives. Then Tennant, the more prominent one, told the curious press, "You don't know anything about ABBA's sex life, either." True, but one knew or assumed that ABBA's "private lives" were heterosexual ones; a person's sex life *should* be private, and is only part of their private or personal life. Neil's next approach was to advise the gay press in 1993 that "We don't deny anything. We can sort of have an interview where we discuss whether we regard ourselves as being out or not—which is truly out in itself to discuss it—but I guess we don't give quotes about it." Sounded like a politician!

Neil added that he was resisting coming out because he didn't wish to be a role model to anyone. Yet all celebs are to some degree role models, and heterosexual (including the pretend-hetero closeted ones) celebs shouldn't have a monopoly in the how-to-live-your-life arena. At last, in 1994, Neil Tennant came out: "I just thought it would be pathetic to turn forty and not come out. So I did it." Besides the "big" four-oh, another influence in his coming out was his new boyfriend and "the point of view of me being in love." "I think love gave him the courage to do it," offered Boy George.

For years, PSB had written genderless love songs and odes to intense friendship, love and loss, some inspired by the loss of friends and lovers to AIDS. Chris Lowe reportedly lived for five years with a man who died of AIDS. In '95 in the UK, printed rumors proliferated that Lowe was dying of AIDS. Tennant denied it. In '96 Lowe issued the statement, "Regardless of my sexuality, I would prefer not to be described as gay," the sort of statement which confirms too many homophobes' opinions that gays are ashamed of being gay. One wonders how old Lowe will have to be before he finds a label that he's comfortable with?

Talk about twisted semantics, one UK singer who might as well go nameless took a new tack: told the media that he was a bisexual who'd never had a homosexual experience. *Pity*!

Peter Burns of Dead or Alive peaked in the mid-'80s. Lately he's focused on Japan where he (and a post-Dead partner) remains popular with albums like *Nukleopatra*. *Edge* wrote that Burns "has thrived in Japan like Elizabeth Taylor in a chocolate factory. . . . At one point, poor Michael Jackson had to push back his Japanese tour because (Burns) was ruling Jackson's desired venue with a series of sold-out performances" (Jackson today is more popular overseas than in the USA). In 1996 Burns performed in Los Angeles' Gay & Lesbian Pride Festival. Asked why his band lost popularity, he muttered, "My choice." Is he gay? Declined to so label himself. Bi? Indicated yes. Admitted his first time was with a male, claimed to be with the same woman for eighteen years. Any kids? "No, loathe them." Wouldn't say if it's a sexual relationship, would not give his age, did say he was happier after "it all (fame and fortune) went away," and that he'd like to achieve some of it all in the USA. (Good luck.)

Of course, certain questions pop up interview after interview—often for a reason. In the last several years, most any interview with songstress/ex-movie star Julie Andrews and/or longtime husband Blake Edwards includes the long-running Rumor about each of them. Andrews denies them more vociferously than Edwards, offering as irrefutable proof her statement to *Vanity Fair* (another 'zine which would rather that people *not* be gay) that "I assure you, I am *not* gay!" How egregiously emphatic can you get?

Openly gay Tony-winning actress Cherry Jones has said she knew early on that she was lesbian because "I spent hours counting the freckles on Julie Andrews' face on the back album cover for *The Sound of Music*." Andrews was known to wear pants, simple blouses and sweaters, sported close-cropped hair, and attended *The Sound of Music*'s preview with friend Roddy McDowall.... No wonder Cherry had a crush!

Jason Donovan, a Bondi Beach boy from Australia, became a hit singer in Britain, where the gay rumors pursued him. In London he bizarrely refuted them by declaring that the success of his latest single "just goes to show how thin those rumors were. If people were to have believed what they read, I'm pretty sure they wouldn't have taken to what I've done as well as they have." Guess no one ever told him about the success of Elton, k.d., or Melissa, not to mention Britain's plethora of "bisexual" singers! Then he was featured with other allegedly gay (a legal term required by a homophobic society and law system) celebs in a series of posters emblazoned "Queer as Fuck."

Which brings to mind a USA poster series of gay, lesbian and bi celebs that was reported by a legitimate newspaper. Their information was picked up by a tabloid, which singled out a gay or bi actor—married with child—who then sued. The tab could have won the suit, as it was reporting information, but chose to settle out of court and even printed an apology! The apology was sheer homophobia, the undisclosed settlement—widely reported on TV by indignant news readers—was later revealed to amount to $5, which is about what the actor's "heterosexuality" is really worth.

Jason Donovan next denied by saying, "It's not the way I choose to live my life." Sexuality isn't chosen, a lifestyle is, and gay people have lives, not "lifestyles"—how often does one hear of "the heterosexual lifestyle?" (followed by most hetero and many closeted-gay people). Openly gay interviewer Paul Burston described in print Donovan's home, including the hunky "photographs of Chesney Hawkes plastered around his bathroom mirror." When *The Face* wrote that the singer was secretly gay, Donovan sued; his pitbullish lawyer called it "a poisonous slur."

Not surprisingly, Donovan won the case. But when the money awarded him—"damages," from *The Face*—threatened to sink the periodical, he tried to make amends, later hosting a male beauty pageant and cutting back on the defensiveness. Jason Donovan remains virtually unknown in the USA. *Pity.*

Singer Kirk Brandon sued Boy George for "malicious falsehood"—of *course* it's never malicious to call someone "straight"—when the boy said they'd had an affair in his *Take It Like a Man* memoirs and in his song "Unfinished Business." George won. The court cited "overwhelming evidence" that the men had an affair, plus it denied that the revelations had caused any damage to the faded singer's attempted comeback. Brandon is left (in 1997) with court costs of about 200,000 pounds. But he claims he'll take the same case to court in the USA if that's what it takes "to clear my name."

In 1996 George Michael professed, "I've wondered what my sexuality might be, but I've never wondered whether it was acceptable or not. Anyway, who really cares whether I'm gay or straight?" Apparently *he* does. His quote was given, appropriately, to Britain's *Big Issue* magazine. It was his first interview in six years. George spent much of his long period away disentangling himself from Sony and avoiding the public eye. Boy George, who's often outed Michael, stated, "It's so silly.

Everyone knows which singers give good throat, not necessarily in front of a mike. . . . We have a million singers who say they're gay—Patrick Fitzgerald of Kitchens of Distinction, he's one, he's good. . . . If the public knew the half of it, there wouldn't be all this prejudice and jumping to conclusions about what one is because of the way one acts or dresses." He half-joked, "I'm waiting for someone to do a study on the cause of heterosexuality. Seems only fair. . . ."

American country singer Sid Spencer said, "The word is that George Michael is very involved with someone who has AIDS and is trying to help out . . . . I just wish he hadn't cheapened himself with that book (of memoirs) where he went out of his way to write about purported girlfriends. That flies right in the face of his usual attitude about not caring what people think, or letting them wonder." Music critic Barry Walters wrote, "Michael has shared very little of himself with his audience. He . . . hides behind model-intensive videos, and rarely ever tours." He explained that some of the songs on Michael's comeback album, *Older*, "gain more power if you understand them as Michael's grieving a beau who has died from AIDS complications."

Five and a half years between albums did result in some changes. Michael's first comeback video featured two shirtless boys holding hands through the frames of separate wooden boxes, an image which reappears toward the end. As Michael sings, "You will always be my love," the youths vanish as if they were ghosts. Walters felt, "Michael is far more up-front with who he is and whom he loves than we could ever have expected. . . . It's great to have him back—and nearly out." *Nearly?* When the long-awaited (but to many overly melancholy) CD came out, George—despite evidently having given up any Hollywood dream—did not. Rather, he misinformed *Big Issue*:

"If every gay pop star and actor in the world came out, it wouldn't make any difference to the gay community." *Excuses!* Try telling that to *Ellen* . . . or the gay community.

In April, '97, *4Front* reported that "George Michael has become a regular at Cherry (a West Hollywood gay bar) on Fridays. Rumor has it that the pop superstar has even taken his turn in the DJ booth to advise on music. Many were surprised at the public displays of affection that Michael was dishing out

311

to his boy-toy for the evening. You would think the young thing would be hanging all over him, but the opposite was true."

Remember the 1990 hit "I'm Too Sexy"? It was via Right Said Fred, a trio comprising Fred and Richard Fairbrass, who used to run a gym together, and Rob Manzoli. The group has had no big international hit since, but—like Boy George—has stayed popular in Britain. Since '91, the UK press was hinting that Richard (the sexy, tongue-in-cheek singer) was gay. So in 1994 he came out as bi (the other two men are hetero), explaining to the typically homophobic *Sun*, "I was not going to sit still and be talked about like I was from another planet. I did it (coming out) for a very selfish reason: I wanted to give myself an easy time." Namely, to obviate having the tabloids spying on him for the inside story. Nor did the declaration hurt the group, as the two non-gay men had feared, and brother Fred declared himself pro-gay; when he got propositioned by a man, "I thought, That's nice, and I still think that."

Richard Fairbrass later clarified that bisexual didn't mean twice as horny, and that "I'm mostly gay at the moment," a brave and frank statement. (Paul Jabara once pronounced, "I don't know how it is for the gals, but a guy who says he's bi either hasn't gone through enough repetition to know what he genuinely prefers, or he's not saying that what it is, is he's 80 or 90 percent gay and 20 or 10 percent straight.") Richard came out about the time of Right Said Fred's new CD, *Sex & Travel*. All of whose songs were described by one critic as "very heterosexual." Because they were written by Fred. *Ahem*. Ironically, the album was dedicated to Richard's intimate friend Peter Barton, who'd died of AIDS.

To his credit, Richard does speak out about gay rights and AIDS issues. He should also speak to his brother about including one or two non-heterosexual songs on a future project. Fairbrass expressed the hope of making it big in the USA too, and has the eventual goal of "singing a really romantic ballad about love between two men." Start writing, Richard, and good luck!

Long before Elton and Melissa and k.d. were out, Jimmy Somerville was. As a pioneer, he didn't benefit from more acceptable timing. And being gay rather than not (or than closeted), cute rather than a beach boy-type hunk, British rather than American, etc., he remains a star rather than a superstar in the UK, and in the USA has a cult following. The *Advocate* pointed out in 1995, on release of his *Dare to Love* album, "In America, Somerville's supports are primarily gays and their aerobic instructors, but in England and the rest of Europe, his audience includes moms, dads and kids."

"I still sing, I try new things professionally, and I work for gay rights. What else can I say?" Indeed. As articulate, but less modest and more exhibitionist, Boy George remains shut out of most of America's radio stations. Like Somerville, he tours the USA periodically—he scored a moderate comeback with the title song from the movie *The Crying Game*—but is far more accepted back home. Says George, "When I'm in the States I'll talk about myself. Everywhere else, I talk about me and I talk about being gay." Jimmy says, "They're not crazy for Brits over there, let alone queer ones."

CBS VP Tim Flack observed, "Sexism usually hurts women. But when sexism meets homosexuality, it's the men that get hurt more." As women, very likeable women at that, k.d. lang and Melissa Etheridge's open homosexuality didn't hurt their careers, even though they were still on the upswing. The only icon-status male singer to come out as gay has been Elton John, who came out in two stages—bi, then gay—already a top star each time. The Boy Georges and Jimmy Somervilles, whatever their nationality, won't get a fair shake until the establishment ceases to think of homosexuality as somehow less "awful" for women than for men. . . . (*The Awful Truth* starred Cary Grant; the movie had nothing to do with *that*—unlike the British-American actor, and I do mean *actor.*)

Jack Dunphy was contractually married to fellow dancer Joan McCracken. They split, and she paired with dancer-choreographer Bob Fosse and he with novelist Truman Capote. The two men were partners—not always living together—for almost forty years. Dunphy, who died in 1992 (eight years after Tru) at seventy-seven, gave up dancing to become a writer. "I gave it up before it gave me up," he once said. "Like most men, I think of myself as pretty virile," he told a *Dance Magazine* reporter, "but the dance tends to bring out your paranoia. You check yourself for every little movement, every gesture.

"It's an unwritten law that the dance requires its male participants to create an illusion of total masculinity, be they gay or straight. . . . Somebody said when you're a man and a dancer, you have to keep apologizing." Today's openly gay *danseurs*, from Mark Morris to Morris Freed, have replaced the apology with Apollo. "Dance, for dance's sake," proclaimed Morris, "and in all its forms." His own dance company illustrates dance without restrictions.

Morris Freed learned piano and tap dancing as a boy, along with his identical twin Oliver, in Hendersonville, Tennessee. Morris became a professional dancer, eventually touring in the national company of *A Chorus Line*. Tragically, he died of AIDS at age forty-one in early 1997. A Buddhist and a theatre buff, he was profiled in *POZ* magazine: "His greatest AIDS-related physical challenges were gastrointestinal, and in his last year he rarely ate, relying on IV nourishment. But what kept him alive was his spirituality, and many free theatre tickets from GMHC (Gay Men's Health Crisis)."

Freed had said, "Dance is evolving into new shapes and freedoms as everyone stops to question the old rigidly defined gender roles and prohibitions on our sexuality." (And yes, Oliver Freed is also—openly—gay; studies on twins are confirming that, like left-handedness, sexuality is at least basically inherent. Homosexuality is just as much a "choice" as is heterosexuality, possibly even less so, since everyone is reared and intimidated toward becoming heterosexual.)

While Nathan Lane was being so coy with the press during *A Funny Thing Happened on the Way to the Forum*, its choreographer—and that of Broadway's *Victor/Victoria*—Rob Marshall, was and is openly gay. Ditto his mate of over fourteen years, director John De Luca; they met in the cast of an off-Broadway musical. Speaking of Broadway (pirouetting into a segue here), Eric Shepard, Tommy Tune's longtime agent at ICM, admitted, "If I have any clients who are dancers, I urge them to stay in the closet if they're gay. Unless they only plan to mature into choreographers."

Paul Draper's dance specialty was a mixture of tap and ballet. He died at eighty-six in 1996, at Woodstock. "I was blacklisted, that's no secret. *The* (political) blacklist . . . but there's other blacklists . . . the guy who's said to be 'too light.' Means not butch enough. In the dance world, no one's butch enough. . . . Gene

Kelly (who also died in '96) never missed a chance to 'explain' why his form of dance was *different*. Means butcher. . . . My motto is shut up and dance. After you've danced, shut up again." Due to his popularity and place in the tinsel pantheon, Kelly's bisexuality will be long in the revealing. Also, the establishment is loathe to give up its myth that all successful male dancers are "normal" (the norm, which should be a non-judgmental term). Certainly when it came to Hollywood dance, Kelly was its butch epitome and sexiest exponent; a close second was apparently heterosexual Gene Nelson, the blond hunk who got to Kansas City in *Oklahoma* and went places (mostly boudoirs) in other movies, making a comeback in 1971 on Broadway in Stephen Sondheim's *Follies*. Nelson also died in '96.

Emmy-winning choreographer Billy Wilson noted, "The most athletic dance form is probably ballet, and it's suffered from AIDS more than any other." He cited the Joffrey Ballet, which has lost over two dozen male dancers, among them the very promising twenty-three-year-old Edward Stierle. Choreographer Lester Wilson worked with Travolta in *Saturday Night Fever*, also with Ann-Margret and Peter Allen. "I don't know why, but AIDS does afflict dancers more than singers or actors or. . . . Dancers are so physical, so needy of expression. Unfortunately, dancers have the least chance of making a transition into the big-time." True, a cute female dancer could often leave the ranks of the chorus line for stardom, while a cute male dancer was typically limited by the higher-ups' perception of him as gay (even if he wasn't!).

One disappointed *danseur* was Harold Lang, who had affairs with Leonard Bernstein and Gore Vidal, who called "Harold's ass one of the seven wonders of the world." Lang danced in Jerome Robbins' ballet *Fancy Free*, probably his high-point. He reportedly believed his looks—fore and aft—and his connections could land him in Hollywood. One insider felt Lang was too arrogant, another that his talent didn't measure up, yet another that "If Harold's lovers had been other chorus boys instead of famous fags like Gore Vidal, then word of his nocturnal life wouldn't have preceded him and spoiled his chances."

Emile Ardolino directed *Dirty Dancing*, and also *Sister Act*. His last project before succumbing to AIDS was the Bette Midler telemusical *Gypsy*, which was dedicated to his memory. He told

Variety, "Dance is attracting more straight boys these days. They're not ashamed to be dancers, which they were when I was a kid. . . . Have things improved for boy dancers who aren't straight? Not unless they're Rudolf Nureyev." Though he never came out, and never disclosed his health condition, it was Nureyev who restored the male ballet dancer to international prominence and who came closest to shattering the all-suc-cessful-dancers-are-straight myth. For one thing, he didn't play the *game*—marrying like Nijinsky or fathering or conjoining his public name with a famous actress, etc.

Subsequent information has revealed that Nureyev's defec-tion to the West was at least partly motivated by fear that upon returning to Russia he would be arrested for having had homo-sexual sex. Billy Wilson apprised the *Sydney Morning Herald* upon Rudi's death from AIDS in 1993, "He was headstrong. He did what he wanted, and once he became a star the only thing he was afraid of was harm to his career and losing his looks. . . . He did get a far greater freedom, especially sexually, in France, but he didn't leave Russia for freedom, *per se* . . . the secret police were compiling a thick file on Nureyev over there, and he knew it was a question of time before he was arrested as an example to the (male) dancers who wouldn't give up their boyfriends."

Nureyev left a huge estate comprising homes, art and paint-ings of male nudes, particularly rear views, plus a sizeable pornography collection. Said Wilson, "Everyone knew, because we'd been tipped off, that Nureyev was seeking one item above all others for his collection, and was willing to pay a fortune for it. See, Nijinsky was very well-hung and his young dancer's body was very supple. I guess because of narcissism and guilt, he often indulged in auto-fellatio. And there were supposed to be one or two existing photos of him doing it, taken by Nijinsky's valet and companion, who was a Swiss guy and also gay. Nureyev longed to have that photo." (Pun intended?)

Critics said Nureyev danced too long, well past forty. Then they said he worked too long, directing in Paris from a wheel-chair, looking gaunt and exhausted. His AIDS became an open secret in the dance and opera worlds of Paris, but he wouldn't utter a word about it, terrified of losing work and no doubt of being shunned personally.

British ice skater John Curry was known as "Nureyev on ice." After winning a gold medal at the 1976 Olympics he became a star, producing and headlining his own ice show in London's West End. Unlike the vast majority of his dancing and skating counterparts in Russia, the USA and elsewhere, he was openly gay.

"You can't be proud if you're in hiding," Curry often said. In 1987 he learned he was HIV-positive. He died at forty-four in 1994, and the prior year, upon Nureyev's death, informed the British press, "The more widespread disease is AIDS-phobia. [AIDS] is a disease, not a stigma. Most people with AIDS today are heterosexuals, in spite of the widespread stereotype.... It's up to those of us [with AIDS] to be honest and aboveboard, lest we perpetuate the needless added burden of stigmatizing people who are ill and dying."

Composer John Cage was involved in art and life with dancer/choreographer Merce Cunningham for fifty-five years. But the two men didn't live together until 1970 (until the '92 death of Cage, the senior partner). Cage told Bill Como of *Dance Magazine* in 1972, "Until the laws change, artists must be cautious about their careers. However, each individual who is different from the rest must sooner or later reach a point where his life and living arrangements agree with his inclinations and wishes, else what's a life for?" A Zen Buddhist philosopher and writer, the modern classical composer published several books and toured extensively with Cunningham. Cage advised young people: "If you find pleasure, be careful before you take it. If you find love, and more importantly, enduring love, take it. Embrace it. Hang onto it no matter who it is and no matter what others say." He added, warningly, "Please be aware that life is not a dress rehearsal. As human beings, this is all we have. So live your life!"

The late, gay Lincoln Kirstein discovered the openly and oft-statedly heterosexual choreographer George Balanchine. He financed Balanchine's succession of ballet companies. He lived to eighty-eight and was for over sixty years, thanks to his inheritance, an active patron of the arts. He was an author (in 1933 he went to London to ghost-write a bio-myth-ography of Nijinsky with the dancer's wife) and a husband-of-sorts to the sister of gay painter Paul Cadmus. As a philanthropist with a high-flying social life, a wife was useful; he stayed married to her from 1941 until her death in 1991. A manic-depressive, he felt that he wasn't entitled to too much happiness; Bill Como believed "Kirstein's never resolved his guilt over being different sexually and religiously, and being born rich." Yet Kirstein did declare—as quoted in *Out* magazine—homosexuality to be his "true, not ... accidental preference, my real blood tribe." Pity he had to use Fidelma Cadmus to cover up his truth for so long.

Joe Layton, who died of AIDS in 1994, was a choreographer, a producer, and a Broadway director. He did the musical sequences of the Julie Andrews vehicle *Thoroughly Modern Millie* (1967). When he complained to the film's gay producer Ross Hunter (who was eventually barred from the set by hetero director George Roy Hill) that some of the sequences were "relentlessly straight, not to mention busy and rather cliché," Hunter snapped, "That's the difference between us! I love kitsch, and kitsch *sells*." The greater difference was healthy gay man versus self-loathing and ever-closeted gay man.

Layton produced, choreographed and "conceived" Barbra Streisand's first color TV special, the award-winning *Color Me Barbra*. "My career is a joy to me," said Layton, "but even for it there are personal standards of freedom and dignity that I wouldn't give up now." His memorial service was attended by the likes of Bette Midler, Lauren Bacall, and Carol Channing. Streisand was to have attended, but instead reportedly chose to attend a heterosexual wedding.

"Do you know what dancing is?" asked Morris Freed. "It's moving from *here* to *there*—preferably done with grace and confidence, and with individuality and honesty. Some of us are better dancers than others, and not necessarily the ones who get paid." If all the world's a stage, then each of us is moving from *here* to *there*, hopefully with grace, confidence, individuality, honesty. . . .

Epilogue

"There is a certain silence which appears to be mysterious, but which is only weakness." ——Queen Christina of Sweden

I've been thinking:

That biography of Leonard Bernstein, the one merely alluded to by Paul Moor in *Christopher Street*—he declared in a footnote, "I decline to provide a plug for that despicable piece of shit." Remember where the author had Bernstein weeping at the piano in Judy Holliday's apartment?

The author thought that Bernstein was crying out of sadness because he found himself in a room where everyone was homosexual.

Maybe he was crying for joy . . . *finally.*

Index

2 Live Crew, 107
4 Non Blondes, 290; Perry, Linda, singer for, 290-91
Abraham, F. Murray, 240
Agate, James, 183
Ailey, Alvin, 223
Albee, Edward, 152, 253
Allen, Peter, 101, 130, 267, 270, 271-72, 291, 315; Bell, Chris, partner of, 271
Anacreon, 252
Andrews, Julie, 309
Andrews, Maxene, 292
Ant, Adam, 182, 192
Ardolino, Emile, 315-16
Arlen, Harold, 252
Armstrong, Billie Joe, 286
Armstrong, Louis, 139
Ashman, Howard, 248
Ashton, Sir Frederick, 222
Astaire, Fred, 231, 232, 235-38; Adele, sister of, 236, 237; Ava, daughter of, 236; *Fred Astaire: His Friends Talk*, biography of, 236; and Horton, Edward Everett, 237; Phyllis, first wife of, 237
Audio Two, 107, 108
Avalon, Frankie, 63, 65
Bach, Sebastian, 107
Baez, Joan, 16, 24-25, 111-13, 140, 164; *And A Voice to Sing With*, autobiography of, 112; and Johnson, Don, 112, 113; and Near, Holly, 112
Baker, Josephine, 134, 135-37, 144, 147; *Jazz Cleopatra*, biography of, 135; and Lillie, Beatrice, 167; and Winchell, Walter, 136

Bankhead, Tallulah, 132, 284; and Holman, Libby, 149-50; and Lillie, Beatrice, 168
Barber, Samuel, 32, 39-40, 43; and Menotti, Giancarlo, 40
Barbette, 227
Bates, Katharine Lee, 252
Bauer, Harold, 52
Beatles, 20, 54, 106. *See also* Lennon, John
Beaton, Cecil, 15
Beethoven, Ludwig Van, 32, 33-34, 251; and Karl, nephew of, 33
Beiderbecke, Bix, 260
Bell, Andy, 208-10; Erasure, singer for, 208-09; and Pet Shop Boys, 206-07
Bellini, Vincenzo, 53
Bennett, Michael, 24, 232-33; and Beaton, Cecil, 232; McKechnie, Donna, wife of, 232
Bentley, Gladys, 138-39; *I Am A Woman Again*, autobiography of, 139
Berle, Milton, 92
Bernhard, Sandra, 156-57, 158, 296-97
Bernstein, Leonard, xii, 31, 32, 42-44, 49, 257, 258, 295; Adrian, Max on, 42, 44; and Granger, Farley, 43; and Kert, Larry, 272; and Lang, Harold, 315; and National Endowment for the Arts, xii; Peyser, Joan, biographer of, 42, 257
"Bette Davis Eyes," 152-53
Bladry, "Long" John, 306
Blakely, Michelle, 299
Bleckmann, Theo, 262
Blitzstein, Marc, 38-39, 43; and Houseman, John, 39; murder of, 39

Block, Adam, 119, 196, 205
Bolan, Marc, 181, 184
Bolger, Ray, 250
Bono, Chastity, 295, 298
Bottum, Roddy, 283
Bowie, David, 16, 22, 24, 111, 114, 175–179, 181, 182, 186, 303-04; accused of rape, 178; Angela, wife of, 175, 177; and Queen, 184; and Reed, Lou, 94
Bowles, Paul, 259–60
Boy George, xiv, 17, 19, 23, 24, 70, 140, 192–96, 207, 280, 282, 313; Brandon, Kirk, sued by, 310; and Dunn, Michael, 194, 196; and Michael, George, 198–99, 310–11; on Morrissey, 203; in *Newsweek* cover photo with Annie Lennox, 121, 193
Bragg, Billy, 23–24
Britten, Benjamin, 172–73; and Pears, Peter, 172
Bronski Beat. *See* Somerville, Jimmy
Bronski, Steve (Bronski Beat), 201; and Hellyer, Jonathan, 202
Brooks, Garth, 249
Brown, Joe, 305
Buchanan, Jack, 183
Burns, Peter, 204-05, 308-09
Burton, Gary, 262–63; and lang, k. d., 263
Cage, John, 317
Caine, Michael, 213
Callen, Michael, 102-03, 267, 270–71
Callow, Simon, 250
Cantor, Eddie, 83–84, 280
Cantor, Marjorie, 280
Capote, Truman, 59. *See also* Dunphy, Jack
Carne, Judy, 226, 294; Reynolds, Burt, husband of, 226
Carpenter, Richard, 86
Casey, Waren, 49, 50
Cassidy, Jack, 75–76; David, son of, 100–01; Jones, Shirley, wife of, 76; Patrick, son of, 76; Shaun, son of, 76
Chapman, Tracy, 291
Cher, 149–50
Cherry, Neneh, 290
Chevalier, Maurice, 24, 57, 80–82; and Barbette, 227; and Mayol, Felix, 81; and Mistinguett, 81; subject of bet between Duke of Windsor and his wife, 81
Chopin, Frederic, 32
Christopher Alden, 263–64; David, twin brother of, 264; and McClintock, Peter, 264
Clarke, Vince, 208–10
Clary, Robert, 279–80; Cantor, Natalie, wife of, 280
Clemons, Clarence. *See* Springsteen, Bruce
Cliburn, Van, 266–67
Cobain, Kurt, 272–73, 280–81

Cocteau, Jean, 217, 218, 219, 227
Cole, Jack, 24, 231-32; and Kelly, Gene, 248; *Unsung Genius*, biography of, 231
Communards. *See* Somerville, Jimmy
Como, William, 75–76, 214, 215, 224, 232, 317, 318; on Mathis, Johnny, 104
Connery, Sean, 213
Cooper, Alice, 87
Copland, Aaron, xi, 32, 42–43, 257; and Del Tredici, David, 264
Corigliano, John, 258
Coward, Noel, 32, 37, 51, 81, 82, 90, 170–72, 173, 228, 247–48; *Genius and Lust*, portrayed in, 247; and Grant, Cary, 171; and Harrison, Rex, 171; and Helpmann, Sir Robert, 221; and Lillie, Beatrice, 167–68; and Taylor, Elizabeth, 171
Cowell, Henry, 58
Craig, Michael (Culture Club), 193
Crane, Hart, 74
Crawford, Cindy, 289
Crawford, Joan, 145–46, 154, 250; Christina, daughter of, 146; *Conversations with Joan Crawford*, biography of, 145; and Grable, Betty, 145–46
Crow, Sheryl, 72. *See also* Jackson, Michael
Cukor, George, 130, 160, 162, 164, 250
Culture Club, 192–93, 194
Curry, John, 317
Dahlgren, Eva, 296
Dailey, Dan, 57, 249–50
Daniels, Jimmie, 273–74
Dante, Nicholas, 233
Davis, Bette, 146, 163
Davis, Miles, 260, 261
Davis, Sammy Jr., 92–93; Britt, Mai, second wife of, 93; Gore, Altovise, third wife of, 93; on Joplin, Janis, 116; and Novak, Kim, 93; Tracey, daughter of, 93
De Falla, Manuel, 32, 53, 218
De Luca, John, 314
Deadly Nightshade, 140–41
Dean, Elton, 306
Debussy, Claude, 32, 48, 52, 214
DeGeneres, Ellen, 248
Del Tredici, David, 264
Delph, Paul, 284, 307
Dennis, Sandy, 261
Diaghliev, Sergei, 214, 215, 217, 218-19
Diamond, David, 43, 45
Dietrich, Marlene, 150–52, 153; and Garbo, Greta, 151
DiFranco, Ani, 298
Dire Straits, 192
Divine, 102
Dolin, Anton, 217
Donovan, 190
Donovan, Jason, 309, 310

Draper, Paul, 314-15

Duncan, Isadora, 224-25; and Duse, Eleanora, 225

Dunphy, Jack, 313-14; and Capote, Truman, 313; McKracken, Joan, wife of, 313

Duran Duran, 21, 191-192; and Erasure, 209

Dylan, Bob, 112

Eagles, Jeanne, 147

Ebb, Fred, 253-54

Eddy, Nelson, 24, 82-83; MacDonald, Jeannette, partner of, 82

Edens, Roger, 267-68; and Haines, William, 267; and Lansbury, Angela, 267

Edwards, Blake, 309

Engel, Lehman, 41, 258

Epstein, Brian, 53-55, 190-91, 305-06; and Wooler, Bob, 54

Erasure. See Bell, Andy

Etheridge, Melissa, 270, 288-89, 299; Cypher, Julie, wife of, 289

Everage, Dame Edna, 303

Extra Fancy, 277, 286-88; Grillo, Brian, singer for, 287, 288; Paul V., manager of, 287, 288

Fabian. See "Good Time Rock 'N Roll, Volume IV" concert

Faithfull, Marianne, 304

Fame, Georgie, 305

Farrell, Perry, 285

Feinstein, Michael, 51-52, 254; *Nice Work if You Can Get It*, autobiography of, 255

Fem 2 Fem, 300

Ferrick, Melissa, 298

Fitzgerald, Patrick. See Kitchens of Distinction

Flack, Tim, 256-57, 313

Flea, 285

Ford, Frankie. See "Good Time Rock 'N Roll, Volume IV" concert

Fosse, Bob, 214

Foster, Jodie, 276-77, 303

Foster, Stephen, 24, 32, 37-38; Cooper, George, left wife for, 37-38; as portrayed in *Swanee River*, 38

Frankie Goes To Hollywood, 199-201; Johnson, Holly, singer for, 199-201; Rutherford, Paul, singer for, 22-23, 199-201

Freed, Morris, 314, 318

Gabriel, Juan, 271

Galas, Diamanda, 297

Gales, Larry, 260

Garbo, Greta, 146, 148, 151, 153

Gardel, Carlos, 268

Garland, Judy, 130, 267, 272

Gay, Marvin, 106

Gere, Richard, 289, 305

Gershwin, George, 29-30, 40-41, 51, 255; and Goddard, Paulette, 40; and

Ravel, Maurice, 40-41

Gershwin, Ira, 29-30, 51, 255

Gibb, Andy, 86

Gibson, Mel. 251

Gillespie, Dizzy, 262

Go-Go's, 140

Godfrey, Arthur, 16

"Good Time Rock 'N Roll, Volume IV" concert, 63-64; Fabian, host of, 63, 64; Ford, Frankie at, 63-64

Gore, Tipper, 128, 248, 249

Graham, Martha, 223

Grainger, Percy, 134

Grainger, Porter, 32, 41

Granger, Farley, 266

Gregory, Daniel, 38

Greif, Martin (*The Gay Book of Days*), 33, 74, 98, 112, 134, 177, 217, 250

Grieg, Edvard, 32, 34

Griffes, Charles Tomlinson, 38

Grillo, Rudy, 135, 154

Guilaroff, Sydney, 268

Guns 'N Roses. See Rose, Axl

Haggard, Merle, 106-07

Hahn, Reynaldo, 32, 47; and Proust, Marcel, 47

Hall & Oates, 86

Hammett, Kirk (Metallica), 284-85

Hammond, Dame Joan, 302

Handel, George Fredrick, 32, 35; and Matheson, Johann, 35; and Scarlatti, Alessandro, 35; and Scarlatti, Domenico, 35; and Steffani, Agustino, 35

Hannah, George, 134

Harlow, Jean, 152

Hart, Lorenz (Larry), 24, 29, 56-58; *Rodgers and Hart—Bewitched, Bothered and Bedeviled*, portrayed in, 58; and Rodgers, Richard, 31, 56, 57. See also Dailey, Dan

Hawkins, Sophie B., 299

Heche, Anne, 305. See also DeGeneres, Ellen

Helpmann, Sir Robert, 221-22, 224

Hepburn, Katherine, 268

Herman, Jerry, 32, 47, 253, 254; *Showtune*, memoir of, 254

Herndon, Ty, 278-79; Slate, Johnny, manager of, 279

Hildegarde, 51, 140

Holiday, Billie, 137-38, 139, 294; *Lady Sings the Blues*, film biography of, 137

Holliday, Judy, 162-64; and Mulligan, Gerry, 163, 261

Holman, Libby, 147-49; *Dreams That Money Can Buy*, biography of, 148; and Halliday, Richard, 147; and Jenny, Louisa d'Andelot Carpenter, 148; Reynolds, Smith, husband of, 148; and Webb, Clifton, 228

Horowitz, Vladimir, xiii, 49, 53

Houston, Whitney, 15, 122, 126, 274, 289
Hudson, Rock, 16, 17, 49, 98, 130
Hughes, Langston, 261
Hulse, Tom, 250
Humperdinck, Engelbert, 20-21, 188-89
Hunger, Ross, 318
Hunter, Alberta, 134, 139
Hüsker Dü. *See* Mould, Bob
Ian, Janis, 111, 113-14, 293-95
Indigo Girls, 301, 302
Isherwood, Christopher, 214, 250, 278
Jabara, Paul, 254, 255
Jackson, Michael, 69-70, 71-73, 86, 233, 274, 275-76, 308; and Crow, Sheryl, 72; Joseph, father of, 72, 73; and Mercury, Freddie, 184; Katherine, mother of, 73; and O'Neal, Tatum, 72; Presley, Lisa Marie, first wife of, 275, 276; Prince, son of, 275-76; and Sheilds, Brooke, 72, 276; in *We Are the World*, 71
Jacobs, Paul, 48
Jagger, Mick, 15, 174-76, 304-05; and Bowie, David, 175, 304
Jarman, Derek, 173
Jett, Joan, 153, 296
Jobriath, 96
Johansen, David (Buster Poindexter). *See* New York Dolls
John, Elton, 16, 21-22, 24, 111, 179-82, 186, 197, 207, 306; and Clarke, Gary, 181; on Jackson, Michael, 275; and Kinison, Sam, 182; Renate, wife of, 180-81; Taupin, Bernie, partner of, 180
Johnson, Holly, 304
Jones, Cherry, 309
Jones, Grace, 22, 96, 123, 140, 192
Jones, Tom, 188
Joplin, Janis, 112, 116-18; biographies of, 116; death of, 117; *The Rose*, alluded to in, 116
Kander, John, 253-54
Karpman, Laura, 269-70
Kaye, Danny, 74-75; Fine, Sylvia, wife of, 75
Kelly, Gene, 233, 248-49, 314-15
Key, Francis Scott, 252
Kiedis, Anthony, 285
Kirstein, Lincoln, 317-18; biographer of Nijinsky, 317
Kitchens of Distinction, 205, 311
Knopfler, Mark, 107
Korrie, Michael, 264
Kowalczyk, Steven, 261, 277-78
Kramer, Larry, 278, 280
Laing, Hugh, 222
Lambert, Kit, 305
Landowska, Wanda, 146-47
Lane, Nathan, 283-84, 314; and de la Cruz, Marco, 283
Lang, Harold, 315

lang, k. d., xiv, 21, 25, 119-21, 123, 143, 249, 270, 288, 289, 295
Lauper, Cyndi, 126, 249, 250
Laurents, Arthur, 266
Lawford, Peter, 74, 93
Layton, Joe, 318
Lennon, John, 16-17, 54, 190-91; and Pang, May, 191; Wooler, Bob, beating of, 54. *See also* Epstein, Brian
Lennox, Annie, 21, 121-22; Franklin, Aretha, duet with, 122; Stewart, Dave, partner of, 121, 122. *See also* Boy George
Lerner, Alan Jay, 47, 268, 269
Levanta, Oscar, 265
Liberace, 17, 24, 48-50; and David, Carl, 49; Ina, sister of 50; Lester Lee, nephew of, 50; and Newton, Wayne, 86; Thorson, Scott, biographer of, 49; *The Wonderful World of Liberace*, autobiography of, 48
Lifar, Sergei, 217, 219
Lillie, Beatrice, 157-158; *Every Other Inch a Lady*, memoirs of, 168
Little Anthony, 64
Little Richard, 67-69, 281; Block, Adam on, 68; Boone, Pat covering tunes by, 67-68; *The Quasar of Rock*, autobiography of, 68;
Loewe, Fritz, 47, 268-69
Lotte, Lenya, 155-56; Weill, Kurt, husband of, 155
Love, Courtney, 296. *See also* Cobain, Kurt
Lowe, Chris. *See* Pet Shop Boys
Luft, Joey. *See* Garland, Judy
Lully, Jean-Baptiste, 32, 34; appointed Director of Official Music for Louis XIV, 34
Lutaaya, Philly Bongoley, 92
Mabley, Jackie ("Moms"), 134
Madonna, 126, 156-58; Ciccone, Christopher, 249-50; and Grey, Jennifer, 158
Maggie, Robert, 259
Mahler, Gustav, 32, 65; Alma, wife of, 53
Manilow, Barry, 98-99
Marshall, Rob, 314
Martin, Dick, 75
Martin, Mary, 269. *See also* Merman, Ethel
Massine, Leonide, 217, 218, 222
Mathis, Johnny, 17, 19, 24, 79, 104-05, 154; ; and Mulligan, Gerry, 261; and Streisand, Barbra, 248
McCartney, Paul, 191
McKellen, Sir Ian, 250
McKuen, Rod, 98, 111
McNally, Terrence, 253
McRae, Carmen, 292-93
Meek, Joe, 305
Melchior, Lauritz, 74
Mercury, Freddie, 184-95, 207, 307
Merman, Ethel, 15, 114-15, 268; Borgnine,

Ernest, husband of, 115; and Chanel, Coco, 115; on Joplin, Janis, 118; Martin, Mary, dislike of, 115

Michael, George, 16, 20, 24, 196-99, 284, 310-12; Ridgeley, Andrew and, 196-97

Midler, Bette, 116-17, 121, 128-29, 154

Mills, Gordon, 189

Minelli, Vincent. See Garland, Judy

Mineo, Sal, 86-87, 93; and Johnson, Don, 86-87, 100; and Sherman, Bobby, 86

Miranda, Carmen, 132-33; Sebastian, David, husband of, 133

Mitropoulous, Dmitri, xi, 41, 43

Monroe, Marilyn, 90, 146, 160-62, 231; and Crawford Joan, 161; Mailer, Norman on, 161; *Marilyn Monroe Confidential*, biography of, 161

Moon, Keith, 183-84; and Townshend, Pete, 183

Morris, Gary, 154

Morrison, Jim, 99-100

Morrissey, 25, 45, 202-04; Smiths, singer for, 203

Moss, Jon (Culture Club), 23, 193, 194

Mötley Crue, 107

Mould, Bob, 285-86; and Hart, Grant, 285

Mozart, Wolfgang Amadeus, 250

Mulligan, Gerry. See Holliday, Judy

Murray, Anne, 120

"My Buddy," 154

Navarro, Dave, 285

NdgeOcello, Me'Shell, 297-98

Near, Holly, 118, 119, 293. See also Baez, Joan

Nelson, Gene, 315

Nelson, Rick, 24, 93-94

New York Dolls, 96, 192

Newton, Wayne. See Liberace

Newton-John, Olivia, 192, 272

Nijinsky, Vaslav, 214-15, 216-17, 218, 316; and Bakst, Leon, 214; and Daighliev, Sergei, 214, 215; and Fokine, Michel, 215

Novello, Ivor, 32, 84, 168-70; and Andrews, Bobby, 169; and Churchill, Winston, 182-83

Nureyev, Rudolf, 217, 219-21, 316; and Beaton, Cecil, 220; and Wood, Natalie, 220-21

Nurock, Kirk, 262

Nyro, Laura, 292

O'Donnell, Rosie, 299; Clinton, Kate, writer for, 300

O'Sullivan, Gilbert, 189-90

Olivia Records, 118-19

Olivier, Robert, 221-22

Olivor, Jane, 290

Ono, Yoko, 305. See also Epstein, Brian

Osborne, Joan, 299

Pansy Division, 286

Parnes, Larry, 305

Parton, Dolly, 250, 281, 290

Pavlova, 215, 222

Pet Shop Boys, 206, 307-08

Phranc, 159-60

Piaf, Edith, 131, 141

Pink Flamingos. See Divine

Poole, Wakefield, 219

Porter, Cole, 24, 29, 30-31, 32, 37, 51, 58-60, 118, 182, 189, 247, 255, 267; and Bouvier, John, 59; and Cassidy, Jack, 76; *Genius and Lust*, portrayed in, 247; and Grant, Cary, 59; portrayed in PBS special, 58; Thomas, Linda Lee, wife of, 59, 60; and Wooley, Monty, 58, 60

Poulenc, Francis, 32, 45-46, 47

Presley, Elvis, 20, 67, 96, 153; Ray, Johnny, fan of, 91; spying for J. Edgar Hoover, 96

Preston, Robert, 85

Prince, 67, 69, 70-71, 273, 274-75; Mozart, idol of, 70; in *Purple Rain*, 19, 70

Proust, Marcel. See Hahn, Reynaldo

Public Enemy, 107

Puig, Manuel, 253

Queen. See Mercury, Freddie

Ra, Sun, 260

Rainey, Ma, 134, 135, 138

Ravel, Maurice, 32, 51, 52-53

Ray, Johnnie, 88-90, 152, 278; on Morrison, Jim, 99, 100; Whiteside, Johnny on, 88

Reagan, Ronald Jr., 213

Reardon, John, 75

Reed, Lou. See Velvet Underground

Richard, Cliff, 190

Ridgeley, Andrew. See Michael, George

Right Said Fred, 312

Ritchard, Cyril, 182, 183

Robbins, Jerome, 43, 222-23. See also Bernstein, Leonard

Robeson, Paul, 84-85, 170

Robinson, Tom, 181, 185, 186

Rockwell, 86

Rogers, Ginger, 236, 247

Rolling Stones, 174-75; *Cocksucker Blues*, film about, 174. See also Jagger, Mick

Rollins, Henry, 285

Romanovsky & Phillips, 103-04

Romero, Cesar, 132

Rorem, Ned, 32, 38, 41, 45, 49, 50; on Britten, Benjamin, 173; and Holmes, James, 38; *Paris Diary*, author of, 38

Rose, Axl, 107

Rose, George, 182

Ross, Diana, 69-70, 71, 72-73, 137-38

Roth, Lynda, 293

RuPaul, 281-82, 284

Russell, Jane, 162

Saint-Saens, Camille, 32, 46

Sakamoto, Ryuichi, 304

Schippers, Thomas, 41

Schneider, Fred (B-52's), 282, 284

Schubert, Franz, 32, 35–36; Huttenbrenner, Anselm dying in arms of, 36

Schumacher, Tom, 306

Sedaka, Neil, 86

Shaiman, Marc, 265–66; and Ashman, Howard, 265; and Lauch, Bill, 265–66

Shaw, Ian, 277, 278

Shawn, Ted, 223; St. Denis, Ruth, wife of, 229; Denishawn School of Dance, co-founder of, 229; *Father of American Dance*, biography of, 230; *1001 Night Stands*, memoirs of, 230

Shelley, Pete, 192, 203

Shipley, Thomas, 260

Short, Bobby, 51, 52, 58

Sinatra, Frank, 154–55

Smith Bessie, 134, 138, 139

Smith, "Ice" Tucker, 231

Sobule, Jill, 298

Somerville, Jimmy, 22, 201–02, 203, 207, 312–13; and Bell, Andy, 209; and Coles, Richard, 201–09, 209

Sondheim, Stephen, 31, 32, 43–44, 46–47, 114, 255–56; and Perkins, Tony, 256

Springfield, Dusty, 302-03

Springsteen, Bruce, 26, 95–96; and Clemons, Clarence, 18, 87

Stein, Gertrude, 280

Steinbachek, Larry (Bronski Beat), 22, 201

Stevens, Cat, 250

Stewart, Rod, 191, 306

Stierle, Edward, 315

Stipe, Michael (R.E.M.), 273, 282

Stokowski, Leopold, 41–42; Vanderbilt, Gloria, wife of, 41

Strayhorn, Billy, 259

Streisand, Barbra, 129–30, 153, 154, 248, 318; Gould, Jason, son of; 295–96

Sullivan, Sir Arthur, 32, 34

Summer, Donna, 65

Susann, Jacqueline, 15

Swanson, Gloria, 163

Sylvester, 65–67, 292–93; LaBelle, Patti and, 66

Taylor, Cecil, 260

Tchaikovsky, Modeste, 32

Tchaikovsky, Peter, 32–33, 250; and Sapelnikov, Vassily, 33

Tennant, Neil. *See* Pet Shop Boys

Terrell, Jon, 154

Thibaudet, Jean-Yves, 264–65

Thomas, Michael Tilson, 258

Thomson, Virgil, 32, 38, 43. *See also* Rorem, Ned

Tiny Tim, 75, 273

Tipton, Billy, 55–56; Kitty, wife of, 55

Tomlin, Lily, 290–91

Townshend, Pete, 303. *See also* Moon, Keith

Travolta, John, 233, 250, 292

Tremoglio, Melinda, 118

Tucker, Sophie, 90

Tudor, Antony, 222

Tune, Tommy, 233–34

Turner, Tina, 20, 21, 22, 122–23, 141

Ulrich, Lars (Metallica), 284–85

Valee, Rudy, 76–77; and Valentino, Rudolf, 76

Valentino, Rudolf. *See* Valee, Rudy

Vandross, Luther, 284

Velvet Underground, 94–95; Cale, John, member of, 95; Morrison, Sterling, member of, 95; Reed, Lou, leader of, 94–96, 111; Tucker, Maureen, drummer for, 95; Warhol, Andy, benfactor of, 94, 95

Village People, 20, 32, 96–98; *Can't Stop The Music*, autobiographical movie of, 97–98, 257; Hughes, Glenn, member of, 97; Morali, Jacques, creator of, 257; Rose, Felipe, 98

Villella, Edward, 213–14

Walker, William Lucas, 254–55

Wallace, Sippie, 133–34

Wallace, Stuart, 264

Ward, Samuel A., 252

Warhol, Andy, 178. *See also* Velvet Underground

Waters, Ethel, 134, 135, 139

Webb, Clifton, 147, 227–29, 249; and Bradley, Buddy, 228; Maybelle, mother of, 228, 229

West, Mae, 130–31, 171

Wham. *See* Michael, George

Wilde, Marty, 305

Williams, Andrew, 284

Williams, David, 284

Williams, John, 267

Williams, Sammy, 233

Williamson, Cris, 118, 119, 293

Wilson, Billy, 315

Wilson, Lester, 315

Youmans, Vincent, 48

Zappa, Frank, 31–32, 56, 248, 24